D0947733

REGULATORY POLITICS IN AN AGE OF POLARIZATION AND DRIFT

Regulatory change is typically understood as a response to significant crises like the Great Depression, or salient events that focus public attention, like Earth Day 1970. Without discounting the importance of these kinds of events, change often assumes more gradual and less visible forms. But how do we "see" change, and what institutions and processes are behind it? In this book, author Marc Allen Eisner brings these questions to bear on the analysis of regulatory change, walking the reader through a clear-eyed and careful examination of:

- the dynamics of regulatory change since the 1970s
- social regulation and institutional design
- forms of gradual change—including conversion, layering, and drift
- gridlock, polarization, and the privatization of regulation
- financial collapse and the anatomy of regulatory failure.

Demonstrating that transparency and accountability—the hallmarks of public regulation—are increasingly absent, and that deregulation was but one factor in our most recent significant financial collapse, the Great Recession, this book urges readers to look beyond deregulation and consider the broader political implications for our current system of voluntary participation in regulatory programs and the proliferation of public–private partnerships. This book provides an accessible introduction to the complex topic of regulatory politics, ideal for upper-level and graduate courses on regulation, government and business, bureaucratic politics, and public policy.

Marc Allen Eisner is Dean of the Social Sciences, Henry Merritt Wriston Chair of Public Policy, and Professor of Government at Wesleyan University, US. He is the author of several books, most recently *The American Political Economy, 2e* (Routledge, 2014, named CHOICE Outstanding Academic Title) and (with James Gosling) *Economics, Politics, and American Public Policy, 2e* (Routledge, 2013).

REGULATORY POLITICS IN AN AGE OF POLARIZATION AND DRIFT

Beyond Deregulation

Marc Allen Eisner

NEW YORK AND LONDON

First published 2017
by Routledge
711 Third Avenue, New York, NY 10017

and by Routledge
2 Park Square, Milton Park, Abingdon, Oxon OX14 4RN

Routledge is an imprint of the Taylor & Francis Group, an informa business

© 2017 Taylor & Francis

The right of Marc Allen Eisner to be identified as author of this work
has been asserted by him in accordance with sections 77 and 78 of the
Copyright, Designs and Patents Act 1988.

All rights reserved. No part of this book may be reprinted or reproduced or
utilised in any form or by any electronic, mechanical, or other means, now
known or hereafter invented, including photocopying and recording, or in
any information storage or retrieval system, without permission in writing
from the publishers.

Trademark notice: Product or corporate names may be trademarks or
registered trademarks, and are used only for identification and explanation
without intent to infringe.

Library of Congress Cataloging-in-Publication Data
Names: Eisner, Marc Allen, author.
Title: Regulatory politics in an age of polarization and drift : beyond
    deregulation / by Marc Allen Eisner.
Description: New York : Routledge, 2017. | Includes bibliographical
    references and index.
Identifiers: LCCN 2016037866| ISBN 9781138183421 (hardback :
    alk. paper) | ISBN 9781138183438 (pbk. : alk. paper) | ISBN
    9781315645865 (ebook)
Subjects: LCSH: Industrial policy—United States—History. |
    Deregulation—United States—History.
Classification: LCC HD3616.U62 E37 2017 | DDC 338.973—dc23
LC record available at https://lccn.loc.gov/2016037866

ISBN: (hbk) 978-1-138-18342-1
ISBN: (pbk) 978-1-138-18343-8
ISBN: (ebk) 978-1-315-64586-5

Typeset in Bembo
by Swales & Willis Ltd, Exeter, Devon, UK

For Patricia

CONTENTS

FIGURES

ACKNOWLEDGMENTS

When I began studying regulation in the mid-1980s, scholars were focused on the issue of deregulation, and with good reason. The recent Ford and Carter presidencies had promoted deregulation as a response to the larger macro-economic problems of the 1970s and the difficulty of managing them with traditional fiscal policy. By the 1980s, the Reagan administration embraced deregulation as part of a larger effort to redefine the role of the state in the market. With a few important exceptions—most notably in finance—the major deregulatory initiatives occurred in the 1970s and, by the mid-1980s, deregulation seemed to have run its course. Yet, many contemporary accounts of regulation assume that we are still in a deregulatory era. This book has been written as a response to these claims. The core argument is that we have entered a period when polarization and gridlock in Congress have impeded the passage of significant new statutes to recalibrate the regulatory state. As a result, the disjunction between regulatory authority and the larger environment has only grown greater over time. One response has been a greater reliance on volun-tary programs and partnerships that promise to extend, however imperfectly, regulatory capacity by devolving authority on to regulated parties and leverag-ing their resources. In other cases, policy simply has failed to adapt to the most important changes in industry practice. Regulators continue to regulate, but they often regulate the wrong things—with devastating consequences.

This book, in large part, represents decades of research and teaching on the subject of regulation. Papers that contained some of the arguments and cases that would contribute to the book were presented to other scholars in Boston (Northeastern University), Durham (Duke University), Grenoble (International Conference on Public Policy), Milan (International Conference on Public Policy), Paris (Science Po and OECD), Portland (New England

Political Science Association), San Francisco (American Political Science Association), and Washington DC (Georgetown), and to my students and colleagues at Wesleyan University in Middletown, Connecticut. Along the way, I have benefited greatly from the generosity of fellow travelers, most notably my two friends and coauthors, Jeff Worsham and Evan Ringquist. Evan's untimely death in 2014 left an enormous gap in the lives of those who knew him and a larger universe of scholars who relied on his excellent research on regulation to inform their own work. I have also benefited from fellow scholars and policymakers I encountered in multiple projects organized by the Tobin Project and the Kennan Institute for Ethics at Duke University. In each case, they challenged and refined my understanding of regulation, political economy, and the dynamics of change.

As always, the greatest thanks are reserved for my wife and best friend, Patricia. For more than three decades, she has been a source of encouragement, happiness, and wisdom.

ABBREVIATIONS

AAA	Agricultural Adjustment Administration
AEC	Atomic Energy Commission
AEI	American Enterprise Institute
AFL-CIO	American Federation of Labor and Congress of Industrial Organizations
AIG	American Insurance Group
ANWR	Arctic National Wildlife Refuge
APA	Administrative Procedure Act
BOEMRE	Bureau of Ocean Energy, Management, Regulation and Enforcement
BOP	Blowout preventer
BTU	British Thermal Units
CBO	Congressional Budget Office
CCP	Cooperative Compliance Program
CERCLA	Comprehensive Environmental Response, Compensation, and Liability Act
CFR	Code of Federal Regulations
CFTC	Commodity Futures Trading Commission
COWPS	Council on Wage and Price Stability
CPI	Consumer Price Index
CSI	Common Sense Initiative
DIDMCA	Depository Institutions Deregulation and Monetary Control Act
EMS	Environmental management system
EO	Executive Order
EPA	Environmental Protection Agency
FDA	Food and Drug Administration

FDIC	Federal Deposit Insurance Corporation
FSLIC	Federal Savings and Loan Insurance Corporation
FTC	Federal Trade Commission
GAO	Government Accountability Office
GDP	Gross Domestic Product
GLBA	Gramm–Leach–Bliley Act
GMAC	General Motors Acceptance Corporation
GOP	Grand Old Party (Republican Party)
GSE	Government sponsored enterprise
HACCP	Hazard analysis and critical control point
HEW	Department of Health, Education, and Welfare
HHS	Department of Health and Human Services
HIV	Human immunodeficiency virus
HUD	Department of Housing and Urban Development
ICC	Interstate Commerce Commission
IMF	International Monetary Fund
INPO	Institute of Nuclear Power Operators
ISO	International Organization for Standardization
MBS	Mortgage-backed security
MMS	Minerals Management Service
MMTCE	Million metric tons of carbon equivalent
MSHA	Mine Safety and Health Administration
MSRC	Marine Spill Response Corporation
NAAQS	National ambient air quality standards
NEPT	National Environmental Performance Track
NGO	Nongovernmental organization
NIOSH	National Institute for Occupational Safety and Health
NIPCC	National Industrial Pollution Control Council
NLRB	National Labor Relations Board
NOW	Negotiated order of withdrawal
NPDES	National Pollutant Discharge Elimination System
NRA	National Recovery Administration
NRC	Nuclear Regulatory Commission
OCC	Office of the Comptroller of the Currency
OIRA	Office of Information and Regulatory Affairs
OMB	Office of Management and Budget
OPA	Oil Pollution Act
OSH Act	Occupational Safety and Health Act
OSHA	Occupational Safety and Health Administration
OSHRC	Occupational Safety and Health Review Commission
RARG	Regulatory Analysis Review Group
REGO	Reinvention of government
S&Ls	Savings and loans

SEC	Securities and Exchange Commission
SGE	Special Government Employee
SHARP	Safety and Health Recognition Program
TSCA	Toxic Substances Control Act
USCG	US Coast Guard
USDA	United Stated Department of Agriculture
VPP	Voluntary Protection Program
VPPPA	Voluntary Protection Program Participants Association

1

A TALE OF TWO CRISES

In 2007 and 2008, the financial crisis unfolded with a rapidity and ferocity few would have imagined possible, giving rise to the deepest recession since the Great Depression. Following more than a decade of appreciation in the housing market, the bubble burst. Much of the debt that fueled the housing bubble had been securitized. That is, mortgages had been purchased, pooled, and transformed into mortgage-backed securities. Many of the highly leveraged financial institutions that had issued mortgage-backed securities and/or retained them in their portfolios were left in ruins. The credit ratings of Fannie Mae and Freddie Mac—the government-sponsored enterprises (GSEs) that had purchased mortgages from lenders to push liquidity into the real estate markets—were downgraded; they were forced into conservatorship, and saved with a massive infusion of public funding. While Lehman Brothers went bankrupt, other institutions that had become emblematic of Wall Street survived, albeit only after receiving lines of credit from the Treasury and the Federal Reserve. The crisis forced the Fed to go well beyond its normal regulatory duties. Its regulatory authority did not extend to the investment banks like Bear Stearns, J.P Morgan, and Goldman Sachs, or the American Insurance Group (AIG) that had issued credit-default swaps to insure the mortgage-backed securities. The Fed drew creatively on Section 13(3) of the Federal Reserve Act, which permitted it to lend money to "any individual, partnership, or corporation" under "unusual and exigent circumstances." Under conditions of crisis, "the Fed could no longer pretend that it supervised banks and someone else supervised the shadow banking system."[1] After brief hesitation, Congress provided additional support: The Emergency Economic Stabilization Act of 2008 authorized the Treasury to spend up to $700 billion to prevent the collapse of the financial system through a newly created Troubled Assets Relief Program.

The crisis was not confined to the financial system, but spread rapidly into the larger economy, creating the deepest recession since the Great Depression. A nation that had combined record levels of both homeownership and indebtedness proved particularly vulnerable. Households' net wealth had reached an unprecedented $66 trillion in the second quarter of 2007, in large part reflecting the inflation of real estate prices. In the next two years, it would plunge by $17 trillion. Some 3.6 million jobs were lost in 2008, with another 4.7 million jobs in 2009. Unemployment spiked at 10.1 percent and the underemployment rate almost doubled from 8.8 percent in December 2007 to 17.4 percent in October 2009.[2] Things might have been far worse if not for the efforts of the Federal Reserve and the Treasury to stave off the further collapse of the financial system and the Obama administration's success in securing passage of the American Recovery and Reinvestment Act of 2009, providing $787 billion for stimulus.

In April 2010, the unemployment rate edged up from 9.7 percent to 9.9 percent, with 15.3 million unemployed. Yet, the worsening economic news and fears that the tepid recovery had stalled were driven from the headlines by a second regulatory crisis, this time in the Gulf of Mexico. On April 20, BP's Deepwater Horizon, a semi-submersible oil rig located 50 miles off the Louisiana coast, exploded, killing eleven workers. Two days later, the rig sank and severed the connection to the Macondo well, some 5,000 feet below the surface. As crude oil gushed from the seabed at a rate of between 52,700 and 62,200 barrels a day, industry experts searched, seemingly in vain, for solutions.[3] President Obama gave voice to the growing sense of dread when he made the Deepwater Horizon disaster the centerpiece of his first Oval Office address, on June 15. He described the spill as "the worst environmental disaster America has ever faced." He likened it to an "an epidemic, one that we will be fighting for months and even years" and admitted what was becoming increasingly evident: "Because there has never been a leak this size at this depth, stopping it has tested the limits of human technology."[4]

Deep water (deeper than 1,000 feet) and ultra-deep water (deeper than 5,000 feet) exploration and production are technologically complex, requiring equipment that can function under extreme conditions characterized by high pressures, low temperatures, and extreme variations in currents.[5] Prior to the Deepwater disaster, some 14,000 deepwater wells had been drilled without any significant problems. "Although the industry knew of the potential risks," a report from Lloyd's of London explained, "planning for a major deepwater pollution event and its subsequent environmental impact was based upon other types of offshore spills, deepwater field tests and modeling of the likely flow dynamics."[6] And thus, as the crisis unfolded, successive attempts to stop the leak and capture, contain, or disperse the oil proved largely ineffective. In the end, after a series of actions that appeared, at times, *ad hoc*, it would take 87 days to seal the leak temporarily through the placement of a cap and 152 days to seal permanently the reservoir through the injection of mud and cement through an intersecting relief well.[7]

The Deepwater Horizon was the greatest oil spill in US history, vastly eclipsing the previous record set by the Exxon Valdez spill in 1989. When the Exxon Valdez ran aground on Bligh Reef in 1989, it spilled an estimated 250,000 barrels of crude oil in Alaska's Prince William Sound. This was approximately 5 percent of the 4.9 million barrels that exuded from the Macondo well. Exxon was forced to pay $3 billion for the cleanup and damages. Although it will be years before the final figures are available, the costs associated with the Deepwater Horizon disaster are estimated to be in excess of $60 billion—a figure that does not include the losses in market capitalization endured by BP's partners and other firms in the petroleum industry, and, more importantly, the damages to the ecosystems of the Gulf of Mexico.[8] As the Report of the National Commission to study the crisis concluded

> Because the Deepwater Horizon spill was unprecedented in size, location, and duration, deepwater ecosystems were exposed to large volumes of oil for an extended period. . . . Unfortunately, except for studies that have focused on rare and specialized communities associated with rocky outcrops or seeps, scientific understanding of the deepwater Gulf ecosystem has not advanced with the industrial development of deepwater drilling and production.[9]

The Crises in Context

These events were two tragic regulatory failures: the largest financial crisis in the postwar period and the greatest oil spill in recorded history. Yet, other than their temporal proximity, they would appear to have little in common. In the case of finance, many critics would attribute the collapse to deregulation. There is undoubtedly some truth to this story. The financial regulatory policies put in place during the New Deal were designed to induce stability. Core statutes created distinct financial industries, each with its own set of regulators. Policies governing the services, products, and interest rates that could be offered were designed to prevent competition. The decades of stability following the introduction of the New Deal regime (the "Quiet Period" in US banking) led many to discount the potential for the kinds of collapses that had been relatively routine in earlier decades.[10] But the high inflation of the 1970s placed enormous pressures on regulated financial firms. Money market mutual funds could offer rates of return that were far in excess of the interest rates permissible under the Federal Reserve's Regulation Q. Mutual funds and state banks could offer services that were prohibited under regulations. Congress responded by passing a series of statutes that facilitated competition by deregulating interest rates, allowing banks and savings and loans to offer new financial products, and permitting a broader range of investments. While deregulation had significant impacts, the extent of deregulation should not be overstated. In inflation-adjusted terms, the budgets of financial regulatory agencies had increased steadily over time. In 2007, on the eve of the financial crisis, federal financial regulators spent $2.6 billion. Adjusted for inflation, this constituted a 292 percent increase over the amount spent in 1980.[11]

In sharp contrast to finance, Congress did not pass any deregulatory statutes regarding oil spills. Between 1970 and 1990, the policies for oil spills evolved in synch with the larger body of environmental protection regulations. Between the passage of the Water Quality Improvement Act of 1970 and the Oil Pollution Act of 1990, Congress repeatedly strengthened the oil spill regime. The Oil Pollution Act, passed in the wake of the Exxon Valdez spill of 1989, was a landmark piece of legislation that broadened the scope of liability, imposed new technological mandates on shippers (e.g., requirements for double-hulled ships), and created a new Oil Spill Liability Trust Fund capitalized at $1 billion to cover the costs of cleanup. Moreover, it sought to prevent catastrophic spills by requiring that industry engage in "worst case scenario" contingency planning.[12] Over the course of the next few decades, the number of spills—and more importantly, the number of large spills—fell significantly. Between 1973 and 1990, an average of 11.86 million gallons were spilled on an annual basis. In the period 1991–2009, the annual average fell to 1.9 million gallons—a figure that includes spills of 8 million gallons following Hurricane Katrina and 1.8 million gallons following Hurricane Rita, both in 2005.[13]

Beneath the surface of these two regulatory failures, however, one can find at least two commonalities that are representative of larger changes in regulation. First, regulatory authority rested on dated statutes that failed to account for the significant changes in the respective industries. In finance, deregulation, while important, did not constitute the creation of a new regulatory architecture to meet the needs of the contemporary financial system. New Deal era regulations were eliminated or relaxed in hopes of allowing regulated depository institutions to compete more effectively in an environment of high inflation. But the decades leading up to the collapse witnessed the rise of securitization and the growth in the sale and repurchase (or repo) market, which combined to create the so-called "shadow banking system." Securitized debt was held in the portfolios of large financial institutions and used more generally as collateral by institutions seeking to borrow short-term funds. Many of the participants in this system—hedge funds, insurance companies, pension funds, investment banks, private equity funds—were not the kinds of entities that one had historically associated with banking.[14] While regulators were regulating *banks*, they were no longer regulating *banking* or the repo market, which had grown from $372 billion in 1990 to $2.6 trillion in 2007.[15] In short, regulators were regulating, but they were regulating the wrong things.

In the case of oil exploration and production, the 1990s witnessed a revolution in offshore oil production. Advances in 3-D seismology, drill and rig technologies, and subsea engineering made it economical to develop deepwater fields with far greater production capacity than wells on the continental shelf.[16] As oil exploration moved into deep- and ultra-deep water locations, "industry and government had embarked on development of petroleum resources in areas that presented significant increased risks—the likelihoods and consequences of system failures—while in some cases employing systems that had not kept pace with these higher risk operations."[17] While there was clear recognition within the industry that a catastrophic blowout of a deepwater well constituted the genuine worst-case scenario, the regulatory environment—shaped in large part by the Oil Pollution Act of 1990—was framed by the increasingly irrelevant precedent of the Exxon Valdez. As with finance, Congress failed to pass new regulatory statutes to adjust the oil spill regime to the significant technological changes that had occurred in the industry. Regulators, once again, were regulating the wrong things.

A second common point: both regulatory systems assigned *de facto* authority to private and quasi-private entities. In the case of finance, there was a growing reliance on the GSEs—Fannie Mae and Freddie Mac—to meet public housing goals by adding liquidity to the market via the purchase of loans in the secondary market.[18] Because the GSEs received a host of benefits (most importantly, their debt carried an implicit guarantee from the federal government that translated into a subsidy estimated at $14–22 billion a year), they had "an affirmative obligation to facilitate the financing of affordable housing for low- and moderate-income families in a manner consistent with their over-all public purposes, while maintaining a strong financial condition and a reasonable economic return."[19] Private credit rating agencies (Standard and Poor's, Moody's Investors Service, and Fitch) were entrusted to evaluate the quality of securitized debt with minimal government oversight. The ratings they awarded determined the extent of the market. That is, many institutions and funds function under ratings-based restrictions on the securities they can purchase, and thus credit rating agencies serve as gatekeepers to the market. The holders of securitized debt could mitigate their exposure to risk through the purchase of credit-default swaps, derivatives that were also largely unregulated. Regulators worked on the assumption that market actors had the incentives, the knowledge, and the technical sophistication to manage their own risk. As Federal Reserve Chairman Alan Greenspan remarked in 1997, "it is critically important to recognize that no market is ever truly unregulated. The self-interest of market participants generates private market regulation."[20]

Tragically, Greenspan's assumption was tested in the financial crisis. The GSEs, which guaranteed or owned half of the $12 trillion mortgage market, were highly leveraged and forced into conservatorship when the asset bubble burst.[21] As rising default rates and downgrades on mortgage-backed securities ballooned, it was discovered that the ratings assigned by the credit rating agencies were inflated—a product of flawed methodologies, the perverse incentives created by the "issuer pays" compensation model, and the failure to verify the data provided by securitizers.[22] As AIG's credit rating was downgraded, it became clear that it failed to set aside the collateral and capital reserves to support the credit-default swaps it had issued.[23] In the wake of the collapse, Greenspan appeared chastened as he testified before Congress. "Those of us who have looked to the self-interest of lending institutions to protect shareholders' equity, myself included, are in a state of shocked disbelief." He concluded that "This modern risk-management paradigm [that] held sway for decades . . . collapsed."[24]

A similar deference to private sector actors was evident in the oil spill regime. The Oil Pollution Act required that corporations engage in contingency planning for worst-case scenario spills and maintain the personnel and equipment necessary to implement them. Rather than creating a firm-specific response capacity, the industry formed the non-profit Marine Preservation Association that, in turn, established the Marine Spill Response Corporation (MSRC). In recognition of the fact that the resources for future cleanups would need to come from the private sector, Congress supported this effort. Indeed, the Conference Committee for the Oil Protection Act, which was conducting its work as a consortium of twenty oil companies, was developing the industry response explicitly cited it as an organization with which the US Coast Guard National Response Unit should work as it engaged in its contingency planning.[25] Members of the Marine Preservation Association could enter into service contracts with the MSRC, a decision that carried two benefits. First, it shielded oil companies from liability for damages related to cleanups. Second, by pooling resources, the industry could draw on $100 million worth of cleanup equipment. The MSRC maintained 400 personnel and 15 large oil-recovery ships positioned in five regional response centers and twenty-three staging areas.[26]

While the industry efforts may have appeared impressive at the time, they would be shown to be tragically inadequate when faced with the catastrophe of Deepwater Horizon. The contingency plan was littered with inaccurate information and was largely an "infamous cut and paste plan that included referenced impacts to walruses, sea lions, and sea otters, creatures that do not exist in the Gulf."[27] Drawing on the example of the Exxon Valdez, the worst-case scenario was defined as 250,000 barrels—not what became 4.9 million barrels. The regulatory oversight of contingency planning, exercised by the Department of Interior's Minerals Management Service, was largely cursory. Although the MSRC dispatched four skimmers within hours of the explosion, it had nothing in its arsenal designed to collect oil at depths of 5,000 feet. Its capacity was simply outmatched by the nature and magnitude of the crisis. Spill response technology had not kept pace with the revolution in deepwater and ultra-deepwater oil exploration. As the national commission created to investigate the disaster reported: "Though incremental improvements in skimming and boom had been realized in the intervening 21 years, the technologies used in response to the Deepwater Horizon and Exxon Valdez oil spills were largely the same."[28] In the words of Mark Davis, "Clearly, the working assumption was that nothing really bad could happen and if it did, industry would be ready."[29] This assumption, ironically, echoed the words of Alan Greenspan in the decade preceding the financial collapse.

Deregulation or Drift

Many would argue that our two crises could be characterized as the tragic but unsurprising products of neoliberalism. The concept of neoliberalism is often contested and imprecise. In some cases, it is used to describe an ideology of laissez-faire or free market fundamentalism. For others, it describes a coherent program of policy and institutional change. Regardless of its usage, at the core of neoliberalism stands a skepticism regarding the role of the state and a celebration of markets and the capacity of self-interested parties, subject to the discipline of the market, to manage their own affairs. As Colin Crouch notes:

> There are many branches and brands of neoliberalism, but behind them stands one dominant theme: that free markets in which individuals maximize their material interests provide the best means for satisfying human aspirations, and that markets are in particular to be preferred over states and politics, which are at best inefficient and at worst threats to freedom.[30]

Since the late 1970s, the US and other wealthy democracies have witnessed changes in public policy that are broadly consistent with the tenets of neoliberalism. There has been a broad departure from Keynesian fiscal policies and the promotion of monetarism and—at least rhetorically—balanced budgets. There has been a rejection of progressive taxation as a tool of redistribution and support for reduced tax rates and a flatter tax structure. Means-tested social welfare programs have been reformed to make them more market-conforming. There has been the broad promotion of trade liberalization and a rejection of various forms of protectionism, particularly when employed by less developed countries. This combination of policy preferences has included privatization of formally nationalized industries and, in the US where nationalization was quite limited, deregulation. Critics of neoliberalism argue that excessive deregulation—the elimination of the kinds of policies that once governed the behavior of economic actors—had the predictable consequences exhibited in the vignettes presented above. Faith was placed in the market, and the market failed.

The story of neoliberalism's ascendency—the rise of the free market and the diminution of the state—can be challenged on theoretical and empirical grounds. One may observe, for example, that the support for the "free market"—itself a theoretical construct—and deregulation was largely rhetorical. Drawing on the work of Karl Polanyi, Fred Block and Margaret R. Somers argue that self-regulating markets exist "only in ideology; in reality, markets are always and everywhere embedded in social structures of politics, law, and culture."[31]

They argue that rather than a process of *de*regulation, the nation witnessed a process of *re*regulation. They write:

> By the term reregulation . . . we aim to push back against the belief that the success of neoliberal ideology since the mid-1970s has been matched by markets being increasingly freed from regulations and government management. On the contrary, regulations did not go away; they simply changed. Those that had previously been written to protect employees or consumers were systematically rewritten to support business interests and reduce previous restrictions on business practices.[32]

The reregulation of the economy may have been framed with free market ideology that acknowledged little role for the state. But it was a product of political mobilization designed to recast regulation—to employ the state—to further the interests of business. To the extent that it succeeded, some of the wealth it generated was recycled back into politics to fund conservative think tanks that propagated free market solutions and the campaigns of supportive candidates and incumbents.

Many regulatory scholars, while less indebted to Polanyi, would agree that the extent of deregulation is frequently overstated. Even where it has occurred, it is but one part of a much richer story that is not simply reducible to the triumph of free and unfettered markets. Analysts have documented the emergence of a fluid and complex network of private governance that serves, in many ways, a regulatory function. Corporations have powerful incentives to manage risk and to act in ways that minimize their costs (including environmental and occupational safety and health liabilities) and meet the demands of key stakeholders (e.g., investors, customers, members of the supply chain, nonprofit organizations). Trade associations seek to manage industry reputations, and can require that members abide by codes of conduct or international standards with third-party auditing that can often demand far more than could be achieved under traditional forms of regulation. Rather than ceding authority to unfettered markets, regulators have learned how to employ market mechanisms to further regulatory goals (e.g., through pollution trading). They have discovered that rather than relying on traditional command and control regulations— policies that prescribe rigid technological standards backed with penalties—there is much to be gained by designing policy to leverage private sector actors and resources. Government no longer dictates. It cooperates and coordinates, helping to orchestrate a broad network of actors and institutions. Yes, markets are in some sense freer than in the past, but there are also more rules, some public and others private.[33] The older system of top-down regulation, in short, has evolved into a networked system of regulatory capitalism, with regulatory goals integrated into the activities of private sector actors and public regulation integrated with a broader network of private regulation.[34]

Where some regulatory scholars celebrate the emergence of regulatory capitalism, critics see it as little more than a smokescreen that obscures the reckless privatization of government regulation. Regulatory agencies that have been stripped of authority and starved for resources simply lack the capacity to oversee the behavior of the corporations and industries they are nominally regulating. Corporate commitments, associational codes of conduct, and international standards can be used to create the impression that capitalism has somehow internalized the goals traditionally associated with public regulation. But there is often little empirical evidence that these forms of private regulation actually generate the promised results. Absent vigorous government oversight, everything will depend on the enlightened self-interest and beneficence of profit-seeking firms. As the financial crisis and the Deepwater Horizon spill revealed, such faith is often misplaced. In sum, the combination of deregulation and a systematic underinvestment in public agencies has created a system prone to disaster.[35]

Each of these positions has merit, but they are lacking in important ways. The neoliberal critique emphasizes deregulation but often grossly overstates the extent to which deregulation has occurred (a point that will be developed in Chapter 2, as we examine the growth in federal regulations and regulatory budgets). There is much to suggest that the crises discussed earlier in this chapter were not simply or even primarily the products of deregulation. As noted above, the financial collapse found its origins in parts of the financial system that had never been regulated in the first place (and hence, could not be "deregulated"). Deregulation certainly was not a factor in the Deepwater Horizon. Oil spill policy, as other social regulatory policies, has been relatively immune from formal deregulation. However, something else was occurring. Congress, increasingly beset by polarization and gridlock, proved incapable of passing new legislation. Regulators, as a result, were either regulating the wrong things (the case of finance) or working under statutory authority that was antiquated and did not grant them the authority to manage the growing complexity of the activities in question (the case of Deepwater Horizon). While these events may be the most salient given the magnitude of the economic and environmental damages, they are not unique. As a generalization, Congress has failed to pass significant new social regulatory statutes in decades, leading to an ossification of the regulatory state.

Scholars of regulatory capitalism are correct in noting that a dynamic network of governance arrangements has emerged in recent decades, and in some ways it can serve functions analogous to public regulation. Corporations have adopted a host of management systems to identify, track, and reduce the factors that contribute to pollution and occupational injuries and diseases. Trade associations have developed codes that incorporate some of these systems, in some cases providing their members with training and peer review. International standards have become ubiquitous. In the US context, most regulatory agencies have made use of some of these efforts, forming public–private partnerships and programs. But in most cases, these programs have been less a product of deliberate design and more a product of necessity—a response to the conditions noted above. Agencies compensated for the absence of new statutory authority by placing an ever-greater reliance on corporate voluntarism and public–private partnerships. Yet, for reasons that will be explored in this volume, agencies have been denied the flexibility to integrate the programs with existing regulations. As a result, they have been layered on top of a rigid set of policies inherited from the past. The same inflexible structures that impede integration limit oversight, creating a situation rightfully denounced by the critics of neoliberalism.

It is a core assertion of this volume—one that will be developed in subsequent chapters—that contemporary regulation cannot be understood through the lens of neoliberalism and some zealous but misplaced commitment to deregulation. Rather, contemporary regulation is increasingly shaped by ossification and drift that are, themselves, a product of institutional failure. The past several decades have witnessed growing polarization and gridlock in Congress, which have rendered it incapable of passing significant new statutes. This is particularly problematic in the area of regulation, because it means that administrators have often lacked the statutory authority to address changes in the organization and activities of the industries they govern. As Congress has proven incapable of recalibrating the regulatory state, the disjunction between what regulators are regulating and the larger environment has grown, creating a condition known as drift. If the lack of regulations resembled the kinds of policies that could be justified by neoliberalism, it was a neoliberalism by default, one borne of institutional failure.

The impact of polarization and gridlock has been evident in key social regulatory areas like environmental protection. To simplify a bit, at a critical juncture in the history of these regulations, Congress adopted a particular strategy of institutional design—it passed detailed statutes and imposed complex procedures—intended to prevent regulatory capture and limit presidential influence over the regulatory state. As Congress constrained the discretionary authority of regulators, it inadvertently denied them the flexibility to adjust their activities to address emerging regulatory problems. When Congress subsequently entered a period of polarization, the gap between agency authority and the larger regulatory environment expanded. The growing reliance on public–private partnerships and voluntary programs was one response to drift. But without the statutory authority to integrate these programs into the existing regulatory structure, their impact was necessarily limited. While the result appeared to some to resemble a networked order of regulatory capitalism, it was more of an uneven patchwork that lacked the level of integration celebrated by its advocates.

Let us be clear on a key point: Regulation continues to serve a vital function. Each day, agencies issue permits, conduct inspections, and enforce regulations. In 2015, for example, the Environmental Protection Agency conducted 15,400 inspections and evaluations. The civil cases that were concluded resulted in more than $200 million in administrative and civil judicial penalties and forced corporations to make investments of $7.3 billion (injunctive relief). It opened 213 criminal cases, charging 185 defendants. The criminal cases that were concluded resulted in 129 years of incarceration, $200 million in fines and restitution, and $4 billion in court-ordered environmental projects.[36] Hazardous and toxic wastes were prevented from entering the soil and the groundwater; contaminated water and wetlands were restored; citizens were protected from particulate matter in the air they breathe. Regulation prevented unnecessary diseases and premature deaths. While the EPA is the largest regulator, a similar story could be told about other agencies. The central point is not that regulation has been abandoned. Much of what the EPA and other agencies do on a daily basis continues to make the environment cleaner, workplaces healthier, and food, drugs, and consumer products safer. But regulatory authority, grounded in decades' old statutes, cannot be easily extended to address emerging problems in an era when Congress is seemingly incapable of passing new laws to recalibrate the regulatory state. As suggested by the two crises that have been the subject of this chapter, the gaps in regulation can have widespread and devastating consequences.

Notes

1 David Wessel, *In Fed We Trust: Ben Bernanke's War on the Great Panic* (New York: Crown Business, 2009), 159.
2 Financial Crisis Inquiry Commission, *The Financial Crisis Inquiry Report: Final Report of the National Commission on the Causes of the Financial and Economic Crisis in the United States* (New York: Public Affairs, 2011), 390–91.
3 National Commission on the BP Deepwater Horizon Oil Spill and Offshore Drilling, *Deep Water: The Gulf Oil Disaster and the Future of Offshore Drilling* (Washington DC: US Government Printing Office, 2011), 167.
4 Barack Obama, Remarks by the President to the Nation on the BP Oil Spill, June 15, 2010. White House Office of the Press Secretary. Available at www.whitehouse.gov/the-press-office/remarks-president-nation-bp-oil-spill.
5 Curry L. Hagerty and Jonathan L. Ramseur, *Deepwater Horizon Oil Spill: Selected Issues for Congress*, CRS Report R41262 (Washington DC: Congressional Research Service, 2010), 2.
6 Andrew Rees and David Sharp, *Drilling in Extreme Environments: Challenges and Implications for the Energy Insurance Industry* (London: Lloyd's, 2011), 17.
7 Deepwater Horizon Study Group, *Final Report on the Investigation of the Macondo Well Blowout* (Berkeley, CA: Center of Catastrophic Risk Management, 2011), 6–8.
8 See Yong-Gyo Lee and Xavier Garza-Gomez, "Total Cost of the 2010 Deepwater Horizon Oil Spill Reflected in US Stock Market," *Journal of Accounting and Finance* 12, 1 (2012): 73–83.
9 National Commission on the BP Deepwater Horizon Oil Spill and Offshore Drilling, *Deep Water*, 182.
10 Gary B. Gorton, *Slapped by the Invisible Hand: The Panic of 2007* (New York: Oxford University Press, 2010), 14.
11 Jerry Brito and Melinda Warren, *Growth in Regulation Slows: An Analysis of the U.S. Budget for Fiscal Years 2007 and 2008* (Arlington, VA and St. Louis, MO: Mercatus Center/Weidenham Center, 2007), 17, 20.

12 Russell V. Randle, "The Oil Pollution Act of 1990: Its Provisions, Intent, and Effects," *Environmental Law Reporter* 21 (1991): 10119–35.
13 US Coast Guard, *Polluting Incidents in and around U.S. Waters. A Spill/Release Compendium: 1969–2011* (Washington DC: United States Coast Guard, 2012), 8.
14 Gorton, *Slapped by the Invisible Hand*, 58.
15 Wessel, *In Fed We Trust*, 117.
16 See National Commission on the BP Deepwater Horizon Oil Spill and Offshore Drilling, "The History of Offshore Oil and Gas in the United States," Staff Working Paper No. 22, 2011.
17 Deepwater Horizon Study Group, *Final Report*, 89.
18 See Wayne Passmore, "The GSE Implicit Subsidy and the Value of Government Ambiguity," Washington DC: Federal Reserve Board, Finance and Economic Discussion Series, 2005–05 (2005).
19 12 U.S.C. §4501(7).
20 Alan Greenspan, "Government Regulation and Derivative Contracts." Remarks at the Financial Markets Conference of the Federal Reserve Bank of Atlanta, Coral Gables, Florida, February 21, 1997. Available at www.federalreserve.gov/boarddocs/speeches/1997/19970221.htm.
21 Charles Duhigg, "Loan-Agency Woes Swell from a Trickle to a Torrent," *New York Times*, July 11, 2008. Available at www.nytimes.com/2008/07/11/business/11ripple.html.
22 John C. Coffee, "Ratings Reform: The Good, the Bad, and the Ugly," *Harvard Business Law Review*, 1 (2011): 244–49.
23 Financial Crisis Inquiry Commission, *The Financial Crisis Inquiry Report*, 352.
24 Edmund L. Andrews, "Greenspan Concedes Error on Regulation," *New York Times*, October 24, 2008, B1. Available at www.nytimes.com/2008/10/24/business/economy/24panel.html.
25 Randle, "The Oil Pollution Act of 1990," p. 10129.
26 Joe Stephens and Mary Pat Flaherty, "Oil Industry Cleanup Organization Swamped by BP Spill," *Washington Post*, June 29, 2010. Available at www.washingtonpost.com/wp-dyn/content/article/2010/06/29/AR2010062905384.html.
27 Mark Davis, "Lessons Unlearned: The Legal and Policy Legacy of the BP Deepwater Horizon Spill," *Washington and Lee Journal of Energy, Climate, and the Environment* 3 (2012): 166.
28 National Commission on the BP Deepwater Horizon Oil Spill and Offshore Drilling, *Deep Water*, 132–33.
29 Davis, "Lessons Unlearned," 166.
30 Colin Crouch, *The Strange Non-Death of Neoliberalism* (Cambridge, UK: Polity Press, 2011), vii.
31 Fred Block and Margaret R. Somers, *The Power of Market Fundamentalism: Karl Polanyi's Critique* (Cambridge, MA: Harvard University Press, 2014), 219.
32 Ibid., 20.
33 See Steven K. Vogel, *Freer Markets, More Rules: Regulatory Reform in Advanced Industrial Countries* (Ithaca, NY: Cornell University Press, 1996).
34 See John Braithwaite, *Regulatory Capitalism: How It Works, Ideas for Making It Work Better* (Cheltenham, England: Edward Elgar, 2008).
35 See Charles Perrow, "Cracks in the 'Regulatory State,'" *Social Currents* 2, 3 (2015): 203–12.
36 Environmental Protection Agency, "Enforcement Annual Results Numbers at a Glance for Fiscal Year (FY) 2015." Available at www.epa.gov/enforcement/enforcement-annual-results-numbers-glance-fiscal-year-fy-2015.

2

MAKING SENSE OF REGULATORY CHANGE

This book explores the dynamics of regulatory change in the contemporary period with the goal of better understanding what has occurred in the decades since the early 1970s. Before we turn to this examination, it is necessary to cover some important preliminary issues—some empirical, others theoretical. This chapter begins with a broad historical overview of the growth of the regulatory state. Despite the common wisdom that the United States entered a period of long-term regulatory retrenchment in the decades since deregulation began, the empirical record suggests otherwise. For all of the rhetoric regarding the return to the market and the triumph of neoliberalism, the regulatory state has never been larger. To cite one indicator: When Ronald Reagan was elected president in 1980, the federal government spent $7.3 billion on regulation. Three decades later, that sum had grown to $52.6 billion.[1] Adjusted for inflation, the spending increased by more than 310 percent, despite the fact that this was supposedly a deregulatory era. Did this expansion lead to better outcomes for the environment, workers, and consumers? Were regulators regulating the right things? These are profoundly important questions that cannot be derived from figures on spending. After establishing the empirical record, we turn briefly to consider competing explanations for regulatory growth. This, in turn, will lead to a discussion of regulatory change, both the significant changes that often accompany dramatic shocks or salient examples of regulatory failure, and the subtler, incremental changes that may fail to attract comparable levels of attention. The chapter concludes with an overview of the volume.

The Empirical Record

Before we explore the dynamics of regulatory change in the contemporary period, it is important to cover some preliminary material and briefly address the historical record. The term *regulation* describes the array of public policies explicitly designed to govern the economic activity of individuals or organizations (e.g., firms, banks, unions). From a technical perspective, analysts often view the decision to regulate through the lens of market failure. Perfectly functioning markets exist when a number of ideal conditions hold. For current purposes, the most important conditions are: (1) there is shared information; (2) there is no monopoly power; and (3) there are no externalities. When information is lacking, it is difficult for consumers to know whether a given market transaction would actually improve their welfare and they can be subject to exploitation. Regulations can address problems of informational asymmetry by requiring the disclosure of information. This has been an important justification for regulations in consumer protection and finance, in particular. When monopoly power exists, prices are not set by competitive markets but established administratively or through the collusion of potential competitors. The prevention of monopoly power has been the focus of antitrust regulation. Where natural monopolies persist due to large fixed costs or economies of scale, regulation has turned instead to price- and rate-setting. Externalities exist whenever there are costs or benefits that are not incorporated into the price mechanism. In the context of regulation, negative externalities attract the greatest attention. In these cases, costs (e.g., pollution, workplace accidents or diseases) are borne by society. These social costs can be reduced or eliminated by requiring that corporations prevent these problems through changes in the production process (e.g., through the application of pollution control technology), incorporating the resulting costs into the price mechanism.

Although all regulation is economic in the broadest sense, scholars traditionally draw a distinction between economic regulations and social regulations. *Economic regulations* govern conditions under which actors can enter or exit a market, permissible competitive practices, the size and organization of economic actors, key features of products and services, and pricing. With the notable exception of antitrust policy, economic regulations are imposed on an industry-specific basis (e.g., finance, agriculture, air transportation). *Social regulations*, in contrast, force corporations to assume greater responsibility for the welfare of consumers, workers, and members of society who would otherwise be forced to bear the costs of industrial production—the kinds of negative externalities described above. Social regulations may also be used to address broader social problems (e.g., equal opportunity in employment, accessibility for disabled citizens). In contrast with economic regulations, social regulations are economy-wide in scope.[2]

Even though the period since the late nineteenth century exhibited a combination of economic and social regulations, the mix has changed over time. Most major economic regulatory statutes were enacted in the period from the passage of the Interstate Commerce Act (1887) through the 1930s. During this period, significant new regulatory initiatives covered railroads (1887), corporate competition and organization (1890), commercial banking (1914), hydroelectric power (1920), agriculture (1933), investment banking (1933), communications (1934), organized labor (1935), trucking (1935), public utility holding companies (1935), merchant marine (1936), and commercial aviation (1938). Although there were social regulations in this earlier period (e.g., the Pure Food and Drug Act of 1906), social regulations became far more prominent in the postwar period, most notably in the decades since the late 1960s. Congress passed ambitious new regulatory statutes covering air and water pollution (1970, 1972), hazardous chemicals and toxic waste (1976, 1980), occupational safety and health (1970), and consumer protection (1972). The early 1970s was a period of dramatic regulatory expansion, with the introduction of the most ambitious and costly regulations in the nation's history. Buffeted by high inflation and slow growth, the remainder of the decade brought a wave of deregulation. Congress revoked or relaxed many of the earlier economic regulatory policies and eliminated well-established agencies, including the Interstate Commerce Commission and the Civil Aeronautics Board. Deregulation would continue into subsequent decades, particularly in the financial services industry.

As noted in Chapter 1, although the deregulation that began in the 1970s was important, one can easily overstate its significance with respect to the growth of the regulatory state. The budgetary impact of old-style economic regulations was relatively small when compared with the costs of the new social regulations. In 1980, the Civil Aeronautics Board and the Interstate Commerce Commission—the two largest agencies that would be eliminated by deregulation—had budgets of $28 million and $80 million respectively. The panoply of agencies responsible for regulating finance and banking had combined budgets of $392 million. In sharp contrast, the Environmental Protection Agency—the flagship of social regulation—had a budget of $4.7 billion.[3] Regulatory spending (1960–2014), adjusted for inflation, is presented in Figure 2.1. A few points are worth noting. First, the real growth in regulatory spending has been rather dramatic. Between 1970 and 2014, total inflation-adjusted spending increased by 770 percent. Second, the vast majority of this growth was driven by social regulation. Thus, during this period, spending on social regulation increased by 912 percent, whereas economic regulatory spending grew by a more modest 450 percent. Third, although major political shifts reduced or moderated regulatory spending, the effects were sporadic and short-lived. Ronald Reagan was elected in 1980 promising to reduce the regulatory burden. Between 1980 and 1983, inflation-adjusted spending fell by almost 12 percent. But then it began to increase and by 1987, it exceeded any levels of spending on record. Similarly, in 1994, Republicans claimed unified control of Congress for the first time since the Eisenhower presidency. Armed with the Contract with America, the new GOP majorities promised, once again, to rein in regulation. While spending was briefly moderated and actually declined by 2.3 percent in 1996, growth quickly resumed.

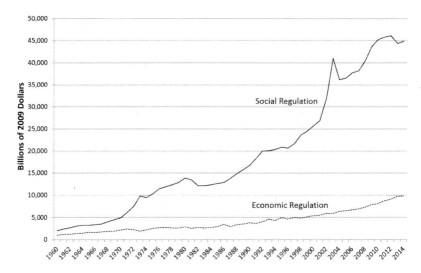

FIGURE 2.1   Regulatory Spending

Source: Susan Dudley and Melinda Warren, *Regulator's Budget Increases Consistent with Growth in Fiscal Budget: An Analysis of the U.S. Budget for Fiscal Years 2015 and 2016* (Washington DC: Regulatory Studies Center, George Washington University, 2015), Table A-5.

Budgetary figures do not provide the only indicator of regulatory growth. Another indicator of levels of regulatory activity is rulemaking activity. Under the Administrative Procedure Act, agencies are required to publish proposed and final rules in the *Federal Register*. The data represented in Figure 2.2 provides a representation of the trend since 1977. Two things are evident. First, there was a significant reduction in the number of rules and proposed rules during the early 1980s. As will be noted later in this chapter (and more expansively in Chapter 4), President Reagan introduced a new regulatory review process via Executive Order 12291 (1981), requiring executive branch agencies to submit regulatory impact analyses for major rules to the Office of Management and Budget. These new demands, when combined with the budget cuts noted above, undoubtedly explain the reduction in rulemaking activity from the levels achieved in the Carter presidency. Second, these reductions were temporary. By the 1990s, the number of new rules exceeded the levels that existed prior to the Reagan presidency.

Figures on annual rulemaking are important. But it is critical to remember that the rules generated in a given year are added to those already in effect. Once rules are promulgated, they are published in the Code of Federal Regulations (CFR). The CFR, issued annually, codifies all of the rules that are currently in force and thus the changes in the number of pages can give us a rough indicator of the aggregate growth of the regulatory state. Given what was presented above,

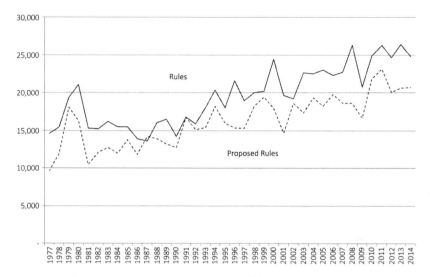

FIGURE 2.2   Rules and Proposed Rules

Source: Office of the Federal Register.

one should not be surprised that the CFR has grown dramatically over time. As one might expect, there were some brief periods when the CFR shrunk—and unsurprisingly, these periods correspond with the Reagan presidency and the mid-1990s when the Republicans assumed unified control of Congress. But the larger story in Figure 2.3 is the trend line. Between 1975 and 2014, the number of pages in the CFR more than doubled, from 71,000 pages to more than 175,000 pages. Going beyond page counts, one can seek to gain some knowledge of how many restrictions are contained in the regulations in any given year. Scholars at the Mercatus Institute at George Mason University have conduced a textual analysis of the digitalized CFR in an effort to quantify the number of restrictions imposed by the regulations. A textual analysis of the CFR from 1997 to 2012 searching strings that impose restrictions (i.e., the words "shall," "must," "may not," "prohibited," and "required") revealed that the number of restrictions increased from some 830,000 to over 1 million during this period.[4]

By way of summary, several key points are worth reiterating. First, there has been a significant growth in regulation over time, whether one is looking at inflation-adjusted spending or rulemaking activity. Second, the vast majority of this growth has occurred in the area of social regulation rather than economic regulation. Third, contrary to the common wisdom, there is little evidence that events like the election of Ronald Reagan or the Republican ascendance in Congress had more than a transitory effect on the growth of the regulatory state. Although deregulation was important in many ways, its primary effects were in the area of economic regulation rather than in the social regulatory arenas that

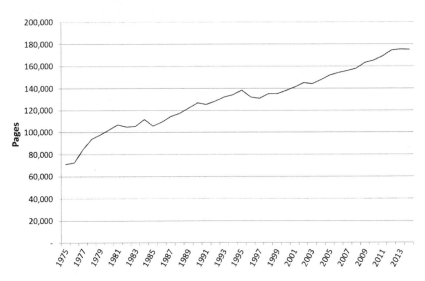

FIGURE 2.3   Code of Federal Regulations

Source: Office of the Federal Register.

were responsible for most of the growth. We turn now to consider explanations for this pattern of regulatory growth.

The Growth of Regulation

Regulation has continued to expand in the United States, even in a period that is often viewed—incorrectly—as a deregulatory era. This raises an important question: How can one explain regulatory growth? A number of factors can be cited to explain the long-term growth in regulation. To simplify a bit, we can begin by viewing the growth of regulation as being the product of demand. Rapid or significant economic change can be highly disruptive. New technologies can threaten existing producers, determining the fate of regional economies and creating great uncertainty for workers and consumers. Unsurprisingly, it can generate heightened popular and elite demands for public intervention. For example, the rise of the large-scale corporate economy in the late nineteenth century threatened small producers, raised the specter of monopoly, and stimulated populist demands for a regulatory response that could limit the power of the large corporation and trust. While contemporary analysts might provide a formal justification for regulation through appeals to market failure induced by market power or informational asymmetries, much of the discourse surrounding policy was explicitly political. As Senator John Sherman (R-OH) argued with respect to the trusts, the powers they exercised were "a kingly prerogative, inconsistent with our form of government . . . . If we would not submit to an emperor we should not submit to an autocrat of trade."[5] New regulations in antitrust, railroad regulation, and food and drug safety quickly became part of the regulatory state.

The demand for regulation may spike as a response to triggering events as well. Thomas Birkland provides a useful definition of a focusing event as

> an event that is sudden, relatively uncommon; can be reasonably defined as harmful or revealing the possibility of potentially greater future harms; has harms that are concentrated in a particular geographical area or community of interest; and that is know to policy makers and the public simultaneously.[6]

In the Progressive Era, Upton Sinclair's book *The Jungle* exposed the unsanitary conditions in Chicago's meatpacking industry, raising the demand for a regulatory response (in this case, the Federal Meat Inspection Act and the Pure Food and Drug Act of 1906).[7] Six decades later, highly salient events and exposés illustrated in graphic terms the problems of pollution, unsafe consumer products, and dangerous workplaces. When taken as a whole, they combined to force changes in the perceptions of risk and the government's proper role in mitigating risk. The salience of these focusing events was intensified by the larger ideological context, as New Left activists argued that environmental, occupational and consumer safety problems were a direct result of business practices, which had been condoned by a political system that worked under the assumption that the public interest was synonymous with ongoing profitability. The result was the wave of new social regulatory statutes noted above, which fundamentally recast the role of regulation and the demands placed on business.[8]

Much of the scholarship on regulatory change—like public policy more generally—is viewed, explicitly or implicitly, through a combination of punctuated equilibrium theory and path dependence. Punctuated equilibrium theory seeks to make sense of the basic pattern exhibited in so many policy arenas: Periods of stability are followed by episodes of rapid and significant change, which are often followed by new periods of stability. Following Frank R. Baumgartner and Bryan D. Jones, under normal conditions, most policy subsystems are at equilibrium.[9] Stability emanates from various sources. There is a common policy image (e.g., a shared understanding of policy problems, underlying causality, and goals). There is a broad consensus regarding appropriate policy instruments, relevant actors, and acceptable distributions of costs and benefits. Baumgartner and Jones use the evocative term "policy monopoly" to refer to these subsystems and convey the sense that they work quite effectively to exclude actors that might challenge the dominant policy image, thereby controlling the terms, direction, and rapidity of change.

The concept of policy monopoly fits well with the second component of the story: path dependence.[10] The basic insight from theories of path dependence is that decisions made early in the creation of an institution often places it on a particular trajectory of development that continues over time. Once Congress passes statutes, agencies engage in rulemaking to produce new regulations to implement the authority they have been delegated. This process continues, often repeatedly, as they make incremental adaptations to changing circumstances or refine policy in light of experience. Agencies are created. They professionalize and create the administrative capacity to develop the technical foundations for policy, conduct inspections, and engage in enforcement. They develop enduring relationships with interest groups, other agencies, and congressional committees, and these relationships provide additional support for path dependent development. Under normal conditions, actors make commitments and investments based on the assumption of stability, and this, in turn, creates incentives to preserve the status quo and raise the costs of significant change.

Every regulation has a constituency, and thus there is pressure to retain regulations once promulgated, even if they become antiquated. Businesses (and their organizational representatives), for example, may decry government interference. But they routinely lobby to preserve existing regulations and promote new regulations as a means of insulating themselves from competitive market forces and securing wealth transfers from consumers. Regulations can create barriers to entry for potential competitors, thereby stifling innovation and allowing incumbent firms to exercise some monopoly power. They can establish prices, thereby circumventing the market. The economic theory of regulation models the regulatory process as an exchange between profit-maximizing firms and vote-maximizing politicians. Elected officials are willing to meet the demands of organized business groups in exchange for political resources,[11] one of the many positive feedback loops that can support path dependence. This tendency is further reinforced by resources constraints. Given limited budgets, agencies are far less likely to invest in rulemakings to revoke obsolete regulations when they can simply decide to shift enforcement priorities. As a result, one should expect to see an accretion of regulations over time, an expectation that fits the data on the growth of the Code of Federal Regulations presented earlier in this chapter.

Policy monopolies can exert control over public policy for extended periods of time. But they can also be highly vulnerable. Crises, exogenous shocks, or salient examples of regulatory failure can punctuate the equilibrium, forcing issues out of the policy monopoly and on to the streets, the floors of Congress, and the White House. Policies that previously attracted little public attention can suddenly become central to political discourse. Political entrepreneurs and interest groups previously excluded from the policy monopoly may move quickly to exploit the changing circumstances, hoping to redefine the dominant policy image in such a way as to emphasize different political values and with them, a new universe of relevant actors. At times, these episodes may not bear much fruit: Actors who were central to the existing policy monopoly have great incentives to preserve the status quo and bring policy disputes to closure as quickly as possible. At other times, the changes can be transformative. More commonly, however, old policies are supplemented with new policies and institutions that may be grounded in very different sets of assumptions. Once this occurs, one should expect some changes in the trajectory of development—although the extent of change may well be limited by the factors noted above—and a new equilibrium. Moreover, while the episodes may result, on occasion, in a contraction of public authority, more commonly they result in an expansion of government.[12]

In sum, policy evolves along a particular trajectory, a product of path dependence and the monopolies that form around public policies. The policies may evolve to meet the needs of members of the policy monopoly. Regulated businesses may profit from regulatory barriers to entry. Members of Congress may benefit from the political support of regulated interests. Agencies may enjoy stable and increasing budgets. But the path dependent process of development may generate policies that are increasingly irrelevant to the regulatory problems that exist in the larger environment, a disjuncture that can generate crises that further add to the growth of the regulatory state.

Regulatory Regimes and the Dynamics of Large-scale Change

The history of regulation is replete with evidence to reaffirm the basic model presented above. Sometimes the shocks are limited to a single policy area. By way of illustration, consider the regulation of nuclear energy. In the immediate postwar period, the industry was under the supervision of the Joint Committee on Atomic Energy, which had jurisdiction over all legislation involving atomic energy, and the Atomic Energy Commission (AEC). With the passage of the Atomic Energy Act of 1954, Congress and the Eisenhower administration promoted nuclear energy and the AEC assumed dual responsibilities: to promote both the commercial development of the industry and to promote safety. By the late 1960s, concerns that safety regulation was being compromised for commercial development led to growing dissent within the AEC. By the 1970s, internal documents challenging the adequacy of coolant systems had been leaked and publicized by the Union of Concerned Scientists; Ralph Nader and environmental organizations had filed suit, attempting to force the closure of nuclear facilities. Ultimately, Congress passed the Energy Reorganization Act of 1974, eliminating the AEC and, three years later, the Joint Committee on Atomic Energy. Henceforth, the two missions would be separated, with safety regulation assigned to a newly created Nuclear Regulatory Commission and congressional oversight spread across multiple committees.[13]

Other times, in contrast, the shocks can be so significant as to force change across multiple policy arenas. The stagflation of the 1970s, for example, highlighted the limitations of fiscal policy. Keynesian theory predicted a stable tradeoff between inflation and unemployment, as represented by the Phillips Curve. When policymakers proved incapable of responding to the high inflation and high unemployment of the period, attention turned to competing macroeconomic theories. Ultimately, policymakers discarded standard Keynesianism and gravitated toward a combination of rational expectations, supply side economics, and monetarism.[14] As these debates were unfolding, critics used the chaotic environment to relitigate core welfare and regulatory policies. A period of welfare reform commenced that would end, two decades later, in the elimination of Aid for Families with Dependent Children. As attention turned to economic regulations—indicted as contributing to inflation and slow growth—Congress turned to the process of deregulation, rapidly eliminating well-established policies in several agencies and policy monopolies that had been stable for decades.

When seeking to understand the broader changes in regulation—those that cut simultaneously across multiple regulatory policy areas—it makes sense to work at a higher level of aggregation and focus on regulatory regimes. In a previous work, *Regulatory Politics in Transition*, I defined a regulatory regime as a historically specific configuration of policies and institutions that structures the relationship between social interests, the state, and economic actors.[15] In this context, regulatory regimes incorporated regulatory policies in multiple substantive issue areas simultaneously. The core argument was relatively straightforward. Exogenous shocks or momentous changes in issue salience can trigger the mobilization of social interests and elites. Shocks may be so profound—the example of stagflation, above—that they lead to mobilization around multiple policies simultaneously. Alternatively, salient events that punctuate the stable equilibrium in one policy area can make policy elites and the public far more responsive to information about related problems in other areas. The salient events—often emotionally charged accounts of tragedies—may be worst-case scenarios that are highly improbable. But they are often perceived as representative of risks more generally. These events can have a cascading effect, rendering the public more responsive to occurrences in other areas, thereby fomenting change in multiple issue areas more or less simultaneously.[16]

Following a crisis, higher levels of political mobilization are common, but the demands of mobilized groups and elites may be diverse and inchoate. There may be sharp contestation over the nature of the crisis—its origins, the responsible parties, the underlying causal factors at work—and, thus, whether an appropriate response involves incremental adjustments to existing policies or significant departures from the status quo. Policymakers and political elites compete to provide some structure by drawing on prevailing political and economic theories to frame problems in ways that favor their preferred set of policy responses. Inevitably, established elites seek to channel demands in ways that are compatible with existing policies, institutions, and coalitions. That is, they strive to preserve the extant policy monopolies. At times, this may be successful and the status quo proves relatively robust. At other times, these efforts fail. In these cases, one should expect to see significant changes in electoral outcomes that create the space for the introduction of a new configuration of policies, institutions, and actors. One should not be surprised that new regulatory regimes have often emerged out of realigning elections or periods when there were enduring shifts in existing party coalitions.

When new policies are introduced in multiple regulatory issue areas, accompanied by substantial institutional changes, a new regulatory regime emerges. The policy initiatives may engage a host of different and seemingly unrelated substantive issues, but one can often discover a set of analogous goals that surmount the problems intrinsic to a given industry or sector of the economy. Similarly, the administrative forms, policy instruments, and procedures developed to make and implement policy and incorporate social and economic interests into the policy process may reflect certain common features across policy areas. This coherence stems from several factors, including the common reference point (e.g., the exogenous shock) and a shared set of political-economic and administrative doctrines. Importantly, in a point we will return to below, the creation of a new regulatory regime does not constitute the wholesale elimination of previous policies and institutions. Rather, the new regime is often superimposed upon or incorporates elements of previous regimes. All of this compromises the extent to which the new regime can dramatically alter the trajectory of policy, while creating incongruities and sources of friction that may generate new problems over time.[17]

We can identify several regulatory regimes, the emergence of which followed this basic pattern.[18] The panic and depression of the 1890s led to an electoral realignment and a sustained period of Progressive reform. New policies were enacted to regulate the conduct of railroads, anticompetitive practices in the corporate economy, the fragility of the financial system, and the safety of food and drugs. Reflecting the concerns with the rise of the large corporate economy, many of the regulations were designed to force a heightened level of corporate responsibility and decentralize corporate power. The initiatives of the period delegated significant powers to the newly created agencies, reflecting the Progressive faith in neutral expertise. Moreover, the design of newly created agencies—as exhibited in the Federal Reserve or independent regulatory commissions like the Federal Trade Commission—reflected a willingness to experiment with new institutional forms.

A few decades later, the financial collapse of 1929 and the Great Depression, led to another massive electoral realignment and the rise of the New Deal. The sources of the collapse were within the financial system, and thus, New Deal reformers turned quite naturally to banking regulation. Congress passed legislation to separate commercial and investment banking. It created the Federal Deposit Insurance Corporation to prevent bank runs and the Securities and Exchange Commission to regulate the issuance and trading of stocks and bonds. In essence, new policies constituted distinct financial sub-industries, each with its own regulator and set of regulations. But regulatory change extended well beyond finance. In less than a decade, important new regulatory statutes were passed to extend public authority over the agricultural economy, industrial relations, communications, civil aeronautics, trucking, and public utility holding companies. These initiatives were grounded in the belief that regulatory policy could limit ruinous competition and coordinate the activities of economic actors in ways that would bring greater stability to a chaotic environment and that new administrative agencies had the capacity to promote the public interest and support recovery.

The postwar period witnessed changes of similar magnitude. The late 1960s and early 1970s brought the rise of the New Left, the antiwar, environmental and consumer movements, all of which placed intense pressure on the fraying New Deal coalition. Highly publicized accounts of pollution and workplace deaths created the kind of risk cascade addressed earlier, leading to extraordinary levels of political mobilization. Within the span of a few years, Congress passed by wide margins the most ambitious and expensive regulatory statutes in the nation's history. New policies were created to regulate air pollution, water pollution, toxic wastes, occupational safety and health, and consumer product safety. New agencies proliferated—most notably the Environmental Protection Agency, the Occupational Safety and Health Administration, and the Consumer Product Safety Commission—with complicated procedures to ensure oversight and the participation of groups previously excluded from the regulatory process. Other agencies, like the Federal Trade Commission, were reorganized and revitalized with vast new regulatory powers. Once again, these initiatives embodied the New Left critique of earlier regulations and corporate capitalism (a point that will be developed in greater detail in Chapter 3).[19]

While the 1970s began with a dramatic expansion of new social regulations, the decade was also distinguished by stagflation—the politically noxious combination of high inflation and unemployment. Although the economic problems of the decade could be causally linked to a combination of macroeconomic policies and growing competition from abroad, they nonetheless punctuated several stable regulatory (and non-regulatory) subsystems, as noted above, and created a window of opportunity for profound change. A network of conservative think tanks successfully linked inflation and slow growth to the burdens imposed by economic regulations. Congress, in turn, pursued market-based deregulation in finance, communications, energy, and air and surface transportation. A series of presidents imposed new regulatory review processes, ultimately forcing executive branch regulators to justify new regulations through the application of cost–benefit analysis. Earlier regimes had focused on the need to force higher levels of corporate accountability, albeit grounded in different theoretical understandings of the economy and the role of the state. The new regime, in sharp contrast, privileged market competition and forced higher levels of governmental accountability. It was premised on the assumption that markets were often superior to government regulations. The state, in turn, should intervene only under conditions of market failure, and then, only if the benefits exceeded the costs.

When Regimes Prove Robust

While crises can create a window of opportunity for regulatory regime change, this outcome is not inevitable. As noted in Chapter 1, the crises that marred the first decade of the new millennium were of extraordinary significance when viewed in historical context. The financial collapse was the greatest economic catastrophe since the 1929 crash and generated the deepest and most prolonged recession of the postwar period. The BP Deepwater Horizon disaster was the greatest oil spill and arguably the greatest environmental cataclysm in US history. The larger context—US involvement in two unpopular wars, rapid growth in the national debt, plummeting public faith in government—would seem to set the stage for the kind of rapid and significant change that, in the past, brought a new regulatory regime. Yet, the extent of regulatory change was quite limited. The Deepwater Horizon disaster stimulated some bureaucratic reorganization: The Minerals Management Service, responsible for overseeing the industry, was eliminated, its duties assigned to three new agencies in the Department of the Interior. But Congress failed to pass new statutes that would recalibrate policy to meet the challenges of deep and ultra-deep oil exploration. The case of finance is a bit more complicated. Significant new legislation was passed, but the Dodd–Frank Wall Street Reform and Consumer Protection Act of 2010 did little to create a new regulatory architecture covering the parts of the financial industry that were central to the collapse, a point that will be developed in far greater detail in Chapter 9.

This raises an obvious question. Why did these events fail to force substantial change in regulation? In *The Politics of Precaution*, David Vogel observes "rather than a risk 'availability cascade,'" the period since 1990 has

> been characterized by a risk "availability blockade." Widely publicized disagreement about the credibility of many of the alarm bells rung by activists made it more difficult for the influential segments of the public to be persuaded that additional stringent and comprehensive regulations were needed to protect them.[20]

While Vogel's argument hinges on changes in public opinion and a public complacency tied to the perceived success of earlier regulations, one can argue that there is an important institutional component to the story as well. There is strong empirical support for two key assertions: First, during the period in question, Congress became far more polarized. Second and related, it became far less capable of passing significant new statutes. The extensive hearings that used to provide a means of raising the popular salience of regulatory issues are far less common, and when they occur, they are far less likely to result in substantial new regulatory statutes.

In the past, Congress was vitally important in passing the statutes that provided the foundation for new regimes, often at the urging of the president.

Roosevelt's New Deal would have been stillborn absent a Congress that was capable of passing a long series of landmark statutes. Similarly, while Nixon adopted the environment and occupational safety and health policy, and interest groups mobilized in support of policy change, absent a Congress that was capable of high levels of legislative productivity, the period would have left little imprint on the history of regulation. Certainly, regulatory agencies are more than passive organizations buffeted by Congress. There is a long history of administrative creativity in building on existing statutory authority to address emergent problems. Yet, there are limits to what can be accomplished absent new legislation. All of this raises some interesting questions that will be reserved for later in this book. Has polarization created insurmountable barriers to the kind of regime change that has occurred in the past? If so, what are the implications for the future of regulation?

Forms of Gradual Change

Even if polarization has created institutional barriers to the passage of significant new regulatory statutes—and thus the kind of sweeping transformations that marked the history of regulation—regulatory change continues to occur. The forms that change takes are subtler, however, and may be more difficult to detect. Gradual forms of change are nothing new, of course. The basic model presented above focuses on long periods of stability punctuated by periods of rapid and substantial change. Critics correctly note that while our attention is drawn quite naturally to these periods of transformative change rather than the periods of stability, the latter are only stable in the most superficial sense.

Beneath the stability, change and conflicts are constantly occurring albeit in ways that are not always obvious to external observers.[21] In part, this may be a product of ambiguities in institutional design. Conflicts between competing groups may force compromises that create new opportunities for the losers to contest earlier decisions. Those seeking to preserve the original victories and distributions of costs and benefits, in turn, may need to mobilize resources on an ongoing basis. The rules that constitute institutions, even if relatively formalized, are routinely open to interpretation, creating additional opportunities for contestation. As James Mahoney and Kathleen Thelen note: "Actors with divergent interests will contest the openings this ambiguity provides because matters of interpretation and implementation can have profound consequences for resource allocations and substantive outcomes."[22] And beyond the ongoing distributional struggles, there are processes of policy learning that may lead to a reframing of core problems. The introduction of new ideas or bodies of expertise may shift the focus of implementation. All of this can have substantial consequences for policy, even if institutions appear to be relatively stable.[23]

Without discounting the importance of dramatic episodes of rapid change, regulatory policy history is more than a discontinuous succession of qualitatively different regimes, separated by the occasional exogenous shock.[24] This realization has stimulated much scholarship in comparative political economy and historical institutionalism, leading to the identification of several different processes of change, including displacement, layering, drift, and conversion.[25] To these, I would add a fifth process of change: devolution. These forms of change may exist within a discrete policy arena or agency; they may also be exhibited at a higher level of aggregation within a larger configuration of institutions.[26] Moreover, multiple forms of change may occur simultaneously. They are by no means mutually exclusive. Let us explore the various forms of change, focusing on their relevance for regulation.

Displacement

Displacement involves the replacement of one set of rules or institutions for another. The changes may be quite sudden, following the passage of new statutes, or they may prove more protracted. The history of regulation is replete with examples of displacement. Consider the example of workplace regulation. Historically, unionization had been highly contested and struggles for union recognition were often marred by violent conflict and industrial warfare. With the passage of the National Labor Relations Act (1935), which built on the National Industrial Recovery Act (1933), workers were granted a legally recognized right to organize. A new agency, the National Labor Relations Board, was established to regulate industrial relations. More than three decades later, the Occupational Safety and Health Act (1970) established a legal obligation on the part of employers to provide workplaces "free from recognized hazards that are causing or likely to cause death or serious physical harm to his employees."[27] This obligation displaced a system grounded in a patchwork of common law and state workers compensation statutes.

Displacement can take far more gradual forms. By way of illustration, one can look at changes in antitrust policy. During the 1970s, the Justice Department's Antitrust Division was professionalized with economists, who came to play an increasingly central role working with attorneys in making decisions about enforcement. At the beginning of the decade, these decisions were informed by the structure–conduct–performance paradigm, which focused on the concentration of market power in a given industry as setting the preconditions for various forms of anticompetitive behavior. Under the assumptions of this framework, there was ample justification for forcing corporate divestment or preventing mergers that would raise levels of industrial concentration. However, as economists were gaining a greater role in making enforcement decisions, the Chicago school gained prominence in industrial organization economics. The Chicago school discounted the role of economic structure, arguing that in many cases it was the result of successful performance rather than the harbinger of anticompetitive behavior. Rather than focusing on mergers and levels of concentration, the Chicago school was more concerned with standard price-fixing, which was a per se violation of the Sherman Antitrust Act. Despite the fact that the agency heads appointed by President Ford and President Carter supported a broad enforcement agenda, increasingly, the agency bureaucracy generated enforcement decisions that were largely what one would expect under the more conservative assumptions of the Chicago school. Agency professionalization combined with changes in economic theory displaced a more populist enforcement agenda, in essence, locking in a pattern of prosecutions that would subsequently be associated (incorrectly) with the Reagan revolution.[28]

Layering

Layering, unsurprisingly, occurs when new laws, regulations, or management systems are superimposed upon existing systems, without fully displacing them. The concept of layering finds its clearest exposition in Eric Schickler's work on Congress. As he explains:

> New coalitions may design novel institutional arrangements but lack the support, or perhaps the inclination, to replace preexisting institutions established to pursue other ends . . . the layering of successive innovations results in institutions that appear more haphazard than the product of some overarching master plan.[29]

This process can generate new tensions within an institution, as layers often prove incongruous. In Schickler's words: "the effects of institutional change . . . are mediated by tensions between that new arrangement and an entrenched authority structure designed to serve other interests."[30] As layers multiply, the difficulties of managing the friction between them grow in significance. This, in turn, creates new sources of ambiguity that may be fruitfully exploited by various interests seeking additional policy or institutional change.

There are powerful incentives to retain regulations, even when they no longer serve the intended function. Each regulation has a constituency that is intent on preserving it to the extent possible, even if only for symbolic purposes. From the perspective of an agency, changing or rescinding regulations can be costly, given the requirements of notice-and-comment rulemaking and the potential for judicial review. Agencies may simply choose to avoid these battles, retain old regulations, and simply fail to enforce them.[31] Regulated parties, in turn, may seek to exploit the inconsistencies and gaps between the new and the old. They may engage in regulatory arbitrage, seeking out the most favorable treatment among competing rule systems. As new regulations are layered upon the old, regulators, in turn, must devote ever-greater attention to managing the problems engendered by inconsistent regulations and the conflict/competition among firms that were organized under different and competing regulatory orders.

Examples of regulatory layering are myriad. In some of the oldest regulatory arenas, policies and institutions have been layered for more than a century. The system for financial regulation, for example, has elements dating back to the Civil War banking acts (the Comptroller of the Currency), the Progressive Era (the Federal Reserve), the New Deal (the Securities and Exchange Commission and the Federal Deposit Insurance Corporation), and the post-1980 era of deregulation. Policies dating back for more than a century have been layered one upon another, creating multiple sources of friction and problems of coordination.[32] But layering is evident even in more recent additions to the regulatory state. In environmental protection, the Environmental Protection Agency (EPA) must execute its own mandates while managing some of the environmental damages caused by the policies of the USDA and the Department of Interior, many of which find their origins in the nineteenth century.

Although layering can be found in many policy areas, it can also be found across multiple regulatory policy arenas. Consider the case of regulatory review. In the 1970s, Congress passed detailed statutes that constrained the president's capacity to control the regulatory state. Beginning with Reagan's Executive Order 12291 (1981), executive branch agencies were required to complete a regulatory impact analysis grounded in cost–benefit analysis.[33] According to Executive Order 12291, section 2b: "Regulatory action shall not be undertaken unless the potential benefits to society . . . outweigh the potential costs." The Office of Management and Budget Office of Information and Regulatory Affairs (OMB-OIRA) served a gatekeeper function, reviewing the impact analyses and requiring that agencies refrain from publishing advanced notice of rulemaking if proposed regulations failed to yield net benefits. This created significant problems for social regulatory agencies, in particular, the EPA. Given the prevalence of upfront costs, the intrinsic difficulties of monetizing social regulatory benefits and the need to discount future benefits to present value, many proposed regulations were defeated by the regulatory review processes.[34] Two rule systems, premised on different sets of normative assumptions, created ongoing conflicts between agencies and the OMB-OIRA, enhancing the power of the executive while depleting scarce resources that might otherwise be used to promote regulatory goals.

Drift

The concept of *drift* finds its clearest expression in Jacob Hacker's work on social policy.[35] Oftentimes, an institution or policy may appear superficially stable. That is, there are no obvious signs of retrenchment, no revocations of core statutes, or significant cuts in spending. But at the same time, institutions and policies are not routinely updated and thus they fail to continue to serve their intended purposes. As Wolfgang Streeck and Kathleen Thelen observe: "institutions require active maintenance; to remain what they are they need to be reset and refocused, or sometimes more fundamentally recalibrated and renegotiated, in response to changes in the political and economic environment in which they are embedded."[36] Drift may be a product of path dependence. That is, an institution's evolutionary trajectory may be shaped by early decisions rather than ongoing reappraisals of and adjustments to changes in the larger environment. Interests that prevail under established policies—members of the policy monopoly, to employ the language used earlier—have powerful incentives to impede changes that would alter the distribution and magnitude of costs and benefits or the balances of power within an industry. Alternatively, those who would welcome outright retrenchment may lack the political resources to bring it about. Given the number of veto points in the American political system, they can nonetheless block efforts to recalibrate existing policies and institutions.

The history of regulation is rife with examples of drift. Agricultural regulation remains premised on assumptions inherited from the New Deal, despite the dramatic changes in technology and the scale of production. When Congress passed the Agricultural Adjustment Act of 1933 creating a system of income and price-support mechanisms, the farm population constituted more than 25 percent of the overall population. Eighty years later, comparable policies play a very different role in an industry that employs less than 2 percent of the workforce and is dominated by agribusiness.[37] Environmental statutes enacted in the 1970s have played an important role in reducing pollutants. Yet, these statutes have not been updated to address emerging challenges like global climate change. Indeed, when the EPA sought to strengthen the regulation of greenhouse gas emissions in 2010, it was required to draw on authorization granted in the Clean Air Amendments passed in 1970, the year the *Washington Post* devoted a front-page story to warnings that scientists were predicting a new ice age.[38] Both of the crises introduced in Chapter 1 had elements of drift. Regulations had not been revised to take into account the rise of securitization (in the case of finance) or deep- and ultra-deepwater exploration (in the case of oil spill policy). As these examples illustrate, the consequences of drift can be catastrophic.

Conversion

Conversion involves the redirection of existing institutions to achieve new goals or to serve new purposes. The roots of conversion may be found in original institutional design, a product of compromise and coalition building. Originally, an agency may have been given a broad statutory mandate—or multiple and potentially contradictory missions—creating space for political actors to shape creatively the focus of regulation.[39] Conversion may be driven by ideas, as new theories or bodies of expertise are adopted in policymaking and alter the interpretation of agency mandates.[40] It may be the product of interest group politics, as political actors reinterpret existing missions to favor their constituents. Conversion may be imposed from without, as Congress passes new statutes and superimposes them on an existing institution (what was described as layering, above) in such a fashion as to redirect an agency toward a new set of goals or constituents.

In regulation, capture theory is essentially a theory of conversion, as agencies evolve to nurture the very interests they were charged with regulating.[41] Even if the concept of capture is often poorly specified and its frequency commonly overstated,[42] the history of regulation nonetheless provides clear cases of agencies that have changed their orientation over time, often to meet the demands of the businesses they were charged with regulating. The Interstate Commerce Commission (ICC), for example, was empowered to set *maximum* rates, authority it used routinely to meet the demands of shippers and agricultural commodity producers. With the Transportation Act of 1920, however, Congress directed the ICC to set *minimum* rates to guarantee a specific rate of return, a conversion that favored the now undercapitalized railroads.[43] By the 1930s, the ICC had gained authority to regulate trucking. Interstate motor carriers could only operate if they had a certificate of public convenience and necessity, and the difficulties of acquiring a certificate and of receiving approval for new routes proved to be potent barriers to entry that protected established firms.

The history of the Federal Trade Commission (FTC) is replete with examples of conversion, albeit without the same explicit capture that one sees in the ICC. Created in 1914 with the vague mandate to bring proceedings against "unfair methods of competition in commerce," commissioners creatively used the FTC to promote regulated competition via trade practice conferences, which they used to foster agreements among competitors as to kinds of activities that were disruptive.[44] In the 1970s, after decades of passivity and following a significant reorganization and under pressure from the consumer movement, the FTC became a vigorous consumer protection advocate. Armed with new authority for industry-wide rulemaking, it was routinely referred to as the second most powerful legislature in Washington. Unsurprisingly, activism carried a high political cost: Following a congressional backlash in the late 1970s, the FTC of the 1980s began applying cost–benefit analysis to identify rules ripe for revocation, a task that actually outpaced the promulgation of new regulations.[45]

Devolution

A final form of change takes the form of devolution. This involves the assignment of governmental duties to private parties, in essence replacing governmental provision with a far more complex configuration of actors involved in defining and implementing public policy. The past few decades have witnessed a far greater reliance on third parties in most areas of public policy, as governmental functions have been devolved increasingly on to nongovernmental actors. Whether one refers to the phenomenon as "third-party government,"[46] "government by proxy,"[47] the "hollow state,"[48] or the "submerged state,"[49] governmental functions have been devolved increasingly on to nongovernmental actors. As Lester Salamon explains:

> The federal government in particular does increasingly little itself, at least in the domestic sphere. Instead, it operates through other entities— states, cities, counties, banks, industrial corporations, hospitals, nonprofit organizations, and a host of other nonfederal third parties. Indeed, we have created a system of third-party government, in which government establishes priorities and generates funds but leaves the actual delivery of services and the operation of public programs to a variety of nonfederal third parties.[50]

In regulation, devolution to nongovernmental actors has a long history. As noted above when discussing conversion, the FTC relied on trade practice conferences as a means of generating new rules on fair competition. This was part of a larger trend in the 1920s commonly referred to as "associationalism." Herbert Hoover, then Secretary of Commerce, promoted this vision of governance, arguing that the state should coordinate the self-regulation of industry via trade associations as a means of capturing some of the benefits of planning without expanding the bureaucracy.[51] During the 1930s, several of the New Deal initiatives in regulation devolved authority on to private parties. For example, the Securities and Exchange Commission adopted a model of government-supervised self-regulation. It regulated the exchanges which, in turn, regulated their members. The Maloney Act of 1938 amended the Securities Exchange Act to recognize the National Association of Securities Dealers as the sole self-regulatory organization for the over-the-counter market. In Thomas McCraw's words, it "assumed the functions and structure of a regulatory agency."[52]

In the past few decades, devolution in regulation has become more commonplace. In nuclear energy, the Nuclear Regulatory Commission and an industry association, the Institute of Nuclear Power Operators, have shared regulatory authority since the Three Mile Island incident.[53] In environmental protection, the EPA responded to problems of drift by relying more heavily on voluntary programs and partnerships that could allow it to leverage private resources and expertise to reach problems that were beyond existing statutory authority. In food safety, regulators from the Food and Drug Administration and the Department of Agriculture depend on firms to develop and implement their own "HACCP" (hazard analysis and critical control point) plans, subject to third-party auditing. In workplace safety, the Occupational Safety and Health Administration uses private inspectors—volunteers trained and deputized as Special Government Employees but paid by their corporate employers—to oversee the quality of the plans implemented by firms in the Voluntary Protection Program. In finance, regulators rely on credit rating agencies to evaluate the risks associated with securities which, in turn, impacts on the size of the market and the levels of collateral that banks must maintain.

In each of these cases, private and quasi-private organizations play a vital role in the implementation chain. Arguably, in some cases devolution is driven by the technical complexity of the issues at hand and the difficulties that regulators might face in accessing quality information. But in other cases, it may reflect the fact that agencies lack the statutory authority to regulate, and are thus forced to rely on voluntary participation in partnerships if they are to manage the problems of drift.

The Argument in Brief

This volume is concerned primarily with the dynamics of regulation in the contemporary period.[54] Even a casual observer of regulation can note three of the most remarkable changes:

1. *The dearth of significant new regulatory statutes.* During the 1960s and 1970s, Congress was marked by extraordinary levels of legislative productivity. It passed a long series of landmark regulatory statutes that literally recast the role of the state in the economy. But as of this writing, the statutory framework for major social regulations is largely the same as it was more than a quarter century ago for environmental protection, and almost a half-century for occupational safety and health.
2. *The rise of presidential unilateralism.* As Congress has become incapable of passing significant new statutes and gridlock has often impeded the execution of normal governmental functions, presidents have embraced unilateral action. In the area of regulation, this has often meant creating extra-legal programs and promoting rulemaking that may exceed the authority previously granted by Congress.
3. *The growing tendency to devolve authority on to regulated parties.* In some agencies like EPA and OSHA—once denounced routinely for their heavy handed, adversarial approach to regulation—there has been a growing reliance on voluntary programs and public–private partnerships. In other cases, there has been an assumption that industry actors have the information, incentives, and capacity to manage the risks they assume, often with the lightest of regulatory oversight.

It is the core argument of this book that these changes are causally related and have important implications for the quality of regulation. Moreover, understanding this relationship can give us some analytical traction in explaining the most striking contemporary examples of regulatory failure: the financial crisis and the Deepwater Horizon spill. The concepts developed earlier are particularly important in framing the argument.

Let us return briefly to three of the processes of change identified above: conversion, layering, and drift. What conditions favor one form of change over another? Following Jacob S. Hacker, the process of change that prevails can be understood as a product of (1) the extent to which institutions are internally malleable and (2) the extent to which the political environment facilitates large-scale external change, for example, the passage of new statutes.[55] Where institutions are malleable but the political environment impedes external change, one can expect to see *conversion*. That is, administrators have sufficient discretionary authority to introduce new goals, policy instruments, or coalition members. They can creatively adjust the functions that an institution serves, redirecting their efforts to incorporate policy learning or address emerging problems.[56] When, in contrast, institutions are too rigid to forestall internal change but external change is nonetheless possible, one can expect to see a process of legislative change. Absent the kinds of crisis that could lead to rapid, transformative change, new statutory authority or institutional arrangements are *layered* upon the old. Finally, when internal and external environments create impediments to change, one should witness a process of *drift*. Opponents of existing policy may lack the political support to pass new statutes, for example, but they can succeed in blocking new laws that could update existing institutions, thereby rendering them increasingly irrelevant. Over time, the disjunction between existing institutions and the larger environment they are charged with managing grows greater, such that the institutions no longer serve their intended purpose even if normal metrics of agency performance (e.g., inspections, citations, prosecutions) suggest otherwise.

The core argument of the book is relatively straightforward and will be developed in somewhat greater detail in the next section. During earlier periods of rapid policy change—the Progressive Era and the New Deal, to be precise—Congress passed statutes that delegated broad discretionary authority to administrators. There was a shared belief that administrators possessed the neutral expertise to regulate in the public interest, and should be given the latitude to do so. Beginning in the late 1960s, in contrast, concerns over potential regulatory capture, the representational capacity of the administrative state, and the compatibility of congressional and presidential policy priorities, combined to support a much different approach to institutional design. Congress passed exhaustively detailed statutes and imposed complex processes that sharply reduced bureaucratic discretion, and thus the flexibility to adapt existing institutions to new tasks. This limited the extent to which conversion could occur. This may not have been a great concern at the time—indeed, it was the intent. Large bipartisan majorities passed the core regulatory statutes and there was little reason to suspect that similar majorities would not be available in the future. However, by the early 1990s, growing partisan polarization and gridlock essentially foreclosed the passage of significant new statutes.

The predictable result of this combination of factors was regulatory drift—growing disjunctions between what institutions were designed to do and the demands of the larger regulatory environment. In some cases, presidents engaged in unilateral action in an attempt to compensate for drift. Key agencies relied increasingly on private–public partnerships and voluntary programs to extend regulatory capacity. Although many of these initiatives bore a resemblance to alternative models of regulation that had been and remain of some scholarly interest, they were largely superimposed on top of rigid institutions rather than integrated into existing policies. This dramatically limited the quality of oversight and their efficacy more generally. In other regulatory policy areas, there may have been less of a dependence on partnerships and voluntary programs. Nonetheless, the failure to update the core statutes led to significant gaps in the exiting regulatory structures. As activities changed within the relevant industries—sometimes in revolutionary ways—regulations premised on dated premises no longer provided the level of protection or accountability that should be central to public regulation, setting the stage for some of the most striking examples of regulatory failure in US history.

Overview

When trying to understand contemporary social regulation, attention must turn to two issues. First, one must look to critical decisions in institutional design (the subject of Chapters 3 and 4). Second, one must look to the problem of polarization (the subject of Chapter 5). Combined, these factors have generated the problem of drift. Chapter 3 explores competing approaches to institutional design in the history of regulation, focusing on the period beginning in the late 1960s. During this period, Congress passed landmark social regulatory statutes, most importantly, in the areas of environmental protection and occupational safety and health. The context was shaped by the prevailing critique of regulation and the administrative state. Earlier economic regulatory statutes provided broad grants of authority to agencies, reflecting faith in the neutrality and competence of administrators. By the 1960s, this faith was roundly renounced. Scholars and activists portrayed many agencies as either moribund and sclerotic or, worse yet, captured by the very business interests they were charged with regulating. Congress sought to prevent a similar fate from befalling the newly created social regulatory agencies by adopting a variety of expedients, including writing exhaustively detailed statutes that limited the discretionary authority of administrators. These same expedients could limit the capacity of presidents and future Congresses to depart from the preferences of those responsible for the core regulatory statutes. Moreover, contemporaneous concerns about the representational capacity of the administrative state informed the decision to create new mechanisms for representing regulatory advocates (e.g., via expanding access to the courts and the rulemaking process).

While the early 1970s was a period of dramatic regulatory expansion, it was quickly followed by a wave of deregulation and, more importantly, the imposition of new regulatory review processes centralized in the executive branch. Chapter 4 examines these phenomena, focusing on regulatory review. When Congress adopted the strategy examined in Chapter 3, it did so, in part, to constrain the president's control over the executive branch regulatory agencies and freedom to depart from congressional policy preferences. The unprecedented costs of the new regulations in an era of high inflation and slow growth created powerful incentives for presidents, beginning with Richard Nixon, to impose review processes within the Executive Office of the President. While early efforts at regulatory review had limited impact, President Reagan's imposition of new cost–benefit analysis-based regulatory review requirements via Executive Order 12291 (1981) marked a sea change. Although regulatory review was a centerpiece of Reagan's antiregulatory agenda, it was also part of a larger inter-branch struggle over the administrative state. By imposing new review requirements and vesting authority in the OMB-OIRA, the executive order provided a means of reclaiming presidential control, an interpretation that is reinforced by the fact that regulatory review has only been strengthened in subsequent decades, by Democratic and Republican presidents. From a practical perspective, agencies that were already working under enormous statutory constraints, now faced additional impediments to translating their statutory mandates into regulations.

During the 1980s, the complexity of the social regulatory statutes, the protracted nature of rulemaking, and the friction between agency missions and cost–benefit-analysis-based regulatory review created significant hurdles for regulation. Things became significantly more challenging subsequently as partisan polarization increased in Congress—the subject of Chapter 5. This polarization had important implications for regulatory budgets and the approval of appointees. But its most profound consequences came in the legislative arena. As noted earlier, it was increasingly rare for Congress to hold extensive hearings in response to salient cases of regulatory failure (an institutional variant of Vogel's "risk availability blockade"). Moreover, while Congress continued to legislate, it failed to pass the kind of substantively important regulatory statutes that had laid the foundations of contemporary regulation. Agencies were forced to base their regulatory actions on increasingly dated statutes (the problem of drift, described above). At the same time, a gridlocked Congress provided greater latitude for unilateral actions on the part of presidents, who authorized extra-legal means of extending regulatory capacity.

The failure to recalibrate institutions led to their growing obsolescence and increased the incentives to extend regulatory capacity via devolution. In the 1990s, the Clinton administration sought to "reinvent government." The nominal aspiration was to apply some of the lessons of the corporate sector to government, thereby creating a system that was lean, entrepreneurial, and more responsive to the needs of citizens (or "customers," as they were frequently called). Many of the reinvention projects devolved authority onto private sector actors through voluntary programs and public–private partnerships, and in so doing, appeared to embody some of the alternative models of regulation that had emerged in scholarly debates. These efforts, largely continued under Presidents Bush and Obama, were most pronounced in the two flagship social regulatory agencies: EPA and OSHA. Once we place reinvention and the ongoing support for regulatory voluntarism in the larger political context, we can better understand it in relation to the problems of polarization. Clinton's reinvention coincided with the resurgence of the GOP and, following the 1994 midterm elections, unified Republican control of Congress. New regulatory statutes were already a rarity by this point, and the pattern of congressional polarization and gridlock would only become more pronounced over time. Agencies lacking new statutory authority and forced to work within severe budget constraints found partnerships and voluntary programs as convenient means of leveraging private sector resources and extending the reach of regulation.

Chapter 6 focuses on the EPA, the largest social regulatory agency and the place where reinvention found its most striking expressions. During the 1990s, dozens of voluntary programs and partnerships were introduced in multiple areas, some as narrow as the Ruminant Livestock Efficiency Program (designed to reduce methane emissions from livestock) others as broad as the Climate Wise Recognition Program (a collaborative program to cut greenhouse gas emissions). The EPA also experimented with a new regulatory green track, the National Environmental Performance Track, designed to provide high-performing firms with a host of regulatory benefits (e.g., public recognition, enhanced compliance assistance, streamlined permitting). Chapter 7 turns to OSHA. Drawing on a Reagan-era innovation, the agency increasingly assisted firms in implementing safety programs under its Voluntary Protection Plan, incentivizing participation with fewer routine inspections and reduced fines. New strategic alliances were formed on an industry-specific basis to encourage firms to find better means of reducing risks in their workplaces. In both agencies, one might argue, initiatives of this kind were relatively unobjectionable, particularly when voluntary programs facilitated efforts to extend agency activities beyond what was permitted under the dated statutes. Yet, given the rigid nature of the regulatory bureaucracies and the lack of statutory foundations, these new programs were not integrated with mandatory regulations. Moreover, there is little evidence that the agencies developed the capacity to evaluate performance and determine whether the programs actually bore results. Indeed, in an age of constrained resources, they may have depleted the budgets available for standard regulation.

Social regulations at EPA and OSHA provide some insights in agency efforts to manage the problems of drift. Chapters 8 and 9 turn to explore two of the largest regulatory failures in the nation's history, arguing that polarization and drift set the foundations for these crises. Chapter 8 focuses on a single case study: oil spill policy. Although there is a long history of legislation designed to assign liability for oil spills, the contemporary regime was a response to the Exxon

Valdez disaster of 1989, which spilled 250,000 barrels of North Slope crude oil into Alaska's Prince William Sound. The spill revealed in stark terms the limitations of existing policy and, following an extended set of congressional hearings, Congress passed the Oil Pollution Act of 1990. The Act imposed new technology-based standards for shippers, created a new Oil Spill Liability Trust Fund, and required that industry develop worst-case scenario contingency plans and maintain the capacity to execute them. As noted in Chapter 1, the decades following the Exxon Valdez disaster were marked by a technological revolution in oil exploration, as firms began to drill in deep- and ultra-deep environments. In 2010, as the BP Deepwater Horizon disaster unfolded, several things became clear. First, because Congress had failed to update the oil spill regime to take into account the dramatic changes in industry practices, it was woefully outdated—a situation of regulatory drift. Second, although Congress had devolved authority for contingency planning and emergency response on to the industry, the industry had failed to execute its responsibilities. Third, the Department of Interior's Minerals Management Service clearly lacked the capacity to monitor industry compliance or oversee the response to the spill.

Chapter 9 turns to the financial crisis. Although many accounts of the crisis interpret it as a product of excessive deregulation, this interpretation is open to challenge. Since the mid-nineteenth century, successive regulatory statutes have been layered one upon another. Beginning in the late 1970s, Congress responded to the difficulties these regulations created for financial institutions under conditions of high inflation by deregulating interest rates and allowing greater latitude in the services that institutions could offer. By the late 1980s, profound changes were taking place in the financial industry. Banks that formerly issued mortgages with the intention of holding them in their portfolios were increasingly selling them to investment banks that were pooling them and selling mortgage-backed securities. The quasi-private government-sponsored entities were directed by Congress and the Department of Housing and Urban Development to purchase a growing percentage of low- and moderate-income mortgages as a means of adding liquidity to real estate markets and facilitating increases in the homeownership rate. These mortgages were subsequently securitized as well. Private credit rating agencies were given the duty of evaluating the quality of the securities and assigning risk-based ratings. Institutional purchasers could manage their remaining risk by buying credit-default swaps, derivatives that guaranteed repayment should mortgage holders fail to meet their obligations. The higher quality debt was entering the portfolios of major institutions and being used as collateral in short-term borrowing in money markets. Although this was clearly banking, it was not being conducted by regulated financial intermediaries and Congress had failed to pass new legislation to create a new regulatory architecture for the most dynamic portion of the financial system. As in the case of oil pollution, a combination of regulatory drift and devolution combined to create the preconditions of regulatory failure.

Chapter 10 concludes the volume with some reflections on contemporary regulatory dynamics and the limitations of the system that have emerged since the early 1990s. Traditionally, public regulation was deemed necessary because markets fail. Profit-seeking firms may collude or erect barriers to entry to undermining market competition and elevate prices. They may fail to provide consumers with sufficient information, hoping to profit from their ignorance. They impose externalities—costs like pollution and industrial injuries that are foisted on to society rather than incorporated into the price mechanism. Regulation could provide a remedy for these and other problems, essentially elevating the public interest over the private interests that prevail in a market economy. While the new agencies wielded significant power, there were mechanisms in place to force transparency and accountability. Certainly, this portrayal of regulation was something of an ideal. But even if there were cases of regulatory failure—some quite tragic—there is strong empirical evidence that regulatory policies often succeeded, whether one is speaking of pollution, occupational diseases, or the safety of food and consumer products.

The key question is whether this record can be extended under the conditions explored in this book. The devolution of regulatory authority on to private sector actors may be a valuable adjunct to mandatory regulations, if the resulting programs are integrated into policy and subject to sufficient oversight. Yet, the institutional design expedients adopted in the 1960s and 1970s created substantial impediments. For several decades, voluntary programs and partnerships have been superimposed on a rigid structure, and without statutory authorization and budgetary support, it is difficult for agencies to evaluate the success of these initiatives. Similarly, as the cases of the Deepwater Horizon and the financial crisis suggest, polarization and gridlock have created extraordinary impediments to updating the regulatory structure to accommodate the dynamics of the market economy. Without ongoing recalibration of regulatory policies and institutions, the system becomes more vulnerable to crises. Under conditions of polarization and gridlock, the system becomes less capable of responding to these crises when they occur.

Notes

1   Susan Dudley and Melinda Warren, *Economic Forms of Regulation on the Rise: An Analysis of the U.S. Budget for Fiscal Years 2014 and 2015* (Washington, DC: Regulatory Studies Center, George Washington University, 2014), Table A-1.
2   Marc Allen Eisner, Jeff Worsham, and Evan J. Ringquist, *Contemporary Regulatory Policy*, 2nd ed. (Boulder, CO: Lynne Rienner, 2006), 3.
3   For a comparison of regulatory spending by category and year, see Dudley and Warren, *Economic Forms of Regulation on the Rise*, Table A-1.
4   Omar Al-Ubaydli and Patrick A. McLaughlin. "RegData: A Numerical Database on Industry-Specific Regulations for All US Industries and Federal Regulations, 1997–2012," Mercatus Working Paper, Arlington, VA: Mercatus Center, January 2015.
5   Congressional Record, 51st Cong., 1st sess/. March 21, 1890, 21: 2457.

6 Thomas A. Birkland, "Focusing Events, Mobilization, and Agenda Setting," *Journal of Public Policy* 18, 1 (1998): 54.

7 Upton Sinclair, *The Jungle* (New York: Doubleday, Jabber & Co., 1906).

8 For a detailed discussion of the consumer movement and its impact on the evolution of regulatory policy in this period, see Michael Pertschuk, *Revolt against Regulation: The Rise and Pause of the Consumer Movement* (Berkeley, CA: University of California Press, 1982), 5–45.

9 See Frank R. Baumgartner and Bryan D. Jones, *Agendas and Stability in American Politics*, 2nd ed. (Chicago, IL: University of Chicago Press, 2009), and James L. True, Bryan D. Jones, and Frank R. Baumgartner, "Punctuated Equilibrium Theory: Explaining Stability and Change in Public Policymaking," in *Theories of the Policy Process*, ed. Paul A. Sabatier (Cambridge, MA: Westview Press, 2001), 155–87.

10 See Paul Pierson, "Increasing Returns, Path Dependence, and the Study of Politics," *American Political Science Review* 94, 2 (2000): 251–67, and Paul Pierson, "Not Just What, But When: Timing and Sequence in Political Processes," *Studies in American Political Development* 14 (2000): 72–92.

11 George J. Stigler, "The Theory of Economic Regulation," *The Bell Journal of Economics and Management Science* 2, 1 (1971): 3–21.

12 See Robert Higgs, *Crisis and Leviathan: Critical Episodes in the Growth of American Government* (New York: Oxford University Press, 1987).

13 See John L. Campbell, *Collapse of an Industry: Nuclear Power and the Contradictions of U.S. Policy* (Ithaca, NY: Cornell University Press, 1988).

14 See Mark Blyth, *Great Transformations: Economic Ideas and Institutional Change in the Twentieth Century* (Cambridge: Cambridge University Press, 2002), 152–201.

15 See Marc Allen Eisner, *Regulatory Politics in Transition* (Baltimore, MD: Johns Hopkins University Press, 1993), 2–3.

16 See Cass Sunstein, *Laws of Fear: Beyond the Precautionary Principle* (Cambridge, UK: Cambridge University Press, 2005), 94–98.

17 This argument is developed in Marc Allen Eisner, "Policy Regimes in Political Time: Path Dependency, Regime Change and the Case of US Financial Regulation," paper delivered at the International Conference on Public Policy, Grenoble, France, June 26, 2013.

18 See Eisner, *Regulatory Politics in Transition*, for a detailed development of these regimes.

19 The best account of this period can be found in Richard A. Harris and Sidney M. Milkis, *The Politics of Regulatory Change: A Tale of Two Agencies*, 2nd ed. (New York: Oxford University Press, 1996).

20 David Vogel, *The Politics of Precaution: Regulating Health, Safety, and Environmental Risks in Europe and the United States* (Princeton, NJ: Princeton University Press, 2012), 41.

21 B. Guy Peters, Jon Pierre, and Desmond S. King, "The Politics of Path Dependency: Political Conflict in Historical Institutionalism," *The Journal of Politics* 67, 4 (2005): 1275–1300.

22 James Mahoney and Kathleen Thelen, "A Theory of Gradual Institutional Change," in *Beyond Continuity: Institutional Change in Advanced Political Economies*, ed. Wolfgang Streeck and Kathleen Thelen (Oxford: Oxford University Press, 2005), 11.

23 For a case study of how different bodies of knowledge can shape policy outcomes, see Marc Allen Eisner, *Antitrust and the Triumph of Economics: Institutions, Expertise, and Policy Change* (Chapel Hill, NC: University of North Carolina Press, 1991).

24 Marc Schneiberg, "What's on the Path? Path Dependence, Organizational Diversity and the Problem of Institutional Change in the US Economy, 1900–1950," *Socio-Economic Review* 5 (2007): 47–80.

25 Wolfgang Streeck and Kathleen Thelen, "Institutional Change in Advanced Political Economies," in *Beyond Continuity: Institutional Change in Advanced Political Economies*, ed. Wolfgang Streeck and Kathleen Thelen (Oxford: Oxford University Press, 2005), 1–39.

26 Richard Deeg, "Path Dependency, Institutional Complementarity, and Change in National Business Systems," in *Changing Capitalisms? Internationalization, Institutional Change, and Systems of Economic Organization*, ed. Glenn Morgan, Richard Whitley, and Eli Moen (Oxford: Oxford University Press, 2005), 21–52.

27 29 U.S.C. §654, 5(a)1–2.

28 See Marc Allen Eisner and Kenneth J. Meier, "Presidential Control versus Bureaucratic Power: Explaining the Reagan Revolution in Antitrust," *American Journal of Political Science* 34, 1 (1990): 269–87.

29 Eric Schickler, *Disjointed Pluralism: Institutional Innovation and the Development of the U.S. Congress* (Princeton, NJ: Princeton University Press, 2001), 15.

30 Ibid., 16.

31 Daniel T. Deacon, "Deregulation through Nonenforcement," *New York University Law Review* 85 (2010): 795–828.

32 See Eugene Nelson White, "The Political Economy of Banking Regulation, 1864–1933," *The Journal of Economic History* 42, 1 (1982): 33–40.

33 See Thomas O. McGarity, *Reinventing Rationality: The Role of Regulatory Analysis in the Federal Bureaucracy* (Cambridge, UK: Cambridge University Press, 1991), and Robert V. Percival, "Checks without Balance: Executive Office Oversight of the Environmental Protection Agency," *Law and Contemporary Problems* 54, 4 (1991): 127–204.

34 On the conflicts between the regulatory review process and environmental protection regulation, see Frank Ackerman and Lisa Heinzerling, *Priceless: On Knowing the Price of Everything and the Value of Nothing* (New York: The New Press, 2004).

35 See Jacob S. Hacker, "Privatizing Risk without Privatizing the Welfare State: The Hidden Politics of Social Policy Retrenchment in the United States," *American Political Science Review* 98, 2 (2004): 243–60, and Jacob S. Hacker, *The Great Risk Shift* (New York: Oxford University Press, 2006).

36 Streeck and Thelen, "Institutional Change in Advanced Political Economies," 24.

37 Statistical History of the United States, Series K-2, and US Bureau of Labor Statistics, "Employment by Major Industrial Sector." Available at www.bls.gov/emp/ep_table_201.htm.

38 David R. Boldt, "Colder Winters Held Dawn of New Ice Age: Scientists See Ice Age in the Future," *The Washington Post*, January 11, 1970, A1.

39 See Gerald Berk, *Louis D. Brandeis and the Making of Regulated Competition, 1900–1932* (Cambridge, UK: Cambridge University Press, 2009).

40 On the role of economic ideas in deregulation, see Martha Derthick and Paul J. Quirk, *The Politics of Deregulation* (Washington DC: The Brookings Institution, 1985). On the impact of changing economic doctrines on the exercise of prosecutorial discretion, see Eisner, *Antitrust and the Triumph of Economics*.

41 See Marver H. Bernstein, *Regulating Business by Independent Commission* (Princeton, NJ: Princeton University Press, 1955), and Samuel P. Huntington, "The Marasmus of the ICC: The Commission, the Railroads, and the Public Interest," *Yale Law Journal* 61 (1952): 467–509.

42 See Daniel Carpenter and David Moss, eds, *Preventing Regulatory Capture: Special Interest Influence and How to Limit It* (Cambridge, UK: Cambridge University Press, 2013).

43 Eisner, *Regulatory Politics in Transition*, 68–70.

44 See Marc Allen Eisner, *From Warfare State to Welfare State: World War I, Compensatory State Building, and the Limits of the Modern Order* (University Park, PA: Pennsylvania State University Press, 2000), 121–38.

45 Harris and Milkis, *Politics of Regulatory Change*, 302–31, and Pertschuk, *Revolt against Regulation*.

46 Lester M. Salamon, "Rethinking Public Management: Third-Party Government and Changing Forms of Government Action," *Public Policy* 29, 3 (1981): 255–75.

47 Donald F. Kettl, *Government by Proxy: [Mis?]Managing Federal Programs* (Washington DC: CQ Press, 1988).

48 H. Brinton Milward and Keith G. Provan, "Governing the Hollow State," *Journal of Public Administration Research and Theory: J-PART* 10, 2 (2000): 359–80.

49 Suzanne Mettler, *The Submerged State: How Invisible Government Policies Undermine Democracy* (Chicago, IL: University of Chicago Press, 2011).

50 Lester M. Salamon, "The Changing Tools of Government Action: An Overview," in *Beyond Privatization: The Tools of Government Action*, ed. Lester M. Salamon and Michael S. Lund (Washington DC: The Urban Institute, 1989), 9.

51 See Eisner, *From Warfare State to Welfare State*, 89–138.

52 Thomas K. McCraw, "With the Consent of the Governed: SEC's Formative Years," *Journal of Policy Analysis and Management* 1, 3 (1982): 359.

53 See Joseph V. Rees, *Hostages of Each Other: The Transformation of Nuclear Safety since Three Mile Island* (Chicago, IL: University of Chicago Press, 1994).

54 An earlier version of this argument was first presented in Marc Allen Eisner, "Beyond Deregulation: Explaining the Dynamics of Contemporary Regulatory Change," paper delivered at the 2nd International Conference on Public Policy, Milan, Italy, July 3, 2015.

55 See Jacob S. Hacker, "Policy Drift: The Hidden Politics of US Welfare State Retrenchment," in *Beyond Continuity: Institutional Change in Advanced Political Economies*, ed. Wolfgang Streeck and Kathleen Thelen (Oxford: Oxford University Press, 2005), 40–82.

56 See Kathleen Thelen, *How Institutions Evolve: The Political Economy of Skills in Germany, Britain, the United States and Japan* (Cambridge, UK: Cambridge University Press, 2004), 36.

3

COMPETING APPROACHES TO INSTITUTIONAL DESIGN

In 1914, Congress passed the Federal Trade Commission Act. The congressional aspirations were expansive: to create an independent regulatory commission that would exercise economy-wide jurisdiction with the overriding mandate to implement a prohibition on "unfair methods of competition." But the term "unfair methods of competition" remained undefined by Congress. As the Conference Report noted: "It is impossible to frame definitions which embrace all unfair practices. There is no limit to human inventiveness in this field." The Senate report on the bill noted that the committee had to decide whether to attempt to prohibit specific acts "or whether it would, by a general declaration condemning unfair practices, leave it to the commission to determine what practices were unfair." It adopted the second course of action.[1] The Federal Trade Commission (FTC) was given the authority to conduct investigations and write detailed regulations of what constituted "unfair methods" (a legislative function). It was also granted the authority to file complaints against corporations that violated the rules (an executive function) and adjudicate the complaints itself (a judicial function). The broad mandate and concentration of powers would have been impossible absent a strong belief in the neutral competence of administrators, something that many of the Progressive Era initiatives exhibited.

Almost six decades later, when Congress entered a new period of statutory activism in the area of regulation, it adopted a far different approach to regulatory design. In the Clean Air Act Amendments of 1970, for example, Congress dictated numerous deadlines, specified emissions limitations for new automobiles (by 1975, "a reduction of at least 90 per centum from emissions and carbon monoxide and hydrocarbons" from 1970 levels),[2] and even recommended (via the Senate report) standards for several criteria pollutants.[3] The debates surrounding regulation were replete with references to agencies—including the FTC—that had failed to use their power and expertise to control corporate activity and protect consumers. Where Progressives saw neutral competence, a new generation of reformers feared *ex parte* communications between regulators and the regulated, the ubiquitous revolving door, and the undue influence by members of Congress and presidents seeking to promote the interests of their donors at the cost of the public interest. There were concerns that agencies were prone to become captive to the interests they were charged with regulating.[4] The new regulatory statutes, in contrast with their predecessors, would be exhaustively detailed, granting far less discretionary authority to administrators and providing multiple mechanisms for review and participation by the public.

Two of the most important regulatory statutes in the nation's history were borne of very different periods, embedded in and informed by very different assumptions about institutional design. In this chapter, we explore the competing approaches to institutional design evident in the history of US regulation. While the discussion focuses on the period since the late 1960s, it is necessary to preface it with a brief examination of the Progressive Era and the New Deal. During these earlier episodes, presidents and legislators held very different assumptions regarding the role of the administrative state. Later critics would respond to these assumptions, citing them as providing the structural preconditions for capture and regulatory failure more generally.

Progressivism and the Origins of the Regulatory State

We begin our examination with the Progressive Era, the period from the 1890s to the 1920s that witnessed the rise of the regulatory state. Although a full account of regulation during this period is beyond the scope of this chapter, we will focus briefly on a few key elements: the assumptions embraced by Progressive reformers and their implications for key regulatory design decisions. This discussion of this period and the New Deal (below) is important if one wants to better understand the regulatory and deregulatory decisions made during subsequent episodes of change. Progressivism was, in part, a response to the significant changes that had been occurring over the course of the nineteenth century. The advent of the large corporation and the proliferation of trusts, the growth of organized labor, and the national expansion of the railroads all marked the transition of the United States to a modern industrial economy. Growing problems of industrial violence, urban poverty, monopolistic behavior, and financial instability created demands for reform. The panic of 1893 and the subsequent depression created the preconditions for electoral change, ending ultimately with the election of William McKinley and an extended period of Republican control. Progressivism as an intellectual and political movement cut across both parties, however, providing support for electoral and policy reforms at the local, state, and national levels. There was a shared belief among Progressive intellectuals that electoral reforms could be used to eliminate political machines and provide policymakers with a clearer understanding of the public will. At the same time, there was a commitment that scientific and social scientific expertise could be of great assistance in better diagnosing the problems facing the nation and designing public policies to address them.[5]

While it is convenient to view Progressivism as a unified reform movement, there were nonetheless deep divisions over the role of the state in the economy. While these divisions cut across the period, they were the most pronounced in the election of 1912, which pitted the incumbent Republican President William Howard Taft, against former president Theodore Roosevelt (running as a Progressive), Woodrow Wilson the Democrat, and Eugene Debs, the Socialist.[6] All of the candidates recognized the growth of big business and the problems of monopoly. However, they offered very different solutions. Taft's position was the most conservative, calling for a continuation of antitrust prosecutions guided by past precedents. Unsurprisingly, Debs was the most radical insofar as he welcomed the ongoing consolidation of industry as an inevitable step toward nationalization. The most important contributions to the debate came from Roosevelt and Wilson. Their competing positions would continue to influence debates over the regulatory state for the next several decades.

As president, Roosevelt had gained a reputation, perhaps undeservedly, as a trustbuster. Yet, he increasingly came to the conclusion that the rise of the large corporation was inevitable, a product of economic evolution that could not be repealed by legislation or antitrust prosecutions. In his words: "Business cannot be successfully conducted in accordance with the practices and theories of sixty years ago unless we abolish steam, electricity, big cities, and . . . all the modern conditions of our civilization."[7] Under his program, the New Nationalism, Roosevelt called for a strengthened Bureau of Corporations, which had been created in 1903 as part of the Department of Commerce and Labor, or a new agency comparable to the Interstate Commerce Commission. The agency would supervise, control, and regulate corporations on an economy-wide basis, even engaging in price setting where necessary. "Our aim should not be to punish the men who have made a big corporation successful . . . but to exercise such thoroughgoing supervision and control over them as to insure their business skill being exercised in the interest of the public."[8] The overarching goal was to direct industrial evolution through regulatory means. Corporations that eschewed cooperating with the new regulatory agency (the "bad trusts") would be subjected to vigorous antitrust prosecution.

Roosevelt's vision was rejected by Woodrow Wilson, as part of his program, the New Freedom, on three counts. First, Wilson found any distinction between "good" and "bad" trusts to be fatuous. Trusts were monopolists and any attempt to regulate them was inferior to forcing market competition. Second, he feared that any institutional arrangement that took the form of the New Nationalism and concentrated so much power in the hands of a single agency would open the door to capture. In his words: "If the government is to tell big business men how to run their business . . . [d]ont you see that they must capture the government, in order not to be restrained too much by it?"[9] Third, it threatened to render the welfare of individuals and the nation as a whole dependent on the benevolence of large institutions. Far superior, in Wilson's mind, was to create a commission staffed with accountants and attorneys who could investigate the strategies corporations adopted to create market power and produce detailed regulations to stop monopoly in its incipiency. Ultimately, Wilson would win the election of 1912, but strands of these two positions can be found in many of the regulatory debates and initiatives of the period. Indeed, they continued to be influential during the New Deal.[10]

Progressives promoted experimentation in institutional design. As Wilson famously observed, the difficulties with the Constitution—its system of checks and balances—were a product of its Newtonian foundations. However, "government is not a machine, but a living thing . . . accountable to Darwin, not to Newton." He concluded: "All that progressives ask or desire is permission—in an era when 'development,' 'evolution' is the scientific word—to interpret the Constitution according to the Darwinian principle."[11] One of the most important institutional innovations was the independent regulatory commission. Although the commission form was first introduced when Congress created the Interstate Commerce Commission in 1887 to regulate railroads, the FTC, discussed briefly in the introduction to this chapter, provides the best single example. Given a broad mandate (to prevent "unfair methods in competition" on an economy-wide basis), it was staffed with experts (many of whom were drawn from the Bureau of Corporations) and given the flexibility to conduct research and promulgate detailed regulations. Reflecting the fluidity of constitutional forms, it exercised a combination of legislative, executive, and judicial powers that had been separated under the Constitution. The FTC was governed by five commissioners, appointed by the president and confirmed by the Senate, with no more than a simple majority from the same political party.[12]

Similar experimentation can be found in the Federal Reserve.[13] Cognizant of sectional conflicts and fears over Wall Street dominance of the banking system, the Federal Reserve Act of 1913 established twelve regional reserve banks. Member banks with national charters were required to purchase the stock of, and maintain their reserves in, the regional banks, which remained private. The boards of directors for each regional bank consisted of three representatives selected by member banks, three drawn from businesses within the district, and three selected by the Federal Reserve Board. The Board, in contrast to the regional banks, was wholly public. An independent agency, it consisted of seven members appointed by the president and confirmed by the Senate. As one might expect, given the period, the Act established broad objectives (e.g., providing an elastic currency, creating the means of discounting paper, enhancing bank supervision, and providing a system of credit to meet the needs of the nation), but the precise means by which the goals were to be met were not specified in great detail. In part, this reflected the practical fact that the statute represented a hard-fought compromise. But, as John Woolley notes, it "was conceived in the spirit of other Progressive reforms that stressed faith in expertise, faith in the effectiveness of tinkering with the machinery of government, and distrust of politicians."[14]

The most ambitious experiment in institutional design was also the least permanent. As the United States prepared to enter into World War I, it was clear that it simply lacked the administrative capacity and the data to oversee the economic mobilization process. The response came in the form of the War Industries Board, which served—albeit briefly, from July 1917 to January 1919—as an economy-wide regulatory agency. The War Industries Board consisted of representatives of large economic interests and branches of the armed services, serving under the direction of Bernard M. Baruch, a Wall Street financier with a vast knowledge of the American economy. The Board worked through a decentralized network of fifty-seven commodity sections, each of which was staffed by a "dollar-a-year" man drawn from industry and government representatives. The sections negotiated with war service committees, which were staffed by the relevant industrial trade association (where none existed, an association would be created and certified by the US Chamber of Commerce). This organizational scheme, designed in large part to compensate for the lack of administrative capacity in the public sector, was used to draw on the expertise of industry actors. The voluntary cooperation of industry undoubtedly reflected some combination of patriotism and self-interest. Prices were set to draw even the high-cost producers into the mobilization process, thereby providing a windfall for the large corporations that dominated the war service committees. But it also reflected the fact that firms that failed to participate could find themselves starved of resources and access to the railroads. Ironically, Wilson's War Industry Board would bear a far greater resemblance to Roosevelt's New Nationalism than to the kinds of agencies envisioned by his New Freedom.[15]

The New Deal and the Expansion of Economic Regulation

The New Deal, unsurprisingly, was shaped both by the crisis of the Great Depression and the intellectual and administrative legacy of Progressivism. The severity of the crisis was best reflected in the employment data. In 1929, the unemployment rate was 3.2 percent. By 1933, it had reached 24.9 percent.[16] Although Franklin Roosevelt and his administration would ultimately gravitate toward Keynesian fiscal policy, for much of the 1930s, there would be a reliance on broader regulatory schemes. Some members of Roosevelt's Brain Trust (most notably Rexford Tugwell and Adolph Berle) had come to the conclusion that the growing organizational density of the economy left markets, in many cases, irrelevant. Large corporate bureaucracies, working alone or in concert, dictated production and pricing decisions free from the forces of supply and demand. As Tugwell wrote, justifying the New Deal policies:

> There is no invisible hand. There never was. If the depression has not
> taught us that, we are incapable of education. . . . We must now supply
> a real and visible guiding hand to do the task which that mythical, non-
> existent, invisible agency was supposed to perform, but never did.[17]

In this context, recovery would require subjecting corporate decisions to regulatory controls. Of course, this strain of thought could be tied to the New
Nationalist strand of Progressivism; in terms of organizational forms, it could
draw on the legacy of wartime planning.

In 1933, Congress passed the National Industrial Recovery Act, largely
on the model of the earlier War Industries Board, and created the National
Recovery Administration and a network of code committees to govern
decisions regarding product features, flow to market, and pricing. Similarly,
Congress created the Agricultural Adjustment Administration to control levels
of production in the farm economy in an effort to eliminate surplus production and raise incomes. Both of these initiatives were ultimately declared
unconstitutional.[18] While the Agricultural Adjustment Administration was res-
urrected and placed on new statutory foundations, the National Recovery
Administration was not. Ultimately, there was a proliferation of new regulatory agencies (little "NRAs") in multiple sectors of the economy that adopted,
in some fashion, a similar model, albeit with less authority delegated to industry actors. Regulatory commissions governed key decisions regarding pricing,
permissible products and services, and conditions of entry and exit. In some
agencies, economic interests found representation in rate-setting bureaus.[19] In
the case of the Securities and Exchange Commission (SEC), authority was
delegated to industry actors (e.g., the exchanges, a newly created National
Association of Securities Dealers), which functioned as surrogate regulators
under the supervision of the agency.[20]

Of course, one could readily identify another regulatory response to the prevalence of administrative pricing, one with roots in the New Freedom strand of
Progressivism. During the early phases of the New Deal, there was little support
for active antitrust enforcement relative to government-supervised cartelization
or the imposition of regulatory controls. Some of Roosevelt's key advisors (most
notably Felix Frankfurter and Robert Jackson) made the case that antitrust policy
should be vigorously enforced to eliminate the market power of large corporations, albeit to no avail. Following the recession of 1937, however, Roosevelt
delivered an address on curbing monopolies, declaring his intention "to stop
the progress of collectivism in business and turn business back to the democratic competitive order." To that end, he called for an updating of the antitrust
laws informed by "thorough study of the concentration of economic power
in American industry" and more vigorous enforcement.[21] Roosevelt appointed
Thurman Arnold to lead the Department of Justice's Antitrust Division, where
he embarked on a path of vigorous enforcement and a creative use of consent

decrees to force industrial restructuring. Ultimately, the effort to reinvigorate antitrust fell victim to the demands of World War II mobilization.[22]

Although the New Deal regulatory initiatives may have been grounded in different theoretical arguments, they shared some commonalities. First, like the laws passed during the Progressive Era, the new regulatory statutes were quite skeletal, once again calling on agencies to act in the "public interest." As Thomas K. McCraw observes:

> Legislative draftsmen inserted the phrase repeatedly into the flood of regulatory law . . . . The "public interest" occurs a dozen times in the Communications Act, a dozen and a half in the Securities and Exchange Act, and more than two dozen in the Civil Aeronautics Act, as a guide for regulators and as a justification for the immense discretionary powers those statutes bestowed.[23]

With little statutory guidance, the agencies could become the arenas for debate and contestation over decisions that could have massive economic ramifications. A second commonality was the faith in expertise. Once again, quoting McCraw: "The single overarching idea that tied the competing philosophies together was the conviction shared by a majority of New Dealers that economic regulation by expert commissions would bring just results."[24]

James M. Landis, who assisted drafting the Securities and Exchange Act and served on the FTC and the SEC, provided the strongest defense of the role of the expert commission in *The Administrative Process* (1938). The regulation of business was possible only because administrators possessed a degree of expertise that was not to be found among legislative generalists. As Landis explained:

> With the rise of regulation, the need for expertness became dominant; for the art of regulating an industry requires knowledge of the details of its operation, ability to shift requirements as the condition of the industry may dictate, the pursuit of energetic measures upon the appearance of an emergency, and the power through enforcement to realize conclusions as to policy.[25]

Rather than seeing the administrative state as a mere extension of the executive, he argued that it must be granted "that full ambit of authority" necessary "to plan, to promote, and to police . . . an assemblage of rights normally exercisable by the government as a whole."[26] One should expect that the number of agencies would proliferate, reflecting the complexity of the economy:

> If the administrative process is to fill the need for expertness, obviously, as regulation increases, the number of our administrative authorities must increase . . . . Efficiency in the processes of governmental regulation is best served by the creation of more rather than less agencies.[27]

And these agencies—staffed by expert administrators—should be insulated from partisan politics and given the power to make, interpret, and implement regulations free from the debilitating system of checks and balances.[28]

Unsurprisingly, there were dissenting voices. Landis' *Administrative Process* was delivered, in part, as a response to the 1937 report of the President's Committee on Administrative Management (the Brownlow Committee), which had been charged with developing recommendations for executive branch reorganization. The report described an administrative state that had grown "without plan or design." It famously observed that it had become "a headless 'fourth branch' of the Government, responsible to no one, and impossible of coordination with the general policies and work of the Government as determined by the people and through their duly elected representatives."[29] More contemporary critics would add that what appeared to be expedient and pragmatic in an era of rapid policy change, created the preconditions for subsequent concerns over the legitimacy of the administrative state. As James O. Freedman argues, Congress failed

> to provide many administrative agencies with either a coherent ideology of regulation or with clear statutory standards by which to act . . . . Statutory vagueness in the delegation of power may be appropriate when an agency is first created to deal with a problem not yet fully understood. But when such vagueness is permitted to persist over decades, it becomes, first, a signal of Congress' refusal to provide the agency with a sense of mandate, and, then, a temptation to private groups to exert pressure and influence.[30]

Some of the concerns raised by the Brownlow Committee were addressed through executive reorganization. The Reorganization Act of 1939 authorized the President to create a new Executive Office of the President and consolidate several agencies as a means of exerting greater managerial control. Following World War II, Congress turned again to the issue of political accountability. It passed the Administrative Procedure Act (APA) in 1946. The APA established the procedures that agencies must follow in the development of rules, requiring the publication of advanced notice of rulemaking and providing opportunities for public participation. It also created standards for adjudication and articulated the scope of judicial review, allowing courts to declare agency decisions or actions to be invalid if arbitrary, capricious, or an abuse of the discretionary authority delegated by Congress. As Keith Werhan explains, in the wake of the APA,

> reformers largely broke free from the tethers to Progressive and New Deal thinking . . . . Inevitably, in light of the prevailing skepticism of administrative expertise and corresponding disenchantment with agency autonomy, reformers no longer treated agencies as uniquely situated to engage in policy formation.[31]

Capture, Representation, and Institutional Design

By the mid-1960s, whatever faith had existed in administrative neutrality and competence had been greatly eroded.[32] An administrative state that was once believed capable of promoting the public interest—however defined—was increasingly viewed as being particularly prone to failure. Several prominent social scientists contributed to the critique of the administrative state.[33] In the 1950s, the most prominent critics were drawn from political science. Samuel Huntington's critique of the Interstate Commerce Commission, for example, described a process of decline leading, ultimately, to its dependence on the railroads. In his judgment, the ICC had lost "its objectivity and impartiality by becoming dependent upon the support of a narrow interest group." It was no longer in the public interest "to have an agency independent of all administrative supervision, masquerading as an impartial tribunal."[34] Similarly, Marver Bernstein's analysis of regulatory commissions suggested that they were subject to a life cycle, where gestation and youth are followed by maturity—when regulatory standards reflect the desires of industry—and ultimately decline. The commissions "lacked an affirmative concept of public interest; they have failed to meet the test of political responsibility in a democratic society; and they tend to define the interest of the regulated groups as the public interest."[35]

Capture theory reemerged in the 1960s, this time through the work of Left historian Gabriel Kolko, whose *Triumph of Conservatism* offered a radical reinterpretation of the Progressive Era and concluded that the core regulatory initiatives were designed at the bidding of regulated interests and were premised on the assumption that the public interest was consonant with corporate interests.[36] The work of Kolko and other historians would contribute to a broader critique of capitalism. For the New Left, society was dominated by large governmental, military, and corporate bureaucracies that negotiated the key features of an order that ensured ongoing profitability while seducing the population with the promise of ongoing consumption.[37] Ironically, an analogous critique of regulation would emerge from the opposite end of the political spectrum in the Chicago school. The economic theory of regulation modeled policy as the product of mutually beneficial exchanges between profit-seeking businesses, vote-maximizing members of Congress, and regulators, the first of these securing benefits (e.g., barriers to entry, established prices) that would not be available in the market and foisting the costs on consumers.[38] While one cannot effectively gauge the effect this scholarship had on activists, it certainly found a popular expression in the exposés of regulatory failure written by Ralph Nader and Nader's Raiders.[39]

Beginning in the late 1960s, Nader's Raiders—a group of lawyers and law students—wrote highly visible critiques of the major regulatory agencies. The investigation of ICC—entitled *The Interstate Commerce Omission*—combined elements of the New Left critique of capitalism and concerns over regulatory capture. In the words of Ralph Nader:

For generations the ICC has operated as a shield, protecting and pre-serving economic groups from the discipline of the marketplace, yet has declined to institute the pro-public interest pattern of regulation that was its original *raison d'être*. Long before it became a pattern of our politi-cal economy, the ICC and the transport industries forged a corporate state that utilized power for private pursuits . . . . All of the now-familiar trappings of such a condition appeared early in the ICC—routine move-ment of personnel into the industry, absence of rigorous Congressional scrutiny, heavy political overtones to agency decisions, rigid barriers to a citizen-consumer access to and participation in ICC proceedings, wholly unjustified secrecy, poor analytic and fact gathering performances, fail-ure to base decisions on reasoned explanations, and a gross dereliction in helping to shape a fair-sighted transportation policy.[40]

The report held little hope for reform, concluding that the ICC "should be abolished in its present form" and "[a] transportation regulatory agency should be created from the ground up."[41] Similar conclusions were issued for a host of agen-cies. These reports, which regulatory historian Thomas K. McCraw described as "immature, predictable, but incisive," contributed to shaping the debates.

By the 1970s, the "public interest" as a credible standard for interpreting regulatory behavior had few defenders. In its place reigned the "capture" thesis, which was rapidly nearing the status of a truism, a cliché of both scholarship and popular perceptions.[42]

Obviously, the critique of regulation could have wildly different implications for reform. On the one hand, it could be used to justify efforts to revitalize estab-lished agencies that had fallen into irrelevance. The Federal Trade Commission, for example, was reorganized, professionalized, and given a new infusion of resources in response to critiques issued by Nader's raiders and the American Bar Association.[43] Given expansive new powers, the "Little Old Lady of Pennsylvania Avenue" became a muscular agency—at least temporarily—with a broad and ambitious mandate.[44] On the other hand, the critique of regulation—when art-fully linked to the problems of inflation—could be used to justify deregulation. As will be discussed in Chapter 4, the 1970s witnessed deregulation in multiple industries and the elimination of core regulatory agencies, including the ICC. Democrats and Republicans, consumer advocates and Chicago school econo-mists may have disagreed on many fundamental issues. But there was a shared perception that regulators, in many cases, had failed to perform as one might have hoped, and capture was an important part of this story.

Although the capture theory was developed in reference to old-style eco-nomic regulations, concern over capture also informed the debates over the new social regulation. Some of the concerns seem misplaced. Economic regulations are fundamentally different than the new social regulations. Economic regulations provide regulated interests with concentrated benefits on an industry-specific basis while imposing diffuse costs on consumers and taxpayers. Arguably, this mix of costs and benefits (and the general opacity of policy) both facilitates capture and impedes the mobilization of opposition. The new social regulations, in contrast, imposed concentrated costs on regulated interests on an economy-wide basis while delivering diffuse benefits. The concentrated costs should engender an adversarial relationship between the regulators and the regulated, rather than contributing to capture. Business subject to social regulations should have a strong incentive to mobilize in opposition. At the same time, the diffuse and probabilistic nature of benefits and the complexity of the policies in question can impede the broad mobilization of support. Ultimately, this mix of costs and benefits renders social regulatory policies vulnerable to political assault, particularly after the core policy problems are displaced on the policy agenda.[45] All of this places a premium on the political entrepreneurship of elected officials and the vigorous oversight and mobilization of supportive interest groups.

Reforming the Administrative State

The new social regulations emerged in a rather unique context. Certainly, capture was perceived as a key problem in regulation. But it was emblematic of a larger problem of an administrative state that was no longer effective in executing its functions, no longer accountable to democratically elected officials, and seemingly incapable of representing the public interest, however conceived. As William T. Gormley, Jr., explains, there were key differences between the reformers of the Progressive Era and the 1970s:

> To the Progressives, the bureaucracy was the solution to a whole fist-ful of problems, including corrupt party bosses, meddlesome judges, and unscrupulous businessmen. To the reformers of the 1970s, the bureaucracy itself was the problem—self-directing (but not self-correcting) organizations that seemed increasingly out of control. . . . the reformers of the 1970s were "fixers" who found themselves repairing institutional machinery that had grown dilapidated over time.[46]

Some of the broad reforms of the period aspired to enhance the provision of information (e.g., the Freedom of Information Act of 1966, as amended in 1974). Other statutes, including the Federal Advisory Committee Act (1972) and Government in the Sunshine Act (1976), mandated open meetings. These statutes were grounded in the belief that access to information is essential for forcing heightened levels of accountability. Here we are primarily concerned with those that addressed the regulatory process and the discretionary authority granted to bureaucrats.

Capture theory is, in essence, a critique of interest representation. Certain interests (in this case the regulated) are over-represented in the policy process, whereas other interests (in this case, environmental, labor and consumer groups that collectively embody the "public interest") receive minimal representation. One should not be surprised that the representation of interests in the rule-making process attracted particular attention. Section 553 of the Administrative Procedure Act establishes the basic features of the rulemaking process. Under the notice-and-comment rulemaking process—the process by which the majority of regulations are developed—an agency is required to publish a "Notice of Proposed Rulemaking" in the *Federal Register*, describing the proposed rule, the underlying legal authority, and the date the rule will be enacted. At that point, it must solicit public comments. After the comment period closes (usually after 30 to 60 days), the agency promulgates the final rule. Notice-and-comment rulemaking is often referred to as informal rulemaking to contrast it with formal rulemaking. Congress can require by statute that agencies engage in formal rulemaking, which requires an agency to hold trial-like hearings, testimony, cross-examinations, and create a formal record. But by default, informal rule-making has been the norm.[47]

The Administrative Procedure Act set a relatively low bar for judicial review of the rules generated via informal rulemaking. In effect, the courts were to defer to the judgment of the agencies unless rules were "arbitrary and capricious." By the early 1970s, however, the courts were demanding a more comprehensive record that would permit informed oversight.[48] Through a series of decisions by the US Court of Appeals (DC Circuit), by the 1970s, informal rulemaking "had increasingly taken on the tone of adjudications, with the public airing of conflicting testimony, formalized rebuttal requirements, a discrete record, and occasionally full-blown trial-type techniques."[49] So-called "hybrid rulemaking" appealed to the courts because it could generate a record that would permit a more searching judicial review of administrative rules. But it also had the effect of providing greater opportunities for the representative of interests when there were conflicting claims. As a contemporaneous observer, Richard B. Stewart, noted:

> Faced with the seemingly intractable problem of agency discretion, courts have changed the focus of judicial review (in the process expanding and transforming traditional procedural devices) so that its dominant purpose is no longer the prevention of unauthorized intrusions on private autonomy, but the assurance of fair representation for all affected interests in the exercise of the legislative power delegated to agencies.[50]

Congress joined the courts in imposing hybrid rulemaking requirements via statute. As Gormley argues:

Congress's enthusiasm for hybrid rulemaking stemmed more from a commitment to fairness and full disclosure than from the need for tough judicial review. Ironically, the Congress saw hybrid rulemaking as a form of due process, while the courts saw it as a precondition for effective oversight.[51]

While the Administrative Procedure Act permits "interested parties" to participate in rulemaking and these opportunities were enhanced as a result of the trend toward hybrid rulemaking, resource asymmetries could sharply limit the extent to which public interest representatives could actually participate. One response to this situation was the introduction of intervenor funding designed to reimburse citizen groups for the costs of participation. Although compensation for participation in rulemaking had been considered in various venues beginning in the late 1960s, Congress first authorized intervenor funding for the Federal Trade Commission in the Magnuson-Moss Warranty Act of 1975. Intervenor funding—authorized by Congress or introduced administratively—spread to a number of agencies, including the Environmental Protection Agency, the Consumer Product Safety Commission, the Food and Drug Administration, and the National Highway Traffic Safety Administration. On several occasions, bills were also introduced in the House and Senate, albeit unsuccessfully, to authorize reimbursement for most agencies.[52] Moreover, Congress created statutory provisions permitting citizen suits as a means of forcing agencies to execute their nondiscretionary functions. It also provided the beneficiaries of regulation with an enhanced role in inspections. In each of these cases, institutions were designed to create new points of access for citizen groups, enhancing participation and representation.

Principals, Agents, and Institutional Design

As noted above, during the Progressive Era, reformers were often highly skeptical of Congress relative to the bureaucracy, which was elevated as a bastion of expertise, professionalism and neutral competence. Congress passed broad regulatory statutes, directing agencies to regulate in the "public interest," thereby granting administrators tremendous discretionary authority. By the 1960s, it was clear that many regulatory bureaucracies were failing to execute their mandates in ways that were broadly consistent with any rendering of the public interest. Reformers could look to the earlier period and note that institutional design decisions were partially to blame for subsequent performance.

It is useful to view the issue of institutional design through the lens of agency theory.[53] When Congress passes legislation, it necessarily delegates authority to administrators. Every act of delegation opens the door to principal–agent problems. There will always be some slippage between what a principal desires and what an agent delivers, a product of dissonant incentives and miscommunication. The slippage can be magnified if the agents shirk their responsibilities (e.g., they simply fail to implement policy with sufficient vigor) or engage in opportunistic behavior (e.g., they pursue a course of action favored by regulated parties in hopes of claiming some benefits). One would expect delegation to be the greatest in complex regulatory policies where the quality of decisions will depend on technical expertise that is often beyond what Congress, as a body of generalists, possesses. The resulting informational asymmetries complicate political control of the bureaucracy. Standard oversight may prove insufficient, forcing Congress to rely on the vigilance of interest groups that possess both the specialized knowledge and the incentives to monitor bureaucratic performance (so-called "fire alarm" oversight).[54]

Complications abound when we recognize that in the American system, bureaucrats are responsible to multiple principals. Congress and the president may have very different preferences with respect to policy and each has the unilateral power to reward or punish their agents. The president's appointees to an agency, for example, may promote a given regulatory action (e.g., a new occupational safety rule) while Congress thwarts its development (e.g., through appropriations riders prohibiting work on the rule). Things only become more complex when you realize that in Congress is a collective principal: Power is divided between two chambers and multiple committees and subcommittees that may share jurisdiction over a given policy area. Agents may receive multiple and mixed signals regarding principal preferences, discovering that efforts to comply with the demands of one set of demands provokes a sanction from another of its principals. Under these conditions, one should expect agency slippage to be a far greater problem than in the simple case of a unitary principal delegating authority to a unitary agent.[55]

An additional complication is worth noting. When Congress passes legislation that represents its preferences (or the preferences of the interests it represents), it does so at a specific point in time. Future congresses and presidents may not share the same policy preferences and priorities of their predecessors. To draw on the cases to be explored in this volume, pollution and workplace safety may have been salient issues in 1969 or 1970, driven by a series of focusing events. But there is an issue attention cycle.[56] The political salience of a given set of problems can peak in response to focusing events, then decline rapidly; new problems can move on to the policy agenda to displace the old. Within a few years of the passage of the landmark social regulatory statutes, for example, the problem of high inflation and sluggish growth assumed center stage and attention turned to the role of regulation in shaping macroeconomic performance (see Chapter 4). The challenge for principals is to bind both today's agents and tomorrow's principals, in hopes that an uncertain future will not bring a reversal of today's legislative victories.

All of this leads to important questions. When designing new regulatory institutions, how can one control for principal–agent problems? How can principals ensure that policy outcomes will reflect their preferences and those of the coalition of interests they represent? How can they insulate today's victories from an uncertain future? There are a few possibilities worth discussing, each of which could be used in isolation or in combination. First, there is the question of organizational form and location. The independent regulatory commission—an attractive option during the Progressive Era and the New Deal—had been discredited as an organizational form as a result of the critiques of regulation and regulatory capture noted above. One could assign regulatory responsibilities to a new agency and place it within an existing cabinet department, but only if there were reason to believe that the new duties would be reinforced by the department's core mission and supported by existing clientele groups. Occupational safety and health issues, for example, might be vested in an agency within the Department of Labor, a department with close and enduring ties to labor organizations that had lobbied hard for the passage of new regulatory legislation. But a similar strategy might not be available for environmental protection, given that the most obvious host departments (e.g., the Department of the Interior, the Department of Agriculture) had close ties with commercial interests and long histories of promoting precisely the kinds of practices that contributed to environmental degradation.

A second means of preventing agency problems would be to depart from past practices of enacting broad statutes. Rather than delegating authority to administrators in the hope that they would pursue the public interest, Congress could write exhaustively detailed legislation, thereby sharply circumscribing the discretionary authority of bureaucrats. Legislation, for example, could specify quantifiable goals and decision criteria, impose decision-making procedures, dictate policy instruments, and impose mandatory compliance timetables, in essence programming implementation. Exhaustive statutes, in this sense, are analogous to detailed commercial contracts. Of course, there will always be delegation in complex policy areas; administrators must make decisions and assumptions that cannot be dictated or foreseen by Congress. But legislators can nonetheless constrain bureaucratic discretion via statutory design.

Third and related, institutions could be designed to give the coalition of interests that have supported the legislation enhanced access to the policy process. There can be mandatory reporting of information on agency activities (e.g., inspections, enforcement) that can enhance oversight. Congress can require open meetings and require that interests are granted substantive representation in policymaking (e.g., through expanded rulemaking procedures). Participation in rulemaking can be subsidized participation via intervener funding. Statutes can create institutional mechanisms that allow interests to sue indolent or resistant agencies for a failure to execute their non-discretionary duties or bring suit against corporations that violate the existing regulations, once again allowing compensation for legal expenditures.[57]

These strategies—all of which were adopted in the design of the new social regulation—may facilitate the management of principal–agent relations. But in practice, whatever benefits they promised were diminished by three facts. First, the strategy of programming implementation via exhaustive statutes may limit the flexibility to depart from principal preferences. But it simultaneously compromises the capacity for bureaucrats to manage the inevitable problems and tradeoffs that may have been unanticipated by legislators or to adapt policy and practices to accommodate policy learning about the underlying regulatory problems or the efficacy of competing policy instruments. This may not be a significant problem if Congress periodically updates the statutes. Second, the strategy of enhancing access to and representation in the policy process is a two-edged sword. Regulated parties have proven quite adept at participating in agency deliberations and accessing the courts, often bringing to bear far greater financial and analytical resources than labor, environmental and consumer groups. Finally, advocates of policy do not have dictatorial control over issues of institutional design. The legislative process involves coalition building and compromise. Opponents of policy have powerful incentives to promote institutional designs that thwart the rapid and effective implementation of policy, further complicating administration. As Terry Moe notes:

> Political compromise ushers the fox into the chicken coop. Opposing groups are dedicated to crippling the bureaucracy and gaining control over its decisions, and they will pressure for fragmented authority, labyrinthine procedures, mechanisms of political intervention, and other structures that subvert the bureaucracy's performance and open it up to attack.[58]

From Regulation to Governance

When Congress passed the core social regulatory statutes in environmental protection and occupational safety and health, it adopted many of the expedients discussed above. Although a more detailed discussion will be reserved for Chapters 6 and 7, a few brief comments at this juncture are necessary. In the area of the environment, Congress passed a series of statutes to manage the problems of air pollution, water pollution, and hazardous and toxic wastes. These statutes were exhaustively detailed and sharply limited the discretionary authority of the EPA, mandating substances to be regulated, the policy instruments to be employed, and establishing ambitious timetables backed with stiff penalties. In contrast, OSHA was given broad rulemaking authority to develop health and safety standards. In both cases, agencies embraced their new mandates and engaged in an aggressive pattern of enforcement. The concerns over capture that had informed the legislative debates seemed largely irrelevant. The new social regulatory agencies, in contrast to their staid predecessors, had sharply adversarial relationships with the businesses they regulated.

The unprecedented expansion of the regulatory state in the 1970s generated a growing body of research on regulation. Much of this began as a critique of overly detailed prescriptive regulations that were viewed as problematic when compared with alternative policy instruments that imposed fewer administrative costs and permitted greater levels of innovation among regulated parties. But as the research evolved, it also turned to the underlying administrative model. Perhaps the hierarchical and dyadic relationships that had been intrinsic to previous regulatory models had been mistaken? Perhaps there were models that could integrate public regulation and private self-regulation and employ a broader range of instruments than those traditionally employed by the government (e.g., association codes of conduct, environmental management systems, international standards)?

The term "command-and-control" is often employed pejoratively as part of a broader critique of regulation as a dictatorial and bureaucratic exercise in social engineering. When used correctly, it is usually used to describe prescriptive regulations that are backed with penalties. In the world of environmental protection or occupational safety and health policy, command-and-control regulations often take the form of technology-based standards. With respect to environmental protection, Kenneth R. Richards notes: "command-and-control regulation provides relatively little or no discretion to the polluting private party." It "employs a technology-based standard that specifies (*de jure* or *de facto*) the technologies that regulated firms must use to abate pollution."[59] Comparable statements could be made regarding the role of command-and-control regulations in other social regulatory arenas.

In the wake of the massive expansion of social regulation, a number of scholars identified some of the intrinsic weaknesses of command-and-control regulations. Let us consider briefly three critiques, acknowledging at the outset that the literature in this area is vast. In a world of complete and perfect information and unlimited budgets, standard-setting would be an exercise in engineering. Regulations could be tailored to the precise technologies and practices of each firm. However, this world does not exist. Agencies work under budgetary constraints, incomplete information, and often demanding implementation timetables imposed by Congress or the courts. Under these conditions, they have little option but to settle for "one-size-fits-all" (or more correctly, "one-size-fits-many") solutions. Overly inclusive standards may over-regulate some firms, while under-regulating others. Thus, a first critique of command-and-control regulation focuses on the unnecessarily high costs and inefficiencies.

A second and related critique of command-and-control regulation involves technology. Once again, in an ideal world, regulators would have the capacity to adjust standards on an ongoing basis to reflect changes in industry practices, control technologies, and the broader understanding of regulatory problems. But in reality, highly prescriptive regulations—once in place—may lock in a particular set of technologies. They can limit the scope for experimentation that could, in theory, lead to superior results. Firms may have few incentives to search for (or develop) new technologies if regulations do not provide them with the flexibility to adopt them. This creates obvious inefficiencies, as dated practices and technologies become ossified, and firms that have already invested in regulatory compliance have powerful incentives for firms to oppose the updating of regulatory standards.

A final critique focuses on the highly adversarial context that was both a source and consequence of command-and-control regulation. Prescriptive rules were a product of high levels of distrust. As noted earlier, those involved in regulatory design had a profound concern about regulatory capture and the perceived failure of past regulations. As David Vogel notes in his book *National Styles of Regulation*: "For environmentalists and other pro-regulation constituencies, there was no middle ground between capture and coercion. The notion of cooperation between business and government was inherently suspect."[60] Highly detailed regulations with strict timetables, technology forcing provisions, and significant penalties were a product of this distrust. They could demand certainty of results and limit the scope of delegation to administrators and regulated parties. At the same time, the high costs of compliance created strong incentives to litigate, which, in an adversarial legal culture, raises the overall costs of regulation without contributing to the outcomes. As Robert A. Kagan and Lee Axelrad observe with respect to the US, the adversarial legalism "adds friction costs that are not characteristic of other economically advanced democracies." What makes this frustrating in a comparative context is that

> for all the legal proceedings, legal bills, and penalties associated with American social regulation, the European and Japanese operations of multinational enterprises often achieve levels of environmental protection and product safety that are comparable to, if not better than, those met by firms' facilities in this country.[61]

If command-and-control regulation is problematic for all the reasons suggested above, what are the alternatives? Following Cary Coglianese and David Lazer, one way to get to this issue is to consider regulatory design along two dimensions: (1) the homogeneity of regulated entities and (2) the regulatory capacity to assess outputs.[62] In cases where there is a high level of homogeneity—that is, regulated units use comparable technologies and processes—there is a strong case to be made for technology-based standards (i.e., command-and-control regulations). But as heterogeneity increases, the challenges of designing adequate standards increase, leading to the production of overly inclusive standards that treat heterogeneous entities as if they were, in fact, the same (the "one-size-fits-all" problem noted above). The second dimension may also prove quite important. If, in fact, there is a high capacity to monitor outputs (e.g., air pollution emissions), then there is a strong case for performance-based standards. Regulators can be less concerned with the specific technologies adopted by firms (thus alleviating the problem of unit heterogeneity), focusing instead of the outputs of interest (e.g., emissions of specific chemicals). In essence, firms are granted greater flexibility in determining how to meet their legal obligations, thereby reducing the administrative and budgetary demands placed on regulators.

In practice, the arguments supporting performance-based standards over technology-based standards began to gain traction in the late 1970s, particularly in the area of air pollution regulation. A decade later, it would provide the foundations for the efforts to manage acid rain under the Clean Air Act Amendments of 1990. Under this statute, Congress required that coal-fired utility plants work within emissions caps for sulfur dioxide and nitrogen oxides. These budgets, in turn, would decline over time, as a means of reducing acid rain. As one might expect, the Clean Air Act Amendments provided utilities with considerable flexibility over the precise means by which the goals would be achieved. Moreover, Congress authorized a system of emissions trading so that firms with lower marginal costs of abatement that could more efficiently exceed regulatory goals could specialize in pollution reduction and sell excess allowances on emissions markets. In the end, the cap-and-trade system generated impressive results at a fraction of the costs that were anticipated in 1990. Indeed, the EPA's own analysis, conducted in 2011, concluded that the benefit–cost ratio was 30:1 (i.e., $2 trillion, compared with $65 billion in costs, 2020) and potentially as high as 90:1.[63] One should not be surprised that the performance of the acid rain policy led to great interest in the application of a cap-and-trade architecture to other policy problems.

Thus far, technology-based standards appear to be quite appropriate when there are high levels of homogeneity. Performance-based standards are justified when the outputs are easily measured. But what can we say when neither of these conditions hold? Returning to Coglianese and Lazer, under these conditions, there is a strong case to be made for management-based regulation:

> Assuming the government has a general understanding of the social objectives (even though it cannot measure or monitor them well), it may be possible to establish criteria for planning and general parameters for effective management, and then to enforce management practices that are consistent with these planning requirements and with firms' own plans.[64]

Firms have an informational advantage over regulators in these cases, and thus there are great benefits that might be achieved via delegation of authority.

One example that illustrates the point can be found in the area of nanotechnology—materials or structures between 1 and 100 nanometers in size (a nanometer is one-billionth of a meter). There are growing concerns over exposure to nanoparticles. One simply cannot infer the toxicity of exposure to nanomaterials from their macro-scale counterparts. Given the relationship between mass and surface area and the novel properties of nanoparticles, there is uncertainty about the applicability of standard risk assessment methodologies.

Moreover, standard approaches to regulation are difficult to employ for obvious reasons. Nanoparticles are used in a wide array of applications, from pharmaceuticals and cosmetics to information technology, and as a result, the firms in question are highly heterogeneous. At the same time, the particles are so small that they are not easily detectable through the deployment of cost-effective technologies. The technologies that are used to detect particulate matter, for example, deal with particles that are hundreds of times the size of nanoparticles.[65] Under these conditions, the EPA has continued to collect information while working collaboratively with partners to address systems for managing exposure to, and release of, nanomaterials.

In nanotechnology, as in other cases of management-based regulation, all will depend on whether firms actually embrace the goals of regulation and implement credible plans. To what extent can firms be trusted to engage in some form of self-regulation? Public regulation had long been premised on the belief that corporations were narrowly focused on profit maximization. They had a fiduciary responsibility to maximize shareholder wealth. The state served a critical function in this context, using regulatory policies to force corporations to assume responsibility for the social costs they would otherwise foist onto society. In sharp contrast, one of the assumptions that gained some credibility, beginning in the 1990s, was that positive social performance reinforced corporate profitability. In some cases, the argument rested on the existence of cost-based advantages that could be gained through socially responsible production. Pollution prevention, for example, could be understood as a prevention of waste that could contribute to greater efficiency (or "eco-efficiency" to use the term then in vogue).[66] Safe workplaces could reduce liabilities and prevent disruptions in production stemming from occupational injuries and diseases. In other cases, analysts considered differentiation-based advantages. Consumers, investors, suppliers, and distributors might reward firms that sought to manage proactively the kinds of externalities that had long provided a justification for public regulation. They could pay a premium for goods produced in ways that were socially responsible.[67]

Yet, even if there is a business case for socially responsible production, there is much evidence that firms routinely fail to embrace it. One can identify at least three reasons. First, it may simply be the case that the economic case for socially responsible production is overstated. Demand may be weaker than supposed or consumers may be unwilling to pay a sufficient price premium. Alternatively, claims of social responsibility may have become sufficiently ubiquitous that it is difficult to claim a differentiation advantage.[68] Second, some firms may be organizationally incompetent. That is, even if there is an incentive to embrace the goals of cleaner or safer production, some companies may lack the expertise or the human resources to implement even a rudimentary management system. Third, there may be regulatory impediments. As Michael E. Porter and Claas van der Linde argued, US regulation "often deters innovative solutions or renders them impossible . . . by concentrating on cleanup instead of prevention, mandating specific technologies, setting compliance deadlines that are unrealistically short, and subjecting companies to unnecessarily high levels of uncertainty." In short, regulation as currently constituted "discourages risk taking and experimentation."[69] Certainly, one could remedy some of these problems by moving toward performance-based standards or management-based regulation, as suggested earlier, thereby delegating greater discretionary authority to firms. But is there any assurance that companies would execute this grant in ways that are consistent with the larger goals of regulation?

One response to this question emerged via discussions of institutional design. Following the work of John Braithwaite, there were compelling arguments that regulatory institutions should be designed to distinguish between firms based on their capacity for self-regulation, employing an explicit enforcement pyramid.[70] In what Ian Ayers and John Braithwaite described as "responsive regulation," authorities could deploy an escalating range of enforcement strategies, extending from government-supervised self-regulation to command-and-control regulation.[71] Some firms may lack the administrative capacity, resources, or incentives to manage their environmental, safety and health problems, even if they were given the flexibility to innovate. They would be subjected to traditional regulation with prescriptive rules. At the other end of the spectrum, one would find companies that employ credible management systems, collect data to evaluate their performance, subject to third-party verification. For these organizations, regulators could serve a role more akin to that of a consultant. Collaboration would take the place of traditional enforcement.

Other scholars looked to the larger institutional field within which firms were situated. In what Neil Gunningham and Darren Sinclair described as "regulatory pluralism,"[72] regulators could use traditional policy instruments, but supplement them with a variety of regulatory surrogates (e.g., trade associations, standard-setting organizations, third-party auditing) that could leverage supply chain and market forces. A number of prominent trade associations have developed standards for their members, in the hope of forestalling new public regulations that could emerge in response to salient cases of industry failure. In the United States, the most important example was drawn from the nuclear energy industry. In the wake of the Three Mile Island disaster of 1979, the nuclear industry created the Institute of Nuclear Power Operators (INPO) to develop and implement practices that would prevent accidents, in the belief that another occurrence could result in the end of the industry.[73] While INPO worked closely with the Nuclear Regulatory Commission, creating a system of co-regulation, this was quite exceptional. In practice, most associations developed far looser relationships with regulators. Absent integration with existing regulations comparable to what existed with INPO, critics questioned whether these arrangements were credible supplements to traditional regulation or exercises in public relations by associations committed to managing the reputation of industry actors.[74]

Attention also turned to internal management systems. During the 1990s, the International Organization for Standardization (ISO) developed its ISO 14000 series of standards for an environmental management system (EMS). A quality EMS, grounded in total quality management, required organizations to identify all environmental impacts, assign goals for their reduction, collect information on performance, and routinely evaluate performance, before beginning the process again to achieve further gains. Firms that had an EMS in place (with third-party auditing) could receive ISO certification. The rapid dissemination of ISO 14001 certificates was quite stunning. By the end of 1996, the year ISO 14001 was released, 1,491 organizations in 45 countries were certified. A decade later, there were 128,211 organizations in 141 countries. As of 2014, there were 324,148 organizations in 170 countries.[75] Some trade associations (e.g., the American Chemistry Council) amended their own codes to facilitate certification under ISO 14001.

The appeal of a certified EMS may be best understood through the lens of club theory.[76] Certified firms discriminate in favor of other certified firms when making contracting decisions, thereby constituting a *de facto* club that reserves for members a host of benefits that are denied to nonmembers. If you want to do business in the automobile industry, for example, you need to be ISO 14001 certified. Ford, General Motors, Chrysler, Honda, and Toyota require that their suppliers be certified. But to be most effective, EMS standards could be integrated with public regulations. This would require government to mandate a particular form of EMS, while delegating to regulated parties greater responsibility for setting goals, assigning responsibility, collecting data, and monitoring performance. Indeed, certification with third-party auditing could be integrated into the top tier of the kind of enforcement pyramid discussed earlier.

Reinventing Regulation without New Statutes

In the three episodes of regulatory change in the twentieth century discussed above, prevailing theories of institutional and regulatory design found an expression in the passage of significant new regulatory statutes. The contemporary critiques of command-and-control and the movement toward a more decentralized form of regulatory governance failed to have a comparable impact in the United States for a simple reason that will be explored in greater detail in Chapter 5. Under conditions of growing polarization and gridlock, Congress failed to pass significant new statutes that could authorize the kinds of models that had gained greater currency among scholars of regulation. The design decisions of earlier decades became increasingly ossified, as a result. The lack of new statutory authority has contributed to a problem of drift, as noted in Chapter 2, and a growing disjunction between regulatory authority and the larger environment. Ironically, it is in this context that the new learning in regulation found an opening, albeit with some significant limitations.

While the literature on regulatory design was rapidly evolving, it found practical expressions in policy design and implementation, beginning in the Clinton presidency. During the 1980s, a number of US businesses were restructured, reducing layers of management, increasing the role of information technology, and emphasizing entrepreneurship, total quality management, and an enhanced customer orientation. Books like Osborne and Gaebler's *Reinventing Government: How the Entrepreneurial Spirit Is Transforming the Public Sector*[77] explicitly explored the ways in which the lessons learned from the business world might be applied to make government more efficient, effective, and responsive. Coercive hierarchies could be replaced with cooperative partnerships. Citizens could be engaged as stakeholders or customers. Elected officials could leverage private sector resources to serve public purposes—an appealing thought given the salience of budget deficits and debt. In Bill Clinton's words, "All the . . . changes were developed according to a simple credo: protect people, not bureaucracy; promote results, not rules; get action, not rhetoric."[78]

As Peri E. Arnold observed, the reinvention of government (or REGO, as it was called) was both an attempt to acknowledge "a widespread, public distaste for government" and "an effort to cut the knot of fiscal constraints" in an environment in which "large budgetary deficits and political sensitivities over taxes severely constrained President Clinton's freedom for generating new policy initiatives."[79] After the 1994 midterm elections, when the Republican Party assumed control of the House and the Senate, these factors were only reinforced by a Congress that would prove unwilling to condone budgetary growth or the passage of new statutes unless they explicitly called for retrenchment. Clinton assured the nation that the era of big government was over. And as a result of the Clinton administration's National Performance Review and reinvention of government efforts, between 1993 and 2000, the federal civilian workforce was reduced by 426,300 positions, 640,000 pages of agency rules were eliminated, 250 programs and agencies were abolished, all at a saving of some $136 billion.[80]

Arguably, the most profound effects of REGO came in the area of social regulation, where a new emphasis was placed on cooperation. Concerns that traditional notice-and-comment rulemaking was cumbersome and tended to result in adversarial proceedings and protracted litigation led the Clinton administration to encourage negotiated rulemaking or "reg neg" as part of its set of REGO reforms. Under reg neg, representatives of regulated interests and the agency are encouraged to cooperate to develop a consensus-based proposal for a rule under the supervision of a convener. While the rule must still go through the normal comment period, at the time, recent experience with negotiated rulemaking suggested that negotiated rules generated fewer comments and a lower incidence of lawsuits after the fact (a point that has been contested subsequently).[81] Based on this experience, Congress had previously given agencies some latitude to employ reg neg with the Negotiated Rulemaking Act of 1990. Clinton's National Performance Review promoted reg neg and in 1993,

Clinton's Executive Order 12866 instructed agencies to "explore and, where appropriate, use consensual mechanisms for developing regulations, including negotiated rulemaking."[82]

Outside of rulemaking, cooperation was promoted through the development of myriad public–private partnerships and voluntary programs. These initiatives were adopted for a variety of reasons. In some cases they could be used to address problems that were simply beyond the reach of existing statutes (e.g., climate change, repetitive stress injuries). In other cases, they could be used to experiment with novel approaches to regulation and self-regulation (e.g., green tracks, standards-based self-regulation, management-based regulation) that were not authorized by statute but held some potential to contribute to the performance of firms willing to go "beyond regulation." Voluntary programs had the added advantage of leveraging industry resources and expertise to supplement stagnant or declining regulatory budgets. Under conditions of drift, there was much to recommend this strategy. Indeed, one might argue that there were few other avenues available.

While one might have expected that these initiatives would have run their course by the end of the Clinton presidency, many were carried forward into subsequent administrations. Although the longevity of these efforts can be explained by the larger argument of this book, whether it is justified in terms of performance is a question we shall reserve for later when we examine the recent history of the two flagship social regulatory agencies, EPA and OSHA. The key question is simple: Did the voluntary programs and partnerships contribute to a genuine expansion of regulatory capacity? Unfortunately, this question is difficult to answer with a high level of certainty. Programs often lacked clear and measurable goals and administrative oversight was tenuous at best. Moreover, what performance data that existed were often fragmentary or provided voluntarily without third-party verification. In some cases, the programs may have made important contributions to the realization of regulatory goals. In other cases, they may have been of little more than symbolic or political importance. Of course, to the extent that these programs demanded scarce agency resources that might have been used for other purposes, they carried potentially high opportunity costs.

Conclusion

Since the Progressive Era, policymakers have struggled with two major questions. First, what role should the state play in regulating the economy? Second, what is the best means of designing regulatory institutions? This second question, the subject of this chapter, has been a complicated one because it touches on so many important practical and normative issues, and these issues have only multiplied over time. Initially, one might have been content with providing administrators with broad grants of authority, on the assumption that they had the specialized knowledge of an industry to understand the most important regulatory problems and the expertise to design appropriate responses. But as administrative agencies proliferated, it became clear that agencies executed more than a narrow technical function. Rather, the policies they developed and implemented addressed some of the most important and contested issues in a market economy, and thus some means had to be found to guarantee greater transparency and provide opportunities for participation. The Administrative Procedure Act, by imposing new requirements for agency rulemaking and judicial review, sought to achieve these goals.

Yet, the immediate postwar decades raised heightened concerns over agency performance. Were regulatory agencies naturally prone to capture by the very businesses they were charged with regulating while neglecting to represent the broader public? Was there some intrinsic logic by which agencies passed through a life cycle of sorts, becoming overly accommodative to regulated interests before sliding into a period of sclerosis and seeming irrelevance? As the nation entered a new period of legislative activism, resulting in the passage of a long series of significant social regulatory statutes, Congress, analysts, and interest group representatives pondered these questions. The broad delegations of authority, so common in the first half of the twentieth century, were anathema to a new generation of reformers. Detailed statutes that constrained the discretionary authority of the newly created agencies were combined with far more complicated procedural safeguards designed, in part, to keep the new regulators in alignment with congressional preferences and guarantee access by supportive interest groups.

As the experience with the new social regulations accumulated, scholars devoted enormous attention to better understanding the preconditions for successful use of various kinds of policy instruments. This led to prolonged discussions of the merits of technology-based standards (so-called "command-and-control" regulations), when compared with alternative approaches (e.g., a reliance on performance-based standards or management-based regulation). It also generated a fascinating literature on alternative models of regulation. Systems could be designed to treat regulated parties differently, based on their exhibited performance in meeting or exceeding expectations. Firms that had implemented high-quality management systems that reduced the incidence of pollution or workplace injuries could be subject to lighter oversight than those that proved unwilling or incapable of meeting their legal obligations. More broadly, regulatory agencies could be understood as one element in a much larger configuration of public and private institutions. They could leverage association codes, international standards, third-party auditing, and other devices to reinforce traditional regulations.

Unfortunately, the institutional design decisions made decades earlier set hard limits on the extent to which this new learning could be applied. Congress, as noted earlier, had written exhaustively detailed statutes that provided little flexibility for administrators, and thus, all would depend on statutory change. In Chapter 5, we will examine the barriers to the passage of new statutes in an era of polarization and gridlock. First, we must turn to the imposition of regulatory review processes by presidents that would further deplete the flexibility granted to regulators. This is the subject of Chapter 4.

Notes

1 Quoted in John B. Dash, "The Federal Trade Commission," *The Yale Law Journal* 24, 1 (1914): 49–50.
2 Public Law 91–604, Sec. 202 (b) (1) (a).
3 R. Shep Melnick, *Regulation and the Courts: The Case of the Clean Air Act* (Washington DC: The Brookings Institutions, 1983), 30.
4 James O. Freedman, "Crisis and Legitimacy in the Administrative Process," *Stanford Law Review* 27, 4 (1975): 1042–43.
5 See Marc Allen Eisner, *The American Political Economy: Institutional Evolution of Market and State*, 2nd ed. (New York: Routledge, 2014), 43–48.
6 For an excellent overview of these debates, see Daniel A. Crane, "All I Really Needed to Know about Antitrust I Learned in 1912," *Iowa Law Review* 100 (2015): 2025–38.
7 Theodore Roosevelt, "The Trusts, the People, and the Square Deal," *Outlook*, November 18, 1911, 653.
8 Ibid., 655.
9 Woodrow Wilson, *The New Freedom: A Call for the Emancipation of the Generous Energies of the People* (New York: Doubleday, Page & Co., 1913), 201–2.
10 See Ellis W. Hawley, *The New Deal and the Problem of Monopoly* (Princeton, NJ: Princeton University Press, 1965).
11 Wilson, *New Freedom*, 47–48.
12 See Marc Allen Eisner, *Antitrust and the Triumph of Economics: Institutions, Expertise, and Policy Change* (Chapel Hill, NC: University of North Carolina Press, 1991), 55–60.
13 This discussion draws on Allan H. Meltzer, *A History of the Federal Reserve*, vol. 1 (Chicago, IL: University of Chicago Press, 2003), 65–73.
14 John T. Woolley, *Monetary Politics: The Federal Reserve and the Politics of Monetary Policy* (Cambridge, UK: Cambridge University Press, 1986), 40.
15 See Marc Allen Eisner, *From Warfare State to Welfare State: World War I, Compensatory State Building, and the Limits of the Modern Order* (University Park, PA: Pennsylvania State University Press, 2000), 45–85.
16 See Robert A. Margo, "Employment and Unemployment in the 1930s," *Journal of Economic Perspectives* 7, 2 (1993): 41–59.
17 Rexford G. Tugwell, "Design for Government," *Political Science Quarterly* 48, 3 (1933): 330.
18 The National Industrial Recovery Act was declared unconstitutional in *A.L.A Schechter Poultry Corp. v. United States*, 295 U.S. 495 (1935). The processing tax that financed the Agricultural Adjustment Act was declared unconstitutional in *United States v. Butler*, 297 U.S. 1 (1936).
19 Colin Gordon, *New Deals: Business, Labor, and Politics in America, 1920–1935* (Cambridge, UK: Cambridge University Press, 1994), 287.
20 See Thomas K. McCraw, *Prophets of Regulation* (Cambridge, MA: Harvard University Press, 1984), 197–200.
21 Franklin D. Roosevelt, "Message to Congress on Curbing Monopolies," April 29, 1938. Available at www.presidency.ucsb.edu/ws/?pid=15637.

22 See Gene M. Gressley, "Thurman Arnold, Antitrust, and the New Deal," *The Business History Review* 38, 2 (1964): 214–31.

23 Thomas K. McCraw, "Regulation in America: A Review Article," *The Business History Review* 49, 2 (1975): 161–62.

24 McCraw, *Prophets of Regulation*, 212.

25 James M. Landis, *The Administrative Process* (New Haven, CT: Yale University Press, 1938), 23–24.

26 Ibid., 15.

27 Ibid., 24.

28 Cass R. Sunstein, "Changing Conceptions of Administration," *Brigham Young University Law Review* 3 (1987): 931–32.

29 The President's Committee on Administrative Management, *Administrative Management in the Government of the United States* (Washington DC: US Government Printing Office, 1937), 30.

30 Freedman, "Crisis and Legitimacy in the Administrative Process," 1055.

31 Keith Werhan, "The Neoclassical Revival in Administrative Law," *Administrative Law Review* 44, 3 (1992): 584.

32 See Ibid., 577–85.

33 See William J. Novak, "A Revisionist History of Regulatory Capture," in *Preventing Regulatory Capture: Special Interest Influence and How to Limit It*, ed. Daniel Carpenter and David A. Moss (New York: Cambridge University Press, 2014), 25–48.

34 Samuel P. Huntington, "The Marasmus of the ICC: The Commission, the Railroads, and the Public Interest," *Yale Law Review* 61 (1952): 508.

35 Marver H. Bernstein, *Regulating Business by Independent Commission* (Princeton, NJ: Princeton University Press, 1955), 296.

36 Gabriel Kolko, *The Triumph of Conservatism: A Reinterpretation of American History, 1900–1916* (New York: The Free Press, 1963).

37 See Gabriel Kolko, *Railroads and Regulation, 1877–1916* (Princeton, NJ: Princeton University Press, 1965), James Weinstein, *The Corporate Ideal in the Liberal State, 1900–1918* (Boston, MA: Beacon Press, 1968), G. William Domhoff, *The Higher Circles: The Governing Class in America* (New York: Random House, 1970), and Charles A. Reich, *The Greening of America* (New York: Random House, 1970).

38 George J. Stigler, "The Theory of Economic Regulation," *The Bell Journal of Economics and Management Science* 2, 1 (1971): 3–21.

39 See Thomas W. Merrill, "Capture Theory and the Courts: 1967–1983," *Chicago-Kent Law Review* 72, 4 (1997): 1061–65.

40 Robert Fellmeth, *The Interstate Commerce Omission: Ralph Nader's Study Group Report on the Interstate Commerce Commission* (New York: Grossman Publishers, 1970), vii–viii.

41 Ibid., 324.

42 McCraw, "Regulation in America," 164.

43 See Edward F. Cox, Robert C. Fellmeth, and John E. Schulz, *"The Nader Report" on the Federal Trade Commission* (New York: Richard W. Baron Publishing, 1969).

44 See Eisner, *Antitrust and the Triumph of Economics*, 150–83. Of course, the commitment to a revitalized FTC was short-lived. See Michael Pertschuk, *Revolt against Regulation: The Rise and Pause of the Consumer Movement* (Berkeley, CA: University of California Press, 1982).

45 On the impact of the distribution of costs and benefits, see James Q. Wilson, *Political Organizations* (New York: Basic Books, 1973), 331–37.

46 William T. Gormley, Jr., *Taming the Bureaucracy: Muscles, Prayers, and Other Strategies* (Princeton, NJ: Princeton University Press, 1989), 36.

47 See Aaron L. Nielson, "In Defense of Formal Rulemaking," *Ohio State Law Journal* 75, 2 (2014): 237–92.

48 See Patrick M. Garry, "Judicial Review and the 'Hard Look' Doctrine," *Nevada Law Journal* 7 (2006): 151–70.

49 Reuel E. Schiller, "Rulemaking's Promise: Administrative Law and Legal Culture in the 1960s and 1970s," *Administrative Law Review* 53, 4 (2001): 1160.

50 Richard B. Stewart, "The Reformation of American Administrative Law," *Harvard Law Review* 88, 8 (1975): 1712.

51 Gormley, *Taming the Bureaucracy*, 94.

52 See Ibid., 77–81, Joan B. Aron, "Citizen Participation at Government Expense," *Public Administration Review* 39, 5 (1979): 477–85, and Carl W. Tobias, "Of Public Funds and Public Participation: Resolving the Issue of Agency Authority to Reimburse Public Participants in Administrative Proceedings," *Columbia Law Review* 82, 5 (1982): 906–55.

53 See Terry M. Moe, "The New Economics of Organization," *American Journal of Political Science* 28, 3 (1984): 739–77.

54 Matthew D. McCubbins and Thomas Schwartz, "Congressional Oversight Overlooked: Police Patrols vs. Fire Alarms," *American Journal of Political Science* 28 (1984): 165–79.

55 Daniel L. Nielson and Michael J. Tierney, "Delegation to International Organizations: Agency Theory and World Bank Environmental Reform," *International Organization* 57, 2 (2003): 247–49.

56 See Anthony Downs, "Up and Down with Ecology: The Issue-Attention Cycle," *The Public Interest* 28, 3 (1972): 38–40.

57 See Terry M. Moe, "The Politics of Bureaucratic Structure," in *Can the Government Govern?*, ed. John E. Chubb and Paul E. Peterson (Washington DC: The Brookings Institution, 1989), 267–329, and Matthew D. McCubbins, Roger G. Noll, and Barry R. Weingast, "Administrative Procedures as Instruments of Political Control," *Journal of Law, Economics, and Organization* 3 (1987): 247–65. On enhancing interest representation in the bureaucracy, see Gormley, *Taming the Bureaucracy*, 62–89.

58 Moe, "The Politics of Bureaucratic Structure," 276.

59 Kenneth R. Richards, "Framing Environmental Policy Instrument Choice," *Duke Environmental Law and Policy Forum* 10, 2 (2000): 239.

60 David Vogel, *National Styles of Regulation: Environmental Policy in Great Britain and the United States* (Ithaca, NY: Cornell University Press, 1986), 254.

61 Robert A. Kagan and Lee Axelrad, "Adversarial Legalism: An International Perspective," in *Comparative Disadvantages? Social Regulations and the Global Economy*, ed. Pietro S. Nivola (Washington DC: Brookings Institution Press, 1997), 147, 180.

62 See Cary Coglianese and David Lazer, "Management-Based Regulation: Prescribing Private Management to Achieve Public Goals," *Law and Society Review* 37, 4 (2003): 691–730.

63 Environmental Protection Agency Office of Air and Radiation, *The Benefits and Costs of the Clean Air Act from 1990 to 2020* (Washington DC: Environmental Protection Agency, 2011).

64 Coglianese and Lazer, "Management-Based Regulation," 706.

65 See Marc Allen Eisner, "Institutional Evolution or Intelligent Design? Constructing a Regulatory Regime for Nanotechnology," in *Governing Uncertainty: Environmental Regulation in the Age of Nanotechnology*, ed. Christopher J. Bosso (Washington DC: Resources for the Future, 2010), 28–45.

66 See Livio D. DiSimone and Frank Popoff, *Eco-Efficiency: The Business Link to Sustainable Development* (Cambridge, MA: The MIT Press, 1997).

67 The distinction between cost- and differentiation-based sources of competitive advantage is drawn from Michael E. Porter, *Competitive Advantage: Creating and Sustaining Superior Performance* (New York: The Free Press, 1985).

68 See David Vogel, *The Market for Virtue: The Potential and Limits of Corporate Social Responsibility* (Washington DC: The Brookings Institution, 2006).

69 Michael E. Porter and Claas van der Linde, "Green and Competitive: Ending the Stalemate," *Harvard Business Review*, September–October 1995, 129.

70 John Braithwaite, "Enforced Self-Regulation: A New Strategy for Corporate Crime Control," *Michigan Law Review* 80, 7 (1982): 1466–507.

71 Ian Ayers and John Braithwaite, *Responsive Regulation: Transcending the Deregulation Debate* (New York: Oxford University Press, 1992). For an excellent review of the regulatory discussions that emanated from this piece, see Robert Baldwin, Martin Cave, and Martin Lodge, *Understanding Regulation: Theory Strategy and Practice*, 2nd ed. (Oxford: Oxford University Press, 2012), 259–80.

72 Neil Gunningham and Darren Sinclair, "Regulatory Pluralism: Designing Policy Mixes for Environmental Protection," *Law and Policy* 21, 1 (1999): 49–76.

73 See Joseph V. Rees, *Hostages of Each Other: The Transformation of Nuclear Safety since Three Mile Island* (Chicago, IL: University of Chicago Press, 1994), and Neil Gunningham and Joseph V. Rees, "Industry Self-Regulation: An Institutional Perspective," *Law and Policy* 19, 4 (1997): 363–414.

74 See Edward J. Balleisen and Marc Eisner, "The Promises and Pitfalls of Coregulation: How Governments Can Draw on Private Governance for Public Purposes," in *New Perspectives on Regulation*, ed. David Moss and John Cisternino (Cambridge, MA: The Tobin Project, 2009), 127–49.

75 ISO survey 2014 is available at www.iso.org/iso/iso-survey.

76 See Aseem Prakash and Matthew Potoski, *The Voluntary Environmentalists: Green Clubs, ISO 14001, and Voluntary Environmental Regulations* (Cambridge, UK: Cambridge University Press, 2006).

77 David Osborne and Ted Gaebler, *Reinventing Government: How the Entrepreneurial Spirit Is Transforming the Public Sector* (Reading, MA: Addison-Wesley, 1992).

78 Bill Clinton, *My Life* (New York: Alfred A. Knopf, 2004), 648.

79 Peri E. Arnold, "Reform's Changing Role," *Public Administration Review* 55, 5 (1995): 414.

80 Yuhua Qiao and Khi V. Thai, "Reinventing Government at the Federal Level: The Implementations and the Prospects," *Public Administration Quarterly* 26, 1/2 (2002): 109.

81 Jeffrey S. Lubbers, "Better Regulations: The National Performance Review's Regulatory Reform Recommendations," *Duke Law Journal* 43, 6 (1994): 1171. On the debates over the supposed efficiency of reg neg, see Cary Coglianese, "Assessing the Advocacy of Negotiated Rulemaking: A Response to Philip Harter," *New York University Environmental Law Journal* 9, 2 (2001): 386–447.

82 Executive Order 12866, "Regulatory Planning and Review," *Federal Register*, 58 51735, Oct. 4, 1993.

4

COSTS, BENEFITS, AND BATTLES OVER THE REGULATORY STATE

On October 17, 1972, President Nixon vetoed the Federal Water Pollution Control Amendments, citing the extraordinary costs. While claiming to be committed to pollution control, he wanted to "attack pollution in a way that does not ignore other very real threats to the quality of life, such as spiraling prices and increasingly onerous taxes."[1] Later that day, as Congress prepared to overturn the veto, a series of legislators dismissed Nixon's concerns over the economic impacts. As Senator Howard Baker (R-TN) noted: "Of course such an ambitious program will cost money—public money and private money." But "study after study, public opinion poll after public opinion poll have revealed that the economy of this Nation can absorb the costs of cleaning up pollution without inflation or without a loss in economic productivity."[2] In the next several years, history would prove Nixon's concerns were well founded. As the nation endured high inflation, unemployment, and slow productivity growth, Congress would initiate a process of deregulation that would eliminate many of the economic regulations inherited from the Progressive Era and the New Deal. The Congress that had made a new commitment to social regulation would insulate its legislative achievements from deregulation. But presidents, whose discretionary authority over the regulatory state had been compromised by Congress, would unilaterally impose new regulatory review requirements to reclaim this authority. Regulation would become mired in inter-branch struggles between Congress and the presidency.

Of course, all of this was embedded in a larger political context. In the 1930s, Congress passed a number of regulatory statutes that sought to regulate competition in a variety of industries, granting regulators the broad authority to set prices, determine acceptable products and services, and control entry and exit.

Four decades later, it once again entered a period of legislative activism, pass-ing a wave of new social regulatory statutes. This time, Congress set ambitious goals to regulate pollutants in the environment and shop floor that had to be measured in parts per million or parts per billion, in many cases with technolo-gies that had yet to be developed. The intrinsic complexity of these regulatory goals was magnified by the experiments in institutional design initiated to force a heightened level of bureaucratic accountability and expand the representational capacity of the administrative state. Regulators had never before been assigned such challenging goals; they had never been granted less discretionary authority to achieve them. Business had never before been forced to absorb compliance costs of this magnitude. Chastened by the regulatory defeats of the early 1970s, businesses mobilized.

Business opposition took multiple forms. Corporations dramatically increased levels of campaign spending via political action committees and expanded their lobbying efforts. But they also engaged in the war of ideas and invested in conservative think tanks that advocated a broad policy agenda that included deregulation and regulatory reform.[3] As noted in Chapter 3, Congress exhibited little concern with regulatory costs when it passed the core regulatory statutes. But these costs became increasingly salient under conditions of stagflation— the politically toxic combination of high inflation and sluggish growth. With macroeconomic policy at an impasse, attention turned to regulation, creating a window of opportunity for policy change.[4] Scholars at conservative think tanks proved quite influential in shaping these debates. The American Enterprise Institute, for example, attributed up to 50 percent of the inflation, 20 percent of the reduction in business investment, and 4 percent of the reductions in growth to regulation.[5] Policymakers intent on responding to broad concerns about the economy could not ignore figures like these.

One outcome of this mobilization and the heightened concern with eco-nomic conditions was a wave of market-based deregulations that eliminated well-established economic regulations in air and surface transportation, finance, energy, and communications.[6] A second, and for present purposes more con-sequential outcome, was the imposition of new regulatory review processes centralized in the Office of Management and Budget. Congress may have directed agencies to execute the tasks it had assigned them by writing detailed statutes that provided few other options, but now, agencies would be required to respond to another principal—the president—and prove that significant new regulations could be justified by cost–benefit analysis before they were promulgated. Another set of procedural requirements grounded on very differ-ent assumptions was layered on top of the statutes passed by Congress, further reducing the flexibility and adaptability of the regulatory state. In this chapter, we briefly explore the politics of deregulation before turning to a more exten-sive discussion of regulatory review.

Deregulation: A Solution in Search of a Problem

The arguments for competitive deregulation existed in one form or another in the 1950s and 1960s, but under conditions of buoyant growth they failed to gain political traction. As Martha Derthick and Paul J. Quirk observe, even in the early 1970s "procompetitive regulatory reform was well and widely articulated as a policy prescription; but it remained a solution in search of a widely perceived problem, and its advocates remained in need of high-level political leadership."[7] But over the course of the next several years, changes in the larger economic and political environment were instrumental in elevating deregulation on the policy agenda. The key changes involved the growing and persistent problems of stagflation. The decades since World War II had been characterized by noninflationary growth. Economic policymakers reveled in their capacity to fine-tune the economy. But suddenly, this economy was in disarray and policymakers were left in search of a solution. Deregulation, when backed with heightened interest group mobilization, and the success of think tanks in shaping the larger debates over economic policy, provided that solution.

Stagflation

If deregulation was a solution waiting for a problem to happen, the problem was found in stagflation. During the late 1960s, high levels of fiscal stimulus connected to the Vietnam War and expanded social spending had produced a growing problem of inflation. Nixon responded, initially, with a slightly contractionary policy (known as "gradualism"), followed by mandatory wage-price controls. But when controls were lifted, exogenous shocks—failed world harvests and the 1973–74 oil embargo—led to inflation rates that were, at times, double those experienced in the late 1960s. Worse yet, the full employment economy of the 1960s gave way to high and persistent unemployment. In 1975, the US endured the worst recession thus far of the postwar period. The unemployment rate, like the inflation rate, was more than double what it had been only a few years ago.

During the 1960s, economic policymakers had remarkable faith in their capacity to fine-tune the economy, guided by Keynesian theory. Keynesianism offered important insights into how to manage the business cycle, and the Phillips Curve provided guidance on the tradeoff between inflation and unemployment. Certainly the tradeoff was not static; one could achieve higher levels of employment without the inflationary consequences if it was accompanied by productivity increases.[8] But under the conditions of the 1970s, Keynesian theory seemed increasingly incapable of offering solutions. The combination of high inflation and unemployment led many to conclude that the inverse relationship between inflation and unemployment represented by the Phillips Curve was no longer operative.[9] Under these conditions, growing attention turned to the issue of regulation. In the 1975 *Economic Report of the President*, the Council of Economic Advisors reported that the costs of regulation could be as high as 1 percent of gross national product. As a result, reform "could save billions of dollars by releasing resources for other uses, helping combat inflation, and making the economy more efficient and more productive in future years."[10] The same issue was reiterated in 1976 and, by the 1977 *Economic Report*, Ford's introductory letter called for a "comprehensive review to ascertain the effects of present controls" and develop a "corrective program that will cut across administrative boundaries. Only a sweeping reform will remove the regulatory burden where it is no longer justified and place the initiative for production and distribution back in the more efficient hands of private enterprise."[11]

In 1976, the year Jimmy Carter was elected president, the recent recession had driven inflation from a peak of 12.3 percent to 4.9 percent. But inflation would grow dramatically over the next few years—peaking at 13.3 percent (1979)—reinforcing the difficulties of using traditional macroeconomic tools and thereby keeping deregulation on the agenda. While President Carter dedicated the majority of his introduction to the 1978 *Economic Report of the President* to the goal of full employment and energy policy, he also announced his intention to "put a high priority on minimizing the adverse effects of governmental regulations on the economy," identifying interagency regulatory review as a means to "set priorities among regulatory objectives and understand more fully the combined effects of our regulatory actions on the private economy."[12] By 1979, regulation assumed its own section in the chapter on "Reducing Inflation." The section concluded:

> According to polls, the public continues to believe that improvements in the environment, in health, and in safety are an important national goal. But recently this sentiment has been accompanied by a growing recognition of the very large costs and the inflationary effects of regulation. The effort to improve both the cost effectiveness of individual regulations and the overall management of the regulatory process will continue to be a top priority of this Administration.[13]

Clearly, poor macroeconomic performance had elevated the political salience of regulation. Deregulation and regulatory reform gained bipartisan support as a supplement to traditional fiscal and monetary policy instruments that were failing to perform as they once had.

Interest Mobilization and the War of Ideas

From the perspective of the immediate postwar decades, many of the regulations created during the Progressive Era and the New Deal appeared to be more or less permanent. The macroeconomic problems of the 1970s opened a window of opportunity for revisiting these commitments. But this window would have been of little importance without the mobilization of interest groups from the Left and the Right. Many of the concerns expressed by the New Left and the consumer movement in the debates over the design of new social regulations (see Chapter 3) contributed to the critique of old-style economic regulations. More importantly, business interests that had suffered significant losses in the earlier legislative battles began to mobilize with far greater sophistication. They invested heavily in electoral politics and in the generation and dissemination of arguments and analyses supporting a deregulatory agenda.

One of the changes in the interest group universe involved the growing influence of the consumer movement and its populist critique of government. As noted in Chapter 3, Ralph Nader and colleagues contributed to the debates over regulatory capture with a number of investigative reports with provocative titles like *The Interstate Commerce Omission*, *The Closed Enterprise System*, and *The Monopoly Makers*. As Mark Green and Ralph Nader argued: "the monopolistic practices and results of economic regulation exact their tribute from the American economy and consumer. Excessive rates mean higher consumer prices for both products and services—prices which may bar the lower-income citizen entirely." The policy implications were clear: "If the problem is over-regulation based on irrational economics, then the most effective remedy is deregulation. Where there would be a viable, competitive market but for economic regulation, the industry should be freed from all such restraint."[14] Of course, Green and Nader cautioned that to have truly competitive markets, deregulation could not happen in isolation but would have to be combined with a commitment to vigorous antitrust enforcement to reduce the concentration of corporate power. While Nader and his colleagues would approvingly reference the research of George Stigler, Richard Posner, and Harold Demsetz—main figures in the conservative Chicago school—their work found its greatest audience on the Left. The connection between deregulation and the consumer movement made the issue quite attractive to Senator Ted Kennedy (D-MA). He embraced airline deregulation at the urging of Stephen Breyer, special council to the Judiciary Committee's Subcommittee on Administrative Practice and Procedure, and held a series of highly publicized hearings in 1975 that resulted, ultimately, in the passage of the Airline Deregulation Act of 1978.

In comparative context, the United States has a highly fragmented and institutionally porous state that provides multiple points of access for lobbyists and interest groups seeking to shape public policy. Unsurprisingly, this structure provides distinct advantages for wealthy individuals, corporations, and foundations capable of funding these activities.[15] While the consumer movement embraced the cause of deregulation, its political influence paled in comparison with that of business. The expansion of regulation in the late 1960s and early 1970s stimulated a counter mobilization on the part of business. As David Vogel notes:

In essence, during the 1970s, the fight over government regulation became the focus of class conflict for the first time in American history: it pitted the interests of business as a whole against the public interest movement as well as much of organized labour. The nature of the conflict over regulation became analogous to the struggle over the adoption of the welfare-state and the recognition of unions that defined class conflict during the 1930s.[16]

The business response had several components: the creation and enlargement of a full-time Washington DC-based lobbying organization, the expansion of campaign finance via political action committees, and efforts to shape the policy debates through a variety of means. For present purposes, the most important part of the business mobilization came through the support for advocacy think tanks.

Think tanks have been active in informing policy debates since the early twentieth century, when organizations like the Brookings Institution (1916), the Hoover Institution (1918), the National Bureau of Economic Research (1920), the Council on Foreign Relations (1921), and the American Enterprise Institute (1943) were founded. These academic think tanks—often functioning like *de facto* universities without students—were largely research-driven organizations that rarely embraced a specific ideology or sought to further a specific policy agenda. Given the broad research agendas of established think tanks, one should not be surprised that regulation attracted some attention. For example, between 1967 and 1975, the Brookings Institution sponsored a great deal of research on regulation and deregulation, funded by a $1.8 million grant from the Ford Foundation. But these efforts would quickly be eclipsed by a new generation of think tanks that were focused on changing public policy.[17]

In 1973, Paul Weyrich, Edwin Feulner and Joseph Coors founded the Heritage Foundation as an organization that would depart from the academic think tank model to develop and promote conservative public policy proposals. As the first think tank explicitly devoted to advocacy, Heritage "devised a new business model that was less concerned with scholarly research than advocating policies from a conservative viewpoint."[18] In the next several years, additional conservative think tanks were founded—including the Cato Institute (1974), the Institute for Contemporary Studies (1974), and the International Institute for Economic Research (1975). The advocacy model found an expression in these new organizations and, more importantly, in the well-established American Enterprise Institute (AEI). The publications, briefings, and press releases from this network of conservative think tanks "played an extremely important role in publicizing the costs associated with the expansion of government regulation as well as in promoting public policies aimed at strengthening the supply side of the American economy."[19]

The AEI was the most important of these think tanks. It actively promoted and disseminated research that advocated regulatory reform and deregulation, often in a less technical format that would be accessible to policymakers and elected officials and focused on contemporary debates. In 1977, the *Washington Post* described the AEI as "a prosperous think tank that serves partly as a Republican shadow government in Washington." With "its $6 million budget and an impressive roster of scholars, economists and political thinkers," the AEI had become "the Brookings of the right."[20] While AEI was involved in a number of policy areas, its influence was particularly pronounced in economic policy and social regulation. Scholars—many who had served in previous Republican administrations—found a new home at the AEI's Governmental Regulation Program. The program was directed by Murray Weidenbaum, former Undersecretary of the Treasury for Economic Policy under Nixon, and James C. Miller, III, former Assistant Director of Ford's Council on Wage and Price Stability. Both would assume prominent policymaking positions following the 1980 election of Ronald Reagan. Weidenbaum would be named Chairman of the Council of Economic Advisors and Miller would be appointed executive director of the Presidential Task Force on Regulatory Relief, head of the Office of Management and Budget's Office of Information and Regulatory Affairs, and ultimately Chair of the Federal Trade Commission.

In the 1970s, AEI's rising influence was reflected in its success in shaping the policy debates, taking the research and popularizing it through publications like its magazine *Regulation*, that was coedited by Murray Weidenbaum and Antonin Scalia. One of Weidenbaum's largest contributions to the debates came through his efforts (with Robert DeFina) to quantify the costs of regulation. For 1976, for example, Weidenbaum estimated that the administrative costs for the regulatory agencies totaled some $3 billion. But the direct and indirect costs of compliance were estimated to be $62 billion, for a total of $65 billion "the equivalent to $307 for every man, woman, and child in the United States or to 18 percent of the federal budget." Absent reform, it was projected that the costs could exceed $100 billion by 1979.[21] The influence of these claims was raised by their connection to the problem of inflation. As Weidenbaum explained in 1975, in additional to budget deficits and overly accommodative monetary policy, regulation constituted "a less obvious—and hence more insidious—way in which government can worsen the already severe inflationary pressures affecting the American economy . . . . Literally, the federal government is continually mandating more inflation via the regulations it promulgates."[22] Weidenbaum and other AEI scholars maximized their impact on the debates through a variety of means, ranging from testimony before Congress to dissemination to a broader public. Indeed, Weidenbaum's research at AEI was even published in the *Reader's Digest* under the title "Time to Control Runaway Inflation."[23] Certainly, many could question the underlying methodology and the inattention to the benefits of regulations. But as one critic noted, the figures were so widely reported, "they seem[ed] to have acquired the stature of official statistics."[24] Moreover, lobbyists and business organizations, including the Business

Roundtable, the National Association of Manufacturers, and the US Chamber of Commerce, routinely cited the studies generated by AEI.[25]

The Limits of Deregulation

Returning to Derthick and Quirk's observation—that deregulation in the early 1970s was "a solution in search of a widely perceived problem,"[26] we can take an opportunity to summarize. Under the pressures of stagflation, the Phillips Curve and the entire edifice of Keynesian economics seemed increasingly vulnerable. The impasse in fiscal policy found several expressions (e.g., the growing attention given to alternative theoretical frameworks for economic policymaking, including monetarism, rational expectations, and supply side economics). But thus far we have been primarily concerned with the advocacy of deregulation. The consumer movement and an ascendant business coalition were in agreement that traditional economic regulatory policies imposed unnecessary costs on the economy that contributed to inflation and arguably created barriers to new investment and productivity gains. Those intent on policy change were not forced to master the arcane details of specific regulations because advocacy think tanks proved quite adept at presenting the case for deregulation in terms that were readily accessible to policymakers and a broader public. In the course of less than a decade, Congress passed significant new statutes that deregulated surface and air transportation, electricity, telecommunications, and finance. Agencies that had become emblematic of failed regulation were eliminated.

There were distinct limitations to what could be achieved via deregulation. Business and the consumer movement might offer a common critique of many of the policies and practices that were largely the product of the Progressive Era and the New Deal. But they quickly parted ways when they looked to the new social regulations that were the legacy of the late 1960s and the early 1970s. There was broad recognition that the costs associated with the new environmental and occupational safety and health policies were far greater than those imposed by traditional economic regulations. But strong Democratic majorities in the House and the Senate, vigorous interest group activity, and high levels of public opinion support politically insulated these policies.

The supportive public policy environment might have surprised some analysts, given the growing concerns over inflation and the belief that spikes in public support for policy change are usually temporary, driven by salient events and quickly displaced by new issues. In 1972, for example, Anthony Downs wrote an influential essay on the "issue attention cycle," arguing that each significant domestic problem "suddenly leaps into prominence, remains there for a short time, and then—though still largely unresolved—gradually fades from the center of public attention."[27] Downs' essay, which focused on pollution, concluded that the nation was entering a stage "in which the intensity of public interest in environmental improvement must inexorably decline."[28]

Despite the logic of the issue attention cycle, there is little evidence for the kind of decline that one might have predicted based on this essay. In 1973, the year after the publication of Downs' essay, the Roper Organization asked whether "environmental protection laws and regulations have gone too far, or not far enough, or have struck about the right balance?" From that point through 1980, the percentage of respondents who believed that the laws and regulations had gone too far increased steadily to 25 percent. But remarkably, the percentage that believed that the right balance had been struck or that the laws had not gone far enough remained quite stable (the combined percentages ranged from 65 to 69 percent).[29] Polls conducted by the Roper Organization and the NORC General Social Survey asked whether we were spending too much, too little, or about the right amount of money on improving and protecting the environment. While the percentage responding "too little" was the highest in the early 1970s (56 percent in 1971, Roper), it remained the dominant response in each year, whereas the percentage that believed we spent too much ranged between 5 and 15 percent).[30] As John M. Gillroy and Robert Y. Shapiro observed in 1986:

> Support for environmental protection has been resistant thus far to energy shortages and price increases, recession, Reagan's landslides, and the high costs of environmental programs and regulation. There was little appreciable backlash in public opinion. The proportion of the public wanting less regulation or less spending has remained small, with relatively little change, even as support for deregulation or 'less government' rose at the beginning of the Reagan administration.[31]

Regulatory Review and the Struggle over the Administrative State

The new social regulatory statutes of the early 1970s were framed, in part, by concerns over the propensity of agencies to become overly accommodative to regulated interests or to lose their vigor over time and sink into obsolescence. But the larger political environment was also shaped by sharp inter-branch struggles between the Congress and the presidency. The Congress that expanded the regulatory state also passed landmark statutes restricting presidential control over foreign policy (the War Powers Act of 1973) and the budget (the Congressional Budget and Impoundment Act of 1974). When Congress wrote detailed regulatory statutes, it did so, in part, to prevent presidents and their appointees from circumventing congressional will. Many of these statutes, and the lack of concern with costs they embodied, were passed before the onset of stagflation.

Given the strong public support for social regulation and the fact that the policies were of great importance to core components of the Democratic coalition, there was little chance that Congress would revise the statutes to increase the discretionary power of the president. The new social regulations, protected by

Democrats in Congress, largely avoided the deregulatory fervor and—as a result of original design decisions—they proved difficult to deregulate via administrative means.[32] For presidents intent on controlling regulatory costs and countering the expression of congressional will, another strategy became apparent: the imposition of regulatory review via executive order. Presidents Nixon, Ford and Carter had attempted this in the 1970s, albeit with little effect. These efforts would set the stage, however, for the Reagan administration's far more aggressive use of cost–benefit-analysis-based regulatory review.

Regulatory Review from Nixon to Carter

In the larger story of regulation, 1970 is the year Congress passed the Clean Air Act Amendments and the Occupational Safety and Health Act. Although Congress would legislate with little concern over costs, industry turned to a more receptive ally in the White House. In April of 1970, President Nixon created the National Industrial Pollution Control Council (or NIPCC) via executive order 11523 (1970). Nixon explained the role of NIPCC in the following terms:

> The new Council will allow businessmen to communicate regularly with the President, the Council on Environmental Quality, and other Government officials and private organizations which are working to improve the quality of the environment. It will also provide a direct opportunity for business and industry to actively and visibly support the drive to abate pollution from industrial sources. Both Government and industrial leaders can use this mechanism to stimulate efforts toward the achievement of our environmental goals.[33]

Housed in the Commerce Department, NIPCC included 63 corporate leaders from firms including DuPont, Exxon, Ford, General Motors, Rockwell International, US Steel, and Westinghouse Electric, with minimal representation for smaller businesses and no representation for environmental advocates. Unsurprisingly, NIPCC made the case repeatedly for the application of cost–benefit analysis to environmental policy, either directly or through Commerce Secretary Maurice Stans. By June 1971, Nixon aide John Ehrlichman had created the Quality of Life Committee in the White House Domestic Council, which would ultimately turn to centralized regulatory review.[34]

During the Johnson administration, cost–benefit analysis had been used by the Systems Analysis Group of the Secretary of the Army to evaluate the projects and regulations of the Army Corps of Engineers.[35] But the Quality of Life Committee's work would lead to a much broader application. On October 5, 1971, OMB Director George Shultz sent a memorandum to the heads of departments and agencies "to establish a procedure for improving the inter-agency coordination of proposed agency regulations, standards, and guidelines."

The Quality of Life review process required agencies to submit to the OMB a schedule of regulations for the upcoming year that would have a significant impact on the activities of other agencies, impose significant costs, or create demands on agencies that exceeded their budget requests. Thirty days before the scheduled announcement of regulations, agencies were required to submit the regulations to the OMB along with a summary that identified the principle objectives, a comparison of costs and benefits, alternatives to the proposed action that were considered, and the justification for the chosen alternative.[36] Analyses would be conducted by the personnel from the System Analysis Group, who had been transferred to the OMB for this purpose and would remain central to regulatory review for the remainder of the decade.

While the Quality of Life review was formally applicable to all regulations generated by executive branch agencies, in practice, it focused on a single agency: the EPA. Given the economic impact of environmental regulations, one should not be surprised that the agency generated so much attention. The review process, even at this early stage, had some negative ramifications. First, it resulted in lengthy delays. Although the OMB's informal policy was to complete reviews in 30 days, the median time between transmission of regulations to agencies for comments and submission to the *Federal Register* was 104 days, of which 56 days were spent in OMB review. Second, because EPA officials viewed OMB review as an implicit threat, they subjected each regulation to an intra-agency review process that required clearance by all EPA assistant administrators. During this process, there were concerns that administrators anticipated all possible objections, compromised their agency's goals, and generated more lenient regulations, thereby blunting their environmental impact.[37]

By the Ford presidency, inflation had assumed central stage in the list of policy concerns. On August 24, 1974, Congress statutorily authorized a new Council on Wage and Price Stability (COWPS) to review the inflationary consequences of government activities, including, most notably, regulations. On October 8, 1974, in an address to a Joint Session of Congress on the economy, President Ford proposed a broad package of policies to "whip inflation right now." Part of the package involved deregulation and a more vigorous enforcement of the antitrust laws. But for present purposes, the most important element was regulatory review. President Ford announced:

> Hereafter, I will require that all major legislative proposals, regulations, and rules emanating from the executive branch of the Government will include an inflation impact statement that certifies we have carefully weighed the effect on the Nation. I respectfully request that the Congress require a similar advance inflation impact statement for its own legislative initiatives.[38]

While Congress failed to acquiesce to President Ford's request, in November 1974, Ford issued Executive Order 11821, requiring that all executive branch agencies submit an inflation impact statement to the OMB for all major legislative proposals, regulations, and rules (the inflation impact statement would be replaced by a broader economic impact statement under Executive Order 11921 in 1976).

Under the system established by Ford, COWPS played an active role in evaluating significant regulations. It conducted analyses, participated in rulemaking, and testified in agency hearings, thereby making its concerns part of the formal rulemaking record.[39] Yet, there were distinct limitations to COWPS' influence. James C. Miller, III, who directed the regulatory review work of COWPS during the final year of the Ford presidency, argued that the primary impediment to effective review was the lack of an enforcement mechanism.

> To improve the performance of the regulatory agencies, simply requiring them (or someone else) to perform an economic analysis of their proposals' likely effects was not enough: someone outside the agency needed to be empowered to tell an agency it could not regulate unless its proposals made common (that is, economic) sense.[40]

The same basic limitations were exhibited during the Carter administration. In March 1978, Carter issued Executive Order 12044, which required executive agencies to publish a semiannual agenda of regulations in the *Federal Register* and, more importantly, to conduct a regulatory analysis for all significant regulations (defined as those with an annual economic effect of $100 million or more) under the supervision of a new Office of Regulatory Information Policy in the OMB. Although agencies were not required to conduct formal cost–benefit analysis, they were informed that regulations should achieve their goals "effectively and efficiently. They shall not impose unnecessary burdens on the economy, on individuals, on public or private organizations, or on State and local governments."[41] Carter also established a new interagency Regulatory Council to address duplicative regulations and, more importantly, a Regulatory Analysis Review Group (RARG), chaired by the Council of Economic Advisors. RARG was directed to evaluate intensively up to ten of the most significant regulations annually, placing their analyses in the rulemaking record.[42]

While the discussion thus far has focused on executive action, by the end of the Carter presidency, a Democratically controlled Congress also provided some statutory support for regulatory review. In September 1980, Congress passed the Regulatory Flexibility Act, further complicating the rulemaking process by amending the Administrative Procedure Act to mandate that agencies evaluate the impact of their regulations on small businesses and, where deemed significant, adopt a less burdensome alternative. Under the law, agencies were required to publish an Initial Regulatory Flexibility Analysis along with the proposed rule in the *Federal Register*, provide notice to affected small entities, solicit comments during public hearings, and publish a Final Regulatory Flexibility

Analysis along with its final rule. They were also required to review their rules periodically to assess the burdens on small businesses and publish biannual regulatory agendas.[43] Congress also passed the Paperwork Reduction Act (1980), requiring that all agencies receive OMB clearance before imposing information requirements on the public.[44] Implementation authority was assigned to a newly created Office of Information and Regulatory Affairs (OIRA). All agencies were required to provide OIRA with "a copy of any proposed rule which contains a collection of information requirement" before publication of notice of proposed rulemaking in the *Federal Register*.[45]

The Reagan Administration and Executive Order 12291

The decade prior to the election of Ronald Reagan witnessed the evolution of regulatory review, as shown above. The review process was centralized in the OMB. Executive branch regulators were required to submit proposed and final rules and a discussion of alternatives considered by the agency. These materials were to be accompanied by an economic analysis, even if there was some inconsistency as to whether a full-blown cost–benefit analysis was required. While the initial Quality of Life review process may have appeared somewhat *ad hoc*, over the course of the decade, the OMB had developed an impressive institutional capacity to review regulations.[46]

During the Carter presidency, scholars and former government officials at AEI gave careful consideration to regulatory review. It became clear that the primary problem with the older processes was the lack of any mechanism for overriding agency decisions. James C. Miller III, a Ford administration veteran responsible for the regulatory review efforts of COWPS and then co-director of AEI's Center for the Study of Regulation, developed the conceptual model for a new review process. It could mandate cost–benefit-analysis-based regulatory review *ex ante* and grant the OMB the authority to stop regulations that failed the review. Optimally, these requirements would be imposed by statute. But the election of Ronald Reagan in 1980 left the House of Representatives in the control of the Democratic Party, thus foreclosing a legislative strategy. Reform would have to be introduced by executive order, a new set of procedures layered on top of existing statutory authority.[47]

Reagan moved quickly on the regulatory front, announcing the creation of the President's Task Force on Regulatory Relief on January 22, 1981—two days after his inauguration. This cabinet-level task force was placed under the direction of Vice President George H. W. Bush. Reagan also placed a sixty-day freeze on final regulations promulgated in the final weeks of the Carter presidency and eliminated COWPS and the Carter-era Regulatory Council. But the greatest impact came in the area of regulatory review. Miller, who had joined the Reagan transition team, was appointed both as head of OIRA and as executive director of the Presidential Task Force on Regulatory Relief. There he worked with

C. Boyden Gray (Counsel to the Task Force) to draft Executive Order 12291, which was signed by Reagan on February 17, 1981. Miller understood that the new executive order "would be seen as a serious taking of power from the regulatory heads." As he would later recall, moving quickly was of the essence:

> the danger lay in delaying too long. If the regulatory agencies began to be filled by Reagan appointees, and if these appointees (with encouragement from the bureaucracy and the agency's other constituents) began to feel their oats, it would be difficult, if not impossible, to get the executive order through the approval process.[48]

Ronald Reagan's Executive Order 12291 marked a dramatic change in the history of regulatory review. It required executive branch agencies to submit proposed rulemaking and final rules to OMB-OIRA before they could be published in the *Federal Register*. Major rules required a cost–benefit-analysis-based regulatory impact analysis. A major rule was any regulation that had an annual economic impact of $100 million per year, had major increases in costs or prices, or had "significant adverse effects on competition, employment, investment, productivity, innovation, or on the ability of United States-based enterprises to compete with foreign-based enterprises in domestic or export markets."[49] The OMB was given the authority, however to determine whether any rule should be treated as a major rule or whether a set of related rules should be treated together, thus extending regulatory review far more broadly.[50] Agencies were instructed "regulatory action shall not be undertaken unless the potential benefits to society . . . outweigh the potential costs" and then "the alternative involving the least net cost to society shall be chosen."[51] In addition to conducting a cost–benefit analysis, regulators also had to include a discussion of alternative means of achieving the regulatory goals at a lower cost. Under the executive order, agencies were directed to "refrain from publishing" in the *Federal Register* until the conclusion of the review and could be required to respond to concerns raised by the OMB-OIRA if rules were returned for reconsideration.[52] In practice, the review process imposed significant costs and delays; approval would be forthcoming only if the agencies could demonstrate to the satisfaction of OMB-OIRA that they would generate net present benefits. If there were disagreements between OIRA and the agencies, the only recourse was to appeal to the President's Task Force on Regulatory Relief. Regulatory review was further strengthened with Executive Order 12498 (1985), which required agencies to submit an annual regulatory program that identified all significant regulations that were planned or in progress. Henceforth, the OMB-OIRA could return for reconsideration any rule that had not been included in the regulatory program, regardless of whether it would meet the requirements of EO 12291.[53]

The executive countermovement was made more consequential by a shift in the posture of the courts. In a series of decisions in the late 1970s and 1980s, the Supreme Court retreated from its earlier emphasis on enhancing the representational capacity of the administrative state. It prohibited the imposition of hybrid rulemaking procedures that exceeded the minima of the Administrative Procedure Act, restricted the reviewability of agency actions, and limited private action. Most strikingly, in *Chevron v. Natural Resources Defense Council* (1984) the Court required deference to regulatory agencies' interpretation of laws where Congress failed to speak precisely to an issue and the agencies' interpretation was based on a permissible construction of the statute.[54] As Keith Werhan notes:

> The thrust of Chevron [was] startling: Courts are to relinquish control over statutory meaning when reviewing agency action. This control is to be asserted either by Congress, which can "command" a particular interpretation by legislating unambiguously, or, failing such a clear command, by the agencies, as long as they do so reasonably.[55]

By increasing the discretionary authority of administrators, *Chevron* expanded the president's control of the regulatory state.

Executive Order 12866 and the Institutionalization of Review

When Bill Clinton was elected president in 1992, there was great hope within the public interest community that the era of regulatory review would draw to a close. Although Clinton revoked the Reagan-era executive orders, he replaced them with a new regulatory review process via Executive Order 12866 (1993) that retained cost–benefit analysis and continued the role of the OMB-OIRA in the review process.[56] The Clinton administration improved on the earlier system by only requiring review and regulatory impact analyses on economically significant rules (i.e., those that imposed costs of $100 million annually, were inconsistent with other policies, or raised novel legal or policy issues). Critics of Executive Order 12291 had condemned the obsession with quantifiable costs and benefits as stacking the deck against regulations, the benefit of which were often difficult to express in monetary terms. The Clinton order directed each agency to

> assess both the costs and the benefits of the intended regulation and, recognizing that some costs and benefits are difficult to quantify, propose or adopt a regulation only upon a reasoned determination that the benefits of the intended regulation justify its costs.[57]

It also forced a higher level of transparency by governing interactions between OIRA and outside actors (including a log of oral and written communications) and access to documents exchanged between OIRA and agencies. The Clinton order also explicitly noted that the president or the vice-president would resolve conflicts between OIRA and agencies.

Following the 1994 midterm elections, which created Republican majorities in the House and Senate for the first time since the Eisenhower administration, Congress sought to provide statutory foundations for regulatory review. The Regulatory Reform and Relief Act, introduced as part of the Job Creation and Wage Enhancement Act of 1995, would have amended the Administrative Procedure Act to require agencies to submit cost–benefit-analysis-based regulatory impact analyses for OMB approval for all major rules (defined as having an annual economic impact of $50 million). Following the earlier precedents, it would have required agencies to adopt the least costly approach and refrain from promulgating a major rule unless approved by the OMB (a more detailed account of this and related legislation will be reserved for Chapter 6). While the Act passed the House of Representatives, it failed to gain traction in the Senate. In 1996, however, Congress added an amendment to the Omnibus Consolidated Appropriations Act that mandated regulatory accounting. Henceforth, the OMB would be required to estimate on an annual basis the total costs and benefits of regulation and report them to Congress.[58]

Clinton's Executive Order continued to provide the foundation for regulatory review in the George H. W. Bush and Obama presidencies, albeit with some modifications that further expanded the role of review without departing from cost–benefit analysis. Concerns that agencies were bypassing OIRA review led President Bush to issue Executive Order 14422 (2007), which extended the coverage of 12866 to guidance documents. Bush's OIRA head, John Graham, promoted additional disclosure, requiring that documents used in OIRA review and logs of communications with outside parties be made available on line. Yet, there was a growing insistence that agencies involve OIRA at an earlier stage in the development of rules, essentially inserting OIRA's staff in agency deliberations at a point before communications would be logged under the provisions of Executive Order 12866.[59]

Upon assuming office, President Obama revoked the Bush-era executive orders and asked the OMB to consult with the heads of the regulatory agencies to collect recommendations that could be incorporated into a new system of regulatory review—two actions that created hope that he would depart significantly from the system put into place under Executive Order 12866. Two years into his presidency, Obama issued Executive Order 13563 (2011). Under Executive Order 13563, each agency "to the extent permitted by law," must:

(1) propose or adopt a regulation only upon a reasoned determination that its benefits justify its costs (recognizing that some benefits and costs are difficult to quantify); (2) tailor its regulations to impose the least burden on society, consistent with obtaining regulatory objectives, taking into account, among other things, and to the extent practicable, the costs of cumulative

regulations; (3) select, in choosing among alternative regulatory approaches, those approaches that maximize net benefits (including potential economic, environmental, public health and safety, and other advantages; distributive impacts; and equity); (4) to the extent feasible, specify performance objectives, rather than specifying the behavior or manner of compliance that regulated entities must adopt; and (5) identify and assess available alternatives to direct regulation, including providing economic incentives to encourage the desired behavior, such as user fees or marketable permits, or providing information upon which choices can be made by the public.[60]

As noted earlier, the Reagan and Clinton orders applied to proposed regulations. Agencies were required to conduct a cost–benefit analysis before a policy had been enacted rather than retrospectively, when they could better evaluate policy performance. The Obama order required that agencies "consider how best to promote retrospective analysis of rules that may be outmoded, ineffective, insufficient, or excessively burdensome, and to modify, streamline, expand or repeal them in accordance with what has been learned."[61] Subsequently, President Obama issued Executive Order 13610 (2012), which required agencies—in consultation with OIRA—to invite public suggestions on regulations that required retrospective review.

Cass R. Sunstein, Obama's OIRA head, described Executive Order 13563 as "a kind of mini-constitution for the regulatory state."[62] Others were less impressed. Lisa Heinzerling counters that what was most striking "is how notnew it was; much of the order simply repeats, verbatim, the language" of the Clinton Era 12866. She continues: "Any hope that President Obama would use the new executive order as an occasion to fundamentally reshape the relationship between the White House and the agencies, or to loosen the grip of cost–benefit analysis on regulatory policy, was dashed."[63] Indeed, the fact that the cost–benefit-analysis-based regulatory review process established under EO 12291 remains in place—albeit with some modifications—more than three decades later suggests that an appeal to Reagan's antiregulatory position provides an incomplete explanation.[64] Congress wrote exhaustive statutes limiting the discretionary authority of bureaucrats and future presidents. In this context, the reassertion of executive authority in regulatory review can be best understood as an institutional countermovement, an effort on the part of presidents to reclaim the authority to manage the executive branch or, at the very least, reduce the political and economic impacts of what they could no longer control.

Evaluating Regulatory Review

The new system of regulatory review raised several serious concerns for critics, some of which have diminished in intensity since the early days of the Reagan presidency as review has become institutionalized. We will focus on four chief critiques: (1) regulatory review concentrates power in the hands of the president and, correspondingly, diminishes the authority of Congress; (2) the process functions chiefly as another channel of influence for corporate interests, a fact that is often obscured by the lack of transparency; (3) even if one can dispel the claim that review enhances corporate influence over regulation, cost–benefit analysis—central to regulatory review—stacks the deck against social regulations; and (4) the process misallocates scarce agency resources and provokes avoidance strategies that may compromise the extent to which regulators can execute their mandates.

Regulatory Review and the Growth of Presidential Authority

The introduction of regulatory review significantly strengthened the president's control of the regulatory state and, in so doing, engaged a fundamental question about the balance of power between the branches. As Terry M. Moe and Scott A. Wilson explain, regulatory review

> captures the essence of the institutional battle between the president and Congress. Presidents have imposed new procedures on regulatory agencies in a sustained attempt . . . to gain control over agency rule-making and assert presidential priorities. During the same time, agencies and their legislative supporters have vigorously protested, claiming the bureaucracy is being denied the autonomy and discretion it needs to fulfill its mandates.[65]

As explained in the last chapter, Congress wrote detailed statutes that constrained the president's authority over executive branch agencies. The presidential response, from Nixon forward, has involved successive and more or less consistent efforts to reclaim this authority. As Christopher DeMuth, former OIRA head observed:

> It is remarkable to find this degree of policy constancy across Republican and Democratic administrations, including one very conservative and one very liberal president. If the same presidents had issued executive orders on administering health care, Social Security disability, or wage-and-hour programs, the documents would have been highly dissimilar.[66]

The battles over regulatory review and the expansion of presidential control of the bureaucracy have been intense, in part, because they engage a core constitutional question. If Congress passes statutes that direct executive branch agencies to promulgate regulations, does the president have the legal authority to dictate the substance of these regulations? Certainly, Article II of the US Constitution vests executive power in the president and directs the president to "take care that the laws be faithfully executed." But there is great disagreement over whether the framers envisioned a unitary executive—a hierarchical executive branch under the direction of the president. Proponents of regulatory review have gravitated toward the unitary executive position, whereas opponents have viewed the extension of presidential authority, particularly after Executive Order 12291, as doing damage to the Constitution.

Lawrence Lessig and Cass R. Sunstein suggest that one can draw a distinction between strong and weak versions of the unitary executive. In the strong version, the president

> has plenary or unlimited power over the execution of administrative functions, understood broadly to mean all tasks of law-implementation. All officers with such functions must either be removable at the President's discretion or be subject to presidential countermand in the context of policy disagreements.

Under the weak version, there is recognition of some genuinely executive functions over which the president exercises plenary power, but "Congress has a wide degree of authority to structure government as it sees fit. Under this view, unitariness is a significant constitutional value, but it is not a trumping constitutional value."[67] As they conclude, following a careful analysis of the constitutional debates and early court decisions, the framers had a pragmatic understanding that provides little support for a strong, unitary executive.

Despite this conclusion, Lessig and Sunstein develop an argument for a stronger unitary executive grounded in core constitutional values. Following their argument, the framers were particularly concerned with establishing administrative accountability and controlling the effects of faction. In the wake of the New Deal, the proliferation of regulatory agencies exercising discretionary authority has compromised accountability. "To the extent that we multiply (and specialize) the bodies exercising lawmaking power (without a presidential or congressional check), we increase geometrically the opportunities and the costs of faction." Given the changing circumstances, "it would not be faithful to the original design to permit officers in the executive branch, making discretionary judgments about important domestic issues, to be immunized from presidential control."[68]

A similar position is struck by John O. McGinnis. Under the Constitution, the combination of bicameralism and a presidential veto—what he refers to as tricameralism—imposed a supermajority rule, to protect the public interest from special interest legislation. However, this system

> has declined with the rise of the modern administrative state because, pursuant to congressional delegation, administrative agencies may impose regulations without overcoming the hurdle of legislative passage in two

houses and presidential approval. Special interest groups can have substantial influence over administrative regulations, and the regulations may reflect less broad-based deliberation and consensus than laws and regulations that are passed under the tricameral procedures.[69]

In this context, the regulatory review processes established under Executive Order 12291 and 12866 are not violations of the original constitutional design. Quite the contrary. In the view of McGinnis, regulatory review is an act of constitutional restoration.

Transparency, Accountability, and Corporate Interests

While advocates of a strong, unitary executive interpret regulatory review as a means of forcing accountability, some critics have charged that, in practice, the review process has had the opposite result. In the years following Executive Order 12291, critics charged that regulatory review had seriously compromised transparency and accountability. As noted earlier, COWPS and RARG had made their reviews part of the rulemaking record. In contrast, OIRA reviews occurred earlier in the process and were largely veiled in secrecy, even if OIRA grudgingly made public some documents from outside parties after 1986. An argument can be made that secrecy was a strength of the process. As former OIRA administrators Christopher DeMuth and Douglas Ginsberg argued with respect to regulatory review:

> like any other deliberative process, it can flourish only if the agency head or his delegate, and the OMB as the president's delegate, are free to discuss frankly the merits of a regulatory proposal . . . . The administration's deliberative process would be significantly compromised if the preliminary rounds in any such disagreement were routinely publicized.

Yet, both also recognized the liability insofar as it put the OMB "at a disadvantage in responding to allegations that it does, or at least could, act as a 'conduit' for information or influence to be introduced illicitly into the agency's decision calculus."[70] In the words of Robert V. Percival, the secrecy fueled the charges that "OMB had served as a vehicle for secret, back door lobbying by industry."[71]

Clinton's Executive Order 12866 resolved some of the problems. Under the order, the OIRA administrator was the only one who could receive oral communications with parties outside of the executive branch and that when such communication occurs, agency representatives must be invited. It also required that all substantive oral and written communications with parties outside of the executive branch be included in a publicly available log. Furthermore, OIRA was required to disclose written communication with executive branch agencies after the publication of the rule, thereby allowing for public scrutiny. Oral communications between OIRA and executive branch actors need not be disclosed, however, to preserve executive privilege.[72] Yet, critics charge that even with the changes under 12866, secrecy and bias remain the order of the day. As an analysis from the Center for Progressive Reform covering the period 2001–11 concluded: OIRA has "routinely flouted these disclosure and deadline requirements" regardless of the occupant of the White House. "The most important consequence of these secretive practices is the nondisclosure of communications between OIRA and the agencies, which makes it impossible for the public to undertake a systematic, rule-by-rule analysis of the impact of OIRA review."[73] More troubling, what information exists reveals a pattern of industry overrepresentation. Of the 5,759 individuals (excluding agency officials) appearing at OIRA meetings, approximately two-thirds (68 percent under Bush, 62 percent under Obama) represented industry interests, suggesting that "the dominance of industry groups over public interest groups in the meeting process is an inherent feature of OIRA reviews, essentially unaffected by changes in administration."[74]

The Intrinsic Limitations of Cost–Benefit Analysis

Leaving aside the political and institutional dimensions of regulatory review, some critics have focused on the intrinsic biases of cost–benefit analysis—the analytical hard core of the process. At a conceptual level, cost–benefit analysis is relatively intuitive. The goal is to determine the extent to which a policy intervention yields net present costs or benefits—that is, whether it detracts from, or contributes to, social welfare. Analysts must identify and quantify the costs and benefits of a policy. While costs are usually expressed in monetary terms (e.g., the costs of installing new pollution control technology, as expressed in dollar terms), benefits must be monetized to be incorporated into the analysis. Because costs and benefits frequently occur at different points in time, the streams of costs and benefits need to be brought to present value via discounting before one can calculate a summary statistic (e.g., the cost–benefit ratio, net present value). If one assumes that the regulatory budget is fixed—there is a limited amount of budgetary resources and a limit to the costs that can be imposed on the economy—it makes intuitive sense that agencies should be cognizant of whether they are maximizing their impact.

Cost–benefit analysis was initially conducted to evaluate projects proposed by the Army Corps of Engineers, as noted earlier in this chapter. Although the application of this methodology to large infrastructure projects may prove unproblematic, social regulations generate benefits that may prove difficult to quantify and monetize. The risk assessment process that is used to project the impact of interventions on the frequency of diseases is often laden with uncertainty, reflecting the complexity of the underlying models of disease processes and the lack of good data. As the EPA notes: "The risk estimates provided in risk assessments and ultimately addressed in EPA decisions are driven by the uncertainty and variability inherent in practically all the information and meth-odologies EPA uses."[75] Once benefits are quantified, monetization can prove equally difficult. Agencies commonly monetize lives saved through the use of the "value of a statistical life," a monetary figure derived from wage-mortality studies. Other benefits may prove more difficult to assign a monetary value (e.g., what is the value of a cancer averted or a unique ecosystem preserved?).

Discounting is particularly problematic in areas like environmental policy. The basic notion of discounting—that a dollar today is worth more than a dollar at some future point—seems relatively unproblematic when viewed at the level of individual preferences. If one assumes a discount rate of 7 percent, one may be quite willing to accept that a $100 benefit today is worth $87.34 received in two years. But this same process applied over lengthy periods of time, may make it nearly impossible to justify regulations that would impose large costs today to assure that future generations would have the same basic environmental amenities enjoyed by this generation. As Richard L. Revesz and Michael A. Livermore note:

> Deciding how much to spend today in order to reduce environmental risks for future generations is not a question of time preferences for any group of people, but is an allocation question between people living at different times. Fundamentally, such allocation decisions are moral.[76]

And yet, in practice, they are treated the same.

The Bureaucratic Response

In the current context, the imposition of executive-based regulatory review is of the greatest interest because of the effects it has had on the regulatory process. In the wake of Executive Order 12291, agencies faced significant difficulties. Consider the EPA. The election of Ronald Reagan resulted in immediate budget cuts, from $4.7 billion (1980) to $3 billion (1981). The nominal budget would not exceed 1980 levels until 1987.[77] During this same period, the agency was responsible for preparing regulatory impact analyses that ranged in cost from $210,000 to $2.38 million per rule.[78] Under conditions of large budget cuts, the costs of complying with regulatory review reduced the pace of rulemaking (a decline that likely also resulted from the appointment of administrators who embraced the administration's anti-regulatory philosophy). As Abner J. Mikva explains, Executive Order 12291's review requirements effectively:

> stopped many new efforts in their tracks. By 1986, one-third of all fed-eral regulatory proposals reportedly were vetoed or held up by OMB, including over half of the Environmental Protection Agency proposals in one three-year period, and almost 80 percent of the proposed hazardous waste regulations.

The procedural impediments were tantamount to an effort "to bypass Congress in setting priorities and shaping the specifics of administrative agency actions."[79] Agencies that might have proposed rules that failed to generate net positive benefits may have chosen not to regulate rather than run afoul of OIRA.

Given that agencies must publish notice of proposed rulemaking and final rules in the *Federal Register*, we can look to the number of pages in the *Federal Register* to get some sense of the impact of regulatory review on the pages of new regulation. During the Carter presidency (1977–80), an average of 31,589 pages were devoted to rules and proposed rules on an annual basis. In sharp contrast, the number of pages devoted to rules and proposed rules fell to 27,773 during the Reagan presidency (1981–88), increasing slightly to an annual average of 30,303 pages during the George H. W. Bush presidency. By the last years of the Clinton presidency, the number of pages (38,285–42,425, between 1998 and 2000) would exceed the peak levels during the Carter administration (37,457 pages in 1979), but by that point regulatory review had been largely institutionalized.[80]

During the Reagan and Bush presidencies, there was a great deal of resistance to OMB review within both Congress and the agencies themselves. In Congress, the response was somewhat predictable, setting aside the 104th Congress where the new GOP majority attempted—albeit, unsuccessfully—to give the provisions of Executive Order 12291 statutory foundations. Where possible, Congress sought to further constrain agency discretion as a means of limiting the scope of OMB review. As Robert Percival notes:

> Congress has expressed its dissatisfaction with the consequences of regulatory review by adding more specific statutory controls on agencies' discretion every time it has reauthorized the environmental laws. The result has been a distinct trend toward reduced flexibility for agencies charged with implementing the federal environmental statutes. This congressional desire to control agency discretion is reflected in an increase in the proliferation of statutory deadlines and the specification of more detailed substantive criteria in such legislation.[81]

Ironically, this response added further rigidities to the regulatory process, further diminishing the capacity of administrators to respond to changes in the environment they were charged with regulating.

In the bureaucracy, the response took a variety of forms. Some analysts have observed that agencies can take a number of paths to avoid OIRA review. The executive orders mandate the completion of regulatory impact analyses for rules that reach a certain level of economic significance. Agencies can seek to achieve their policy goals through a variety of instruments other than formal rules (e.g., guidance documents, adjudications, consent decrees or settlements on existing lawsuits, deference to state-level enforcement), thereby bypassing review requirements. They may take what would otherwise be economically significant rules and split them into multiple rules, none of which would meet the monetary thresholds for significance. They may seek to obfuscate, providing opaque or incomplete analyses to raise OIRA's costs of conducting a rigorous review. Agencies may also seek to exploit statutory deadlines or wait until the end of a presidential administration.[82] While there is little question that some of these strategies have been employed, there is disagreement as to their frequency and their effectiveness.

From a practical perspective, it is difficult to understand how these efforts to avoid OIRA scrutiny could bear fruit. Lisa Heinzerling, who served as Associate Administrator of the EPA's Office of Policy during the Obama presidency, argues:

> Most of the EPA rules OIRA reviews are not economically significant, so fussing around to make a rule or package of rules not econom- ically significant won't help to avoid OIRA review. OIRA, in any event, lavishes skeptical attention on EPA's estimates of regulatory costs. Moreover, . . . OIRA continues to review agency guidance, so denominating an action as guidance will not avoid OIRA review. And in my experience, OIRA personnel keep an eagle eye on EPA—on its public announcements, website, etc.—to make sure EPA does not sneak something past it.[83]

Efforts to package regulatory actions, in short, run afoul of a simple reality: "OIRA reviews pretty much anything it wants to review and fits anything it must into the catch-all category, 'novel legal or policy issues.'"[84] From a strategic perspective, as Nina A. Mendelson and Jonathan B. Wiener argue, a reliance on tactical ploys could prove overly myopic. Agencies "can expect to deal with OIRA in a continuing repeat–play relationship, so that no tactic or response can be viewed in isolation." In the end, those agencies that gain a reputation for avoidance tactics may well discover that "OIRA might review more aggres- sively all the agency's rule submissions . . . . This could increase overall delays and resource demands on the agency."[85]

Even if agencies may be less inclined to dodge OMB-OIRA review through an array of strategic maneuvers, the realization that cost–benefit analysis will carry the day on most rules most of the time may have a pernicious effect on agency decision-making. Agencies work under tight budget constraints. Each decision to develop one rule or standard diverts resources from other potential areas of regulation. Agency officials understand that they can clearly quantify and monetize the benefits of intervention in some areas (e.g., clean air rules). Comparable calculations may be far more difficult when regulating toxic and hazardous wastes, for example, because of the intrinsic complexities of risk assessment (e.g., the myriad assumptions that must be made about disease pro- cesses, the shape of the dose response curve, cessation lags) and the difficulties of monetizing benefits (e.g., the value of non-fatal cancers averted). Rather than devoting scarce resources to rulemakings that might be embroiled in lengthy disputes with OIRA or be rejected altogether, they may focus their efforts in areas of limited resistance. Over time, rules governing some aspects of an agency's responsibilities may continue to advance, whereas others simply languish.[86]

Regulatory agencies, quite predictably, responded to the imposition of regulatory review in another way: by expanding their analytical capabilities to conduct analyses in house. As Thomas O. McGarity observes: "In most regulatory agencies, the central regulatory office might be characterized as a 'mini-OMB,' but in no other agency does this description apply with greater force than in EPA."[87] The EPA's economists are concentrated in its Office of Policy, part of the Office of the Administrator responsible for rulemaking, but economists also staff positions in the program offices that compose the regulatory impact analyses for the various rules. The agency also draws on outside consultants to assist in preparing the majority of regulatory analyses.[88] As Michael A. Livermore notes:

> the sheer resources that EPA can bring to bear in support of a rule making vastly outstrip OIRA's. EPA has a team of professionals charged with preparing the regulatory-impact analysis, often augmented by outside consultants. OIRA has a single desk officer, or at most a small group within the office.[89]

Certainly, OIRA still has the power to block regulations. But following Livermore, the regulatory agencies have developed the capacity to structure the terms of debate with respect to cost–benefit methodology and the empirical foundations of specific rules.

Conclusion

When Congress passed the new social regulatory statutes of the early 1970s, they did so with a seeming disregard for cost. Yet, as the nation entered a period of stagflation, the costs became increasingly salient, giving rise to a period of sustained deregulation that eliminated some of the more important economic regulations inherited from earlier episodes of regulatory expansion. As noted earlier, the public interest community broadly supported deregulation. But the debates were framed by a new network of conservative think tanks that had effectively linked regulation to inflation and stagnant growth and popularized the case for deregulation. While the new social regulations were largely insulated from deregulation, the debates over the costs of regulation and their economic ramifications provided support for the introduction of regulatory review processes grounded in cost–benefit analysis. Of course, regulatory review could also serve an important role as part of the larger presidential response to the strategies of institutional design embraced by Congress.

When designing the new social regulations in environmental protection and occupational safety and health, Congress designed a system to prevent capture and limit bureaucratic discretion. In so doing, it constrained the power of the president over the executive branch. This, in turn, stimulated a counter-movement in the form of regulatory review centralized in the OMB-OIRA. Cost–benefit-analysis-based review provided presidents with an enhanced ability to control executive branch regulatory agencies and forestall the promulgation of new regulations that could impose significant costs. Certainly, Reagan's Executive Order 12291 could be seen as part of his larger program to scale back the regulatory state. But subsequent presidents proved quite adept at using regulatory review free from Reagan's larger ideological agenda.

After decades of regulatory review centralized in the OIRA—decades that spanned presidencies as ideologically diverse as Ronald Reagan and Barack Obama—it is clear that what was once viewed as an ideological attack on the administrative state has become institutionalized. It is no longer a partisan affair. Agencies that were once encouraged to regulate with little or no concern for the costs imposed by their actions now routinely consider the cost–benefit rationale for the decisions they make. The EPA, as the most frequent target of regulatory review, has adapted to the changing institutional environment and developed a powerful analytical capability, one that rivals that of the OMB. Whether the inclusion of cost–benefit criteria is a positive occurrence remains a point of serious contention. There is little consensus on whether it has resulted in better public policy. But for present purposes, its primary importance is found elsewhere. These requirements have only added to the complexity and rigidity of the regulatory process, making agencies far less capable of responding to changing circumstances. The importance of this fact will become clear in Chapter 5, as we turn to the problem of gridlock and polarization.

Notes

1 Richard Nixon, "Veto of the Federal Water Pollution Control Act Amendments of 1972, October 17, 1972." Available at www.presidency.ucsb.edu/ws/?pid=3634.
2 Federal Water Pollution Control Act Amendments of 1972 Veto Message. Congressional Record-Senate, October 17, 1972: 36871. Available at http://abacus. bates.edu/muskie-archives/ajcr/1972/CWA%20Override.shtml.
3 See Kay Lehman Schlozman, "What Accent the Heavenly Chorus? Political Equality and the American Pressure System," *The Journal of Politics* 62, 2 (1984): 1006–32, and David Vogel, "The Power of Business in America: A Re-Appraisal," *British Journal of Political Science* 13, 1 (1983): 19–43.
4 See John L. Campbell, "Institutional Analysis and the Role of Ideas in Political Economy," *Theory and Society* 27, 3 (1998): 377–409.
5 J. Craig Jenkins and Craig M. Eckert, "The Right Turn in Economic Policy: Business Elites and the New Conservative Economics," *Sociological Forum* 15, 2 (2000): 321–22.
6 See Martha Derthick and Paul J. Quirk, *The Politics of Deregulation* (Washington DC: The Brookings Institution, 1985).
7 Ibid., 38.

8 See Herbert Stein, *Presidential Economics: The Making of Economic Policy from Roosevelt to Clinton*, 3rd ed. (Washington DC: The AEI Press, 1994), 89–101.

9 See Campbell, "Institutional Analysis and the Role of Ideas in Political Economy."

10 Council of Economic Advisors, *Economic Report of the President* (Washington DC: US Government Printing Office, 1975), 159.

11 Council of Economic Advisors, *Economic Report of the President* (Washington DC: US Government Printing Office, 1977), 8.

12 Council of Economic Advisors, *Economic Report of the President* (Washington DC: US Government Printing Office, 1978), 17.

13 Council of Economic Advisors, *Economic Report of the President* (Washington DC: US Government Printing Office, 1979), 91.

14 Mark Green and Ralph Nader, "Economic Regulation vs. Competition: Uncle Sam the Monopoly Man," *Yale Law Journal* 82, 5 (1973): 883.

15 John L. Campbell and Ove K. Pedersen, "Policy Ideas, Knowledge Regimes and Comparative Political Economy," *Socio-Economic Review* 2015: 7.

16 Vogel, "The Power of Business in America," 36.

17 Derthick and Quirk, *The Politics of Deregulation*, 36.

18 John L. Campbell and Ove K. Pedersen, *The National Origins of Policy Ideas: Knowledge Regimes in the United States, France, Germany and Denmark* (Princeton, NJ: Princeton University Press, 2014), 46.

19 Vogel, "The Power of Business in America," 38.

20 Rudy Maxa, "Playing Politics for Keeps and Laughs," *Washington Post*, December 4, 1977, 317.

21 Murray L. Weidenbaum, "On Estimating Regulatory Costs," *Regulation*, May/June 1978: 17.

22 Murray L. Weidenbaum, *Government-Mandated Price Increases: A Neglected Aspect of Inflation* (Washington DC: American Enterprise Institute, 1975), 1–2.

23 Murray L. Weidenbaum, "Time to Control Runaway Inflation," *Reader's Digest*, June 1979, 98.

24 John Schwarz, quoted in Stan Luger, "Administrative Law, Regulatory Policy, and the Presidency," *Presidential Studies Quarterly* 23, 4 (1993): 719.

25 Jenkins and Eckert, "The Right Turn in Economic Policy," 321–22.

26 Derthick and Quirk, *The Politics of Deregulation*, 38.

27 Anthony Downs, "Up and Down with Ecology: The 'Issue-Attention Cycle,'" *The Public Interest* 28 (Summer 1972): 38.

28 Ibid., 46.

29 Robert Y. Shapiro and John M. Gillroy, "The Polls: Regulation-Part II," *The Public Opinion Quarterly* 48, 3 (1984): 668.

30 John M. Gillroy and Robert Y. Shapiro, "The Polls: Environmental Protection," *The Public Opinion Quarterly* 50, 2 (1986): 273.

31 Ibid., 271.

32 Robert B. Horwitz, "Judicial Review of Regulatory Decisions: The Changing Criteria," *Political Science Quarterly* 109, 1 (1994): 160.

33 Richard Nixon, "Statement on Establishing the National Industrial Pollution Control Council," April 9, 1970. Available at www.presidency.ucsb.edu/ws/?pid=2454.

34 Peter Cleary Yeager, *The Limits of Law: The Public Regulation of Private Pollution* (Cambridge, UK: Cambridge University Press, 1993), 136–38, and Henry J. Steck, "Private Influence on Environmental Policy: The Case of the National Industrial Pollution Control Council," *Environmental Law* 5 (1974–75): 241–81.

35 See Jim Tozzi, "OIRA's Formative Years: The Historical Record of Centralized Regulatory Review Preceding OIR's Founding," *Administrative Law Review*, 63 (2011): 37–69.

36 George P. Shultz, "Memorandum for Heads of Departments and Agencies: Agency Regulations, Standards, and Guidelines Pertaining to Environmental Quality, Consumer Protection, and Occupational Safety and Health." Executive Office of the President, Office of Management and Budget, October 5, 1971. Available at www.thecre.com/ombpapers/QualityofLife1.htm.

37 See "Special Report: Office of Management and Budget Plays Critical Part in Environmental Policymaking, Faces Little External Review," *BNA Environmental Reporter—Current Developments* 7 (1976): 693–97, and Yeager, *The Limits of Law*, 204–5.

38 Gerald R. Ford, "Address to a Joint Session of the Congress on the Economy," October 8, 1974. Available at www.presidency.ucsb.edu/ws/index.php?pid=4434.

39 Tozzi, "OIRA's Formative Years," 51.

40 Jim Miller, *Fix the U.S. Budget: Urgings of an "Abominable No-Man"* (Stanford, CA: Hoover Institution Press, 1994), 1.

41 Executive Order 12044, §1.

42 Thomas D. Hopkins, "The Evolution of Regulatory Oversight: CWPS to OIRA," *Administrative Law Review* 63 (2011): 71–77, and Tozzi, "OIRA's Formative Years," 52–53.

43 Paul R. Verkuil, "A Critical Guide to the Regulatory Flexibility Act," *Duke Law Journal* 2 (1982): 230–31.

44 See Cecelia Wertz, "Paperwork Reduction," *Administrative Law Review* 34, 2 (1982): 155–58.

45 Paperwork Reduction Act (1980), §3504.

46 Jim Tozzi, a veteran of regulatory review at OMB, persuasively argues that these features were evident in the Quality of Life review process, which "set the template for action taken by the Ford, Carter, and Reagan Administrations." Tozzi, "OIRA's Formative Years," 47.

47 James C. Miller, III, "The Early Days of Reagan Regulatory Relief and Suggestions for OIRA's Future," *Administrative Law Review* 63 (2011): 93–101.

48 Miller, *Fix the Budget*, 2.

49 Executive Order 12291, §1 (b).

50 Executive Order 12291, §3 (b).

51 Executive Order 12291, §2.

52 Executive Order 12291, §3 (f).

53 See Robert V. Percival, "Rediscovering the Limits of the Regulatory Review Authority of the Office of Management and Budget," *Environmental Law Reporter* 17 (1987): 10017–23, and Curtis W. Copeland, "Federal Rulemaking: The Role of the Office of Information and Regulatory Affairs," *CRS Report for Congress*, RL32397 (Washington DC: Congressional Research Service, 2009).

54 467 U.S. 837 (1984).

55 Keith Werhan, "The Neoclassical Revival of Administrative Law," *Administrative Law Review* 44, 3 (1992): 593.

56 See Richard H. Pildes and Cass R. Sunstein, "Reinventing the Regulatory State," *The University of Chicago Law Review* 62, 1 (1995): 1–129.

57 Executive Order 12866, §1 (6).

58 See Robert W. Hahn, "Government Analysis of the Benefits and Costs of Regulation," *Journal of Economic Perspectives* 12, 4 (1998): 201–10.

59 Lisa Heinzerling, "Inside EPA: A Former Insider's Reflections on the Relationship between the Obama EPA and the Obama White House," *Pace Environmental Law Review* 31 (2014): 335.

60 Executive Order 13563, §1 (b).

61 Executive Order 13563, §6.

62 Cass R. Sunstein, "The Office of Information and Regulatory Affairs: Myths and Realities," *Harvard Law Review* 126 (2013): 1846.

63 Heinzerling, "Inside EPA," 341.

64 William F. West, "The Institutionalization of Regulatory Review: Organizational Stability and Responsive Competence at OIRA," *Presidential Studies Quarterly* 35, 1 (2005): 76–93.

65 Terry M. Moe and Scott A. Wilson, "Presidents and the Politics of Structure," *Law and Contemporary Problems* 57, 2 (1994): 37.

66 Christopher DeMuth, "OIRA at Thirty," *Administrative Law Review* 63 (2011): 16.

67 Lawrence Lessig and Cass R. Sunstein, "The President and the Administration," *Columbia Law Review* 94, 1 (1994): 8–9.

68 Ibid., 105, 119. For a discussion of regulatory review as a response to factions, see James C. Miller III, William F. Shughart II, and Robert D. Tollison, "A Note on Centralized Regulatory Review," *Public Choice* 43, 1 (1984): 83–88.

69 John O. McGinnis, "Presidential Review as Constitutional Restoration," *Duke Law Journal* 51, 3 (2001): 902–3.

70 Christopher C. DeMuth and Douglas H. Ginsburg, "White House Review of Agency Rulemaking," *Harvard Law Review* 99, 5 (1986): 1085–86.

71 Robert V. Percival, "Checks without Balance: Executive Office Oversight of the Environmental Protection Agency," *Law and Contemporary Problems* 54, 4 (1991): 151.

72 Pildes and Sunstein, "Reinventing the Regulatory State," 21–24.

73 Rena Steinzor, Michael Patoka, and James Goodwin, *Behind Closed Doors at the White House: How Politics Trumps Protection of Public Health, Worker Safety, and the Environment* (Washington DC; Center for Progressive Reform, 2011), 7.

74 Ibid., 20.

75 Environmental Protection Agency, *Risk Assessment Principles and Practices*. Office of the Science Advisor, Staff Paper EPA/100/B-04/001 (Washington DC: Environmental Protection Agency, 2004), 141.

76 Richard L. Revesz and Michael A. Livermore, *Retaking Rationality: How Cost–Benefit Analysis Can Better Protect the Environment and Our Health* (New York: Oxford University Press, 2011), 107. Also, see Frank Ackerman and Lisa Heinzerling, *Priceless: On Knowing the Price of Everything and the Value of Nothing* (New York: The New Press, 2004).

77 EPA's Budget and Spending. Available at www2.epa.gov/planandbudget/budget.

78 Environmental Protection Agency, *EPA's Use of Benefit–Cost Analysis, 1981–1986* (Washington DC: Environmental Protection Agency, 1987), S-2.

79 Abner J. Mikva, "Deregulating through the Back Door: The Hard Way to Fight a Revolution," *The University of Chicago Law Review* 57, 2 (1990): 530.

80 *Federal Register* and CFR Publication Statistics. Available at www.federalregister.gov/uploads/2015/05/OFR-STATISTICS-CHARTS-ALL1-1-1-2014.xls.

81 Percival, "Checks without Balance," 175.

82 "Note: OIRA Avoidance," *Harvard Law Review* 124, 4 (2011): 994–1015, and Jennifer Nou, "Agency Self-Insulation under Presidential Review," *Harvard Law Review* 126, 7 (126): 1755–837.

83 Heinzerling, "Inside EPA," 348.

84 Ibid., 349.

85 Nina A. Mendelson and Jonathan B. Wiener, "Responding to Agency Avoidance of OIRA," *Harvard Journal of Law and Public Policy* 37, 2 (2014): 513–14.

86 See the discussion in Heinzerling, "Inside EPA," 352.

87 Thomas O. McGarity, *Reinventing Rationality: The Role of Regulatory Analysis in the Federal Bureaucracy* (Cambridge, UK: Cambridge University Press, 1991), 256.

88 Michael A. Livermore, "Cost–Benefit Analysis and Agency Independence," *University of Chicago Law Review* 81 (2014): 626–29.

89 Ibid., 635.

5

POLARIZATION, GRIDLOCK, AND REGULATORY DRIFT

In the past, significant new regulatory initiatives have often emerged as the product of a related chain of events. A focusing event—a new book or report, a well-publicized case of policy failure, a catastrophic tragedy—raises the media attention to a particular issue and triggers a heightened demand for policy change. Advocacy groups and policy entrepreneurs play a central role in this process, as they promote issue expansion. That is, they seek to change elite and public opinion and leverage the focusing event to make the case for larger changes in public policy and institutions. On occasion, the impacts may spread well beyond the confines of a discrete policy. A series of focusing or triggering events can contribute to much broader concerns about risk, unleashing a "risk availability cascade" that fundamentally changes the ways in which other sources of risk are understood and, ultimately, supporting broader demands for policy change.[1] For example, heightened concerns over environmental risks in the late 1960s and early 1970s spread to other policy areas—occupational health and consumer product safety—leading to a wave of new regulatory statutes that literally recast the regulatory state and produced the most complicated and expensive regulatory initiatives in the nation's history.

The most notable cases of regulatory change, as suggested in Chapter 2, often follow the basic punctuated equilibrium model. Institutional structures that limit access to sites of policymaking (policy monopolies) are combined with a dominant policy image, creating a good deal of stability overtime. But the kinds of triggering events noted above can punctuate the structurally-induced equilibrium, creating the opportunity to introduce a new policy image, incorporate new interests, build new institutions, and usher in a period of rapid, non-incremental change.[2] As a result of this dynamic, regulation—like many policy areas—has exhibited "institutionally reinforced stability interrupted by bursts of change. These bursts of change have kept the US government from becoming a gridlocked Leviathan despite its growth in size and complexity since World War II."[3] But what if these bursts of change cease to occur?

There is much to suggest that the system has become far less responsive to the kinds of triggering events that formerly forced momentous changes in public policy and institutions. This chapter explores the problem of polarization as it impacts on regulation. It is the core assertion of this chapter that the dearth of new significant regulatory statutes in the post-1990 period has been a product of growing polarization and gridlock. Institutional failure has foreclosed the opportunities for policy change. This, in turn, has contributed to the regulatory drift and created the preconditions for greater unilateralism on the part of presidents. Before addressing polarization in greater detail, it is useful to compare two episodes drawn from environmental protection to better understand how salient events can trigger—or fail to trigger—significant changes in policy.

Crisis and Response

The late 1960s and early 1970s witnessed the rise of the modern environmental movement, the growing political salience of pollution, and the passage of the most ambitious regulatory statutes in the nation's history. Attention to the environment predated the period, of course, but it usually took one of two forms. Preservationists focused on maintaining pristine wilderness areas. Section 2 (c) of the Wilderness Act of 1964 defined wilderness in poetic terms as "an area where the earth and its community of life are untrammeled by man, where man himself is a visitor who does not remain." Such areas, if preserved, would provide "outstanding opportunities for solitude or a primitive and unconfined type of recreation." In contrast, conservationists were concerned with stewarding existing natural resources to accommodate economic activity. In 1960, Richard Nixon ran unsuccessfully for president on a platform that recognized conservation, but placed it in the context of economic growth ("A strong and growing economy requires vigorous and persistent attention to wise conservation and sound development of all our resources").[4] Environmental protection, in contrast, would aspire to reducing environmental risks more broadly and to preserve the intrinsic virtues of the ecosystem while creating a healthy context for this and future generations. Unlike preservation or conservation, environmental protection would require imposing new and costly restrictions on industrial activity and promulgating standards that would force regulators to work at the intersection of law, science, and economics. The shift from preservation/conservation to environmental protection is an excellent example of changes in policy images, one which emerged as a product of political mobilization.

There were a number of focusing events during the period—the Torrey Canyon oil spill (1967), the burning Cuyahoga River (1969), the Santa Barbara oil spill (1969), the Lake Eerie fish kills—that reinforced the core messages

Hayes, who hoped "to bypass the traditional political process" and viewed "traditional characterizations of left and right are irrelevant at this stage of the environmental movement," declined the invitation.[13]

The spike in environmental activism in 1970 propelled the legislative process. President Nixon was committed to wresting the issue of the environment from Senator Edmund Muskie (D-MN), a potential candidate for the presidency in 1972. The central role of the environment in the State of the Union Address and Nixon's proactive decision to create the Environmental Protection Agency that same year were two expressions of the commitment. In February 10, 1970, President Nixon delivered a special message to Congress to announce "a comprehensive, 37-point program, embracing 23 major legislative proposals and 14 new measures being taken by administrative action or Executive Order" to "move us dramatically forward toward what has become an urgent common goal of all Americans: the rescue of our natural habitat as a place both habitable and hospitable to man."[14] Several of these proposals involved the problem of air pollution. Nixon called for an extension and strengthening of the 1967 Clean Air Act, including mandating reductions in automobile emissions and national standards for stationary sources. During March and April, the House Interstate and Foreign Commerce Committee held hearings and, on June 10, the House passed amendments to the Clean Air Act by a 375–1 roll call vote. The Senate Public Works Committee followed suit, voting unanimously on September 17 to report a bill that would receive a unanimous roll call vote (73–0) five days later. On December 18, the conference committee report was passed by voice vote in the Senate and the House and the President signed the Clean Air Act Amendments into law on December 31. Nixon celebrated the "cooperative effort" of both parties at the signing ceremony, a ceremony that occurred in the absence of one of the bill's chief architects—Senator Muskie—who had not been invited by the White House.[15]

In 1971, the Senate turned its attention to water pollution. It passed amendments to the Federal Water Pollution Act by a unanimous vote, mandating the elimination of discharges into the nation's waters by 1985 and authorizing $16.8 billion in spending, $14 billion of which was for the construction of sewage treatment plants. The bill was passed too late for consideration by the House. Nixon's opposition to the spending and the concentration of powers in the federal government, combined with heavy industry lobbying regarding the abatement deadlines, had little impact. The House passed a version of the bill on March 29, 1972 by a 380–14 roll call vote. While the House and Senate versions of the bill differed significantly, the conference committee retained the goals of achieving fishable, swimmable waters by 1981 and zero discharges by 1985, imposed ambitious implementation deadlines, and increased the authorized spending to $24.7 billion. Nixon vetoed the bill in the final moments of October 17, proclaiming that its "laudable intent is outweighed by its unconscionable $24 billion price tag" which was four times what the administration had proposed. The President conceded "I am prepared for the possibility that my action on this bill will be overridden" but warned that if the bill were "rammed into law" he would use his discretionary authority to "put the breaks on budget-wrecking expenditures."[16] At 1:30 am on October 18, the Senate voted 52–12 to override the veto; later that day, the House followed suit, voting 247–23. What was arguably the most demanding environmental statute in the nation's history became the law of the land on an overwhelmingly bipartisan vote.[17]

From Earth Day to Deepwater

Almost forty years to the day after the first Earth Day, methane gas exploded in the BP Deepwater Horizon drilling rig, unleashing what would become a 4.9 million barrel spill in the Gulf of Mexico. As noted in Chapter 1, as the nation became aware of the magnitude of the crisis, it became clear that industry had failed to develop effective contingency plans and marshal the resources necessary to respond, despite the legal requirements that had been in place for two decades. Policymakers seemed equally incapable of offering any assurances other than the industry would be held responsible. Ultimately, after 87 days the leak was plugged, although the task of remediation would take years. The Deepwater Horizon was the largest spill in recorded history—an environmental disaster that was far greater than anything experienced at the dawn of the modern environmental era. The difference between the responses in 1970 and 2010 is highly instructive.

At first glance, one would expect to have witnessed a compelling policy response. The media attention to the oil spill was intense. Oil spills did not attract much media attention in the months preceding the Deepwater Horizon, despite the fact that 2010 marked the twentieth anniversary of the Exxon Valdez spill, at that point the greatest oil spill in US history. But in the 100 days following the event, news coverage exploded. As a study by the Pew Research Center's Project for Excellence in Journalism noted, this was not the typical "one-week wonder," where coverage spikes then quickly dissipates.

> One of the characteristics that made the BP saga unusual was that the event-driven news coverage—the breaking news aspect of the disaster— never went away. That storyline, which included the ongoing efforts to cap and clean up the flow of oil and the environmental and commercial damage caused, kept evolving, requiring constant attention and effectively keeping the story from simply defaulting to a more partisan or politicized story line.[18]

Newspapers followed the event closely, and devoted 31 percent of the front-page newshole to the topic. Unlike the earlier episode, the Deepwater Horizon occurred in an era of cable news. The cable news networks devoted 31 percent of their airtime to the story, with CNN leading the coverage with a full 42 percent of its airtime. The network news broadcasts followed suit, devoting 29 percent of their broadcast time to the disaster. The story coverage found a strong audience: Surveys revealed that between 50 and 60 percent of Americans were following the story "very closely."[19]

One would expect that the magnitude of the crisis when combined with the high level of media attention would translate into rapid and substantial policy change. Unlike the 1970–72 period discussed above, Congress and the White House were now under unified Democratic control. President Obama had campaigned, in part, on a pledge to tackle climate change and move to a post-carbon economy. The Deepwater Horizon disaster could have been cited as the best possible evidence in support of the claim that the promised changes were necessary. Moreover, one would imagine that the risks associated with oil exploration and the clear evidence of industry's failure to take the necessary precautions would resonate with a public still suffering from the recent financial crisis— another case of corporations assuming risks they proved incapable of managing. Another comparison: During the earlier episode, the federal government had yet to develop expertise in environmental policy. By the Deepwater Horizon, the Congress had four decades of experience with environmental protection. It had passed important statutes designed to prevent the occurrence of, and mitigate the damages caused by, toxic and hazardous wastes. It had learned some important lessons about the design of liability regimes and funding mechanisms for accelerating a response to disasters. These expedients, first introduced in the Comprehensive Environmental Response, Compensation, and Liability Act of 1980, had been used as a model for the Oil Pollution Act of 1990, itself a response to an oil spill crisis.

Yet, the response was muted. President Obama's June 15, 2010, address from the Oval Office reviewed the nature of the crisis, announced a six-month moratorium on drilling and the creation of a commission to study the disaster, and called for a strengthening of regulation. Yet, regulation, by itself, was insufficient. Thus, Obama turned to energy policy, celebrating the House of Representative's 2009 passage of climate change legislation and calling for the promotion of renewable energy resources and a disengagement from fossil fuels. The President warned: "the one approach I will not accept is inaction. The one answer I will not settle for is the idea that this challenge is somehow too big and too difficult to meet."[20] As the *New York Times* editorial board noted: President Obama

> described the oil spill as a signal that the country needed to move quickly to break its reliance on fossil fuels. In so doing, he sought to revive the Senate's flagging efforts to pass an energy and climate bill. Nothing has worked. We hope this will.[21]

The *Washington Post* was less optimistic, finding "Mr. Obama's apparent interest in protecting himself politically rather than seizing the moment to address America's addiction to oil" to be "disappointing" and part of "the White House's rhetorical strategy."[22]

The Deepwater Horizon disaster unfolded in the summer of 2010, and President Obama and the Democratically controlled Congress looked to the upcoming midterm elections with some trepidation. The concern over a potential GOP resurgence in the election undoubtedly loomed large in the decision of Senate Majority Leader Reid (D-UT) to scuttle the climate change bill that had passed the House and shaped the congressional response to the Deepwater Horizon as well. Hearings on the disaster and various oil-spill-related issues commenced almost immediately. Congress held more than 60 hearings in the remainder of 2010, and members of Congress introduced more than 150 bills.[23] Some oil safety legislation made it through the House, only to die in the Senate. "When Republicans began to sense that the voters would increase their numbers in November, they gained resolve to turn back these proposals."[24] When Republicans gained control of the House after the 2010 midterms and eliminated the Democrats' filibuster-proof majority in the Senate, attention turned, ironically, to expanding offshore drilling rather than strengthening regulation. William K. Reilly, former EPA administrator under George H. W. Bush and co-chair of the National Commission on the BP Deepwater Horizon Oil Spill and Offshore Drilling, presented the commission's findings before the House Natural Resource Committee in January 2011. Some two decades earlier, he recalled, the Exxon Valdez disaster had been met with bipartisanship, a Republican administration and a Democratic Congress that worked together to develop the Oil Pollution Act of 1990. This time, he discovered nothing but partisan rancor and an unwillingness to even consider substantive reforms.[25]

On the two year anniversary of the Deepwater Horizon, *Congressional Quarterly* reported:

> In 2010, experts had predicted that the worst oil spill in American history would be a game changer that would spur fundamental changes in environmental policy—just like the 1969 Santa Barbara spill off California that helped lead to the creation of the EPA and the Exxon Valdez accident that resulted in the Oil Pollution Act of 1990. So far, that prediction has been confounded.[26]

We will reserve a more detailed discussion of the legislative response to the Deepwater Horizon for Chapter 8. Suffice it to say that the largest environmental disaster in US history—and a significant regulatory failure—resulted in little more than a set of short-term measures and incremental changes in the regulatory regime for the oil industry. Despite broad recognition that regulations had failed to keep pace with changes in the industry, Congress proved unwilling or incapable of formulating a statutory response.

Beyond the Two Crises

These two vignettes are strikingly different. Temporally, the first series of events clustered at the birth of the modern environmental movement, whereas the Deepwater Horizon occurred precisely four decades after Earth Day 1970. In terms of policy impacts, the first series of events generated a prolonged period of executive and legislative activism that resulted in the creation of the EPA, and over the course of the next decade, the passage of the most demanding and expensive regulatory statutes in the nation's history. Despite the fact that the Deepwater Horizon was the largest environmental catastrophe in the nation's history, it failed to generate any significant new statutes. How can one make sense of the disparate outcomes?

One explanation would posit that there had been a reduction in the popular demand for policy. As noted in Chapter 2, it may be the case that events like the Deepwater Horizon no longer stimulate mobilization and a demand for change. Perhaps citizens have been lulled into a state of complacency by the belief that existing regulations provide them with sufficient protection? Perhaps every attempt on the part of activists to raise the salience of an issue is contested and discredited by the opposition, leading the public and influential elites to discount the magnitude—or the very existence—of the problem in question? As David Vogel argues, these factors may have created a "risk availability blockade," preventing citizens from understanding the connections between triggering events and a broader array of related risks.[27]

One might also argue that the demand for a policy response was muted by the fact that the Deepwater Horizon spill occurred in the midst of the Great Recession. A nation anxious for economic recovery was less concerned about the environment. For decades, public opinion polls had revealed that, when asked to consider the tradeoff between economic growth and the environment, a majority of Americans prioritized the environment. In 2008, in the wake of the financial crisis, survey data revealed that for the first time on record, a larger percentage of respondents prioritized economic growth. Yet, these numbers would shift dramatically following the Deepwater Horizon. On the eve of the disaster (March 2010), 53 percent of respondents favored economic growth over the environment (with 38 percent supporting the environment). A month after the Deepwater Horizon, the positions had almost flipped (50 percent to 43 percent). More precisely, when asked about the tradeoff between the development of energy supplies and environmental protection, energy production won out (50 to 43 percent) in March 2010. By May 2010, protecting the environment took priority (55 to 39 percent).[28] During the period when public opinion was strongly supportive of change—and, as noted above, media attention was intense—the response was limited. One might argue that this was a failure of interest groups. In the late 1960s and early 1970s, environmental interest groups effectively popularized the issue and kept it on the legislative agenda in a period marked by war, impeachment, and stagflation. Yet, one can discount this explanation given that these same groups had evolved subsequently into highly professionalized, well-funded, institutions that were arguably far more capable of asserting an agenda than they had been four decades earlier.[29]

If the explanation is not to be found in the demand for policy, perhaps we need to look to the institutions that supply policy. The key argument to be extended below, is relatively straightforward. The different policy responses to crisis cannot be understood without placing these events in a larger history of Congress. To be more precise, we have to frame our explanation by looking at the growing problems of polarization and gridlock that have rendered Congress increasingly incapable of generating the kind of significant new statutes that formed the foundations of the regulatory state.

The Problem of Polarization

One of the most important and widely discussed changes in the US Congress in recent decades has been the growth in polarization. The most commonly adopted measure of polarization—DW-NOMINATE, developed by Nolan McCarty, Keith T. Poole, and Howard Rosenthal—is based on roll call voting, and can be used to measure the differences between Democratic and Republican legislators over time. Figures 5.2 and 5.3 present a graphical representation of polarization in the House of Representatives and the Senate. According to this and other measures of polarization, several things have occurred. First, the ideological means of the Democratic and Republican parties have become more widely separated than at any time in the past century. Second, both parties have become ideologically more homogenous. Third, and related, moderates in the House and Senate—the conservative Democrats and liberal Republicans that used to be available for coalition building—have virtually disappeared.[30] The changes, which began in the 1970s, have only become more extreme over time.

Arguably, the greatest movement has occurred within the Republican Party. As congressional scholars Thomas E. Mann and Norman J. Ornstein note, polarization is better described as one of "asymmetrical polarization"—"the center of gravity within the Republican Party has shifted sharply to the right." Moderates have diminished in number as "the GOP has become the reflexive champion of lower taxes, reductions in the size and scope of the federal government, deregulation, and the public promotion of a religious and cultural conservatism."[31] Increasingly, the two parties are so divided that each is embedded in its own organizational network. "Orbiting each party is an array of organizations, including advocacy groups, media outlets, ideological foundations, lobbying firms, 527s, and think tanks." These networks are "highly distinct" from one another and "foster partisan distinctiveness."[32] Each side, drawing on a tailored set of facts, values, and policy images, finds few opportunities to engage in consensus building.

How does one explain the growth in polarization? The first and most obvious explanation is that polarization in Congress is simply reflective of a larger

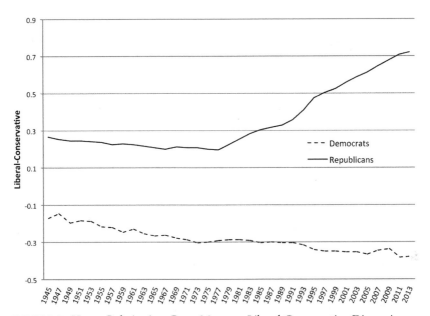

FIGURE 5.2 House Polarization: Party Mean on Liberal Conservative Dimension

Source: DW-Nominate voteview.com.

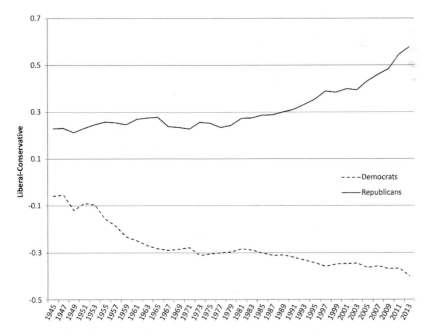

FIGURE 5.3 Senate Polarization: Party Mean on Liberal Conservative Dimension

Source: DW-Nominate voteview.com.

polarization within the electorate—the implication one would draw from the red and blue maps that have become ubiquitous in mass media election coverage. Yet, there is much evidence that citizens have remained moderate in their policy positions and have not become more polarized over time. As Morris P. Fiorina, Samuel A. Abrams, and Jeremy C. Pope note:

> There is little evidence that American's ideology or policy *positions* are more polarized today than they were two or three decades ago, although their *choices* often seem to be. The explanation is that the political figures that Americans evaluate are more polarized.[33]

Indeed, empirical research reveals that members of Congress are more extreme than even the median voters in their own parties, not to mention the median voters in their districts.[34] Although there remains some disagreement on this point,[35] the consensus position supports the contention that polarization is primarily an elite phenomenon.

Thus, we turn to factors that may affect the selection of candidates. Some analysts have considered the role of gerrymandering. The existence of safe districts that virtually guarantee reelection have allowed members of Congress the freedom to eschew broad coalition-building while making them more responsive to donors and primary voters who embrace more ideologically extreme positions. While this explanation may be attractive, it does not help explain the fact that similar levels of polarization have emerged in the House and in the Senate, where all positions are filled in statewide contests.[36] Another possible explanation would focus on the vast increase in the influx of money into the electoral process. While much attention is lavished on political action committees—a main vehicle for corporate campaign spending—there is much to suggest that they strive to maximize access to legislators, and thus tend to be less ideological in their orientations and commonly engage in split giving, donating to candidates of both parties. Individual donors, in contrast, tend to be far more ideologically extreme and support candidates who more closely represent their positions.[37] Even if elected officials are not personally committed to extreme policy positions, preference falsification can be purchased. Members of the House and Senate, anxious to retain their positions, can pre-commit to policy positions that signal their ideological purity to large donors.

Most accounts of polarization focus on long-term historical trends. Some accounts attribute a large role to the partisan realignment of the South, arguably the single most important event in the US political party system in the twentieth century. Traditionally, the South had been solidly Democratic—an enduring legacy of the Civil War. The role of seniority in Congress magnified the influence of Southern legislators. During the New Deal, as Ira Katznelson explains, Southern members of Congress "reduced the full repertoire of possibilities for policy to a narrower set of feasible options that met with their approval, or at least their forbearance." National policymaking occurred in what Katznelson describes as a "southern cage."[38] When conservative Southern Democrats were combined with more liberal Northern Republicans, the two parties were more ideologically diverse and there were opportunities for building bipartisan coalitions. The civil rights revolution, however, marked a critical turning point. In a process that took decades to unfold, Southern conservative whites exited the Democratic Party and moved to the Republican Party. This ideological reshuffling contributed to two more cohesive parties, less need to manage intra-party disputes, and fewer opportunities to forge broad coalitions.

While the Southern realignment was important, there is a strong argument that it does not provide a complete explanation of polarization. As Nolan McCarty, Keith T. Poole, and Howard Rosenthal note, it cannot account for the disappearance of Republican moderates in other sections of the country. Indeed, their careful analysis concludes that polarization has been largely driven by economics, with high-income voters increasingly identifying with the GOP and lower-income voters identifying with the Democratic Party. Income effects were far less pronounced in the immediate postwar decades, but they increased along with elite polarization, beginning in the mid-1970s. It is important to note that the trend in polarization closely tracked another trend: growing income inequality. As they conclude:

> during periods of increasing inequality when the fortunes of different economic groups are diverging, the policies preferred by each will diverge as well. In the current context, the Democratic Party will continue to support policies that redistribute to the poor and collectivize social risks, while the Republicans represent the interests of those whose incomes are growing rapidly and hence support policies to cut taxes and privatize risk.[39]

From Polarization to Gridlock

Certainly, the polarization of American politics has attracted a great deal of academic and media attention. But historically, the kind of moderation of partisan differences that marked the immediate postwar decades was anomalous. As Marc Hetherington notes: "if one views the entire history of the nation rather than just the most recent sixty years, partisan polarization appears to be more the rule than the exception."[40] During the last quarter of the nineteenth century, the US Congress had levels of polarization comparable to contemporary levels. The Democratic and Republican parties then entered a seven-decade period of convergence, with a growing number of moderates. "Put simply, the fraction of moderates grew and the fraction of extreme liberals and extreme conservatives fell from 1900 to about 1975. By the beginning of the twenty-first century, the extremes had come back."[41]

Our first vignette presented above occurred when this process of moderation had reached its historical climax. In the House of Representatives, for example, the percentage of party-line votes (i.e., the percentage of votes when a majority of one party votes against a majority of the other party) had declined steadily from a high of 52 percent during the Truman presidency to 34.5 percent during the Nixon–Ford years.[42] During the immediate postwar period, bipartisan coalitions in Congress ensured high levels of productivity and Congress passed bills of enormous national importance, including a number of significant regulatory statutes. The Constitution had created a system of separation of powers and a bicameral legislature. Without compromise and coalition building, the legislative process would grind to a halt. From today's perspective, this period in US history might seem idyllic. And yet, there was no shortage of critics.

In the immediate postwar period, there was a strong consensus among American political scientists that the nation needed responsible political parties. Rather than the "catch all" parties that seemed to prevail in the American context, political scientists looked longingly at the programmatic parties that were common in European systems. Such parties, particularly if placed in unified control of Congress and the Presidency, could allow for responsible party government. The American Political Science Association's Committee on Political Parties compiled a highly publicized report in 1950 which called for "a democratic, responsible and effective" party system composed of parties that had distinctive programs and "sufficient internal cohesion to carry out these programs." It noted

> the fundamental requirement of accountability is a two-party system in which the opposition party acts as the critic of the party in power, developing, defining and presenting the policy alternatives that are necessary for a true choice in reaching public decision.[43]

As David Mayhew observed, party government "plays a role in political science somewhere between a Platonic form and a grail. When we reach for it as a standard, we draw on abstract models, presumed European practice, and well-airbrushed American experience."[44]

Two ideologically distinct political parties with high levels of cohesion among members would be optimal if the goals are to provide voters with alternative policy agendas—a clear choice—and hold the winners accountable should they fail to follow through on their promises. One might assume that under these conditions, the majority party could be highly productive, particularly if there were unified control of the Congress and the White House. Yet, even under these conditions, majority strategies to limit the influence of the minority and, alternatively, minority strategies to obstruct the legislative process, can combine to create gridlock.[45] In the House, the period of growing polarization coincided with the rising power of the leadership over the Rules Committee, which increasingly imposed procedural hurdles to participation by the minority. The growing reliance on closed rules and the rapid movement to floor votes have impeded amendments. Moreover, since the 1990s, the GOP majority has imposed a "majority of the majority rule" (known colloquially as the Hastert rule). Under this rule, no important legislation will be scheduled for a floor vote unless it receives the support of the majority of the Republican caucus. As Frances E. Lee notes:

> The result is a more centralized, streamlined process in the House, in which a unified majority party can work its will while the minority party enjoys little opportunity to shape outcomes or even put the majority on the record in awkward ways.[46]

While the Senate lacks a Rules Committee and has traditionally functioned under strong norms of collegiality, parallel practices have emerged to limit the power of the minority. As the leadership in the Senate has grown more powerful, it has limited the opportunities for minority amendments by "filling the amendment tree." That is, the majority leader introduces several amendments, often redundant or extraneous, preventing other senators from introducing amendments that might change the substance of the legislation or embarrass the majority.[47] This, in turn, has stimulated a far greater reliance on the filibuster (or the threat of filibuster) on the part of the minority to derail the majority. In the five years between 2007 and 2012, for example, the GOP threatened filibusters 385 times, roughly the same number of times as the entire seven-decade period separating World War I and the end of the Reagan presidency.[48] Because the Senate requires sixty votes to invoke a closure motion to end debate, this has created an anti-majoritarian barrier to passing legislation.[49]

When coupled, the "twin processes of majority tyranny in the House and minority obstructionism in the Senate" have predictable results.[50] Pressing issues that might challenge the prevailing balance of power or disrupt the status quo in public policy are kept off the agenda; legislation that might otherwise pass with bipartisan support is prevented from reaching a vote. In sum, as Sarah Binder explains: "The combination of these two forces—bicameral policy differences reinforced by different sets of institutional rules—affects the prognosis for issues on the agenda."[51] Under high levels of polarization there may be few moderates available for forming coalitions. Given the ideological distance between parties, the majority party may prove unwilling to forge compromises and the minority may prove unwilling to accede to the policy preferences of the majority. The majority has incentives not to compromise; the minority has incentives to impede the legislative process. Both sides have incentives to use obstruction and strategic roll call votes to shape their public image for outside constituencies, in hopes of retaining (or regaining) a majority. Gridlock is the result, and it has had clear negative implications for the productivity of Congress.[52]

Polarization, Gridlock, and Legislative Lethargy

When examining the period of growing polarization, a few things become quite evident. First, there has been a long-term downward trend in the number of laws enacted per year. Between 1961 and 1970 (the 87th through the 91st Congress), an average of 369.6 public laws were enacted per year. This figure declined slightly during the next two decades, falling to 309.1 public laws per year in the 1971–80 period (the 92nd through the 96th Congress) but rose to 312.3 laws per year between 1981 and 1990 (the 97th through the 101st Congress). But between 1991 and 2000 (the 102nd through the 106th Congress), the annual average number of laws enacted fell to 236.2. By the 2001–10 period (the 107th through the 111th Congress), the annual average would fall again, to 220 public laws enacted. To return to our earlier episodes, the Clean Air Act Amendments of the 1970s were passed in the 91st Congress, a Congress that enacted 695 public laws. The Deepwater Horizon disaster of 2010 occurred during the 111th Congress, which enacted a mere 383 public laws. As noted above, no significant oil pollution statutes would be passed during the 112th Congress (2011–12) either, something that might not be a great surprise given that only 283 public laws were enacted that year.[53]

Another comparison is worthy of attention. Congressional subcommittees are where the hard work of legislation and oversight occurs. Agency representatives, experts, and interest group representatives are called to testify, providing Congress with important insights into the sources of problems and potential policy remedies. Between the 91st and 92nd Congress (1969–72) that generated so many significant regulatory statutes and the 111th Congress, the annual number of committee and subcommittee meetings in the House of Representatives declined from 2,545 to 692. In the Senate, the number of committee and subcommittee meetings fell from 1,706 per year to 1,187 per year.[54] The diminution of committees reflects changes in their role in the legislative process. As Thomas E. Mann and Norman J. Ornstein explain, bills that would have been subjected to weeks of hearings are now given a few days, with little systematic analysis. "Much of the action now takes place behind closed doors, with bills . . . put together by a small group of leadership staff, committee staff, industry representatives, and a few majority party members and then rammed through subcommittee and committee with minimal debate."[55] Congressional committees and subcommittees, in short, have become far less important as legislative productivity has fallen dramatically.

Perhaps Congress produced few bills in more recent decades, but nonetheless generated a comparable level of significant statutes. Although there is some debate on what precisely constitutes a "significant statute," the most broadly accepted methodology is that employed by political scientist David Mayhew and as part of his book *Divided We Govern*.[56] While Mayhew's core concern was whether divided government generated a reduction in the passage of significant statutes, the data also reveals something of a decline in the number of significant statutes. Unsurprisingly, during the period from the mid-1960s to the mid-1970s (the 89th through the 93rd Congress), Congress passed an average of 9.8 significant statutes per year. From 2000 to 2012, this number fell to an average of 5.7 per year. The decline in significant statutes has been accompanied by the rapid growth of minor laws as a percentage of the public laws enacted. In the House, minor laws are often passed under the suspension of the rules process whereby debate is limited to 40 minutes, amendments are prohibited, and passage requires a two-thirds vote. Laws passed under suspension of the rules involve such pressing matters as renaming post offices after constituents or designating attractions in one's district as historical sites. According to Don Wolfensberger, between 1983 and 2012, minor laws passed under suspensions have increased from 35 to 79 percent of all laws enacted. In short, "Congress is shying away from more substantive, controversial legislation today, in favor of passing home crowd pleasers."[57]

Let us narrow our focus once again. With respect to regulation, during the period 1965–75, Congress passed 27 significant regulatory statutes that dramatically expanded social regulation, extending policy to consumer protection, environmental protection, and occupational safety and health. In sharp contrast, by the post-1990 period, Congress passed far fewer significant regulatory statutes. Setting aside the economic regulatory statutes that were either deregulatory in focus or passed in response to the financial crisis of 2007–8, let us focus on the social regulatory statutes. There were some consumer protection statutes passed that addressed food and drug safety (the Food Quality Protection Act of 1996, the Food and Drug Administration Modernization Act of 1997, and the FDA Food Safety Modernization Act of 2010) and tobacco regulation (the Family Smoking Prevention and Tobacco Control Act of 2009). But in the area of environmental protection, Congress passed a single significant environmental protection statute (the Safe Drinking Water Act Amendments of 1996). It passed no new statutes on occupational safety and health. As of this writing, the regulation of environmental protection and occupational safety and health is largely the product of statutes that were passed during the early episode of legislative activism of the 1960s and 1970s. In this context, the lack of a legislative response to the Deepwater Horizon disaster should come as no surprise.

Polarization, Gridlock, and the Executive Countermovement

Polarization has had mixed implications for the presidency, simultaneously constraining presidential power and creating incentives for unilateral action to circumvent a gridlocked Congress. Let us consider these in turn. One of the president's greatest powers is the power of appointment. Contemporary presidents appoint judges and justices when vacancies occur and make some 4,000 full-time political appointments, well over 1,000 of which are subject to Senate confirmation.[58] There is good empirical evidence that polarization has resulted in a sharp reduction in the Senate confirmation of appellate court nominees. Under conditions of low polarization (e.g., the 92nd Congress, 1971–72) fully 99 percent of nominees were confirmed. Under conditions of high polarization (e.g., the 109th Congress, 2005–6), the likelihood of confirmation had fallen to 33 percent.[59] Similarly, there is empirical evidence that polarization has contributed to greater delays in the confirmation of agency appointees, even under conditions of unified government.[60] The threat of protracted confirmation hearings may make high-quality appointees far more difficult to attract into public service. These delays, moreover, leave agencies with persistent vacancies. Acting executives and recess appointees may prove reticent to initiate important rulemaking and high-profile enforcement efforts.[61]

Although the president is in control of executive branch agencies, these agencies are nonetheless dependent on budgetary decisions made by Congress. There is good reason to believe that polarization and gridlock have created greater uncertainty about agency budgets. The congressional budget process has been in disarray, particularly since the 1990s. The repeated failure to pass appropriation bills, the need to pass continuing resolutions to fund government, the drama surrounding each increase in the debt ceiling, and the threat and reality of government shutdowns have become quite routine. All of this can impose significant costs on agencies. Resources that are devoted to developing contingency plans for an orderly shutdown cannot be used for implementing policy. Threats of furloughs can impact morale and retention. Agencies that are uncertain about their budgets may shepherd their resources in anticipation of future shortfalls or pursue less costly enforcement actions. In some cases, budgets have stagnated or declined in real terms, creating ongoing pressures with respect to staffing and the priority assigned to various functions. For example, while the EPA's inflation-adjusted budget grew by 21 percent during the decade of the 1990s, by 2015 it had fallen to 89 percent of what it was in 2000.[62]

Even when there is superficial stability in an agency's budget, its adequacy can be undermined in subtle ways. One common strategy, as Joel A. Mintz explains, is what is commonly referred to as Congress' "cost of living trick." Between 1991 and 2010, Congress mandated federal civil service pay increases in every year, with an average adjustment of 3.5 percent annually.[63] While Congress imposed cost-of-living adjustments, it usually refused to provide the necessary budgetary support. Agencies can respond to this situation in a variety of ways. For example, they may leave positions vacant for extended periods of time, functioning at levels below their authorized staffing levels. But a common response has been to divert funds from their extramural budgets to supplement their salary pools. The extramural budgets are critically important for enforcement efforts. They cover the expenses of travel, taking depositions, and contracting expert witnesses or technical support for conducting investigations.

As these funds are depleted, agencies are forced to reorient enforcement priorities, reduce the number of inspections, or delay filing cases. Enforcement budgets appear stable, in short, but they are not providing the resources to support the activities of agency employees.[64]

Congressional obstructionism finds a more explicit expression in the growing tendency to place limitation riders in appropriation bills that earmark funds for narrow purposes or prohibit agencies from using funds to collect data, initiate rulemaking, finalize specific rules, or enforce them. Indeed, during a single ten-year span, the House Appropriations Committee imposed 4,042 limitation riders, 66.6 percent of which prohibited agencies from making specific decisions with policy effects. Many of these riders, as Jason A. MacDonald explains, allow "Congress to block laws/regulations that it would like to overturn with a new law but which it cannot due to antimajoritarian hurdles in the lawmaking process."[65] In some cases, riders can effectively forestall the development of new regulations. When regulations have already been published in the *Federal Register* but Congress passes riders that prevent inspections or enforcement, regulations may retain the force of law, but to what effect? As a Congressional Research Service report explains: "Regulated entities are still required to adhere to applicable requirements (e.g., the installation of pollution control devices, submission of relevant paperwork), even if violations are unlikely to be detected and enforcement actions cannot be taken by federal agencies."[66]

Although polarization and gridlock have had some negative effects on presidential power, it has also enhanced it. As argued in Chapter 4, in the 1970s, Congress adopted regulatory design decisions that constrained presidential control of the administrative state, provoking a presidential countermovement: the imposition of regulatory review. In the post-1990 period, polarization and gridlock have once again created the preconditions for a presidential countermovement—this time, a greater tendency toward unilateralism. As Congress became incapable of passing significant new statutes, presidents have responded by engaging in unilateral action via a greater centralization of control within the White House and the use of executive orders, memoranda, signing statements, waivers, recess appointments, and administrative actions that test the boundaries of statutory authority.[67] In the words of Kenneth S. Lowande and Sidney Milkis: "partisan gridlock seems to have induced presidential aggrandizement."[68] While the expansion of unilateralism was evident under Presidents Clinton and Bush, it reached new levels during the Obama administration. President Obama—plagued by a divided Congress crippled by gridlock—reveled in unilateral action as a means of pursuing goals of importance to core Democratic constituencies and emphasizing Republican obstructionism. In 2011–12, the administration publicized some 45 executive actions as part of its "We Can't Wait" campaign, moving forward on a host of issues including job creation, fuel efficiency standards, immigration, the minimum wage for federal contractors, and educational policy, and dared Congress to respond.[69]

Congress can object to presidential unilateralism as a violation of the constitutional separation of powers—a common refrain from the opposition, regardless of party—but it faces distinct challenges in responding. As Terry M. Moe and William G. Howell observe, if presidents

> want to shift the status quo by taking unilateral action on their own authority, whether or not that authority is clearly established in law, they can simply do it . . . . The other branches are then presented with a fait accompli, and it is up to them to respond. If they are unable to respond effectively, or decide not to, the president wins by default.[70]

Traditionally, Congress has faced enormous disadvantages relative to the president. Congress, unlike the president, has to manage vexing collective action problems and move legislation through a complex set of procedures with multiple veto points. Under the conditions that now prevail, polarization and gridlock have impeded the legislative process, thereby limiting the extent to which condemnations of unilateralism can find an expression in statutory change.

Of course, there are limitations to what presidents can accomplish on their own. They remain more or less constrained by existing statutes and the threat of limitation riders on appropriations bills. Opponents can use the courts to further their claims, and this has become a far more likely avenue as the Obama administration discovered as suits were filed to challenge many of its unilateral actions. Moreover, the policies that presidents put into place via executive action rather than through the legislative process can be more easily reversed by their successors. From a political perspective, voters may view unilateralism as an illegitimate exercise of presidential power. There is strong evidence that while public opinion is more supportive of unilateral action under conditions of congressional gridlock, support remains low, particularly among those who prioritize the rule of law.[71] But the core point remains: The failure of Congress as an institution has created the preconditions for unilateral action, and presidents seeking to change policy may have few other options at their disposal.

Conclusion

While the political and budgetary environment can be vexing, the greatest long-term challenge remains managing the problem addressed earlier: the inability of Congress to pass significant new statutes. Agencies are not simply passive actors in the policy process. While polarization and gridlock have impeded the passage of new legislation, they have also created the preconditions of presidential unilateralism and the space for more entrepreneurial agencies to adjust existing programs and policies to address emerging problems. The extent to which they can succeed in these efforts, however, will depend on a host of factors, including presidential support, budgetary constraints, levels of agency

professionalization, and supportive relationships with other agencies and interest groups. It also depends, most centrally· on the statutory authority they have
been granted in the past.

As noted in Chapter 2, when internal and external environments create
impediments to change one should witness a process of drift. In the case of
social regulation, exhaustively detailed statutes and complicated procedures
sharply limited bureaucratic flexibility. This did not completely foreclose
entrepreneurial activities on the parts of agencies seeking to extend the reach of
regulation under difficult conditions. Indeed, in many cases (as will be detailed
in Chapters 6 and 7), presidents and their appointees promoted new voluntary
programs and public–private partnerships. In some cases, they embodied—
albeit, incompletely—some of the new learning in regulation discussed briefly
in Chapter 3. The EPA provided the most striking example. During the 1990s,
new programs were instituted to collect information, promote collaboration
between regulators and the regulated, and introduce a regulatory green track
designed to provide high-performing organizations with environmental management systems with a number of benefits. At OSHA, firms were encouraged
to implement health and safety management systems that exceeded what could
be compelled by regulation in exchange for a lower inspection priority. The
agency worked closely with a participant association to promote peer review
and the dissemination of best practices. Many of these efforts, which began
in earnest under the Clinton administration, continued through successive
presidential administrations.

Although voluntary programs and partnerships may be commendable as efforts
to manage a complex environment and limit the extent of drift, there are sharp
limits to what can be achieved absent new statutory authority. Without new
legislation, for example, any demands they place on participants (e.g., mandatory information disclosure) are limited by the benefits they can offer, which
are necessarily paltry. The extent to which participants go well beyond what
could be demanded under regulation depends, ultimately, on factors outside the
control of regulators (e.g., the willingness of firms to invest in elevating their
reputations with internal and external stakeholders). Rather than being integrated
with existing policies as part of a regulatory pyramid (see Chapter 3), they have
been layered on top of inflexible and increasingly dated regulatory structures.
Moreover, there are obvious concerns that agencies have not invested sufficiently
in developing metrics to evaluate performance and determine whether the programs and partnerships make verifiable contributions to regulatory goals. Under
the prevailing budgetary conditions, investments in the voluntary programs carry
a high opportunity cost insofar as they can deplete resources that might otherwise
be used for rulemaking or enforcement.

A lack of effective oversight, moreover, can translate into a lack of political
accountability. The Administrative Procedure Act created an orderly process
of notice-and-comment rulemaking that provided interested parties with the

opportunity to participate in the development of regulations. The Freedom of Information Act and open meeting requirements provided access to data that could be valuable in evaluating government performance. Congress passed a series of regulatory statutes that established firm implementation timetables and provided parties with the opportunity to sue agencies for a failure to execute their nondiscretionary duties. Agencies were subject to ongoing congressional oversight. The level of accountability is critical given that a failure of regulation can be measured in deaths and diseases that could have been averted. These mechanisms are no longer operative in the world of regulatory voluntarism. Although the devolution of authority on to the regulated may be expedient, it has potentially serious consequences for transparency and accountability, two of the hallmarks of public regulation.

While the programs at EPA and OSHA may be viewed as being relatively benign, the consequences of drift in other policy areas were far more consequential. It will be argued in Chapters 8 and 9 that two of the largest regulatory failures in US history—the Deepwater Horizon spill and the financial crisis—were products, in part, of regulatory drift induced by polarization. Despite significant changes in oil exploration and extraction—most notably, the movement to deep- and ultra-deep environments—Congress failed to update the Oil Pollution Act of 1990. Despite the growth of securitization and shadow banking, Congress failed to pass new statutes to extend regulation to the most dynamic parts of the financial system. Regulators, as a result, were acting on the basis of antiquated statutes that failed to account for emerging regulatory challenges. While policymakers were aware of the changes in question, they did not have the authority to adapt their policies accordingly. In both cases, regulators were regulating. But they were regulating the wrong things, setting the stage for tragic outcomes that could have been foreseen.

Notes

1 David Vogel, *The Politics of Precaution: Regulating Health, Safety, and Environmental Risks in Europe and the United States* (Princeton, NJ: Princeton University Press, 2012), 37–38. See Timur Kuran and Cass R. Sunstein, "Availability Cascades and Risk Regulation," *Stanford Law Review* 51, 4 (1999): 683–768.
2 See Frank R. Baumgartner and Bryan D. Jones, *Agendas and Instability in American Politics* (Chicago, IL: University of Chicago Press, 1993).
3 James L. True, Bryan D. Jones, and Frank R. Baumgartner, "Punctuated-Equilibrium Theory: Explaining Stability and Change in Public Policymaking," in *Theories of the Policy Process*, ed. Paul A. Sabatier (Cambridge, MA: Westview Press, 2007), 157.
4 "Republican Platform, 1960," in *National Party Platforms, 1840–1960*, compiled by Kirk H. Porter and Donald Bruce Johnson (Urbana, IL: University of Illinois Press, 1961), 612.
5 See Erik W. Johnson and Scott Frickel, "Ecological Threat and the Founding of U.S. National Environmental Movement Organizations, 1962–1998," *Social Problems* 58, 3 (2011): 305–29. See Rachel Carson, *Silent Spring* (Boston, MA: Houghton Mifflin, 1962) and Paul R. Ehrlich, *The Population Bomb* (New York: Sierra Club-Ballantine, 1968).

6 Robert Bendiner, "Man—The Most Endangered Species," *New York Times*, October 20, 1969, 46.
7 Richard A. Harris and Sidney M. Milkis, *The Politics of Regulatory Change: A Tale of Two Agencies*, 2nd ed. (New York: Oxford University Press, 1996), 65.
8 See Baumgartner and Jones, *Agendas and Stability in American Politics*, Appendix A.
9 The data used here were originally collected by Frank R. Baumgartner and Bryan D. Jones, with the support of National Science Foundation grant numbers SBR 9320922 and 0111611, and were distributed through the Department of Government at the University of Texas at Austin. Neither NSF nor the original collectors of the data bear any responsibility for the analysis reported here.
10 Richard Nixon, "Annual Message to the Congress on the State of the Union, January 22, 1970." Available at www.presidency.ucsb.edu/ws/index.php?pid=2921#axzz1Lrd00CYq.
11 Nan Robertson, "Earth's Day, Like Mother's, Pulls Capital Together: All Are Off and Talking," *New York Times*, April 23, 1970, 30.
12 Gladwin Hill, "Earth Day Goals Backed by Hickel: 1,000 Attend Rally Here in Prelude to Today's Events," *New York Times*, April 22, 1970, 1.
13 "Earth Day Sponsors to Stay Together," *New York Times*, April 22, 1970, 35.
14 Richard Nixon, "Special Message to the Congress on Environmental Quality," February 10, 1970. Available at www.presidency.ucsb.edu/ws/?pid=2757.
15 Congressional Quarterly, "Air Quality, 1970 Legislative Chronology." *Congress and the Nation, 1969–1972*, vol. 3 (Washington DC: CQ Press, 1973). Available at http://library.cqpress.com/congress/catn69-0000862782.
16 Richard Nixon, "Veto of the Federal Water Pollution Control Act Amendments of 1972," October 17, 1972. Available at www.presidency.ucsb.edu/ws/?pid=3634.
17 Congressional Quarterly, "Water Pollution, 1972 Legislative Chronology." *Congress and the Nation, 1969–1972*, vol. 3 (Washington DC: CQ Press, 1973). Available at http://library.cqpress.com/congress/catn69-0008167703.
18 Pew Research Center's Project for Excellence in Journalism, *100 Days of Gushing Oil: Eight Things to Know about How the Media Covered the Gulf Disaster* (Washington DC: Pew Research Center, 2010), 4.
19 Ibid., 6–7.
20 Barack Obama, "Remarks by the President to the Nation on the BP Oil Spill, June 15, 2010." Available at www.whitehouse.gov/the-press-office/remarks-president-nation-bp-oil-spill.
21 "The President Confronts the Spill," *New York Times*, May 28, 2010, A22. Available at www.nytimes.com/2010/05/28/opinion/28fri1.html?_r=0.
22 "Lessons from the Gulf Oil Spill: A More Farsighted Approach Is Needed beyond Assigning Blame," *Washington Post*, May 23, 2010, A16.
23 See Jonathan L. Ramseur and Curry L. Hagerty, *Deepwater Horizon Oil Spill: Recent Activities and Ongoing Developments*, CRS Report for Congress, R42942 (Washington DC: Congressional Research Service, 2014).
24 Margaret Kriz Hobson, "A Year after Oil Spill, Urgency Turns to Impasse," *CQ Weekly*, April 18, 2011, 852.
25 Pam Radtke Russell, "Oil Spill Legislation Shows Signs of Slip-Sliding Away," *CQ Weekly*, April 23, 2012, 798.
26 Ibid.
27 Vogel, *The Politics of Precaution*, 41.
28 Art Swift, "Environment over Economic Growth," Gallup Poll, March 20, 2014. Available at www.gallup.com/poll/168017/americans-again-pick-environment-economic-growth.aspx, and Jeffrey M. Jones, "Oil Spill Alters Views on Environmental Protection," Gallup Poll, May 27, 2010. Available at www.gallup.com/poll/137882/Oil-Spill-Alters-Views-Environmental-Protection.aspx.

29 See Christopher Bosso, *Environment Inc.: From Grassroots to Beltway* (Lawrence, KS: University Press of Kansas, 2005).

30 For an overview of the competing explanations of polarization, see Michael J. Barber and Nolan McCarty, "Causes and Consequences of Polarization," in *Solutions to Political Polarization in America*, ed. Nathaniel Persily (Cambridge, UK: Cambridge University Press, 2015), 15–57. For a technical discussion of how levels of polarization can be measured, see Nolan McCarty, Keith T. Poole, and Howard Rosenthal, *Polarization: The Dance of Ideology and Unequal Riches* (Cambridge, MA: The MIT Press, 2006), 15–70.

31 Thomas E. Mann and Norman J. Ornstein, *It's Even Worse Than It Looks: How the American Constitutional System Collided with the New Politics of Extremism* (New York: Basic Books, 2012), 51–52.

32 Frances E. Lee, "How Party Polarization Affects Governance," *Annual Review of Political Science* 18 (2015): 264.

33 Morris P. Fiorina, Samuel A. Abrams, and Jeremy C. Pope, *Culture War? The Myth of a Polarized America*, 2nd ed. (New York: Pearson Longman, 2006), 8–9.

34 See Joseph Bafumi and Michael C. Herron, "Leapfrog Representation and Extremism: A Study of American Voters and Their Members in Congress," *American Political Science Review* 104, 3 (2010): 519–42.

35 See, for example, Alan I. Abramowitz, *The Disappearing Center: Engaged Citizens, Polarization, and American Democracy* (New Haven, CT: Yale University Press, 2010).

36 See Nolan McCarty, Keith T. Poole, and Howard Rosenthal, "Does Gerrymandering Cause Polarization?" *American Journal of Political Science* 53, 3 (2009): 666–80.

37 See Michael Barber, "Ideological Donors, Contribution Limits, and the Polarization of American Legislatures," *The Journal of Politics* 78, 1 (2016): 296–310, and Adam Bonica, "Ideology and Interests in the Political Marketplace," *American Journal of Political Science* 57, 2 (2013): 294–311.

38 Ira Katznelson, *Fear Itself: The New Deal and the Origins of Our Time* (New York: Liveright, 2013), 16.

39 McCarty, Poole, and Rosenthal, *Polarized America*, 192.

40 Marc J. Hetherington, "Putting Polarization in Perspective," *British Journal of Political Science* 39, 2 (2009): 419.

41 McCarty, Poole, and Rosenthal, *Polarized America*, 8.

42 Martin P. Wattenberg, *The Decline of Political Parties, 1952–1984* (Cambridge, MA: Harvard University Press, 1986), 78.

43 "Toward a More Responsible Two-Party System: A Report of the Committee on Political Parties, American Political Science Association," *American Political Science Review* 44, 3 (1950), Supplement: 17–18.

44 David R. Mayhew, *Divided We Govern: Party Control, Lawmaking, and Investigations, 1946–2002*, 2nd ed. (New Haven, CT: Yale University Press, 2005), 198.

45 Lawrence C. Dodd and Scot Schraufnagel, "Party Polarization and Policy Productivity in Congress: From Harding to Obama," in *Congress Reconsidered*, 10th ed., ed. Lawrence C. Dodd and Bruce I. Oppenheimer (Washington DC: CQ Press, 2012), 440.

46 Lee, "How Party Polarization Affects Governance," 269.

47 See Christopher M. Davis, "The Amending Process in the Senate." Congressional Research Service Report for Congress, 98-853 (Washington DC: Congressional Research Service, 2015).

48 Kenneth S. Lowande and Sidney M. Milkis, "We Can't Wait: Barack Obama, Partisan Polarization and the Administrative Presidency," *The Forum* 12, 1 (2014): 9.

49 See David R. Mayhew, "Supermajority Rule in the U.S. Senate," *PS: Political Science and Politics* 26, 1 (2003): 31–36.

50 Douglas Kriner, "Can Enhanced Oversight Repair the Broken Branch?" *Boston University Law Review* 89 (2009): 768.

51 Sarah Binder, *Stalemate: Causes and Consequences of Legislative Gridlock* (Washington DC: The Brookings Institution, 2003), 105.
52 Nolan McCarty, "The Policy Effects of Political Polarization," in *The Transformation of American Politics: Activist Government and the Rise of Conservatism*, ed. Paul Pierson and Theda Skocpol (Princeton, NJ: Princeton University Press, 2007), 223–55.
53 www.govtrack.us/congress/bills/statistics.
54 Data from Vital Statistics on Congress. Available at www.brookings.edu/~/media/ Research/Files/Reports/2013/07/vital-statistics-congress-mann-ornstein/ Vital-Statistics-Chapter-6—Legislative-Productivity-in-Congress-and-Workload_ UPDATE.pdf?la=en.
55 Thomas E. Mann and Norman J. Ornstein, *The Broken Branch: How Congress Is Failing America and How to Get It Back on Track* (Oxford: Oxford University Press, 2006), 170.
56 See Mayhew, *Divided We Govern*, appendix, for a discussion of the methodology. Mayhew's updated data set is available at http://davidmayhew.commons.yale.edu/ datasets-divided-we-govern.
57 Don Wolfensberger, "Number of Laws Congress Enacts Isn't the Whole Picture," *RollCall*, August 11, 2014. Available at http://blogs.rollcall.com/beltway-insiders/ number-of-laws-congress-enacts-isnt-the-whole-picture-procedural-politics/.
58 Bradley Patterson, *To Serve the President* (Washington DC: The Brookings Institution, 2008), 93–94.
59 See Sarah Binder, "Advice and Consent in the 'Slow' Senate," in *The U.S. Senate: From Deliberation to Dysfunction*, ed. Burdett A. Loomis (Washington DC: CQ Press, 2012), 178–98.
60 See Nolan McCarty and Rose Razaghian, "Advice and Consent: Senate Responses to Executive Branch Nominations 1885–1996," *American Journal of Political Science* 43, 4 (1999): 1122–43.
61 Anne Joseph O'Connell, "Shortening Agency and Judicial Vacancies through Filibuster Reform? An Examination of Confirmation Rates and Delays from 1981–2015," *Duke Law Journal* 64 (2015): 1692–93.
62 Susan Dudley and Melinda Warren, *Regulator's Budget Increases Consistent with Growth in Fiscal Budget: An Analysis of the U.S. Budget for Fiscal Years 2015 and 2016* (Washington DC: Regulatory Studies Center, George Washington University, 2015), Table A-2.
63 Patrick Purcell, *Federal Employees: Pay and Pension Increases since 1969*, CRS Report for Congress, 94-971 (Washington DC: Congressional Research Service, 2010), 8. Calculations by author.
64 See the discussion of the "cost of living trick" as it has impacted the EPA in Joel A. Mintz, *Enforcement at the EPA: High Stakes and Hard Choices*, rev. ed. (Austin, TX: University of Texas Press, 2012), 130–31, 174–75.
65 Jason A. MacDonald, "Limitation Riders and Congressional Influence over Bureaucratic Policy Decisions," *American Political Science Review* 104, 4 (2010): 769.
66 Curtis W. Copeland, *Congressional Influence on Rule-making and Regulation through Appropriations Restrictions*, CRS Report for Congress, RL34354 (Washington DC; Congressional Research Service, 2008), 27.
67 Lee, "How Polarization Affects Governance," 272.
68 Lowande and Milkis, "We Can't Wait," 21.
69 Ibid., 9–12.
70 Terry M. Moe and William G. Howell, "The Presidential Power of Unilateral Action," *The Journal of Law, Economics, and Organization* 15, 1 (1999): 138.
71 See Andrew Reeves and Jon C. Rogowski, "Unilateral Powers, Public Opinion, and the Presidency," *The Journal of Politics* 78, 1 (2015): 137–51.

6

ENVIRONMENTAL PROTECTION AND THE PERSISTENCE OF PARTNERSHIPS

In 1969, Congress passed the National Environmental Policy Act and, over the course of the next decade, it passed the most demanding and costly regulatory statutes in the nation's history. While environmental protection is intrinsically complicated, the form that regulation took in the United States made it something of an anomaly when viewed in cross-national perspective. As Robert A. Kagan observes:

> Unique to the United States . . . is the frequency with which Congress has stipulated firm deadlines for the promulgation of particular implementing regulations and for the achievement of pollution reduction goals—deadlines that almost invariably have not been met, resulting in lawsuits by environmental groups demanding compliance. Prescriptive, deadline-laden statutes, moreover, lead to prescriptive, deadline-laden regulations, and at the level of individual regulated enterprises, to permits, remediation plans, checklist for inspectors, and reporting requirements that far exceed in specificity those imposed in other countries.

The US, in sum, is distinctive "in its legal formality, its openness to interest group participation, its adversarial quality, and its subjection to judicial review."[1] The complexity of regulation—in large part, a product of conscious design decisions—has imposed costs, delays, and ongoing conflict. There is much to suggest, moreover, that it has impeded innovation and the search for cooperative solutions to regulatory problems. But it has also insulated regulation from the excessive influence of business interests and the intrusion of presidents that might reject the priority that Congress assigned to the environment during the environmental decade.

Environmental protection, as suggested in Chapter 3, departed in important ways from earlier regulatory initiatives. Traditionally, economic regulatory statutes delegated vast amounts of authority to agencies. There was a presumption that expert administrators, working under broad mandates and with flexible procedures, were best suited to determine what was in the public interest. By the late 1960s and 1970s, this model had come into disrepute. Skeptical of neutral expertise and fearful that broad mandates created the preconditions for capture or subsequent departures from congressional will, Congress passed exhaustively detailed regulatory statutes. They imposed specific timetables backed with strict deadlines, mandated precise reductions in pollutants, and designed processes that minimized the discretionary authority of administrators while maximizing opportunities for participation and oversight. The kinds of institutional designs celebrated by Progressives and their New Deal successors were roundly rejected.

From the perspective of the late 1980s, these decisions seemed sound. Environmental protection regulation had survived a particularly difficult challenge, with the Reagan administration's efforts to slash budgets, appoint hostile administrators, and denigrate policy as being emblematic of excessive government intrusion. Detailed mandates and procedures could not, as a generalization, force activism. But they could limit the extent of change. Yet, detailed mandates—like detailed contracts—can be quite useful, as long as they can be amended to reflect changes in circumstances, knowledge, and the preferences of key actors. As shown in Chapter 5, polarization made such amendments difficult, if not impossible. As Congress became incapable of passing significant new statutes to refine policy in light of experience or adjust policy to engage emerging problems, a condition of drift ensued. This chapter explores in some detail the administrative response to regulatory drift at the Environmental Protection Agency and the problems this response posed. Before we consider the contemporary period, it is important to provide an overview of policy as it evolved in the two decades separating Earth Day and the Clean Air Act Amendments of 1990.

The Environmental Decade

The period from 1969 to 1980 witnessed a dramatic expansion of social regulation, and much of this growth was a product of environmental protection.[2] In 1969, Congress passed the National Environmental Policy Act, creating the Council on Environmental Quality in the Executive Office of the President and mandating environmental impact statements for major federal acts that would have a significant impact on the environment. When President Nixon signed the Act on January 1, 1970, he declared his determination "that the decade of the seventies will be known as the time when this country regained a productive harmony between man and nature."[3] By the end of the year, Congress had passed the Clean Air Act Amendments of 1970 and Nixon had created the Environmental Protection Agency (EPA). In 1972, Congress passed amendments to the Federal Water Pollution Control Act (Clean Water Act) and the Federal Insecticide, Fungicide, and Rodenticide Act. In 1974, Congress passed the Safe Drinking Water Act. In 1976, it turned to toxic and hazardous materials, passing the Resource Conservation and Recovery Act and the Toxic Substances Control Act. The next year, it amended the Clean Air Act and the Clean Water Act. The decade closed with the passage of the Comprehensive Environmental Response, Compensation and Liability Act of 1980, creating a process for remediating sites contaminated with toxic wastes.

The remarkable outpouring of new environmental statutes occurred in a context of divided government, with Republican control of the presidency for the majority of the decade. Much of this can be explained by a simple fact: The environment had become a salient issue, with high levels of media coverage and strong levels of support in public opinion. Under these conditions, there were strong incentives for both Congress and President Nixon. Congress faced the dilemmas discussed earlier in Chapter 3. It needed to find the means to limit both the opportunities for capture and the potential for future presidents to undermine its preferences. For Nixon, the primary concerns were political and institutional. Nixon needed to prevent Senator Edmund Muskie (D-ME)—a potential presidential aspirant—from claiming control of such a popular issue. At the same time, he had to promote institutional designs that would maximize executive control over policy. Let us examine briefly the creation of the EPA and the key decisions made by Congress in the design of environmental regulation.

The Environmental Protection Agency

In his 1970 State of the Union Address, Nixon proclaimed that "restoring nature to its natural state is a cause beyond party and beyond factions . . . . Clean air, clean water, open spaces—these should once again be the birthright of every American."[4] By year's end, the Nixon administration had created the Environmental Protection Agency via bureaucratic consolidation, based in part on the recommendations of the President's Advisory Council on Executive Organization (the Ash Council). The design of the EPA departed from prior practices. The EPA was not placed in an existing department nor was it created as an independent regulatory commission with a plural executive. Rather, the administration consolidated environmental responsibilities in an independent agency that could be subject to executive control through presidential appointment of a single administrator.

When considering the structure of the new regulatory agency, the Ash Council explicitly rejected an organization that focused on medium ("This alternative fails to deal with the fact that forms of pollution tend to be interrelated and interchangeable") and pollution sources ("This alternative produces extreme fragmentation and fails to come to grips with the environment as an entity"). Instead, it called for a functional organization that could "recognize the interrelated nature of pollution problems" and "address the fact that pollutants cut across media lines."[5] Although these recommendations made sense at the time—and even greater sense in subsequent decades—EPA Administrator Ruckelshaus was forced to manage significant bureaucratic and political impediments. The EPA was staffed with 5,743 bureaucrats drawn from "15 components stripped away from five departments and independent agencies," including the Interior Department's Federal Water Quality Administration, the Department of Health, Education, and Welfare's Bureau of Water Hygiene and National Air Pollution Control Administration, and pesticide offices from the USDA, the FDA, and the Interior Department.[6] As Alfred Marcus notes, Ruckelshaus hoped to "maintain the confidence of the inherited bureaucracy" by "avoid[ing] the disruption of its routines that would result from program integration." Moreover, there was the political reality: "A disruption of standard operating procedures would have jeopardized EPA's success in meeting its statutory responsibilities by the prescribed deadlines" and would have fueled bureaucratic dissention, both of which could stimulate a negative response from environmental advocates, Senator Muskie, and Congress.[7]

Ultimately, Ruckelshaus adopted a hybrid design that combined some functional elements and programmatic elements that addressed pollution on a medium-specific basis. By so doing, he avoided bureaucratic recalcitrance. As the EPA hired new staff, it attracted a cadre of committed environmentalists who, in the words of one agency veteran, acted as "shock troops committed to stringent environmental regulation."[8] Indeed, as an early evaluation of the agency observed, the EPA quickly developed "a refreshing élan rarely found in regulatory agencies" and a remarkable capacity to "strike a high profile in the enforcement of the pollution laws." However, if the early decisions allowed for an agency that could "hit the road running," it was nonetheless fraught with difficulties. In Ruckelshaus' words, managing the new agency was more "like trying to run a 100-yard dash while undergoing an appendectomy."[9]

To create an agency that could rapidly implement the new policies also required that environmental duties be delegated to the states. Both the Clean Air Act Amendments (1970) and the Clean Water Act (1972) assigned significant duties to the states, many of which had not yet created regulatory agencies or administered existing policies through general public health agencies.[10] Once the EPA established national ambient air quality standards (NAAQS) for criteria pollutants, for example, the states were required to develop state implementation plans detailing how they would achieve the goals of policy and submit them to the EPA for approval. Under the water pollution legislation, moreover, the states were responsible for assessing and monitoring water quality, permitting, and constructing sewage and water systems. While policymaking was largely centralized in the EPA, ten regional offices—which would come to house some two-thirds of EPA personnel—were created to supervise state activities. Because of the decentralized implementation structure, the success of environmental policy would often depend on the quality of state-level regulation and the supervision of the regional offices.

The Question of Regulatory Design

Detailed statutes and institutional design, as explained in Chapter 3, constitute means of shaping regulatory politics. Let us consider them in turn. The core environmental statutes of the 1970s—most notably the Clean Air Act Amendments of 1970 and the Clean Water Act Amendments of 1972—were exhaustively detailed pieces of legislation. The contrasts between the new legislation and older regulatory statutes could not be more pronounced. As noted in Chapter 3, during the Progressive Era and New Deal, Congress passed broad mandates and delegated vast amounts of authority to administrators, who were instructed to act in the "public interest" with little detailed statutory direction. Agencies were given the flexibility to experiment with different regulatory strategies, and some regulators (like the Federal Trade Commission and the Securities and Exchange Commission) used this flexibility to promote innovative approaches to regulation and co-regulation. As John Graham notes, the basic design of the new environmental statutes marked a "repudiation of the New Deal model." With reference to the Clean Air Act, he writes:

> Under the agency-forcing approach, blind faith in administrative discretion was replaced by strict procedural and substantive demands on bureaucratic policymaking. Activists in Congress, spurred by their allies in consumer and environmental groups, used statutory language and legislative history to specify the ends/means relationships that would be expected to govern administrative decision.[11]

The same could be said of other statutes passed in the environmental decade. Although a comprehensive discussion of the core environmental laws is beyond the scope of this book, a brief consideration of two of the most important statutes is illustrative.

Under the Clean Air Act Amendments of 1970, Congress required that the EPA administrator propose primary and secondary NAAQS for criteria pollutants within 30 days, and after a period for public comment not to exceed 90 days, promulgate final standards. The criteria pollutants included carbon monoxide, hydrocarbons, lead, nitrogen oxide, photochemical oxidants (subsequently changed to ozone), sulfur dioxide, and total suspended particulates. The primary standards were designed to protect public health; secondary standards were to protect public welfare (including animals, crops, vegetation, and buildings). The EPA administrator was also directed to identify and set emission standards for hazardous air pollutants that "may cause, or contribute to, an increase in mortality or an increase in serious irreversible or incapacitating reversible, illness" (§112). The administrator had 90 days from the passage of the Act to publish a list of hazardous pollutants, with emission standards required within 180 days. The Act set detailed requirements for automobile manufacturers, requiring a reduction in tailpipe emissions by 90 percent for carbon monoxide and hydrocarbons by 1975, with comparable reductions in nitrogen oxides by 1976, even though reductions of this magnitude were impossible under existing technologies.[12] Congress assumed that such goals could be achieved, if backed with significant sanctions (in this case, a fine of $10,000 per automobile that failed to meet the standards).

For purposes of achieving the goals of the Act, the nation was divided into 247 air quality control regions. Within nine months of publication of primary and secondary NAAQS, the states were required to submit state implementation plans for EPA approval (and approval was to occur within four months of submission). The state implementation plans were to describe the process for achieving state standards for stationary sources, complete with timetables, a description of monitoring, inspection, and enforcement provisions that would bring the air quality regions into "attainment." The Act required that primary ambient air quality standards be met "as expeditiously as possible" but "in no case later than three years" from the approval of the state implementation plan, although governors could request extensions of up to two years (§101 a). States were given primary responsibility for enforcement, although the EPA retained enforcement powers should states fail to meet their obligations. This posed quite a challenge for the states, given that most states had not yet created their own environmental regulatory agencies. Nonetheless, states that failed to submit plans could face the imposition of plans developed by the federal government and risk losing federal highway and pollution control funds. "Should the states fail to enforce, EPA could undertake more stringent and less flexible enforcement activity than might be politically acceptable to the citizens of a state."[13]

The Federal Water Pollution Control Act Amendments of 1972 (Clean Water Act) established the most ambitious goals in regulatory history. Section 101 (2) declared as a national goal "that the discharge of pollutants into the navigable waters be eliminated by 1985," with the interim goal of "water quality which provides for the protection and propagation of fish, shellfish, and wildlife and provides for recreation in and on the water" by July 1, 1983. These goals were to be achieved through the National Pollutant Discharge System (NPDES). Point sources of pollution (i.e., any single identifiable source of pollution, such as a factory or sewage plant) were prohibited from discharging waste into navigable waters without a permit issued by the EPA or its state-level counterparts. These permits embodied guidelines for national effluent limitations, regulations that were to be promulgated by the EPA by categories of polluters. Under §304 (b), the regulations were to "identify, in terms of amounts of constituents and chemical, physical, and biological characteristics of pollutants, the degree of effluent reduction attainable through the application of the best practicable control technology available for classes and categories of point sources." By 1977, all point sources were required to meet the "best practicable technology currently available" standard, which required "consideration of the total cost of application of technology in relation to the effluent reduction benefits." By 1983, they would be required to meet more demanding requirements, employing the "best available technology economically achievable," a standard that did not require a similar weighing of costs and benefits.[14] At the same time, the Act initiated funding (some $18 billion) for the construction of public treatment plans.

Although the goals established by the Clean Water Act were technically unachievable at the time of passage, from the perspective of the early 1970s, this was irrelevant. As Senator Edmund Muskie (D-ME) proclaimed on the floor of the Senate, Congress's duty was not "to be limited by what is or appears to be technologically or economically feasible." Rather, it was "to establish what the public interest requires" even if it meant "industries will be asked to do what seems to be impossible at the present time."[15] The technical complexity of developing effluent limitation guidelines on an industry-specific basis was combined with administrative complexity. As with the Clean Air Act, a heavy reliance was placed on the states. Under the new water pollution statute, the NPDES was established in every state as a federal program, superimposed upon a patchwork of existing state policies. States were encouraged to apply for EPA approval to operate their own programs, as long as they were consistent with federal law.

In addition to limiting the discretionary authority of regulators, institutions were designed to guarantee advocacy groups a greater role in overseeing and intervening in EPA actions. Writing in 1975, Richard Stewart argued that there had been something of a reformation of administrative law. The courts, increasingly, were providing a "surrogate political process to ensure the fair representation of a wide range of affected interests." In Stewart's account, this shift was partially a response to the critiques of regulation explained in Chapter 3 and a "judicial reaction to the agencies' perceived failure to represent such interests fairly."[16] It would be incorrect, however, to assign responsibility for this reformation solely to the courts. In the case of environmental protection, Congress actively promoted an expansion of standing to grant advocacy groups preferential access to the courts. The citizen suit provisions in the Clean Air Act Amendments (1970) allowed public interest litigants, absent agency action, to sue private polluters in federal court for violating the Act without having to show that they had been injured. This provision, it was hoped, would pressure the EPA to accelerate its own enforcement proceedings. More importantly, it allowed public interest groups to sue the EPA for a failure to execute its non-discretionary duties and allowed the courts to award attorney fees, thereby partially subsidizing the costs borne by advocacy groups. Subsequent amendments (1977) also expanded the EPA's rulemaking process to provide greater opportunities for participation and allowing for the insertion of information into the rulemaking record that could be of use in subsequent litigation.[17]

These provisions gave rise to a very supportive relationship between environmental advocates, the EPA, and congressional committee staff. As the EPA's first administrator, William Ruckelshaus, recalled in his oral history: "we accepted much of the initial agenda of the environmental movement. In fact, the new agency worked with environmentalists, whose demands helped create the EPA in the first place. They were allies, at least in part." Deploying the language of capture, Ruckelshaus describes a

> so-called "iron triangle" relationship between the environmental movement, the EPA staff, and the Congressional committee staffs . . . . There has existed among them a symbiosis, in which the environmental movement used the agency as an antagonist to raise money and get more members; and the agency used the environmental group to sue for objectives they were trying to accomplish but could not otherwise gain. The same is true of the Congressional committees.[18]

While one might argue that the regulatory design decisions were made to *prevent* capture, it might be more accurate to note that they enhanced the influence of interests that were aligned with the goals of environmental protection as a means of keeping the new agency on a path favored by Congress.

The combination of technical complexity, statutory specificity, and labyrinthine institutions and procedures created impediments to the rapid implementation of policy. In the area of water pollution, the Clean Water Act required that all facilities that discharge pollution into public waterways function under permits, with escalating technological requirements (i.e., "best practical" control technology by 1977 and a more rigorous "best available" control technology by 1981). But the permitting process moved at a glacial pace. In part this was a product of the intrinsic complexity of the task. "The technology-based approach to permitting," Evan Ringquist notes, "produced a mind-boggling number of complex requirements for industrial and municipal dischargers." Moreover, standards, once proposed, were subjected to industry litigation. Congress, cognizant of the failure of the action-forcing provisions it imposed on the EPA, responded by providing successive extensions of deadlines in 1977, 1981, and 1987.[19] Much of the system rested on the quality and vigor of state regulation. Some states simply lack the capacity, resources or political will to execute their duties to assess water quality, issue permits, and conduct inspections. More than two decades after the passage of the Clean Water Act, estimates of surface-water quality remained, in the words of Walter Rosenbaum, "sophisticated guesswork" given that assessments covered about one-third of the water. The blame was placed directly on "the states' haphazard water-quality monitoring" that "create[d] massive information deficiencies that frustrate[d] accurate national assessment."[20]

The success of the EPA in its first decade can be attributed to at least two factors. First, one must acknowledge the importance of agency leadership. Nixon's EPA chief, William Ruckelshaus, formerly Assistant Attorney General for the Department of Justice's Civil Division, was an aggressive litigator. As noted above, he embraced an organizational structure and staffing practices that allowed the new agency to move rapidly toward vigorous enforcement. His successor, Russell Train, had strong environmental credentials, as president of the Conservation Foundation (1965–69) and chairman of the Council on Environmental Quality. Under his direction, the EPA expanded on enforcement efforts and dramatically increased its research capacity. President Carter appointed Douglas Costle as EPA Administrator in 1977. Costle, who had led the Connecticut Department of Environmental Protection before assuming the position of Assistant Director for Natural Resources at the Congressional Budget Office, brought experience in environmental regulation and a commitment to transforming the EPA into a public health agency, focusing increasing resources on the regulation of toxic substances and carcinogens. Certainly, the three EPA administrators differed in their approaches to managing the new agency. But they shared a commitment to environmental protection.[21]

A second source of success came from the courts. As noted above, Congress designed the new environmental regulatory system to provide ample opportunities for interest groups to challenge agency regulations, sue the agency to force it to execute its nondiscretionary duties, and directly sue polluting parties, all of which was encouraged by the courts' adoption of a more expansive definition of standing to sue. On several occasions, the courts responded to legal challenges by forcing the EPA to adopt a far more aggressive stance. For example, the court responded to a citizen suit filed by the Sierra Club and prevented the EPA from approving state implementation plans that would achieve NAAQS in nonattainment areas by allowing the degradation of areas that were currently cleaner than required.[22] In a subsequent case brought by the Natural Resources Defense Council, polluters were barred from using dilution or "dispersion enhancement" via tall smoke stacks.[23] While these and other decisions that strengthened regulations and accelerated implementation were celebrated by environmental groups, the courts have neither sword nor purse. They must rely on the EPA to enforce the law and monitor compliance, and this requires budgetary and administrative resources that the courts cannot provide.[24]

The Reagan Interregnum and the Power of Institutional Design

When Congress passed the core environmental statutes, it provided detailed mandates that limited bureaucratic discretion. As argued earlier, this reflected the dual goals of insulating the new policies from future administrations that might be hostile to environmental protection and limiting the vulnerability to undue industry influence or outright capture. These design decisions would be tested in the 1980s, during the Reagan presidency. Candidate Reagan embraced the arguments emanating from conservative think tanks in the 1970s, which attributed the high inflation and sluggish growth of the 1970s, in part, to the excesses of the regulatory state. His economic recovery program was premised on the belief that deregulation and regulatory reform—when combined with tax reductions, stable monetary policy, and a reduction in spending—would usher in a new period of market-based growth and prosperity. Unsurprisingly, the EPA was quickly targeted for reform.

While the 1980 elections brought a new Republican majority to the Senate, the Democratic Party remained in control of the House of Representatives and public opinion remained strongly supportive of environmental protection. In this context, there would be no real opportunity to repeal the Clean Air Act or the Clean Water Act, although proposals were floated. Change would have to occur through administrative means, with a combination of appointments, budget cuts, and the imposition of new regulatory review requirements. These requirements, as presented in Executive Order 12291, required executive branch agencies to complete a cost–benefit-analysis-based regulatory analysis and submit it to the Office of Management and Budget's Office of Information and Regulatory Affairs. Regulatory review increased the managerial control of the president, as noted in Chapter 4. Its greatest impacts would fall on the EPA.

The most significant changes at the EPA occurred during Reagan's first term in office. Reagan appointed Anne Gorsuch, a corporate attorney, to run the EPA. Gorsuch and her team appeared to have few discernible qualifications for the position. As the *New York Times* editorial board remarked: "Seldom since the Emperor Caligula appointed his horse a consul has there been so wide a gulf between authority and competence." Gorsuch was "a telephone company attorney and two-term state legislator who learned about environmental issues fighting Clean Air Act provisions in Colorado." Those she appointed to senior EPA positions were "distinguished only by a lack of relevant qualifications and hostility to environmental regulation . . . a crew of industry lobbyists and lawyers to administer Washington's largest and most complex regulatory agency."[25] (Comparable appointments in other environmentally important agencies raised similar concerns, most notably James G. Watt, who left the presidency of the Mountain States Legal Foundation—a conservative legal foundation that litigated on behalf of development interests—to lead the Department of Interior.) Gorsuch refused to articulate specific positions on policy issues during her confirmation hearings, stating that she would defer to President Reagan. She argued, nonetheless, that the EPA should do more to balance environmental protection and economic growth. Subsequently, she would call for greater delegation to the states (in keeping with Reagan's "new federalism"). With respect to enforcement, she stated "my personal philosophy is that incentives always achieve better results than sanctions." While fines might be warranted for "persistent" violators, "the emphasis has to be on voluntary participation."[26]

The appointment of hostile administrators was combined with deep budget cuts. When Reagan was elected, the EPA's budget was $4.7 billion. By 1982 and 1983, it had fallen to $3.7 billion. In inflation-adjusted terms, the budget had been cut by some 30 percent. These cuts necessitated deep reductions in personnel: The EPA workforce fell from a record high of 13,078 to a low of 10,832 by 1983.[27] While most of these cuts occurred through attrition, "the remaining staff were thoroughly demoralized."[28] The budget cuts were used as a justification for agency consolidation. The Office of Enforcement was merged with the general counsel's office, with some enforcement responsibilities transferred to the divisions responsible for each program (e.g., air, water). This allowed for a reduction in the number of EPA attorneys while simultaneously increasing the EPA administrator's control over enforcement activities. A new Intergovernmental Liaison Office was established to work more closely with the states, which Gorsuch believed should be treated as "equal partners."[29]

One should not be surprised that enforcement lagged dramatically under the direction of Gorsuch. As Joel A. Mintz, chief attorney at the EPA during the Carter administration, notes: "the agency's enforcement programs during this period experienced unprecedented levels of disorganization, demoralization, and internal strife."[30] Placing things in broader historical perspective, he writes:

> The approach of the EPA's early Reagan administration managers . . . led to an almost complete politicization of the enforcement process. This politicization interfered with the agency's remedial application of hazardous waste statutes and its enforcement of other federal laws, objective tasks requiring persistent professional effort and institutional stability. Beyond this, the EPA managers of the early 1980s failed from the outset to enunciate a clear and defensible approach to EPA's enforcement work. In this respect, their efforts stand in sharp contrast not only to the litigious EPA enforcement strategies of the Carter administration but also to the enforcement regimes of the Nixon, Ford, and George H. W. Bush administrations.[31]

All of this generated a highly publicized congressional backlash, investigations into the enforcement of the Superfund, and ultimately the resignation of Gorsuch and nineteen other high-level EPA officials. Gorsuch was found in contempt by Congress after she refused to comply with a subpoena issued by a House committee investigating implementation of the Superfund, claiming executive privilege.[32] Although the Justice Department refused to prosecute, Gorsuch resigned on March 9, 1983.

There were some attempts by the Reagan administration to bring about statutory change. With respect to the Clean Air Act, it proposed legislation that would relax standards for motor vehicle emissions, require the application of cost–benefit analysis in the development of NAAQS and delay deadlines for areas not in attainment, devolve greater authority to the states, and give the EPA greater discretionary authority to mitigate penalties and use private contractors to conduct inspections.[33] With respect to the Clean Water Act, the administration proposed delaying best available technology standards for an additional four years, revoking rules mandating national standards for the treatment of industrial toxic waste, extending the maximum terms for permits, and giving the EPA greater latitude in providing exemptions.[34] Congress exhibited little sustained interest in the proposals, given recent public opinion surveys that revealed strong opposition to relaxing the existing statutes and concerns that activism on this front could carry significant political costs in the 1982 midterm elections. Indeed, following the highly publicized battles with the Reagan EPA, Congress strengthened the environmental laws, passing the Hazardous and Solid Waste Amendments (1984), Safe Drinking Water Amendments (1986), Superfund Amendments and Reauthorization Act (1986), and the Water Quality Act (1987). In the wake of the Bhopal chemical spill, it passed the Emergency Planning and Community Right-To-Know Act (1986), requiring hazardous chemical emergency planning and mandating businesses report on the storage, use and release of hazardous chemicals.

Following the Gorsuch resignation, the Reagan administration sought to retreat from the conflicts involving the EPA, and thus asked Williams Ruckelshaus, the first administrator of the EPA with strong credentials in the environmental community, to return to run the agency. The transition from Gorsuch to Ruckelshaus was, in the words of the EPA's Associated General Counsel for Air and Radiation, "like the liberation of Paris." When Ruckleshaus resigned at the end of Reagan's first term, he was replaced by Lee Thomas, Acting Assistant Administrator for Solid Waste and Emergency Response who was brought into the agency as part of the Ruckelshaus team.[35] Enforcement of the environmental laws was reinvigorated. Rather than continuing the segregation of enforcement activities by medium, the agency began to develop a multimedia focus. Moreover, working with the Department of Justice, it began to develop multi-case enforcement initiatives that could increase their deterrent effects. The new emphasis on enforcement bore fruit. From the mid-1980s until the end of the Reagan presidency, the EPA reported record numbers of criminal referrals, civil referrals and, in 1988 alone, more than $24 million in civil penalties (another record).[36]

When Reagan's two-term presidency drew to a close, it was clear that the EPA had survived its most significant challenge to date. As Philip Shabecoff noted in the *New York Times*, when Reagan assumed office "environmentalists feared the worst" and "expected him to dismantle environmental regulation." However,

Eight years later, people on both sides of the argument say the environmental legacy of the Reagan era is a stalemate: that the Administration
left many serious problems unaddressed and neither revolutionized environmental regulation nor transferred large amounts of public resources to
private industry.[37]

As Richard A. Harris and Sidney M. Milkis observe, because the president
"followed an administrative rather than a legislative strategy, the institutional
bases of the new social regulation were left intact," such that, in the words of a
former Reagan appointee, "environmental protection easily 'could be ratcheted
up later.'"[38]

Indeed, Reagan's vice president and successor, George H. W. Bush, proved
to be far more supportive of environmental protection than many would
have expected, given his previous role running the President's Task Force on
Regulatory Relief (see Chapter 4). In part, this was an acknowledgment that
the Republican Party's electoral success was contingent on its ability to sof-
ten its image and embrace a "kinder, gentler, conservatism." Bush appointed
William K. Reilly, a former senior staffer at the Council on Environmental
Quality and president of the World Wildlife Fund, as EPA Administrator.
Under Bush, the EPA's budget expanded significantly, from $5 billion (1988)
to $6.7 billion (1992), an inflation-adjusted budget that was the largest level
since the Carter presidency.[39] Enforcement continued to improve under Bush,
although it remained bedeviled by bureaucratic fragmentation and ongoing
congressional suspicion over the adequacy of Superfund administration. More
important, the EPA's more vigorous enforcement efforts brought the agency
into conflict with the Council on Competitiveness—the institutional heir of
the Reagan-era Task Force. The activities of the Council, led by Vice President
Dan Quayle, became more activist as the nation experienced a brief recession
and the Bush administration sought to cater to the conservative base as the reelection campaign approached.[40]

More striking, the Bush administration would play a central role in crafting
the 1990 Clean Air Act Amendments to address acid rain. In the past decades,
a solution to acid rain had eluded policymakers insofar as it generated conflicts between Western states that produced low-sulfur (or "clean") coal, Eastern
states that produced high-sulfur (or "dirty") coal, and the industrial Midwest
that was responsible for the emissions that subsequently produced acid rain in
the Northeast.[41] Various schemes to mandate control technologies (that would
permit the use of dirty coal) while grandfathering existing plants and imposing
a national energy tax or allowing performance standards (that would favor clean
coal) were ineffective or politically untenable. Drawing on a proposal from the
Environmental Defense Fund, the Bush administration successfully negotiated
an innovative system of cap-and-trade. Lacking explicit distributional consequences and employing market forces to incentivize reductions, cap-and-trade

was capable of attracting broad political support. This legislative accomplishment would mark the last significant environmental statute before the nation entered a period of sustained polarization.

Polarization and Environmental Protection

The Clean Air Act Amendments of 1990 passed with overwhelming support (93 percent in the House and 89 percent in the Senate). The bipartisan coalition was so strong that it even included the Republican Congressman from Georgia's 6th District, Newt Gingrich. Four years later, Gingrich would lead the GOP to victory in the 1994 midterm elections behind the Contract with America, a platform that pledged to scale back the role of the federal government relative to the states and redefine its role in the economy. While the GOP would claim a majority in both chambers for the first time in four decades, the greatest gains came in the House of Representatives. Among its many promises, the contract vowed to pass a number of new statutes that would mandate procedural reforms that could have potentially dramatic ramifications for environmental protection and regulation more generally.

The first bill submitted for consideration by the new Republican majority was the Unfunded Mandate Reform Act of 1995. It passed within a month with large majorities (360–74 in the House, 86–10 in the Senate). For the past several decades, the federal government had imposed requirements on state and local governments without providing the necessary funding. The new GOP majority championed a balanced budget amendment, and the Act was designed to prevent the federal government from controlling spending by forcing costs on to the states. Under the Act, a public bill or joint resolution imposing a mandate must be submitted to the Congressional Budget Office for a cost estimate that would have to be considered on the floor. Unfunded intergovernmental mandates in excess of $50 million and/or private sector mandates in excess of $100 million, would be subject to a point of order. Administrative agencies, in turn, were required to estimate the costs and benefits of rules with mandates with effects in excess of $100 million. All of this raised concerns for environmental protection regulation, since requirements imposed under past environmental statutes (e.g., the implementation of state implementation plans under the Clean Air Act, a variety of requirements under the Clean Water Act) could be considered unfunded mandates. Yet, it remained unclear whether the statute would have teeth: In Congress, for example, a point of order could be waived by a vote.[42]

Before the House of Representatives passed additional procedural reforms, it passed the Regulatory Transition Act of 1995 (HR 450). The Act would force a moratorium on new regulations. In the past, similar actions had occurred via executive action. For example, one of Ronald Reagan's first actions upon assuming office was to impose a 60-day moratorium on regulations promulgated in the waning days of the Carter presidency; George H. W. Bush had imposed a similar moratorium in 1992, hoping to galvanize the support of conservatives. From this perspective, the Regulatory Transition Act was expansive, preventing agencies from implementing regulations proposed or enacted since November 20, 1994, and banning any significant new regulations until December 31, 1995, or until the passage of regulatory reform bills that emanated from the Contract with America.[43]

The most striking statute introduced in the House of Representatives was the Job Creation and Wage Enhancement Act of 1995 (HR 9). This omnibus bill was divided into several titles, separate acts that focused on key regulatory issues with the potential to dramatically reshape environmental protection. The Private Property Protection Act required the relevant agency (e.g., the EPA, Department of Interior) to "compensate an owner of property whose use of any portion of that property has been limited by an agency action, under a specified regulatory law, that diminishes the fair market value of that portion by 20 percent or more" (§3). If the diminution of value exceeded 50 percent, the federal government could be required, at the discretion of the owner, to purchase that portion for its market value. The Act defined property to include land and "the right to use or receive water." It enumerated the specified regulatory laws to include the Clean Water Act and the Endangered Species Act (§10). Given the Republican efforts to reduce agency budgets, "the net effect of the property compensation requirement would almost surely have been to inhibit agencies . . . from imposing substantial limitations or mitigation on permit applicants."[44]

The Regulatory Reform and Relief Act of 1995 was designed to provide a statutory foundation for the requirements imposed under Reagan's Executive Order 12291. It amended the Administrative Procedure Act to mandate that all agencies prepare cost–benefit-analysis-based regulatory impact analyses for majors rules, defined as any rule having an annual impact in excess of $50 million, resulting in major price increases, or impacting on "competition, employment, investment, productivity, innovation" or US competitiveness (§201). Under §204 (4)(D), these analyses would have to include

> an analysis of alternative approaches, including market-based mechanisms, that could substantially achieve the same regulatory goal at a lower cost and an explanation of the reasons why such alternative approaches were not adopted, together with a demonstration that the rule provides for the least costly approach.

Agencies were prohibited from promulgating a major rule unless the OMB Director approved the analysis. Under §203, agencies would be required to hold hearings on a proposed major rule if more than 100 interested parties requested it. Similarly, the standard comment period of 90 days would have to be extended by an additional 30 days, once again, if requested by more than 100 persons individually. Additionally, the Act imposed new judicial over-sight responsibilities, and authorized small entities to petition for judicial review within a year of its effective date.

The Risk Assessment and Cost–Benefit Act of 1995, §2, stated "public and private resources available to address health, safety, and environmental con-cerns are not unlimited" and "need to be allocated to address the greatest needs in the most cost-effective manner." To accomplish this, Congress mandated that, for each major rule "within a program designed to protect human health, safety, or the environment" an "analysis of the incremental costs and incre-mental risk reduction or other benefits associated with each alternative strategy identified or considered by the agency." The alternatives would have to include "no government action" and those that "employ performance or other market-based mechanisms that permit the greatest flexibility in achieving the identified benefits of the rule" (§201). Final rules could not be promulgated unless the agency certified that (1) its analyses were grounded in "objective and unbiased scientific and economic evaluations"; (2) "incremental risk reduction or other benefits . . . will be likely to justify, and be reasonably related to, the incremen-tal costs incurred"; and (3) other strategies were either "less cost-effective" or "provide less flexibility to State, local or tribal governments" (§202). The Act assigned the OMB the responsibility of overseeing the development and prepa-ration of the analyses (§203). For the purposes of the Act, "any proposed or final clean-up plans for a facility the costs of which are likely to exceed $5,000,000 shall be as a major rule" (§204). It also required agencies to develop an independ-ent and external peer review for any health, safety or environmental program that was likely to result in annual costs of $100 million or more. Peer review panels, under the Act, would include representatives of the regulated industry.[45] As Sally Katzen, Clinton's OMB-OIRA director, noted, the requirements of the Act "would create endless analytical loops and excessive opportunities for litigation," in essence, stopping the regulatory process.[46]

The various components of the Job Creation and Wage Enhancement Act passed the House in March 1995, some three months after the introduction of the omnibus bill and within the 100-day deadline imposed by the leadership. Democratic critics expressed ongoing concerns that the bills were being rushed through the legislation process "after hasty and perfunctory consideration . . . emphasizing speed over deliberation."[47] Much to the dismay of the House majority, the level of enthusiasm for reform was not matched in the Senate. The components of the Job Creation and Wage Enhancement Act languished in the Senate, reflecting a combination of the Democratic majority's successful filibuster threats, President Clinton's promise of vetoes, and Majority Leader Bob Dole's political aspirations in the year preceding a presidential election. As for the Regulatory Transition Act, once passed and referred to the Senate, the Senate stripped the moratorium and passed its own version that would allow Congress a 45-day period after the issuance of significant new regulations to pass a resolution revoking the regulation.[48] Although it failed to pass in its new incarnation, the core provisions would ultimately reemerge in the Congressional Review Act in 1996. We shall reserve a discussion of this Act for Chapter 7.

The Senate, as noted above, stalled the flurry of legislative activity in 1995. But the next several years would nonetheless be difficult ones for environmental protection and regulation more broadly. Efforts to pass new statutes to strengthen existing laws and extend their reach to emerging issues ran afoul of the GOP majority committed to scaling back the reach of government. Even the Superfund tax, central to CERCLA, was allowed to expire in 1995 when Congress failed to pass a reauthorization. The House would retreat from the efforts to pass new statutes and turn, instead, to budgetary politics. In 1995, the House passed an appropriations bill that would cut the EPA's budget by one-third (some $2.4 billion) and enforcement by 50 percent; an additional seventeen riders were added to further constrain the agency. Although the Senate voted for a far more modest cut of 14 percent (with a 21 percent reduction in enforcement) and successfully removed most of the riders, President Clinton vetoed the bill, leading to a six-day partial shutdown of government and the EPA. The next several months would witness temporary spending bills, tense negotiations, and a 27-day government shutdown that furloughed the employees of the EPA (and other agencies). In April 1996, Congress finally passed a spending bill that met President Clinton's

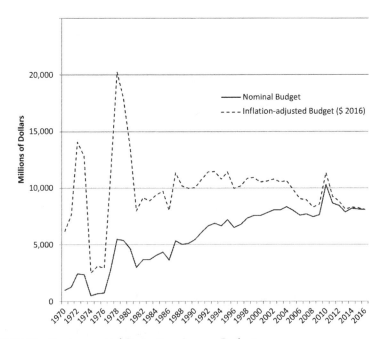

FIGURE 6.1 Environmental Protection Agency Budget

Source: Environmental Protection Agency.

approval.[49] The budget fell from $7.4 billion (1995) to $6.5 billion (1996), but the cuts were far more modest than what the Republican House had advocated.[50]

After the cuts of 1996, the EPA's budget would grow steadily, reaching $7.8 billion by the last year of the Clinton presidency. But as the data in Figure 6.1 reveal, the growth in the nominal budget should not obscure the more important trend. When adjusted for inflation, the 2001 budget was smaller than it had been in the last year of the Bush presidency, and more strikingly, at the peak of the Reagan presidency. Moreover, while the agency had avoided the deep cuts proposed by Congress, the budget battles of the mid-1990s and the resulting furloughs had a negative impact on staff morale. They also had a "chilling effect" on the EPA more generally, creating a hesitancy to undertake enforcement actions that might draw the ire of Congress or demand resources that might not be available in an uncertain environment.[51]

Environmental Protection and Partnerships

The core environmental statutes were written with great specificity, as noted earlier, to constrain executive authority and limit the extent to which even hostile presidents could depart from congressional preferences. While this strategy may have borne fruit during the Reagan presidency, the benefits came at a steep cost. Under conditions of growing polarization and gridlock, Congress no longer proved capable of passing laws that could recalibrate regulation. Regulators were denied the flexibility to address emerging challenges within the confines of existing statutes and thus had to act entrepreneurially to find alternative means. The Clinton administration's promotion of the "reinvention of government" or REGO provided the space for agency experimentation.[52] The 1990s would witness the proliferation of voluntary programs and public–private partnerships designed to compensate for the rigidity of traditional regulation, promote innovation, and leverage private sector resources and expertise. REGO would be one of the most significant legacies of the Clinton administration, and the EPA's new emphasis on forging partnerships and promoting regulatory voluntarism would continue in subsequent presidencies.

In a document entitled "Reinventing Environmental Protection," the Clinton administration noted that "we are in the midst of a critical transitional period for our nation's environmental policy." While the policies of the past twenty-five years yielded important achievements, "we learned a great deal about the limitations of 'command-and-control,'" an approach that "can discourage technological innovation that can lower the costs of regulation or achieve environmental benefits *beyond* compliance."

> We have learned that pollution is often a sign of economic efficiency and business can improve profits by preventing it. We have learned that better decisions result from a collaborative process with people working

together, rather that from an adversarial one that pits them against each other. And we have learned that regulations that provide flexibility—but require accountability—can provide greater protection at a lower cost.

The administration made the case that "using performance standards along with economic incentives encourages innovation. The lowest-cost and most effective strategies earn a greater return in the marketplace." Ultimately, economic and environmental goals "must be mutually reinforcing to produce both jobs and environmental quality."[53]

The Clinton EPA would reiterate these basic points on multiple occasions, pointing to the importance of flexible, performance-based approaches, and declaring its willingness to experiment with third-party auditing and self-certification. It emphasized the importance of eliminating the adversarial relations of the past ("to reinvent environmental protection, we must first build trust among traditional adversaries") and forging new partnerships.[54] As the EPA noted in its *Strategic Plan* (1997), the case for partnerships rested on some practical realities. First, the "EPA alone does not have all the answers," and thus must consult "external stakeholders," including businesses. They "have strong opinions about how federal environmental policies affect their operations and overall competitiveness nationally and abroad." Second, there was the practical reality of resource constraints:

> In a time when Congress and the Administration are eliminating the federal deficit, it is more important than ever to assure that federal dollars achieve the greatest possible gain. Leveraging resources through partnerships can provide this assurance, and help create mutually beneficial situations for the public and private sectors.[55]

The administration's reinvention goals quickly found several concrete expressions. As noted earlier, the core environmental statutes were medium-specific, a focus that was reflected in the EPA's program offices. Redundant regulations, unnecessary costs, and inter-media transfers (e.g., removing pollutants from smokestacks only to produce solid wastes that needed disposal) were long recognized as some of the vexing byproducts of this system. The Clinton EPA sought to address these issues with the Common Sense Initiative (CSI), created in 1994. Under the CSI, the EPA established a council and subcommittees of stakeholders representing six industries (automobile manufacturing, computers and electronics, iron and steel, metal finishing, petroleum refining, and printing) to identify "cleaner, cheaper, and smarter" ways of preventing pollution on an industry-specific basis and develop projects to test innovative approaches.[56]

Ultimately, by the time CSI completed its work at the end of 1998, it was clear that it had failed to generate the results envisioned by those who viewed it as a "flagship program." In part, the lack of results was a product of the decision-making model adopted by the EPA. The approval of subcommittee proposals required consensus, something that was interpreted, in practice, as unanimity. As the difficulties of reaching consensus became clear to subcommittee members, they lowered their expectation and turned to more modest areas where unanimity might be found (e.g., the development of training manuals, voluntary performance targets, public outreach). But there was a more fundamental problem. As Cary Coglianese and Laurie K. Allen explain:

> Unfortunately, because the problems CSI was designed to address were embedded in underlying environmental statutes, EPA came up against some significant limitations in what it could accomplish through administrative actions. EPA cannot change these statutes; in fact, they are written to constrain and direct the kinds of actions EPA takes. Statutes not only direct EPA's priorities, but also stipulate numerous judicially enforceable deadlines that the agency must meet and often specify the regulatory strategies EPA must use in great detail.

Once again, we encounter the problems of original regulatory design: "Existing environmental statutes limit EPA's opportunities to waive statutory requirements and they provide no catchall provision granting EPA authority to develop alternative regulatory systems." Moreover, departures from established regulations—even if sanctioned by the EPA—might result in litigation, as environmental organizations used the opportunities provided in the environmental statutes to file suit against firms.[57]

As CSI was getting started, the Clinton administration introduced Project XL (for eXellence in Leadership) in 1995. It was explicitly created to grant greater flexibility to organizations so that they could test alternative regulatory strategies. As the EPA noted: "Based on the premise that these participants know better than the federal government how to reduce their pollution, Project XL reduces the regulatory burden and promotes economic growth while achieving better environmental and public health projection." The goal was to limit Project XL to a maximum of fifty projects. They would be selected in accordance with eight criteria: "better environmental results; cost savings and paperwork reduction; stakeholder support; test of an innovative strategy; transferability; feasibility; identification or monitoring, reporting, and evaluation methods; and avoidance of shifting risk burden."[58]

Project XL encountered several problems that ultimately limited its efficacy.[59] Potential participants were slow to apply. The review process proved quite protracted, particularly in the early years when the time elapsed between submission and signing of the final project agreement exceeded two years, leading to high regulatory transaction costs. During the first three years, 72.5 percent of the proposals were rejected, withdrawn or simply became inactive. Potential participants were often dissuaded by the *quid pro quo*—greater regulatory flexibility was granted in exchange for superior environmental performance. The EPA would countenance this flexibility only if superior performance were guaranteed under the terms of a consent decree, a requirement that stifled innovation by forcing potential participants to accept any downside risk of failure. In essence, the desire to promote innovation came into conflict with an institutional structure that demanded certainty of results.[60]

Reinvention moved forward rapidly and was placed under the coordination of a new Office of Reinvention under the direction of a new associate administrator. In 1995 alone, the EPA introduced twenty-five REGO projects, under the umbrella "Partners for the Environment," designed to leverage the expertise of corporations, research labs, environmental groups, and state and local regulators to develop means of preventing pollution or going beyond the confines of existing regulations. Some of these partnerships were industry specific (e.g., AgStar, Coalbed Methane Outreach, Energy Star, Green Chemistry, Natural Gas Star, Pesticide Environmental Stewardship Program, Voluntary Aluminum Industry Partnership). Others focused on specific business processes (e.g., Consumer Labeling Initiative, Design for Environment, Environmental Accounting, Environmental Technology Verification). A third class included partnerships that focused on larger environmental problems like climate change (Climate Wise), indoor air pollution (Indoor Air Quality), or municipal solid waste (WasteWise).

The most ambitious, and arguably the most promising REGO initiative, was the National Environmental Performance Track (NEPT), a regulatory green track modeled, in part, on OSHA's Voluntary Protection Program, which will be discussed in Chapter 7. In 2000, the Clinton EPA introduced NEPT, drawing on the experiences of states experimenting with green tracks and EPA Region 1, which had incorporated some of their lessons in its Star Track Program.[61] Like its state and regional predecessors, NEPT was designed to promote high-quality environmental management systems among organizations that had distinguished themselves as leaders. The basic assumption underlying the program was a simple one: Firms with an environmental policy, a commitment to continuous improvement, a high-quality environmental management system or EMS, and a strong regulatory compliance record should be given greater flexibility in managing their environmental impacts and subjected to lower levels of regulatory scrutiny than firms that are organizationally incompetent or fail to exhibit these traits. Given that NEPT was fully implemented during the Bush presidency, we will return to it below.

The EPA promoted these partnerships with a simple message: Environmental management can further corporate profitability. As the agency noted in one of its promotional pamphlets (*Partners for the Environment: Boosting Your Bottom Line*):

> By making improvements that optimize performance, companies are cutting costs, adding value, and increasing market share. That's why many companies—perhaps your competitors—have come to view environmental

management as a fundamental part of smart business strategy. They're protecting the environment and gaining competitive advantages as a result.[62]

The EPA noted that its partners would have opportunities to realize cost savings ("Programs are designed to help companies cut waste and increase efficiency and productivity"), public recognition ("Many partnership programs offer awards, logos, and other distinctions that can be used for marketing purposes"), and technical assistance. For those who might still prove skittish, the agency assured potential participants that a partnership agreement "isn't legally binding, but it does lay out steps the company will take to pursue environmental improvements. These actions might include conducting a self audit to assess water and energy use, installing more efficient equipment, and reporting on progress."[63]

There was a significant level of participation in the EPA partnership programs. By 2000, the EPA reported that more than 11,000 stakeholders (both public and private) were participating in one or more of the voluntary EPA programs. The agency surveyed the members of its partnership programs and reported that in 2000, they had saved $5.9 billion, reduced greenhouse gas emissions by 37.3 million metric tons of carbon equivalent, recycled 17,788 tons of municipal solid waste, saved 603 million gallons of water and 768.8 trillion BTUs, while reducing nitrogen oxide emissions (158,172.5 tons) and sulfur dioxide emissions (288,627.49 tons).[64] Of course, one might question the veracity of the information provided given that there was no requirement of third-party verification of results. Moreover, one might question how much of these results would have occurred absent the partnership programs (if environmental performance genuinely reinforces corporate profitability, one can imagine that corporations would discover this absent a partnership agreement).

The growing reliance on public–private partnerships during the 1990s provides an important example of *devolution*. Given the failure of Congress to update the environmental statutes and support budgetary growth, partnerships held some promise for addressing the limitations of the regulatory system. There were many opportunities for improving the performance of regulated entities. Industrial processes and products could be reengineered to manage environmental impacts across the lifecycle. Companies could set voluntary goals addressing recycling or greenhouse gas emissions. Trade associations could develop industry-specific codes to force higher levels of performance among their members (e.g., the chemical industry's Responsible Care Program). Standard-setting associations could develop standards that could facilitate self-regulation and elevate the role of environmental performance in supply chains (e.g., the International Organization's ISO 14001 standard). Moreover, regulators could leverage corporate resources to fill critical gaps in the EPA's data (e.g., the High Production Volume Chemical Challenge enlisted firms to voluntarily develop toxicological data sets for chemicals that had been grandfathered into the TSCA chemical inventory).[65] Much could be accomplished in the shadow of the environmental laws.

There were ongoing concerns, however, over whether the voluntary environmental programs were actually producing the intended results. Take the example of Climate Wise, a program introduced in 1993 as part of President Clinton's Climate Change Action Plan with the goals of encouraging "the immediate reduction of greenhouse gas emissions in the industrial sector" and "foster[ing] innovation by allowing participants to identify the actions that make the most sense for their organizations."[66] Under Clinton, the US had signed the Kyoto Protocol. But the Byrd–Hagel Resolution of 1997, which the Senate passed by a 95–0 margin, informed the administration that the Senate would oppose any climate agreement that had the broad features of this international agreement. In response, the Protocol was never submitted for ratification. Climate Wise, by default, became one of the EPA's core programs for managing greenhouse gas emissions. Yet, subsequent analyses found little evidence of statistically significant emissions reductions among participants. Indeed, analyses of comparable voluntary programs at the Department of Energy suggest that emissions reductions were actually greater among firms that did not participate than among those that pledged reductions.[67] It may be the case that participation was largely viewed in strategic terms, particularly among firms that were late to join the program. While there is some evidence that early participants cut emissions—albeit less than they pledged—the effects were largely erased by firms that joined subsequently. Late joiners tended to engage in "symbolic cooperation," free-riding on the achievements of earlier participants, essentially using participation as a means of greenwashing their environmental records.[68] The performance of Climate Wise was of legitimate concern given the lack of forward movement on mandatory climate change policy.

Going beyond Climate Wise, the empirical analyses of voluntary environmental programs arrive at mixed conclusions regarding their efficacy. The 33/50 Program, which was introduced in 1991, enlisted firms to reduce voluntarily the emissions of chemicals specified by the Toxic Release Inventory by 33 percent by 1992, and 50 percent by 1995. Subsequent analyses revealed that participants met the goals and realized reductions in other chemical emissions as well. More impressive, they continued to achieve additional reductions of between 20 and 30 percent between 1996 and 2013, after the program was terminated.[69] In contrast, other programs, seem to have had little effect, including the Sustainable Slopes program[70] and the much celebrated National Environmental Performance Track (a point that we shall return to below). Similarly, voluntary programs that were not formally sponsored by regulators have also had a mixed track record. Participation in ISO 14001—the international standard for environmental management systems—has had a modest impact on pollution reduction and regulatory compliance in the US.[71] In contrast, the performance of Responsible Care has been found wanting. Indeed, the empirical analyses conclude that participants actually pollute more than non-participants.[72] Bottom line, one cannot assume that voluntary programs will have the intended effects.

Much will depend on program design: the kinds of demands that can be made of participants, the kinds of benefits they can be offered, the capacity to verify results, and mechanisms to penalize and exclude participants that fail to meet their obligations.

In the end, contemporaneous observers may have viewed the voluntary programs—even if of uncertain effect—to be relatively benign. In the early years of the Clinton presidency, the promotion of compliance assistance, collaboration, and voluntarism created some confusion in an agency traditionally devoted to enforcement. To what extent would the administration's REGO activities be compatible with the EPA's core mission? As things turned out, the EPA would expand its enforcement activities over the course of the 1990s. It would begin using computer databases for targeted national enforcement, turning its focus from individual facilities to entire companies and in some cases industries (including petroleum refining, steel, and coal-fired utilities). Certainly, there were constraints imposed by budgets, ongoing concerns over Congress, and, increasingly, conflicts with the states, which were increasingly under the direction of Republican governors. But there was little to suggest, at least at this juncture, that voluntarism had become a substitute for enforcement.[73]

Reinvention Republican Style

In many ways, the EPA changed course during the George H. W. Bush administration. Under Clinton, the EPA had enjoyed a prolonged period of stability in leadership. Carol Browner's tenure as EPA administrator was unprecedented, extending for a full eight years. In contrast, during Bush's first term, the EPA had two administrators, Christine Todd Whitman and Michael Leavitt, with Stephen L. Johnson serving the entirety of Bush's second term. Particularly in the first term, appointees in key positions exhibited inexperience with the federal bureaucracy, failed to communicate with the professional staff, and asserted centralized control over enforcement activities. Three highly publicized events attracted the ire of critics. First, the EPA withdrew a Clinton-era rule on arsenic in the drinking water, citing questions about the adequacy of the underlying analysis (it was subsequently finalized, after attracting much negative publicity).[74] Second, the administration formally rejected the Kyoto Protocol, which had languished signed but never submitted for Senate ratification. This decision, when combined with a third decision—to revise new source review (NSR) standards applied to electric utilities in response to recommendations by Bush's National Energy Policy Development Group, chaired by Vice President Dick Cheney—raised concerns that environmental policy was being politicized and directed by a White House with close ties to the energy sector.

The NSR standards were particularly troublesome, given the thousands of deaths caused by particulate matter. New source review was implemented as a means of determining when maintenance on coal-fired utilities that had been grandfathered in under the Clean Air Act Amendments was substantial enough to render the facilities, in essence, new facilities subject to a higher set of regulatory standards. The Clinton administration had used NSR as the cornerstone of lawsuits against nine of the nation's largest electric utilities and by 2000 had reached settlements with Tampa Electric, Virginia Electric Power Company, and Cinergy Company. By 2001, the remaining suits, which had been filed as part of the Clinton EPA's targeted national enforcement initiatives, were quickly approaching settlements on terms favorable to the government. Administrator Whitman advised the remaining defendants to defer settlements until work was completed on the revision of the NSR standard for routine maintenance. Ultimately, the revisions permitted utilities to spend as much as 20 percent of replacement costs on an annual basis, thereby undercutting the suits and dramatically limiting the opportunities for future enforcement in this area. The fact that executives from the firms targeted by the EPA had contributed heavily to the Bush campaign—and the energy sector was the single most important source of contributions—raised the concerns that NSR had become captive to electoral politics.[75]

The efforts to limit the expansion of enforcement via policy change were combined with ongoing budgetary pressure. There were minor increases in the EPA's budget from 2001 ($7.8 billion) to 2004 ($8.4 billion), but some of this was connected to expanded duties following the terrorist attacks of September 11, 2001. Thereafter, the budget would decline steadily, falling to $7.4 billion by 2008 (see Figure 6.1). By that point, in inflation-adjusted terms, the EPA was working with a budget that was the smallest since the Reagan presidency.

As noted above, in 2001, the Bush administration formally rejected Kyoto—which had languished, signed but never submitted to the Senate. The next year it announced its goal of reducing greenhouse gas intensity (i.e., emissions levels relative to GDP) rather than abiding by absolute emissions targets. Building on the Clinton administration precedents, the EPA unveiled a new voluntary program, Climate Leaders. Under Climate Leaders, corporations would voluntarily conduct a greenhouse gas inventory using a Greenhouse Gas Inventory Protocol (based on a protocol development by the World Resources Institute and the World Business Council on Sustainable Development). Participants would work with the EPA in developing corporate-wide goals for greenhouse gas reductions and report on their progress annually. Participants were rewarded with various forms of public recognition and technical assistance (e.g., the program published lists of participants in *Newsweek* and *Fortune* magazines).[76] By 2008, there were 251 Climate Leader partners, collectively responsible for 8 percent of total US emissions. The EPA projected that their efforts would prevent some 13.6 MMTCE per year, compared to business-as-usual.[77] While Climate Leaders may have been one of the more high-profile programs, by 2008 the EPA listed 36 different Climate Partnership Programs and claimed "[t]here are now more than 13,000 firms and other organizations participating in climate-related EPA Partnership Programs."[78]

Although the myriad climate-related partnership programs and the high levels of participation may have been celebrated by the Bush administration, critics were unimpressed. The rejection of the Kyoto Protocol, the embrace of greenhouse gas intensity reductions (and goals that were no better than a continuation in the historical trend line), and the promotion of voluntary partnerships were seen largely as an expression of the Bush administration's close ties to the energy sector. As one analyst noted:

> The energy lobby can take well-earned credit for the voluntary (instead of mandatory) measures advocated by President Bush and his Administration to address the climate issue.... Powerful business and individual interests influencing the Bush Administration differ from the pluralist interests (including environmental NGOs) that were shaping the Clinton Administration's climate policymakers.

Indeed, this interpretation of the changed context would proliferate during the Bush presidency: What was once considered "regulatory reinvention" designed to promote innovative approaches to environmental management was now viewed as a subversion of environmental regulation, if not evidence of outright capture.[79]

While the National Environmental Performance Track was a Clinton administration initiative, it came to fruition during the Bush presidency. Under NEPT, participants were given a host of benefits, including public recognition, awards, and the use of the Performance Track logo. The EPA promoted information sharing among members of NEPT via national conferences, regional roundtables, Internet seminars, and mentoring programs. Members also received a set of regulatory benefits, including a lower inspection priority, expedited permitting, and streamlined reporting and paperwork requirements.[80] Between 2000 and 2008, the number of NEPT members increased from 228 to 547, including several top corporations like Xerox, Baxter Healthcare, and Johnson & Johnson, each of which were designated as "Corporate Leaders." Through the Performance Track Network, the EPA had forged relationships with a number of trade associations, some of which (e.g., the American Chemistry Council) had well-developed environmental codes for their members. The EPA also signed memoranda of agreement with fourteen states to coordinate the requirements of NEPT and state-level performance-based programs and secure additional benefits for NEPT members.[81]

According to the Bush EPA, NEPT was "designed to recognize and encourage top environmental performers—those who go beyond compliance with regulatory requirements to attain levels of environmental performance and management that benefit people, communities, and the environment."[82] One should not be surprised that this proved an elusive goal. Cary Coglianese and Jennifer Nash have conducted the most comprehensive evaluation of NEPT to date. Their comparison of NEPT participants and comparable firms revealed no evidence that the performance of the former exceeded that of the latter. As they explain: "nothing in the design or EPA's evaluation of the program enabled the agency to determine that the program in fact recognized top environmental performers within any industrial sector."[83] At best, it attracted "organizational extroverts" that

> appear to have been generally the strongest in their desire for public recognition. Of course, if it were not for opportunity costs and scarcity of governmental resources, there would presumably be nothing inherently wrong with EPA engaging with firms that value the agency's attention and appreciation.[84]

By the mid-2000s, the EPA had some over fifty initiatives, including NEPT. Although the EPA proclaimed the environmental benefits of its programs, evaluations by the EPA Inspector General raised profound concerns. One of the problems came in the area of data collection. In 2006, the Inspector General noted that the greatest barrier to making claims about the performance of these programs was the simple facts that "a partnership program cannot require data submission" and, as a result, "collected data may not be completely accurate." The implications were clear: "Without needed data, these programs may be hindered in their ability to demonstrate program success or adapt to changing partner and participant needs."[85] In 2007, the Inspector General's report found several additional problems that reflected on the lapses in program management and oversight. At the most basic level, the Inspector General encountered difficulties in determining what actually constituted a voluntary program. The EPA lacked a standard definition, and as a result, the EPA's own estimates of numbers of programs ranged from 54 to 133, depending on the year. More important, the EPA failed to implement

> a systematic management approach for developing new programs or for evaluating existing programs. As a result, EPA cannot consistently identify its voluntary program population; determine the overall environmental impact of its broader voluntary program effort; or systematically design, evaluate, and model programs that are effective at achieving environmental results.[86]

There was ample evidence, in short, that the kinds of programs that were once introduced as central to reform were ripe for reform.

Obama and the Temporary Retreat from Regulatory Voluntarism

The 2008 election that brought Barack Obama to the White House was dominated by the financial crisis and deep recession. But the environment, seemingly irrelevant in 2000 and 2004, assumed a prominent role for both Obama and his Republican rival, John McCain, both of whom sought to distance themselves from the policy positions of the outgoing Bush administration. Both candidates promoted cap-and-trade as a means of managing greenhouse gases, although Obama was far more aggressive in his reduction targets. Obama, moreover, combined his support for climate change legislation with the goal of moving to renewable forms of energy, and revitalizing a moribund system of environmental protection.[87] As Elizabeth Bomberg and Betsy Super note: "Most environmentalists greeted Obama's victory with a wave of euphoria, with expectations to match." It "brought a relief so palpable, the promised contrast with Bush so stark, that many environmentalists—like many other constituencies—were unwilling to contemplate the prospect that their expectations might not be met."[88]

The EPA's first administrator, Lisa Jackson, assumed her position following a period of budgetary retrenchment. In inflation-adjusted terms, the 2009 budget of $7.6 billion was 82.5 percent of what it had been during the first year of the Bush presidency (and 67 percent of what it had been when President Clinton assumed office). The workforce had fallen from 18,000 in 2001 to 17,252.[89] Jackson identified some key priorities: "restoring science and science's role in writing regulations" so that EPA would no longer be perceived as "one more political voice in the discussion." She also wanted to restore the rule of law and pursue enforcement with greater transparency, eliminating the "fog that clouded some of the decision-making process" at the Bush EPA.[90] With Democratic majorities in both chambers, the Obama administration was successful in achieving its budgetary goals, at least in the short term. By 2010, the agency's budget had increased to $10.3 billion. However, of the $2.7 billion of increases, only $600 million went to the operating budget (the remainder was passed through the agency to finance infrastructure, in an effort to offset state-level budget cuts).[91]

As part of the reorientation of the EPA, voluntary programs came under greater scrutiny. In March 2009, EPA Administrator Lisa Jackson announced that the National Environmental Performance Track was being terminated. It "was developed in a different era and may not speak to today's challenges," she explained.[92] Memoranda of agreement with the states were canceled and the regulatory incentives provided to NEPT participants were canceled. In September 2010, EPA Assistant Administrator Gina McCarthy followed suit and announced the termination of the Climate Leaders program, noting that "the context in which Climate Leaders is operating is far different from what it was when it was launched in 2002." Partners were encouraged to participate in programs operated by the states and non-governmental organizations.[93] The days of deregulation and novel experimentation that devolved authority on to regulated parties appeared over. At least this was the opening proposition.

The departure from Climate Leaders made sense, given the emphasis the administration had placed on a more vigorous attack on climate change. Candidate Obama had been sharply critical of his predecessor's unilateralism, particularly in foreign policy. But following his inauguration, President Obama's efforts to address climate change would combine four elements, three of which would take the form of unilateral action. First, the administration promoted statutory change. With unified Democratic Control of the Congress, it appeared that the time was finally ripe for the passage of new significant legislation. In 2009, President Obama created a new White House Office of Energy and Climate Change Policy and placed it under the direction of former Clinton EPA Administrator Carol Browner. The Office was given the task of coordinating legislative efforts. While the legislative process was unfolding, the administration promoted investments in renewable energy, new fuel efficiency standards, and the promulgation of new regulations on greenhouse gases. Let us consider them in turn.

The first element in the administration's climate change efforts involved statutory change. The Obama administration strongly supported a cap-and-trade system comparable to what had been developed under the Clean Air Act Amendments of 1990 with the goal of reducing greenhouse gas emissions by 80 percent by 2050.[94] In June 2009, the Democratically controlled House of Representatives voted on the American Clean Energy and Security Act, a complex bill of almost 1,300 pages establishing a cap-and-trade system. The politics surrounding the bill were complicated, pitting East and West coast Democrats against Democrats representing districts that relied heavily on coal for electricity and manufacturing. Republicans were close to unified in their opposition to what they viewed as a *de facto* national energy tax. Environmental groups were divided. Greenpeace, for example, urged a negative vote in response to the insufficient reduction targets and the offsets, both of which were derided as products of heavy business lobbying. Business was divided as well: The US Chamber of Commerce and the National Association of Manufacturers opposed the legislation while some large firms like Ford Motors and Dow Chemical actually supported it. Ultimately, the bill narrowly passed the House (219–212), with the support of 8 Republicans and the opposition of 44 Democrats.[95] With a Democratic majority in the Senate, there was finally a chance that Congress might pass the first significant environmental statute in two decades, thereby ending the reliance on voluntarism and public–private partnerships to extend the EPA's regulatory capacities.

Whatever momentum might have existed for climate change legislation disappeared in the Senate. What remained of the norms of civility in the Senate had disappeared as a result of the contentious battles over other significant pieces of legislation, including the American Recovery and Reinvestment Act (2009), the Patient Protection and Affordable Care Act (2010), and the Dodd–Frank Wall Street Reform and Consumer Protection Act (2010), all of which were narrowly passed with strong Republican opposition. Heavy lobbying from the energy sector and the impending threat of a Republican surge in the upcoming 2010 midterm elections made it highly unlikely that Majority Leader Harry Reid (D-NV) could secure a filibuster-proof majority of 60 votes. The political calculus led Reid to withdraw from a Senate climate change bill written by Senators John Kerry (D-MA), Lindsay Graham (R-SC), and Joseph Lieberman (I-CT), urging his colleagues to pursue a piecemeal approach in the next Congress.[96] In the 2010 midterm elections, Republicans gained 63 House seats—the largest seat change in a midterm election since 1938—sufficient to gain control of the chamber. In the Senate, Republicans claimed six seats, enough to end the Democrats' filibuster-proof majority (historically unprecedented Republican gains came at the state level as well, leaving the GOP in charge of a majority of state legislatures and governorships).[97] If 2009–10 had provided a window of opportunity for new climate change legislation, that window had now closed abruptly.

The second component in the climate change policy involved the promotion of investments that would further the campaign promise of promoting the transition to a low-carbon, green economy. The American Recovery and Reinvestment Act of 2009 provided $787 billion in fiscal stimulus, some of which was used to meet this objective. The Act provided $60 billion in direct spending and $30 billion in tax credits to promote energy efficiency, renewable energy generation, modernization of the electricity grid, mass transit, and carbon capture and sequestration.[98] As the Council of Economic Advisors explained:

> These Recovery Act investments were carefully chosen and provide a soup-to-nuts approach across a spectrum of energy-related activities, ranging from taking advantage of existing opportunities to improve energy efficiency to investing in innovative high-technology solutions that are currently little more than ideas.

The CEA framed the environmental spending as part of the larger recovery program that would simultaneously reduce dependence on oil—thereby enhancing national security—while promoting new jobs in emerging industries that promised to "put the United States on a path to becoming a global leader in clean energy."[99]

Third, in addition to investments under the Recovery Act, President Obama moved unilaterally to achieve an agreement for significant increases in the Corporate Average Fuel Economy (or CAFE) standards. Under the Energy Independence and Security Act (2007), Congress required automakers to achieve 35 miles per gallon by 2020, and authorized the Secretary of Transportation to issue regulations for incremental increases toward this goal. In 2009, President Obama convened representatives of the automobile industry and the United Auto Workers and negotiated an agreement to reach the 2020 goals by 2016, and for Transportation and the EPA to promulgate a CAFE and greenhouse gas standard. Two years later, the White House negotiated a second agreement, this time with a goal of 54.5 miles per gallon by 2025. There were critics in Congress, dismissive of the President's unilateralism and circumvention of the process established in 2007. But President Obama celebrated his accomplishment in achieving a near doubling of fuel efficiency without legislation. As Bruce Oppenheimer notes, Obama's success in aggregating interests "as a means of undercutting potential congressional opposition" could be explained, in part, by a single fact. "Like the president, these groups preferred working with the executive branch rather than struggling with the delay and uncertainty of the contemporary congressional process."[100]

A fourth element of the climate strategy was simultaneously progressing on the regulatory front. In 2007, the Supreme Court ruled that greenhouse gases are air pollutants under the Clean Air Act, and ordered the EPA to determine whether they posed a danger to public health or welfare. The Bush administration was slow to respond, publishing an Advanced Notice of Proposed Rulemaking in July 2008. By April 2009, the Obama EPA published its proposed endangerment findings in the *Federal Register* and following public hearings and more than 380,000 public comments, it published its final endangerment finding in the *Federal Register* in December 2009.[101] At the very least, the foundations were now in place to regulate climate change under the provisions of the decades-old Clean Air Act Amendments, and in 2010 the EPA issued new regulations for motor vehicles and stationary sources. While large stationary sources (like large industrial facilities and utilities) were clearly subject to regulation previously, the EPA decided to extend regulation to smaller sources. Under the Clean Air Act, thresholds for stationary sources (at least 100 or 250 tons of emissions per year, depending on facility type) if applied to greenhouse gases, would embroil the agency in endless permitting. Its solution was to tailor the thresholds to 75,000 to 100,000 tons per year, despite the fact that this was outside of the discretionary authority granted the agency by Congress.[102] The regulations were challenged in court and, ultimately, the Supreme Court issued a decision that recognized the authority to regulate larger stationary sources, but invalidated the attempt to expand regulations to smaller sources and rejected the agency's exercise of its discretionary authority. As the majority decision noted: "An agency has no power to 'tailor' legislation to bureaucratic policy goals by rewriting unambiguous statutory terms. Agencies exercise discretion only in the interstices created by statutory silence or ambiguity."[103]

The House of Representatives sought to preempt these efforts through legislation. For example, in April 2011, the House passed a bill barring the use of the Clean Air Act Amendments to regulate emission of greenhouse gases. It died in the Senate.[104] The upper chamber's ability to block legislation was depleted, however, when the 2014 midterm elections brought a new GOP majority in the Senate. Nonetheless, the Obama administration moved unilaterally. In August 2015, the administration unveiled its Clean Power Plan, which required states to submit implementation plans for emissions reductions in their electric power plants no later than September 2018, to bring carbon emissions to 32 percent below 2005 levels by 2030. Although the Plan provided states with great flexibility in meeting these goals, a failure of states to submit state implementation plans could result in a far less flexible federal implementation plan.[105] As one might expect, the Plan attracted legal challenges from industry and states, claiming that the EPA was exceeding its statutory authority as granted under the Clean Air Act Amendments of 1990. The Supreme Court took the unusual action of issuing a stay, essentially prohibiting the EPA from implementing the Plan until the US Circuit Court of Appeals for the DC Circuit could resolve the legal issues. As Jonathan H. Adler observed: "an unprecedented assertion of regulatory authority may itself have justified an unprecedented exercise of the Court's jurisdiction to stay the agency's action."[106]

While the EPA's authority was challenged by the House and in the courts, the agency was also forced to bear dramatic budget cuts. With the economy in a tepid recovery, the House began to emphasize spending reductions, and this would have significant implications for levels of spending for the EPA. As noted above, the Obama administration had increased the EPA's budget to $10.3 billion (2010). Thereafter, the budget would enter a period of steep decline (e.g., by 2013, the budget had fallen to a low of $7.9 billion, with modest increases in subsequent years). The budget cuts necessitated reductions in staffing, from 17,417 in 2010 to 15,335 five years later,[107] involving buyouts for top civil servants and midlevel managers, including those involved in enforcement. These cuts impacted on a host of other common indicators of agency action, including inspections, criminal cases opened, and hazardous waste cleanups. While the EPA claimed to be better focusing its resources, as Shawn Zeller noted, it was "planning a new approach to enforcement that aims to persuade companies and local governments to comply with the law, rather than go after them for breaking it."[108]

By the end of the Obama presidency, the hope for a comprehensive new regulatory statute addressing the most important environmental challenge had dissipated. Efforts to address the climate through rulemaking on the antiquated Clean Air Act Amendments were mired in the courts. The Office of Energy and Climate Change Policy in the White House had been shuttered. Budgets and staffing had been cut significantly. Although the National Environmental Performance Track and Climate Leaders were eliminated, the EPA would continue to rely on voluntary programs, many of which had now been in place for decades. With no new climate legislation forthcoming, the administration created a new Center for Corporate Climate Leadership that appeared to continue the work of the Bush-era Climate Leaders, which had been initiated to continue the work of the Clinton-era Climate Wise. It joined a long list of existing industry partnerships on climate and energy that included: the Combined Heat and Power Partnership, Energy Star, Green Chill, the Green Power Partnership, the High Global Warming Potential Gases Voluntary Programs (which include the Voluntary Aluminum Industrial Partnership and the Sulfur Hexafluoride Emissions Reduction Partnership for Electric Power Systems), the Methane Reduction Voluntary Programs (which include AgSTAR, Natural Gas STAR, the Global Methane Initiative, the Coalbed Methane Outreach Program, and the Landfill Methane Outreach Program), the Transportation and Air Quality Voluntary Programs (which include the National Clean Diesel Campaign, the SmartWay Transport Partnership, and Clean School Bus USA), the Responsible Appliance Disposal Program, WasteWise, and WaterSense.[109]

Conclusion

In 1995, the EPA celebrated its twenty-fifth anniversary and noted its accomplishments. Since 1970, the emissions of the six criteria air pollutants fell by an average of 24 percent. Particulate matter decreased by 78 percent, and lead emissions by 98 percent. The improvements were impressive, given that during the same period the economy grew by 90 percent, population by 27 percent, and vehicle miles driven by 111 percent. Although the Clean Water Act declared a goal of fishable and swimmable waters by 1978 and zero discharges by 1983, these goals remained elusive. Nonetheless, some 60 percent of surveyed waters were clean enough for fishing and swimming. There were other improvements in toxic wastes and pesticides, all documented by the agency. While the EPA had failed to meet the most ambitious goals established in the early years of the environmental decade, it had accomplished much, particularly given the complexity, costs, and political contestation.[110]

Much of this success could be attributed to the original institutional design decisions. Congress, committed to environmental protection and wary of capture and excessive presidential interference, wrote detailed statutes and imposed demanding implementation timetables. Even when the EPA faced its greatest challenges during the 1980s, the original design decisions limited the extent to which the agency could be deregulated by administrative means. With supportive public opinion and congressional support, the agency would survive, even if it did not flourish. Of course, the 1990s would offer a new set of challenges as Republicans claimed control of Congress, steadfast in their opposition to an expansion of regulatory authority and resources.

The EPA used the opportunity of its anniversary to promote reinvention and new approaches to environmental protection, including the reliance on "consensus-based" solutions: "EPA is bringing industry representatives, environmental groups, concerned citizens and local governments to the negotiating table. With EPA as moderator, these groups are working to resolve their differences and agree on mutually acceptable environmental solutions."[111] This report, issued the year that the new Republican majority assumed unified control of the House and Senate, could not anticipate that the consensus-based solutions would be one of the few ways in which the reach of the EPA could be extended in an age of polarization and gridlock. It could not anticipate that by the forty-fifth anniversary in 2015, the compendium of significant environmental statutes would remain largely the same as it had at that time. By that date, the

Clean Air Act Amendments of 1990 would be celebrating its twenty-fifth anniversary as the last major statutory expansion of EPA authority.

Notes

1 Robert A. Kagan, *Adversarial Legalism: The American Way of Law* (Cambridge, MA: Harvard University Press, 2001), 188.

2 An earlier version of this argument was presented in Marc Allen Eisner, "Environmental Protection in the United States: Fragmentation, Rigidity, and the Problems of Institutional Design," paper delivered at "Governing Sustainable Development: Evolution of Environmental Administration in Europe and the United States," Science Po, Paris, September 21, 2012.

3 Richard Nixon, "Statement about the National Environmental Policy Act of 1969," January 1, 1970. Available at www.presidency.ucsb.edu/ws/?pid=2557.

4 Richard Nixon, "Annual Message to the Congress on the State of the Union, January 22, 1970." Available at www.presidency.ucsb.edu/ws/index.php?pid=2921#axzz1Lrd00CYq.

5 President's Advisory Council on Executive Organization, "Federal Organization for Environmental Protection," April 29, 1970. Available at www.epa.gov/history/org/origins/ash.htm.

6 Robert Gillette, "Environmental Protection Agency: Chaos or 'Creative Tension?'" *Science* 173, 3998 (1971): 705.

7 Alfred A. Marcus, "EPA's Organizational Structure," *Law and Contemporary Problems* 54, 4 (1991): 23.

8 Joseph Krevac, quoted in Richard A. Harris and Sidney M. Milkis, *The Politics of Regulatory Change: A Tale of Two Agencies*, 2nd ed. (New York: Oxford University Press, 1996), 231.

9 Gillette, "Environmental Protection Agency," 706, 703.

10 Evan J. Ringquist, *Environmental Protection at the State Level: Politics and Progress in Controlling Pollution* (Armonk, NY: M. E. Sharpe, 1993), 38.

11 John D. Graham, "The Failure of Agency-Forcing: The Regulation of Airborne Carcinogens under Section 112 of the Clean Air Act," *Duke Law Journal* 1985 (1985): 101.

12 See David Gerard and Lester B. Lave, "Implementing Technology-Forcing Policies: The 1970 Clean Air Act Amendments and the Introduction of Advanced Automotive Emissions Controls," *Technology Forecasting and Social Change* 72 (2005): 761–78.

13 Abigail English, "State Implementation Plans and Air Quality Enforcement," *Ecology Law Quarterly* 4 (1975): 631.

14 "The EPA's Power to Establish National Effluent Limitations for Existing Water Pollution Sources," *University of Pennsylvania Law Review* 125, 1 (1976): 129–30.

15 116 Congressional Record 32901–32902 (1970).

16 Richard B. Stewart, "The Reformation of American Administrative Law," *Harvard Law Review* 88, 8 (1975), 1670, 1728.

17 Joseph L. Smith, "Congress Opens the Courthouse Doors: Statutory Changes to Judicial Review under the Clean Air Act," *Political Research Quarterly* 58, 1 (2005): 141–44.

18 William D. Ruckelshaus, "William D. Ruckelshaus: Oral History Interview." Available at www.epa.gov/history/publications/print/ruck.htm.

19 Ringquist, *Environmental Protection at the State Level*, 55–56.

20 Walter A. Rosenbaum, *Environmental Politics and Policy*, 6th ed. (Washington DC: CQ Press, 2005), 193.

21 See Marc K. Landy, Marc J. Roberts, and Stephen R. Thomas, *The Environmental Protection Agency: Asking the Wrong Questions* (New York: Oxford University Press,

1990), 30–42, Marc Allen Eisner, *Regulatory Politics in Transition* (Baltimore, MD: Johns Hopkins University Press, 1993), 147–50.

22 *Sierra Club v. Ruckelshaus*, 344 F. Supp. 253 (D.D.C. 1972).

23 *Natural Resources Defense Council v. Environmental Protection Agency*, 489 F.2d 390 (5th Cir. 1974).

24 R. Shep Melnick, *Regulation and the Courts:The Case of the Clean Air Act* (Washington DC:The Brookings Institution, 1983), 60–61.

25 "The E.P.A. Wasteland," *New York Times*, February 26, 1983, 22.

26 "Confirmation Seems Likely for Administrator of E.P.A," *New York Times*, May 2, 1981, 10, Philip Shabecoff, "New Environmental Chief Vows to Lift Regulatory Burden," *New York Times*, June 20, 1981, 36.

27 Environmental Protection Agency, EPA's Budget and Spending. Available at www.epa.gov/planandbudget/budget.

28 Phil Wisman, "EPA History (1970–1985)." Available at www.epa.gov/aboutepa/epa-history-1970-1985#burford.

29 Philip Shabecoff, "Environmental Agency Chief Announces Reorganization," *New York Times*, June 13, 1981, 8.

30 Joel A. Mintz, *Enforcement at the EPA: High Stakes and Hard Choices*, rev. ed. (Austin, TX: University of Texas Press, 2012), 58.

31 Ibid., 59.

32 This event marked the first time that Congress had held the head of an executive agency or department in contempt. For a review of this event, see Ronald L. Claveloux, "Conflict between Executive Privilege and Congressional Oversight: The Gorsuch Controversy," *Duke Law Journal* 1983 (1983): 1333–58.

33 Philip Shabecoff, "Plans to Weaken the Clean Air Act Charged to E.P.A.: Democrats Voice Concern," *New York Times*, September 4, 1981, 1.

34 Philip Shabecoff, "Administration Seeks Eased Rules for Industries in Clean Water Act," *New York Times*, April 22, 1982, 1.

35 See "EPA: A Retrospective, 1970–1990." Available at www.epa.gov/aboutepa/epa-retrospective-1970-1990.

36 Mintz, *Enforcement at the EPA*, 70–72.

37 Philip Shabecoff, "Reagan and Environment: To Many, a Stalemate," *New York Times*, January 2, 1989.

38 Harris and Milkis, *The Politics of Regulatory Change*, 261.

39 Environmental Protection Agency, *Summary of the 1994 Budget* (Washington DC: Environmental Protection Agency Office of the Comptroller, 1993), 10.

40 See Mintz, *Enforcement at the EPA*, 87–103.

41 See Bruce Ackerman and William Hassler, *Clean Coal, Dirty Air* (New Haven, CT: Yale University Press, 1981).

42 See Theresa A. Gullo and Janet M. Kelly, "Federal Unfunded Mandate Reform: A First-Year Retrospective," *Public Administration Review* 58, 5 (1998): 379–87.

43 Bob Benenson, "Senate Passes Up 'Freeze' Plan, Substitutes Regulatory Review," *CQ Weekly*, April 1, 1995, 933–34.

44 J. Peyton Doub, *The Endangered Species Act: History, Implementation, Successes and Controversies* (Boca Raton, FL: CRC Press, 2012), 215.

45 For a detailed discussion of this Act and the strengths and weaknesses of risk assessment methodology, see Jeff Gimpel, "Risk Assessment and Cost Benefit Act of 1995: Regulatory Reform and the Legislation of Science," *Journal of Legislation* 23, 1 (1997): 61–91.

46 Bob Benenson, "House Panels Take Quick Action on Risk Assessment Provisions," *CQ Weekly*, February 11, 1995, 450.

47 Bob Benenson, "Complaints Don't Delay Action on Regulatory Overhaul Bills," *CQ Weekly*, February 18, 1995, 520.

48 Benenson, "Senate Passes Up 'Freeze' Plan."

49 Joel A. Mintz, "Neither the Best of Times Nor the Worst of Times: EPA Enforcement During the Clinton Administration," *Environmental Law Reporter* 35 (2005): 1039–41.

50 Data from Environmental Protection Agency, *Budget Summary*, various years.

51 Mintz, "Neither the Best of Times Nor the Worst of Times," 1040.

52 On reinvention at EPA, see Daniel J. Fiorina, *The New Environmental Regulation* (Cambridge, MA: The MIT Press, 2006), 121–55.

53 Bill Clinton and Al Gore, *Reinventing Environmental Regulation* (Washington, DC: The National Performance Review, 1995), 1–3.

54 Ibid., 3.

55 Environmental Protection Agency, *EPA Strategic Plan* (Washington DC: EPA, 1997), 11.

56 See General Accounting Office, *Regulatory Reinvention: EPA's Common Sense Initiative Needs an Improved Operating Framework and Progress Measures*, RCED-97-164 (Washington DC: General Accounting Office, 1997).

57 Cary Coglianese and Laurie K. Allen, "Building Sector-Based Consensus: A Review of the EPA's Common Sense Initiative," Faculty Scholarship, Paper 103 (2003), 12. Available at http://scholarship.law.upenn.edu/faculty_scholarship/103.

58 Environmental Protection Agency, *Partners for the Environment: A Catalogue of the Agency's Partnership Programs* (Washington DC: Environmental Protection Agency, 1998), 41.

59 This discussion of Project XL draws on Marc Allen Eisner, *Governing the Environment: The Transformation of Environmental Protection* (Boulder, CO: Lynne Rienner, 2007), 103–7.

60 See Alfred A. Marcus, Donald A. Geffen, and Ken Sexton, *Reinventing Environmental Regulation: Lessons from Project XL* (Washington DC: Resources for the Future, 2002).

61 See Jerry Speir, "EMSs and Tiered Regulation: Getting the Deal Right," in *Regulating From the Inside: Can Environmental Management Systems Achieve Policy Goals?*, ed. Cary Coglianese and Jennifer Nash (Washington DC: Resources for the Future, 2001), 198–219.

62 Environmental Protection Agency, *Partners for the Environment: Boosting Your Bottom Line* (Washington DC: Environmental Protection Agency, 2000), 2.

63 Ibid., 4, 3.

64 Environmental Protection Agency, *Partnership Programs: Basic Information*. Available at www.epa.gov/partners/about/index.htm.

65 See Eisner, *Governing the Environment*, 153–75.

66 Environmental Protection Agency, *Partners for the Environment: A Catalogue of the Agency's Partnership Programs*, 11.

67 See William A. Pizer, Richard Morgenstern, and Jhih-Shyang Shih, "The Performance of Voluntary Climate Programs: Climate Wise and 1605(b)," RFF Discussion Paper (Washington, DC: Resources for the Future, 2010) and Eric W. Welch, Allan Mazur, and Stuart Bretschneider, "Voluntary Behavior by Electric Utilities: Levels of Adoption and Contribution of the Climate Challenge Program to the Reduction of Carbon Dioxide," *Journal of Policy Analysis and Management*, 19, 3 (2000): 407–25.

68 Magali A. Delmas and Maria J. Montes-Sancho, "Voluntary Agreements to Improve Environmental Quality: Are Late Joiners the Free Riders?" University of California, Santa Barbara, ISBER Paper 07, 2007.

69 See Phi Cong Hoang, William McGuire, and Aseem Prakash, "Is There Life after Death? The Enduring Effects of the 33/50 Program on Emissions Reductions," paper presented at the Agricultural and Applied Economics Association Annual Meeting, Boston, Massachusetts, July 31–August 2, 2016.

70 Jorge Rivera and Peter de Leon, "Is Greener Whiter? Voluntary Environmental Performance of Western Ski Areas," *The Policy Studies Journal*, 32, 3 (2004): 417–37.

71 Matthew Potoski and Aseem Prakash, "Green Clubs and Voluntary Governance: ISO 14001 and Firms' Regulatory Compliance," *American Journal of Political Science*, 49, 2 (2005): 235–48, and Matthew Potoski and Aseem Prakash, "Voluntary Environmental Programs: A Comparative Perspective," *Journal of Policy Analysis and Management*, 31, 1 (2012): 123–38.

72 Andrew A. King and Michael J. Lenox, "Industry Self-Regulation without Sanctions: The Chemical Industry's Responsible Care Program," *Academy of Management Journal*, 43, 4 (2000): 698–716, and Shanti Gamper-Rabindran and Stephen R. Finger, "Does Industry Self-Regulation Reduce Pollution? Responsible Care in the Chemical Industry," *Journal of Regulatory Economics*, 43, 1 (2013): 1–30.

73 See Mintz, "Neither the Best of Times Nor the Worst of Times," 10393, 10408–9.

74 See Cass R. Sunstein, *Risk and Reason: Safety, Law, and the Environment* (Cambridge, UK: Cambridge University Press, 2004), 153–90.

75 Joel A. Mintz, "Treading Water: A Preliminary Assessment of EPA Enforcement During the Bush II Administration," *Environmental Law Reporter*, 34 (2004): 10937–40, and Patrick Parenteau, "Anything Industry Wants: Environmental Policy under Bush II," *Duke Environmental Law and Policy Forum*, 14, 2 (2004): 373–75.

76 See Environmental Protection Agency, *A Program Guide for Climate Leaders* (Washington DC: Environmental Protection Agency, 2007).

77 Environmental Protection Agency, *ENERGY STAR and Other Climate Protection Partnerships: 2008 Annual Report* (Washington DC: Environmental Protection Agency, 2008), 39.

78 Environmental Protection Agency, *A Business Guide to U.S. EPA Climate Partnership Programs*, June 2008 (Washington DC: Environmental Protection Agency, 2008), 3.

79 Odile Blanchard, "The Bush Administration Climate Proposal: Rhetoric and Reality," CFE Policy Paper, March 2003, 12–13. Available at www.ifri.org/files/OB_Bush_Climate_Policy.pdf.

80 See Environmental Protection Agency, *Performance Track Program Guide* (Washington DC: Environmental Protection Agency, n.d.).

81 Environmental Protection Agency, *Performance Track Final Progress Report, May 2009* (Washington DC: Environmental Protection Agency, 2009), 1, 3.

82 Environmental Protection Agency, *Performance Track Program Guide*, 2.

83 Cary Coglianese and Jennifer Nash, "Performance Track's Postmortem: Lessons from the Rise and Fall of EPA's 'Flagship' Voluntary Program," *Harvard Environmental Law Review*, 38 (2014): 62.

84 Ibid., 61.

85 Environmental Protection Agency Office of Inspector General, *Partnership Programs May Expand EPA's Influence* (Washington DC: Environmental Protection Agency, 2006), 13.

86 Environmental Protection Agency Office of Inspector General, *Voluntary Programs Could Benefit from Internal Policy Controls and a Systematic Management Approach* (Washington DC: Environmental Protection Agency, 2007), 7.

87 Michael B. Gerrard, "McCain vs. Obama on Environment, Energy, and Resources," *Natural Resources and Environment*, 23, 2 (2008): 3–7.

88 Elizabeth Bomberg and Betsy Super, "The 2008 US Presidential Election: Obama and the Environment," *Environmental Politics*, 18, 3 (2009): 426.

89 EPA Budget Summary, various years. Calculations by author.

90 Margaret Kriz, "EPA is Back on the Job," *National Journal*, February 28, 2009, 15.

91 Environmental Protection Agency, *FY 2011 EPA Budget in Brief* (Washington DC: Environmental Protection Agency, 2010), 8.

92 Cary Coglianese and Jennifer Nash, "Performance Track's Postmortem: Lessons from the Rise and Fall of EPA's 'Flagship' Voluntary Program," *Harvard Environmental Law Review*, 38 (2014): 32.

93 www.epa.gov/climateleadership/documents/partners_letter_15sep2010.pdf.

94 Council of Economic Advisors, *Economic Report of the President* (Washington DC: Council of Economic Advisors, 2010), 254.

95 John M. Broder, "House Passes Bill to Address Threat of Climate Change," *New York Times*, June 26, 2009, A1.

96 Geof Koss, "The Price of the Climate Stalemate," *CQ Weekly*, September 20, 2010, 2157.

97 Jeremy P. Jacobs, "Devastation: GOP Picks Up 680 State Leg. Seats," National Journal Hotline On Call, November 4, 2010. Available at http://hotlineoncall.national journal.com/archives/2010/11/devastation-gop.php (accessed August 23, 2012).

98 See Jason Walsh, Josh Bivens, and Ethan Pollack, *Rebuilding Green: The American Recovery and Reinvestment Act and the Green Economy* (Washington DC: BlueGreen Alliance and the Economic Policy Institute, 2011).

99 Council of Economic Advisors, *Economic Report of the President* (Washington DC: Council of Economic Advisors, 2010), 243.

100 Bruce I. Oppenheimer, "It's Hard to Get Mileage Out of Congress: Struggling over CAFE Standards, 1973–2013," Center for the Study of Democratic Institutions Working Paper 3-2014 (Nashville, TN: Vanderbilt University, 2014), 29.

101 Environmental Protection Agency, "Timeline of EPA's Endangerment Finding." Available at www3.epa.gov/climatechange/Downloads/endangerment/Endangerment Finding_Timeline.pdf.

102 Peter Glaser, "Symposium: Can the EPA Really Rewrite a Statute? Really?" Scotusblog, February 4, 2014. Available at www.scotusblog.com/2014/02/symposium-can-the-epa-really-rewrite-a-statute-really/.

103 *Utility Air Regulatory Group v. Environmental Protection Agency*, 573 U.S.___ (2014), 21.

104 Geof Koss, "2011 Legislative Summary: EPA Regulatory Rollback," *CQ Weekly*, January 9, 2012, 35.

105 See Environmental Protection Agency, "Overview of the Clean Power Plan: Cutting Carbon Pollution from Power Plants." Available at www.epa.gov/sites/production/files/2015-08/documents/fs-cpp-overview.pdf.

106 Jonathan H. Adler, "Supreme Court puts the Brakes on the EPA's Clean Power Plan," *Washington Post*, February 9, 2016. Available at www.washingtonpost.com/news/volokh-conspiracy/wp/2016/02/09/supreme-court-puts-the-brakes-on-the-epas-clean-power-plan/.

107 EPA Budget Summary, various years.

108 Shawn Zeller, "For EPA, Budget Crunch Is Clear," *CQ Weekly*, March 3, 2014, 314.

109 Descriptions of these programs are available at www3.epa.gov/climatechange/EPAactivities/voluntaryprograms.html.

110 The Environmental Protection Agency, *The U.S. EPA's 25th Anniversary Report: 1970–1995*. Available at www.epa.gov/sites/production/files/documents/report.pdf.

111 Ibid., 58.

7

WORKPLACE SAFETY AND THE RETURN OF THE VOLUNTARY REGULATOR

In 1970, Congress passed the Occupational Safety and Health Act, creating the Occupational Safety and Health Administration (OSHA) and giving it the responsibility to promulgate and enforce regulations on an economy-wide basis. The new agency quickly became renowned for its adversarial relationship with business and became a politically potent symbol of regulatory zealotry. A 1979 analysis by the American Enterprise Institute's Michael Levin noted organized labor's protective stance toward the agency ("For the unions, OSHA is a religion. There is no middle ground") and decried OSHA's enforcement tactics ("treating all employers like criminals"). When speaking of reform, Levin wrote:

> OSHA clearly needs to give employers greater certainty that good performance will be recognized by reduced intervention. It should provide detailed information on major hazards and acceptable controls—and stand behind its advice. It should accept the fact that broad-scale improvement requires government, business, and workers to share responsibility, since no agency can do the job alone. And it should start measuring employers, as well as its own inspectors, by results rather than by compliance with mandatory procedures—admitting, in other words, that it is not omniscient and that there are many roads to the same end.[1]

Such reform proposals would find little traction in a Democratically controlled Congress that retained close links to organized labor and remained protective of the social regulatory advances of the 1970s.

More than four decades following the passage of the Occupational Safety and Health Act, Congress had failed to pass any significant new statutes to extend or update the law. From the 1990s onward, OSHA efforts to extend regulation via rulemaking was mired in procedural complexity and frequently hampered by appropriation riders that prohibited the collection of relevant data and specific rulemaking. Absent substantial increases in resources and new statutory authority, the agency was forced to rely ever more heavily on the Voluntary Protection Program, introduced by the Reagan administration. Employers that participated in the program received lower inspection priority if they implemented their own safety and health management systems to prevent workplace injuries and diseases. Inspections, when they occurred, were often conducted by special government employees—corporate health and safety officers who were deputized to conduct inspections while having their expenses and salaries paid by their employers. Jordan Barab, President Obama's Deputy Assistant Secretary of Labor, addressed the program participants in 2015, thanking them for their "living proof that maintaining a safe workplace is not only a moral imperative, it's also good for the long-term bottom line."[2] Reform had come through administrative means, and ironically along the lines suggested by some of OSHA's harshest critics in the 1970s.

Protecting Occupational Safety and Health

Until the 1960s, the regulation of workplace safety was largely a byproduct of the incentives created by a patchwork of state-level workers' compensation laws layered upon the common law regime. State administration was uneven and reactive, focusing on compensating injured parties after the fact rather than preventing damages in the first instance. The focus on injuries, moreover, did little to address the problems of diseases that resulted from exposure to chemical agents in the workplace. The scientific foundations of occupational health policy were simply beyond the analytical capacity of state workers' compensation programs and absent these foundations, the causal relationship between occupational exposure and disease was difficult if not impossible to prove.

Although the late 1960s witnessed a rise in the number of workplace deaths and injuries, the issue failed to attract much attention from interest groups or issue advocates. Whatever references appeared in President Johnson's speeches, for example, were placed there by one of his speech writers, Robert Hardesty, at the urging of his brother, a bureaucrat working on occupational safety and health in the Department of Health, Education, and Welfare. Ultimately, a proposal for new workplace regulations made it on to the president's legislative program and hearings were held in Congress in 1968, but stiff business opposition was sufficient to quell the passage of legislation.[3]

Things would change rapidly in the next few years. In November 1968, an explosion at a Consolidation Company coal mine in Farmington, West Virginia, claimed seventy-eight victims. As the *New York Times* reported, the "explosions and fires that shattered and scorched Consol's 'modern' mine in West Virginia caused shock waves in Washington." Interior Secretary Stewart L. Udall called for a public conference on coal mine safety, summoning "all the critics, all the crippled angry human castoffs of the coal industry."[4] The 1968 mining disaster raised the salience of occupational safety and health more broadly, and the AFL-CIO increasingly joined forces with the environmental movement to secure a legislative victory.[5] In little more than a year, Congress had passed the Coal Mine Safety and Health Act of 1969, which created the Mining Enforcement and Safety Administration in the Department of Interior and increased the federal regulation of coal mines.[6] While the new act provided additional protections for mine workers, attention would soon turn to broader protection for American workers.

Upon assuming office, President Nixon promoted the cause of occupational safety and health and proposed his own legislative package. In a message to Congress on August 6, 1969, Nixon presented in detail the costs that were being incurred by the nation:

> Consider these facts. Every year in this country, some fourteen thousand deaths can be attributed to work-related injuries or illnesses. Because of accidents or diseases sustained on the job, some 250 million man-days of labor are lost annually. The most important consequence of these losses is the human tragedy which results when an employee—often the head of a family—is struck down. In addition, the economy loses millions of dollars in unrealized production and millions more must be used to pay workmen's compensation benefits and medical expenses. It is interesting to note that in the last five years, the number of man-days lost because of work-related injuries has been ten times the number lost because of strikes.

Nixon argued that policy had failed to keep pace with technological changes. He promised new legislation that could "correct some of the important deficiencies of earlier approaches. It will go beyond the limited 'accident' orientation of the past, giving greater attention to health considerations, which are often difficult to perceive and which have often been overlooked." It will separate standard-setting and enforcement and "provide a flexible mechanism which can react quickly to the new technologies of tomorrow."[7]

Nixon's embrace of occupational safety and health likely reflected a larger political calculus involving several factors. First, because the issue was already on the agenda, Nixon's active participation could allow him greater influence in shaping the outcome. Second, there was a larger goal of garnering the support of organized labor as part of a "blue collar strategy" designed to elevate the Republican Party's appeal to working-class voters.[8] But Nixon also appeared to want to connect workplace health and safety to environmental protection. As noted in Chapter 6, Nixon had adopted the cause of the environment for political reasons. This strategy spilled over into Nixon's message on occupational safety and health:

during their working years most American workers spend nearly a quarter of their time at their jobs. For them, the quality of the workplace is one of the most important of environmental questions. The protection of that quality is a critical matter for government attention.

To add to the salience of the issue, Nixon Labor Secretary George P. Shultz informed the House Committee "during the past four years more Americans have been killed where they work than in Vietnam."[9]

Designing Institutions for Occupational Safety and Health

The debates on occupational safety and health quickly turned to questions of institutional design. Where should the new regulatory authority be vested? What role should the federal government play relative to the states? In Nixon's message to Congress, he had called for the creation of an independent five-member National Occupational Safety and Health Board to be appointed by the president with the advice and consent of the Senate. This board would have the authority to promulgate as "national consensus standards" the standards already developed by "nationally-recognized public or private standard-setting organizations." Where such standards did not exist or were deemed insufficient, the board could "break new ground after full hearings." If the Secretary of Labor or Health, Education, and Welfare (HEW) objected to the board's decisions, implementation would be delayed unless a majority of the board continued to support the standard. Authority would be further decentralized given the role Nixon envisioned for the states. The states would be invited to develop their own plans

> for expanding and implementing their own occupational safety and health programs . . . . When a State presents a plan which provides at least as much protection to the worker as the Federal plan, then the federal standard administration will give way to the State administration, with the Federal government assuming up to 50 percent of that State's costs.

As for federal enforcement, responsibility would be vested with the Secretary of Labor. If the Secretary believed that board standards had been violated, he would "ask employers . . . to comply with them voluntarily." If violations continued, hearings could be held before the board, which would be empowered to issue cease and desist orders that could be enforced via the court system. The board would not have criminal jurisdiction.[10]

Whereas industry had successfully thwarted new regulatory legislation during the Johnson administration, the US Chamber of Commerce now threw its support behind the administration's far weaker proposal and the successive bills that the administration sponsored in hopes of limiting the powers of the new agency and keeping it independent of the Department of Labor. Organized labor and public interest advocates, in contrast, feared that Nixon's independent board would likely become captured by industry. As the AFL-CIO's legislative director noted, the Nixon board would "place management-oriented professional organizations in a commanding position over the crucial area of standard setting."[11] From labor's perspective, standard-setting should be located in the Department of Labor—an institutional home that would better ensure that organized labor's interests would be elevated. Moreover, federal standards should be mandatory rather than a last resort for states that failed to develop their own programs.

Ultimately, when Congress passed the Occupational Safety and Health Act (OSH Act) of 1970, it varied significantly from the original Nixon proposal. Section 5 (a)—the "general duty clause"—stated that each employer "shall furnish to each of his employees employment and a place of employment which are free from recognized hazards that are causing or likely to cause death or serious physical harm to his employees" and "shall comply with occupational safety and health standards promulgated under this act." As Charles Noble explains:

> The OSH Act codified a new, more radical, vision of worker rights. Conventional liberal ideology linked health and safety to individual, voluntary action in markets. But the OSH Act created a universal and substantive right to safety and health. Employers could not buy the opportunity to risk workers' health and safety, despite some workers' willingness to sell it. Moreover, this right was enjoyed by all workers regardless of their market position, income, or occupation.[12]

The contrast with the earlier patchwork of policies was striking. Rather than simply providing monetary payments for injuries *ex post* (the workers' compensation model), the focus turned to prevention. Rather than placing responsibility for safety on the workers, the responsibility was assigned to the employer. Under the general duty clause, the entitlement to a safe workplace had been extended to all private sector employees in firms engaged in interstate commerce.

Authority to set health and safety standards was vested in a new agency, the Occupational Safety and Health Administration. In a major defeat for the Nixon administration, OSHA was placed in the Department of Labor. Formal authority for the promulgation and enforcement of new standards was assigned to the Secretary of Labor and OSHA, which was placed under the direction of an assistant secretary, a presidential appointee requiring Senate approval. Yet, in a concession to the opposition, the larger institutional structure was quite fragmented. The National Institute for Occupational Safety and Health (NIOSH), formerly the Bureau of Occupational Safety and Health, was given the authority to develop and recommend new standards. Rather than placing NIOSH in the Department of Labor, it remained in the Department of Health, Education, and Welfare. The Act also created the independent, quasi-judicial Occupational Safety and Health Review Commission (OSHRC) to adjudicate disputes on enforcement decisions arising between OSHA and employers. A new advisory body, the National Advisory Committee on Occupational Safety and Health, was established to work with the secretaries of Labor and Health, Education, and Welfare. It was to be staffed by representatives of labor, business, the public, and experts in the field of occupational safety and health.[13]

Under the OSH Act, the new agency had broad rulemaking powers. It could initiate the standard-setting process on its own initiative, or in response to recommendations of NIOSH or petitions filed by state and local governments, nationally recognized standard associations, or the organizational representatives of labor or employers. Given that the OSH Act Section 6(b) required a "public hearing" on request of "any interested person," the standard-setting process provided an important access point for organized labor. While normal standard-setting would be governed by the Administrative Procedure Act, OSHA was authorized to issue temporary emergency standards if it believed that workers were in "grave danger." Temporary standards had to be published in the *Federal Register* and would constitute a proposed permanent standard for subsequent rulemaking, which had to be completed within six months. In the hope of accelerating the standard-setting process, Congress authorized the Secretary of Labor to promulgate, during the first two years, any "national consensus standard" (i.e., standards established by nationally recognized standard-producing organization) or "established Federal standard" without going through the notice-and-comment rulemaking mandated by the Administrative Procedure Act.[14]

This legislative function—standard-setting—was combined with an executive function: enforcement. Under the OSH Act, inspections were authorized without advance notice. Anyone giving unauthorized advanced notice of inspections could be fined up to $10,000, imprisoned for six months, or both. Under the OSH Act, the penalties for violations were relatively insignificant (up to $1,000 per violation), with larger penalties ($10,000) for "willful" or repeated violations or failures to correct a violation (up to $1,000 per day). However, a conviction on a "willful" violation that resulted in death could be met with a fine of up to $10,000, six months imprisonment, or both.[15]

As noted above, the Nixon administration initially envisioned an independent National Occupational Safety and Health Board and a deference to state programs. Although Nixon lost on the first issue, a prominent role for the states was retained. This was somewhat of an irony given that federal action was largely a response to the perceived inadequacy and unevenness of state efforts. But given the number of regulated workplaces, state enforcement was a practical necessity. Under the OSH Act, states were permitted to implement standards via their own programs if they were "at least as effective" as their federal counterpart. The approval of state programs would also be contingent on various components that mirrored the federal program (e.g., guaranteed right of access for inspectors, no advance notice of inspections, adequate legal authority and funding). States were given incentives to develop their own programs through federal funding of one-half of their operating costs.[16]

Under the OSH Act, workers and their representatives were given a number of rights. They could participate in standard-setting, have access to agency findings and the right to appeal decisions to OSHRC. Moreover, they had the right to request OSHA inspections and to be present during the inspections. They were also empowered to report violations of the standards or the general duty clause to OSHA without having their identities revealed to the employer.[17] Labor unions responded quickly to the provisions of the OSH Act. The AFL-CIO's Industrial Department established a new Department of Health, Safety, and Environmental Affairs to provide technical support to its affiliated unions, many of which employed full-time health and safety directors following the passage of the Act. Moreover, in the wake of the OSH Act, safety and health guarantees were incorporated into union contracts for the first time, most significantly in the United Auto Workers contracts with Chrysler, General Motors, and the Ford Motor Company.[18]

Standard-Setting in a Procedural Cage

In the 1970s, Congress passed exhaustively detailed statutes for environmental protection, mandating pollution control and mitigation on a media-specific basis. What differences existed on an industry-by-industry basis could be addressed through the permitting process. In occupational safety and health, a somewhat different strategy was required. Given the diversity of conditions of employment and the consequent need to develop more specific rules, Congress placed a much heavier reliance on the rulemaking process to develop health and safety standards. In implementing its mandate, OSHA encountered significant procedural hurdles in the rulemaking process that became only greater over time. Congress imposed some of the hurdles via the OSH Act and subsequent legislation. Others were imposed by the courts or by presidents via executive order. The end result was a highly protracted policy process that generated enormous delays, leading some to suggest that the original mandate is unworkable absent statutory change.[19]

Under the OSH Act (§ 655 (b)(5)), the Secretary of Labor is directed to

> set the standard which most adequately assures, to the extent feasible, on the basis of the best available evidence, that no employee will suffer material impairment of health or functional capacity even if such employee has regular exposure to the hazard dealt with by such standard for the period of his working life.

Under a series of decisions, this section was interpreted as requiring both a finding that current exposure levels posed a significant risk and that the risk would be significantly reduced by the standard. Moreover, the Court determined that standards must be technologically and economically feasible.[20] The technological feasibility of a given standard may require investigating through fieldwork whether favored technologies can be applied on an industry-specific basis. With respect to the issue of economic feasibility, OSHA must determine whether the standard is compatible with long-term profitability and competitiveness. This, in turn, involves the analysis of information gained through fieldwork at individual worksites and industry-wide surveys. Under the Paperwork Reduction Act of 1980, the OMB must approve these kinds of surveys, after a period of public comment.

Once OSHA has arrived at a determination that the risk is significant and can be reduced by a standard that is both technologically and economically feasible, it must comply with the provisions of Executive Order 12866 (1993). As noted in Chapter 4, all significant rules with an impact greater than $100 million must be subjected to a detailed cost–benefit analysis that is submitted to the OMB-OIRA for review. Proposed rules with effects that exceed a threshold of $500 million must have the scientific analysis that serves as a foundation for the rule subjected to a peer review process. If the rule would have a significant impact on small businesses, additional review requirements come into play. Under the Small Business Regulatory Enforcement Fairness Act of 1996, if it is determined that a proposed standard could have a significant economic impact on small entities, OSHA is required to consult a Small Business Advocacy Review Panel, with representatives of small businesses and officials from OMB-OIRA and Small Business Administration's Office of Advocacy.

Once these review processes are completed successfully and the agency has OMB approval, it is finally permitted to publish a Notice of Proposed Rulemaking in the *Federal Register*. Under the OSH Act, the agency must convene public hearings upon request. In practice, this has become an obligatory part of the process, complete with the submission of evidence, testimony, and cross-examination, under the supervision of an administrative law judge. Once the hearings are concluded, OSHA considers the testimony and evidence, along with any additional data that is subsequently submitted as part of the rulemaking docket, and completes a final standard. The standard is again submitted to the OMB before being published in the *Federal Register*.

Thus, while Congress granted OSHA broad rulemaking powers, new standards of judicial review (introduced in the early 1980s), new regulatory review requirements (introduced in 1981, with significant revisions in 1993), and the need to subject rules that affect small businesses to an additional stage of consultation (introduced in 1996), have complicated and elongated the process. In 2012, the Government Accountability Office conducted a review of the 58 significant health and safety standards issued between 1981 and 2010. It found that it took an average of 93 months (7 years and 9 months) to develop and issue a standard. Strikingly—but not surprisingly, given the discussion in

Chapter 5—the 1990s were particularly difficult. During the decade of the 1980s, OSHA finalized 24 standards, requiring an average of 70 months (6 years and 10 months) to complete. By contrast, in the decade of the 1990s, OSHA finalized 23 significant standards, and these required an average of 118 months (9 years and 10 months to complete). In the next decade, the average time to finalize a rule fell to an average of 91 months (7 years and 7 months), but the number of significant standards had fallen to 10. None of this takes into account standards that remained mired in the development process or were abandoned before being finalized.[21]

Under §6 (c) of the OSH Act, the agency is authorized to issue emergency standards if workers are exposed to a grave danger and the standard is necessary to protect workers. The standard must be published in the *Federal Register* and is effective immediately. The emergency standard, once published, serves as the proposed permanent standard. However, under the OSH Act, OSHA is then required to issue a permanent standard within 6 months. Between 1971 and 1983, OSHA used these powers sparingly and issued nine emergency standards. Of the nine emergency standards, five ran afoul of the courts and were stayed or invalidated. Since 1983 when OSHA unsuccessfully issued an emergency standard for asbestos, the agency has issued no emergency standards. Given the difficulties encountered in the courts and the protracted nature of the rulemaking process, OSHA's ability to issue emergency temporary standards within the statutory timeframe has been largely vanquished.

The slow pace of OSHA rulemaking—an average of 7 years and 9 months—is particularly striking when viewed against the rapidity of change in the economy that OSHA is charged with regulating. As Thomas McGarity, Rena Steinzor, Sidney Shapiro, and Matthew Shudtz observe:

> OSHA's rulemaking process is in need of drastic reforms. At the same time chemical manufacturers are creating about 700 new chemicals each year, OSHA is drafting new health standards at a rate of about two per decade. And out of the tens of thousands of chemicals that are already on the market, OSHA has set standards for only about 400. Those standards are almost 40 years old already, and based on science from the 1940s and 1950s.[22]

This is an important example of regulatory drift, albeit one that arises from procedural complexity rather than overly prescriptive statutes. New standards of judicial review and new forms of regulatory oversight are superimposed upon a rulemaking process designed to provide heightened levels of transparency and accountability. As OSHA's rulemaking processes grind on slowly, the disjunction between its regulatory authority and the risks in the larger economy grows ever greater.

In response to the procedural labyrinth that OSHA must negotiate in the rulemaking process and the limited resources available for standard-setting, it has emphasized alternative approaches to achieving its goals. For example, it may seek to educate employers as to specific workplace hazards through the publication of alerts. It may seek to use voluntary partnerships to enlist the assistance of corporations and industry associations. Obviously, far more could be done with the support of the White House and Congress. Many of the procedural requirements stem from executive orders mandating regulatory review; they could be revised to limit the demands placed on agencies like OSHA, albeit at the cost of ceding some of the control that presidents have reclaimed over the regulatory state. Congress could authorize generic rule-making, thereby allowing OSHA to address multiple risks faced by workers in a given industry or simultaneously update multiple rules that are antiquated. This latter approach was attempted in 1988 when OSHA sought to update the permissible exposure limits on 212 substances and extend regulation to an additional 164 substances, based on the recommendations of NIOSH and the American Council of Governmental Industrial Hygienists. The approach was rejected by the court, which demanded that the agency follow the process identified earlier—analyzing the risk and feasibility—for each sub-stance.[23] Similarly, Congress could pass legislation imposing statutory deadlines for rulemaking and streamlined procedures for addressing specific hazards (an approach that was adopted successfully in forcing expedited action on blood-borne pathogens).[24] Reforms of this kind, while strongly warranted, would prove difficult to achieve in the polarized environment described in Chapter 5.

From Design to Practice: The Early OSHA

As with the Environmental Protection Agency, there was great urgency to get the new regulatory bureaucracy up and running as quickly as possible. Congress accelerated the work of the EPA through the passage of significant new stat-utes like the Clean Air Act Amendments of 1970 and the Clean Water Act of 1972. In the case of OSHA, Congress gave the new agency the power to adopt consensus standards via publication for the first twenty-eight months, thereby avoiding the delays of notice-and-comment rulemaking. Assistant Secretary of Labor George Guenther wasted little time, and 4,400 standards were adopted in the first month, claiming some 250 pages in the *Federal Register*. The vast major-ity of these standards were safety standards previously issued by standard-setting organizations. Unfortunately, many of these standards were outdated or trivial. As W. Kip Viscusi notes:

> the standards became the object of widespread ridicule, as OSHA regula-tions began to epitomize the most objectionable aspects of government intrusion in the market. OSHA was widely condemned for establishing standards for the shape of toilet seats, the precise height of fire extinguishers, and the availability of portable toilets for cowboys.[25]

When OSHA began regulating, it faced significant challenges.[26] Given the daunting task of regulating some 5 million workplaces across the country, the agency had few options other than to investigate catastrophic accidents and prioritize industries with the highest injury rates (e.g., long shoring, roofing and sheet metal work, meat processing, construction). While there were initial hopes that state-run programs would compensate for the limited federal resources, these hopes were quickly dashed. As OSHA's own history explains:

> Counting on the bulk of the states to participate, OSHA limited the development of its own staff of enforcement officers. It quickly became apparent that the states were not going to participate as extensively as OSHA had hoped. As a result, the agency soon found itself inadequately prepared to directly enforce the law on a nationwide basis.[27]

The agency's resources were further limited by the broader thrust of Nixon's "New Federalism." Nixon promoted a greater flow of resources to the states on the argument that the federal bureaucracy was too large, too politicized, and too often constrained innovation. In 1973 and 1974—crucial years in the development of the new agency—the budgets for state enforcement ($25 million) were almost as great as the budgets for federal enforcement ($26.2 million).[28] Administration efforts to limit the budgets of the Department of Labor and the Department of Health, Education, and Welfare had troubling consequences for the new agency. NIOSH, for example, was unable to fill one-sixth of its authorized positions, thereby forcing delays in the development of criteria for toxic substances in the workplace. During its first four years, OSHA had managed to develop but two health standards, one for asbestos (1972) and another covering fourteen carcinogens (1974).

Things would improve marginally during the Ford presidency. Under pressure from Congress and with a significant increase in the agency's budget—from $60.7 million (1974) to $139.2 million (1976)—OSHA improved its targeting of enforcement actions and accelerated its development of health standards. Ford appointed Morton Corn, a professor of occupational health and chemical engineering, to head OSHA. Corn promoted agency professionalization through recruitment of qualified inspectors and new in-house training. The Standards Development Office was expanded and OSHA forged closer relationships with NIOSH to expand the focus on occupational health issues. During the Ford presidency, OSHA released new health standards for Vinyl Chloride (1974), coke oven emissions (1976), and a proposed rule for cotton dust. The coke emissions and proposed cotton dust standards mandated expensive engineering controls. This, in turn, raised concerns for Ford. As inflation worsened, Ford cited regulation as one of the prime culprits, as shown in Chapter 4, and OSHA became a prime example of excessive regulation. Speaking to a group of businessmen, Ford recognized that they would like "to throw OSHA into the ocean" and promised that he would not "tolerate the unnecessary and unjustified harassment of citizens" by the agency. In hopes of reigning in regulators, Ford's Executive Order 11821 (1974) required that all executive branch agencies compose an Inflation Impact Statement for major legislative proposals, rules and regulations. According to Corn's estimates, the preparation of these statements was claiming $6.3 million of the $10.8 million budgeted for standards development.[29]

Arguably, the Carter presidency marked a high point for OSHA. In nominal terms, the budget increased by some 43 percent between 1977 and 1980; adjusted for inflation, it would be decades before OSHA would once again have a comparable budget. In addition, the agency had strong leadership. President Carter appointed Eula Bingham, an occupational health scientist from the University of Cincinnati who had experience in cancer research and had advised OSHA on the development of health standards during the previous administration. Under Bingham, the agency took a much more aggressive role in health regulation, promulgating permanent standards for cotton dust (1978), lead (1978), benzene (1978), dibromochloropropane or DBCP (1978), inorganic arsenic (1978), and acrylonitrile (1978). The agency also continued work on a generic cancer policy, releasing its final rule in 1980.[30] As the health standard-setting activities peaked, Bingham used the Standards Deletion project to eliminate more than 900 of the safety standards that had been adopted wholesale in the agency's first months and had served as an ongoing source of ridicule.[31]

While Bingham's tenure at OSHA marked a high point in the agency's history, the problems it encountered were emblematic of the controversies it would face in subsequent years. Although Carter had been strongly supportive of OSHA in the first years of his presidency, the economy intervened much as it had under Ford. By 1978, stagflation had become a household word and critics' attention turned, once again, to the issue of regulation. In addition to the new analytical requirements imposed via EO 12044 (see Chapter 4), OSHA found itself running afoul of the courts. Some matters were relatively trivial. In *Marshall v. Barlow's, Inc.* (1978), the Supreme Court decided that nonconsensual OSHA inspections required a search warrant under the Fourth Amendment.[32] However, because warrants could be obtained with relative ease (e.g., the "existence of administrative probable cause"), it was assumed that most employers would continue to consent to OSHA inspections without a warrant.[33] In *Chamber of Commerce v. Occupational Safety and Health Administration* (1978), the D.C. Circuit Court vacated OSHA's requirements that employees be compensated for time spent accompanying compliance officers during OSHA inspections.[34] More important, in *Industrial Union Department, AFL-CIO v. American Petroleum Institute et al.* (1980), the Supreme Court upheld the US Court of Appeals for the Fifth Circuit's decision that OSHA's benzene standard was invalid.[35] The Court of Appeals had concluded that OSHA failed to show that the exposure limit was "reasonably necessary or appropriate to provide safe or healthful employment" and because the OSH Act does "not give OSHA the unbridled discretion to adopt standards designed to create absolutely risk-free workplaces regardless of costs." The Supreme Court upheld the Circuit Court decision, in essence, requiring that OSHA show that current exposure levels would pose a "significant risk" of developing cancer and that the risk would be "significantly reduced" by the standard. This, in turn, would require a more careful application of risk assessment methodologies. As Antonin Scalia concluded in an analysis of the case: "The most noteworthy feature of the benzene decision . . . is its application of judicial activism in a new direction—to reduce, rather than augment, health and safety regulatory impositions upon the private sector."[36] As noted above, this decision contributed to the procedural complexity of OSHA's rulemaking.

Creating the Cooperative Regulator

If the Carter presidency marked the high point for OSHA, the Reagan presidency would mark its nadir. Ronald Reagan had long opposed OSHA as exhibit A in the case against regulatory zealotry. In 1975, he used his syndicated column to berate OSHA as "a four-letter word that's giving businessmen fits and helping drive up consumer costs."[37] Five years later on the campaign trail, Reagan offered a vision of OSHA that departed dramatically from that envisioned a decade earlier:

> My idea of an OSHA would be if government set up an agency that would do research and study how things could be improved, and industry could go to it and say . . . Would you come and look at our plant and then come back and give us a survey of what should be done?[38]

Unsurprisingly, OSHA was a prime target of regulatory relief for the newly inaugurated Reagan administration. Corporate compliance costs were estimated to be some $5 billion (1981) and many business owners would undoubtedly echo the words of Mike McKevitt of the National Federation of Independent Business, who, in turn, seemed to echo Reagan. Citing the resentments for "OSHA's petty harassment and abuses," he noted: "Of all the Washington acronyms, OSHA is the worst four-letter swear word in small business's vocabulary."[39]

In a sharp departure from past practices, Reagan appointed Thorne G. Auchter, a vice-president of a family construction firm and special events director for the Reagan campaign in Florida, to run OSHA. At his confirmation hearing, Auchter, proclaimed his goal of eliminating OSHA's "prevailing adversary spirit" and promoting greater cooperation with business. The 1982 budget—the first submitted by the Reagan administration—reflected these goals. Overall, OSHA's budget was cut by 6.6 percent, from $209.4 million to $195.5 million and federal enforcement funds were reduced by 7.3 percent.

At the same time, the budget for compliance assistance increased by 8.6 percent. The standard-setting budget fell by 13.6 percent.[40] Thereafter, the pace of standards development fell significantly. By mid-1988, a General Accounting Office study reported the majority of the standards that OSHA was developing "had been under development for over 4 years."[41] All of this brought OSHA into conflict with NIOSH—the agency responsible for generating the scientific findings for rulemaking. NIOSH claimed that OSHA was neglecting the scientific foundations for new rules and more often than not was basing its new standards on questionable science, a claim Auchter characterized as "a lot of hogwash."[42]

The new priority was to turn OSHA into a cooperative regulator. Part of this involved expanding on existing programs. For example, since 1975, OSHA states had been authorized to offer free consulting services for small businesses. Beginning in 1984, OSHA expanded the cooperative assistance program to address workplace safety and health management systems rather than discrete workplace hazards.[43] Participants were granted a one-year exemption from general schedule inspections if they had corrected hazards and instituted a management system.[44] A more impressive initiative took the form of the Voluntary Protection Program (VPP), introduced in 1982. The VPP was based on the experimental Cooperative Self-Inspection Program employed in the 1970s by California OSHA for the construction of the San Onofre Power Plant. The VPP had three tiers. "Star" was reserved for "workplaces having superior safety and health programs that go beyond OSHA standards in providing worker protection." They would be exempted from routine or programmed inspections and given priority when requesting variances. "Try" was a broader program "designed to evaluate alternative internal safety and/or health systems" whereas "Praise" was a recognition program for firms in low-hazard industries.[45] Although labor-management committees were required under OSHA's original proposal (much in keeping with California's Cooperative Self-Inspection Program), this requirement was ultimately dropped. Unsurprisingly, the program met with the opposition of organized labor that viewed it's exclusion as a departure from the original spirit of the OSH Act and as part of the larger regulatory relief program that favored business.[46]

As one might expect, the VPP went through some changes in the next few years.[47] Initially, VPP participants could qualify based on safety alone. In 1985, the requirements were revised to include health hazards. The "Praise" program was eliminated (1985) and a new "Demonstration" program was introduced for experimental projects formerly included in the "Try" program.[48] By 1988, the Try program had been renamed "Merit." In 1989, OSHA released its Voluntary Safety and Health Program Management Guidelines.[49] From the initiation of VPP to October 1989, 124 sites had applied to the VPP, 98 successfully (an approval rate of 78.5 percent). Of the 67 sites that remained in the program by this date, 91 percent were in the top category ("Stars").[50] As participants in VPP grew, so did their political presence. In 1985, VPP participants had formed their own association with annual conferences and outreach efforts. This became formalized in 1991, with the creation of the Voluntary Protection Programs Participants Association (VPPPA). Margaret R. Richardson, who had been in charge of VPP at OSHA, retired from the agency and became executive director of the association, which quickly expanded to create chapters in each of the OSHA regions.[51]

The promotion of cooperation was framed by OSHA as being part of a larger strategy designed to maximize its impact on occupational safety and health within its budgetary constraints. Under the VPP, high-performing employers were granted a lower inspection priority, freeing resources for other uses. The agency, moreover, began to use data on workplace injuries and illnesses to target its inspections, thereby exempting the majority of firms from routine safety inspections. Federal inspections, which had peaked at 71,371 in 1984, had fallen to 58,353 by 1988.[52] This resulted in a reduction in the number of citations for serious and willful violations, a reduction in the magnitude of the penalties, and a greater reliance on informal conferences to reach settlements that would allow, in theory, for a more expeditious elimination of workplace hazards.[53]

There was little evidence, however, that the change in agency orientation was having the promised effects. In 1989, for example, the General Accounting Office's analysis of OSHA practices found little credible evidence that the targeting of resources was amounting to much:

> OSHA tries to target scheduled inspections to worksites thought likely to be hazardous but, in fact, conducts relatively few inspections in high-hazard worksites. For example, in fiscal year 1989, only 10 percent of the worksites OSHA identified as high hazard for safety reasons were inspected. Similarly, only 3 percent of the worksites identified as high hazard for health reasons were inspected. Of these inspections, about half were conducted in response to specific evidence of hazard conditions at a worksite, such as complaints or referrals.[54]

While there would be persistent claims that the new approach was bearing fruit in reduced levels of workplace accidents, the Office of Technology Assessment concluded that any reductions in the injury rate during this period were largely attributable to the deep recession of the Reagan years rather than to OSHA's regulations.[55] To the editorial board of the *New York Times*, the changes in policy were little more than

> a return to self-regulation by industry. Often, inspectors look only at company-kept log books, not actual work sites. Instead of follow-up inspections, violators are supposed to notify the agency of corrective action. Fines are subject to dramatic reduction following informal conferences between violators and agency officials.[56]

Despite these concerns, the legacies of the Reagan administration would continue to find an expression at OSHA in subsequent decades.

As with the EPA, the George H. W. Bush administration brought a newfound vigor at OSHA. The agency's budget grew from $235 million (1988) to $297 million (1992), an increase of some 26 percent. While federal inspections would continue to decline in number, from 58,354 in 1988 to 42,431 in 1992, the growth in the federal enforcement budget (from $111 million in 1988 to $234 million in 1992) permitted a new emphasis on more complicated health inspections.[57] Penalties reached record levels under Bush, suggesting greater success in the targeting of resources. Bush's OSHA head, Gerald F. Scannell initiated important new standards, including exposure to HIV and hepatitis B in the healthcare industry and repetitive stress injuries.[58] Indeed, when the renewed activism at OSHA was combined with parallel changes at EPA and the promotion of the Clean Air Act Amendments (1990) and the Americans with Disabilities Act (1990), conservative critics charged that the Bush administration was marking a departure from the more market friendly posture struck by Ronald Reagan. As William G. Laffer from the Heritage Foundation warned: "Although President Bush often complains about the burden placed on the economy by excessive regulation, only Richard Nixon in the last two decades has done more to add to this burden."[59]

Polarization and Occupational Safety and Health

The problems of polarization explored in earlier chapters found an expression in occupational safety and health as well. As one might expect, the deep cuts of 1982 left OSHA with a budget 15 percent below the peak of the Carter presidency (1979). Given the political context explored in Chapter 5, increases in OSHA's budget would be elusive. Although there was some recovery—as noted above, the budget would actually increase during the presidency of George H. W. Bush—the average inflation-adjusted budget for occupational safety and health would be lower during Clinton's two terms than during the Reagan presidency (see Figure 7.1). The first years of the Clinton presidency witnessed an increase in the federal enforcement budget (from $136 million in 1993 to a peak of $144 million in 1995), but this would be short-lived. For the remainder of the Clinton presidency the average annual enforcement budget would be $130.2 million. At the same time, the budget for compliance assistance would grow substantially, from $40 million (1993) to a record $46 million.[60]

The budgetary limitations were compounded by a failure to pass new statutes. In 1994, the Clinton administration backed legislative reforms that would have been the first significant revision to OSHA's core statute since 1970. The Comprehensive Occupational Safety and Health Reform Act, co-sponsored by Senator Edward M. Kennedy (D-MA) and Representative William D. Ford (D-MI) would have extended OSHA coverage to public employees, increased

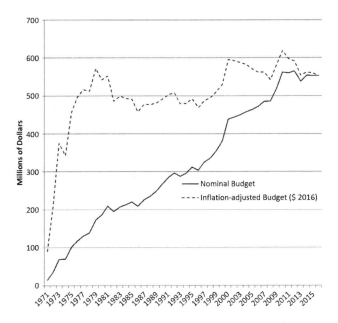

FIGURE 7.1 Occupational Safety and Health Administration Budget

Source: US Budget appendices, various years.

the criminal penalties for "willful violations" that cause death, updated exposure limits for toxic substances, and created an office of construction safety. It would have required all companies to develop and implement comprehensive safety and health programs with employee training and education, a goal that had previously been pursued via voluntary programs like VPP. More important, it would have mandated safety and health committees with worker representation in firms with eleven or more employees.[61] A similar bill had been introduced two years earlier, but had languished. As with the 1992 effort, this bill attracted opposition on several counts, including the unfunded mandates it would place on the states, the increased costs borne by business, and the empowerment of labor. While companies rejected the safety and health committees out of a fear of promoting union strength on the shop floor, unions were hesitant to restrict their role to committees that might be dominated by employers.[62] While the bill passed through the House Education and Labor Committee in March 1994, the Senate failed to act.

With the election of Republican majorities in both chambers, any hopes of new statutes strengthening OSHA were vanquished.[63] The political environment in the 104th and 105th Congresses was far from hospitable. The Republican-controlled House repeatedly attempted to use appropriations bills to hobble the enforcement powers of OSHA—in essence, emphasizing information dissemination and compliance assistance over traditional enforcement—while creating impediments to new rulemaking. In 1995, for example, Representative

Cass Ballenger (R-NC), House Economic and Educational Opportunities Workforce Protections Subcommittee Chairman, introduced a bill that would merge OSHA and the Mine Safety and Health Administration, and require the application of "industry-specific" cost–benefit analysis and risk assessment that had been adopted under the House's Contract with America regulatory reform package. Under his proposal, 50 percent of OSHA's budget would be dedicated to "consultation, training, education and compliance assistance programs." This could be contrasted with the 1995 fiscal year budget, wherein 14 percent was dedicated to compliance assistance. Employers with voluntary compliance programs would be exempt from random OSHA inspections.[64]

While the Ballenger bill and other legislative assaults on OSHA failed to pass, they sent a clear message: The agency was under siege. As Ballenger claimed, the threat embodied by the legislation: "made them change their regulations [and] made them consult with business more than regulate them." David Vladeck, director of Public Citizen's litigation group, concurred, noting that OSHA had been forced to "assume a bunker mentality. This is an agency that has overreacted to threats from Congress to put it on a short leash. There's plenty of evidence of capitulation."[65] Clinton OSHA head Charles N. Jeffress similarly attributed changes in the pace of rulemaking to the new political environment, concluding that the agency had "become more cautious" because of Congress: "I do think that people in the program who do rulemaking are much more cautious that every 'i' is dotted, every 't' is crossed. It has a chilling effect, if you will."[66]

Reinventing Occupational Safety and Health

With no opportunities for supportive new statutes, the Clinton administration turned to reform through administrative means, much as it had at EPA. The overarching goal was to change the "fundamental operating paradigm from one of command and control to one that provides employers a real choice between a partnership and a traditional enforcement relationship." The basic features of the administration's reinvention plans were presented in a 1995 document entitled *The New OSHA: Reinventing Worker Safety and Health.* The core premise was a simple one: "Not all workplaces are alike; not all employers are equally responsible. Yet too often, today's regulatory scheme applies a 'one-size-fits-all' approach that treats all workplaces and all hazards equally." Employing the same insights that informed our earlier discussion of enforcement pyramids, the challenge was to design institutions to differentiate between firms based on their exhibited commitment to occupational safety and health. Employers would be given a "clear choice" between partnership and traditional enforcement. Firms that were "fully committed" and "truly exceptional in eliminating hazards and reducing injuries and illnesses" would be offered a set of benefits including recognition, low priority for programmed inspections ("which, given remaining priorities, means that inspections will be quite rare"), and "the highest priority for assistance, appropriate regulatory relief, and penalty reductions up to 100 percent." Incentives would be structured to promote improvements. Employers that did not have strong and effective programs would face rigorous enforcement "without compromise to assure that there are serious consequences for serious violators." This would be facilitated by a shift of enforcement resources away from high-performing firms.[67]

Of course, the approach embodied in *The New OSHA* might be more accurately described as a retrofit of the Reagan-era VPP. Indeed, in 1995, Vice President Al Gore spoke before the VPPPA and argued that "the new national model of OSHA regulation" was "patterned" on programs like VPP. He used the occasion of his speech to present the National Performance Review Hammer Award to two public servants involved with managing VPP. Joseph Dear, then Clinton's OSHA head, noted that the VPP "is the premier example of partnership between government, management and workers, and a model for virtually all of OSHA's reinvention initiatives."[68]

Voluntary programs like the VPP may have been attractive given OSHA's situation. In an era of stagnant budgets, the ability to leverage corporate resources was appealing. Moreover, the devolution of authority on to regulated parties made practical sense given that with fewer than 2,200 OSHA employees—roughly 1.74 OSHA staff members per 100,000 workers—the probability of any employer receiving an inspection in any given year was remote.[69] But one should not discount the strategic importance in the larger political environment. The Reagan-era origins of the VPP may have limited the potential opposition of Republican legislators. Moreover, by enlisting corporations as partners, OSHA could further manage the opposition. As Gregory A. Huber observes, the VPP "allowed the agency to demobilize a component of the agency's opposition by giving high-performing businesses (and their political allies) an option to partner with OSHA and thereby opt out of traditional adversarial enforcement."[70] The need to engage business was magnified by the decline of OSHA's strongest constituency: organized labor. While one-quarter of private sector employees were union members at the birth of OSHA, by 1995, that figure had fallen to 10.3 percent.[71] Given the decline in labor influence, this strategy of demobilization may have been one of the few options open to the administration.

The VPP expanded significantly during the Clinton presidency. In 1992, there were 104 federal and state VPP sites. Two years later, the number of sites had grown to 180, raising concerns about the resources required to oversee the program. As OSHA admitted: "The rapid growth of the VPP has strained OSHA's ability to conduct the increasing numbers of required pre- and post-approval site reviews and, at the same time, provide the technical assistance and support that interested applicants often need."[72] The budget constraints were managed in two ways. First, in February 1994, OSHA approached the VPPPA with a novel suggestion: Its members could help the agency leverage its scarce resources by providing volunteers—Special Government Employees or

SGEs—to serve as members of onsite review teams to inspect sites that wanted to join VPP. Upon completing a three-day training course, SGEs would be sworn in and appointed to three-year renewable terms, with their salaries and travel expenses covered by their employers. Second, in June 1994, OSHA formalized a VPP Mentoring Program. Under the new program, employers that wanted to join VPP would be paired with an existing VPP site to foster information sharing. The new program was funded by the VPPPA (and was aptly renamed the VPPPA Mentoring Program).[73] These programs and subsequent efforts to facilitate participation by smaller worksites bore fruit. By 2000, the number of VPP sites had increased to 678, more than ten times the number that had existed in the last year of the Reagan presidency.[74]

While the VPP clearly extended the Reagan legacy, the Clinton administration moved forward with a far more ambitious initiative: the Cooperative Compliance Program (CCP). The CCP found its origins in a pilot program, Maine 200, initiated in 1993. Data from 1990 revealed that Maine had a high incidence of workplace illnesses and injuries, some 63 percent above the national average. Under Maine 200, OSHA identified the 200 employers with the highest number of worker compensation claims and targeted them for inspection. These firms employed 30 percent of the state's workers at 1,245 worksites, but were responsible for 45 percent of the workers' compensation injuries, illnesses, and fatalities. OSHA gave employers the option of developing health and safety programs in cooperation with the agency or accepting traditional enforcement. Successful participation was rewarded with a lower inspection priority and technical assistance. Some critics saw obvious incentive problems. The program seemed to provide greater benefits to firms that were targeted based on their poor performance than it did to firms that had proactively developed their own health and safety programs. While employers that had voluntarily developed programs could be eligible for a reduction in the magnitude of penalties, firms under the Maine 200 program were given a *de facto* exemption. Regardless of the critiques, Maine 200 was judged a success in reducing injuries and illnesses.[75]

In the next few years, OSHA introduced variants of the Maine 200 program in other states and in December 1997, the Clinton administration announced that the Maine 200 program was "going national" as the Cooperative Compliance Program. Under CCP, employers would commit "to find and fix hazards, work toward reducing injuries and illnesses, fully involve employees in their safety and health program, share injury and illness data and provide OSHA with information from their annual injury and illness records."[76] In turn, participants would be assigned a lower priority for safety and health inspections. The new program was focused on the 29 states that did not operate their own mini-OSHAs (those that did, were welcome to develop their own versions of CCP). Based on 1996 data, OSHA identified 12,250 workplaces with illness and injury rates that were almost twice the national average. The 500 sites with the worst records were subject to automatic mandatory inspections. The remaining firms could participate in CCP or face mandatory inspections. Under the program design, the data on injuries and illnesses would be reviewed every two years to develop an updated list of worksites that would be subject to mandatory inspection or invited to participate in CCP.

In 1998, OSHA added to its voluntary programs once again with Strategic Partnerships for Worker Safety and Health, designed primarily for employers in high-hazard workplaces. As Assistant Secretary Charles N. Jeffress explained, these partnerships could not be imposed by administrative fiat. Rather, OSHA, business and labor had to recognize that partnership was "in our enlightened self interest."[77] Some of the partnerships were of limited scope (e.g., developing employee training programs to address specific problems). Others were far more comprehensive (e.g., developing and implementing safety and health management systems that could facilitate participation in VPP or the CPP). The partnerships did not carry the same benefits as VPP or CCP. For example, there were no exemptions from programmed inspections—a reflection of the fact that participants lacked comparable levels of performance.[78] By the end of 2000, OSHA had 44 strategic partnerships.[79] As with other Clinton REGO efforts, real expansion would come during the presidency of George H. W. Bush, a point to be developed in greater detail below.

While the OSHA Strategic Partnerships would survive and flourish during the subsequent administration, the same cannot be said of the more ambitious CCP. Although 87 percent of the firms contacted by OSHA agreed to participate in CCP, the US Chamber of Commerce objected, in a letter to its members, that the program was voluntary "like a neighborhood protection racket is voluntary." Like the Godfather, OSHA was giving business "an offer you can't refuse."[80] An industry group, led by the Chamber and the National Association of Manufacturing filed suit in the US Court of Appeals for the DC Circuit. The court granted an emergency stay in February 1998 and struck down the CCP in April 1999, concluding that OSHA's directive was "the practical equivalent of a rule that obliges an employer to comply or to suffer the consequences; the voluntary form of the rule is but a veil for the threat it obscures." Because it was a *de facto* rule, the agency was required to conduct a notice-and-comment rulemaking.[81]

At first glance, one might find industry resistance surprising: Short of eliminating OSHA in its entirety, the CCP seemed to provide business with all that it had sought since the passage of the OSH Act. But there were concerns that the CCP was but an effort to extend OSHA regulations beyond what it could achieve through the rulemaking process (e.g., to the area of ergonomics). Moreover, it could expose companies to greater legal liability. Under CCP, employers were required to identify and control hazards in the workplace, thereby eliminating a common defense against OSHA citations (i.e., that risks were not recognized).[82] "After the setback," Cynthia Eastland writes, "instead of revving up the comparatively ponderous formal rulemaking procedures demanded by the court's ruling, OSHA retreated from comprehensive reform efforts."[83]

The Case of Ergonomics

As the Clinton OSHA focused on reinvention, the development of new standards languished, falling to the lowest levels since the Reagan presidency. Much of this may be explained by the success of Congress in constraining agency activism. While broad legislative assaults on OSHA were prevented, Congress nonetheless was quite successful in limiting the agency's ability to move forward with significant new regulations. The most striking case is found in the ergonomics rule. Repetitive stress injuries are strikingly common in American industry. There was some movement toward the regulation of these injuries during the Reagan and Bush presidencies. In May 1987, OSHA cited Chrysler for ergonomic hazards and entered into negotiations that would result in a comprehensive ergonomics program. In 1990, ergonomic agreements were signed with Ford Motors and General Motors, the latter covering more than 300,000 employees in 138 facilities. In August of 1990, the Department of Labor concluded that repetitive-stress injuries were among the "most debilitating" occupational illnesses and released ergonomic guidelines for the meatpacking industry. Within a year, 30 labor organizations petitioned OSHA to issue an emergency standard for ergonomics. While Bush Labor Secretary Lynn Martin decided against an emergency standard, she directed OSHA to begin the development of a standard via the normal notice-and-comment rulemaking process and by June of 1992, advanced notice of proposed rulemaking was published in the *Federal Register*.[84]

Although the Clinton administration departed from the Bush administration on a number of regulatory policy questions, there was great continuity in ergonomics. The administration declared the development of the ergonomics standard to be one of its regulatory priorities. By the time the draft standard was published in 1995, however, the Republican Party had assumed unified control of the Congress. Over the next several years, Congress used the appropriations process to prevent OSHA from moving forward in its rulemaking. The supplemental appropriations law for 1995 blocked OSHA from issuing the standard; the subsequent House appropriations bill not only prohibited the rule, but barred OSHA from collecting data on repetitive stress injuries. This dynamic would continue to play out for the next few years.

In May 1998, House Appropriations Chair Robert Livingston (R-LA) and Representative Henry Bonilla (R-TX) succeeded in appropriating funding ($490,000) for a National Academy of Sciences study on repetitive-motion injuries. The study concluded that "Musculoskeletal disorders are a serious national problem: estimates of costs range from $13 to $20 billion annually" and "there are interventions that can reduce the problems."[85] When the study confirmed that many of these injuries were occupational in origin, Congress appropriated another $890,000 for a second study. This time, OSHA was not prevented from engaging in rulemaking, although the House passed a bill (that languished in the Senate) prohibiting OSHA from issuing its rule before the second study was completed. The acquiescence on ergonomics may have been a product of the National Academy of Sciences' first study, or the Bureau of Labor Statistics' annual survey of workplace injuries and illnesses that cited repeated trauma disorders as "the dominant type of illness reported, making up 64 percent of the 430,000 total cases" in 1997.[86] This acquiescence, however, was illusory.

By February 1999, OSHA had a draft of its proposed final rule. In November— on the day that Congress adjourned—it announced its timetable for hearings. Although OSHA had hoped to complete the public comment period on the rule by February 2000, it extended its deadline under congressional pressure, making it increasingly unlikely that the rule would be completed and implemented before the end of the Clinton presidency. Waiting once again for the adjournment of Congress, OSHA announced its new ergonomic standard in November 2000. Under the standard, which had yet to be implemented, employers were required to educate workers about prevention of repeated motion injuries. They were required to respond to reported injuries by reconfiguring workspaces to prevent future injuries. If workers' injuries extended seven days or longer, they could claim compensation of up to 90 percent of their wages for up to 90 days.[87] By OSHA's own estimates, the ergonomics rule would cover 1.9 million work sites at a cost of $4.2 billion annually. But by preventing the injuries of some 300,000 workers, it would generate benefits of $9 billion (a combination of productivity gains and reduced sick pay for injured workers).[88] Organized labor could claim a significant victory, more than a decade in coming.

The victory, however, was stillborn. Throughout 2000, business lobbied heavily to defeat the ergonomics rule. The National Association of Manufacturers disputed OSHA's cost estimates, arguing that a survey of its members had led it to project costs of $6.7 billion the first year. Similar critiques came from the National Federation of Independent Business. Representative Cass Ballenger (R-NC), who had been a central critic of OSHA in the 1990s, argued that costs would drive companies hoping to remain competitive to outsource their production or move facilities off shore. In his words, "OSHA's ergonomics regulation will protect workers whose jobs no longer exist."[89] Initially, the House returned to the old strategy of using an appropriations rider to prohibit funding for the ergonomics rule but abandoned it over concerns that it could cost Republicans their seats in the upcoming 2000 elections—a fear heightened by union promises to target 40 GOP moderates.[90]

As the battle over appropriations gave way, business lobbyists developed a new strategy: delay the rule until 2001, when there might be a more hospitable political environment and an hitherto untested tool. In 1996, Congress passed the Congressional Review Act, part of the Small Business Regulatory Enforcement Flexibility Act, coauthored by Senator Don Nickles (R-OK) and Senator Harry Reid (D-NV). Under the Congressional Review Act, Congress could overturn a major regulation via a joint resolution of disapproval, passed by a simple majority with limited time for debate. Once the ergonomics rule was delayed to take effect on January 16, 2001, Congress had 60 days to act and with unified Republican control of the House and Senate and a newly inaugurated George H. W. Bush, the stage was set.[91] On March 6, 2001, the White House released a statement of administration policy in support of the joint resolution disapproving of a "vague and cumbersome" standard with high costs ("significantly more" than estimated by OSHA), "uncertain benefits," and weak empirical foundations ("none of the common musculoskeletal disorders are uniquely caused by work exposures").[92] On March 7, after the maximum 10 hours of debate permitted by the Congressional Review Act, the Senate voted 56–44 to repeal the ergonomics rule. The next day, the House followed with a one-hour debate and a 223–206 vote to repeal the standard. As Minority Leader Richard A. Gephardt exclaimed: "Ten years of work, swept aside in one hour of debate in the House of Representatives."[93]

Upon signing the joint resolution, President Bush repeated his earlier critique, and noted that there "needs to be a balance between and an understanding of the costs and benefits associated with Federal regulations." The ergonomics rule "would have applied a bureaucratic one-size-fits-all solution to a broad range of employers and workers—not good government at work."[94] The Bush administration would subsequently eschew mandatory regulations for a voluntary approach. During the summer of 2001, Secretary of Labor Elaine Chao held a series of public forums (the so-called "Ergo Tour 2001"), inviting the comments of interested parties. Labor leaders were skeptical, noting that the revoked rule had been the product of more than a decade of work. In 2000 alone, OSHA had held ten weeks of public hearings with some 1,000 witnesses. What more was to be learned about the repetitive stress injuries?[95] At the commencement of the tour, Chao testified before the Senate. While she acknowledged the "great strides in improving worker safety over the last century," she suggested in terms reminiscent of Clinton-era REGO reports "the new century, and the new workforce, require a new approach to the safety needs of the American labor force—an approach based on cooperation and prevention, rather than the antiquated, adversarial approach of years past."[96] The next spring, the Bush administration announced its new voluntary guidelines to replace the ergonomics rule. It would involve an outreach committee, the development of industry-specific guidelines, and research, all under existing laws and without any budgetary consequences.[97]

The Return of the Cooperative Regulator

The Bush OSHA, perhaps unsurprisingly, withdrew even further from an activist stance in occupational safety and health. Economically significant rules—those subject to OMB review—declined by 86 percent when compared with the Clinton presidency. Within the first two years, Bush's first OSHA head, John Henshaw, withdrew 26 draft regulations from the regulatory calendar and proved hesitant to issue health warnings, on the theory that they would be used in lawsuits. Health-based standards that had been in development were scuttled, often through the intervention of political appointees. These rules included a rule that could protect hospital workers from tuberculosis (preventing up to 32,700 infections and 190 deaths annually) and a rule to reduce exposure to crystalline silica (averting up to 40 cases of lung cancer and 41 deaths annually). In Henshaw's words: "there wasn't a whole lot of political will for more rules and burdens on industry . . . . We focused on improving what we had."[98] Of the 34 OSHA health standards released since 1972, only 2 emanated from the Bush administration.[99]

During the Bush presidency, OSHA continued to struggle for resources. The nominal budget increase, from $439 million in 2001 to $486 million in 2008, masked a reduction in inflation-adjusted budgets (indeed, by the last year of the Bush presidency, OSHA's inflation-adjusted budget was smaller than what it had been when Reagan assumed office in 1981). Beneath the surface, there was a continuation of trends that were evident under Clinton. The resources for enforcement slipped further from 56.7 percent (2001) to a low of 55.3 percent (2007) of the budget, although OSHA claimed that it was more effectively targeting its efforts through the Enhanced Enforcement Program, created in 2003. At the same time, the resources for compliance assistance increased from 13.2 percent (2001) to a record 15.3 percent of the budget.[100] The growth in compliance assistance reflected the larger philosophies of Henshaw and his successor, Ed Foulke. In Foulke's words:

> my emphasis was on trying to help employers comply with the law and have a better safety program. Hopefully that would help them be more successful and reduce their injuries and illnesses, which means they'd be more profitable, more competitive and able to keep jobs here in the US.[101]

And while the fervor of the Contract with America Congress had long since passed, the Republican-controlled House passed legislation repeatedly to weaken OSHA. The bills would have allowed the Occupational Safety and Health Review Commission to waive the fifteen-day period for businesses to contest citations, expand the commission from three to five members (a move that Democrats denounced as an effort to pack the commission), and requirements that the courts defer to the commission when there were legal disputes over citations. An additional bill would have forced OSHA to reimburse businesses for legal fees when citations were overturned; the agency would have been forced to cover the legal costs out of its budget. These bills, passed in 2004 and again in 2005, died in the Senate.[102]

Voluntary programs remained a focus of the agency, even once the formal reinvention efforts of the Clinton administration had come to a conclusion. By the end of the Clinton presidency, OSHA's most significant voluntary programs included (1) the State Consultation Program, created in 1975 and administered by the states, supplemented in 1984 by its Safety and Health Recognition Program or SHARP, which was created to recognize small firms that participated in the Consultation Program, (2) the VPP, created in 1982 and subsequently expanded, and (3) the Strategic Partnership Program, created in 1998. The Bush administration would add to this mix with a new Alliance Program in 2002.[103] In contrast with the other initiatives, the Alliance program was designed to promote cooperative efforts with employers, trade and professional associations, and labor unions to develop educational programs and better ways of identifying and managing workplace safety and health hazards. The number of alliances would peak at 432 in 2008, with the vast majority supervised by regional or area offices.[104]

Despite the addition of new programs, the VPP remained the centerpiece of OSHA's voluntary programs. In marking the twentieth anniversary of VPP before a meeting of the Voluntary Protection Programs Participants' Association, Bush's OSHA head John L. Henshaw reported that the number of worksites in the program had increased from 9 in 1982 to 100 by 1993 and 864 by 2002 (623 in federal programs and 241 in state programs). Looking to the future, he asked: What can be done to expand the VPP?

> There are only a few more than 850 VPP sites. Eight hundred fifty out of the seven million businesses in the US. In fact, VPP sites only represent approximately one out of every 10,000 companies in America. But WHAT if achieving VPP was not the exception, but the rule?

To expand the number of participants, Henshaw reasoned, it would be necessary to have a "jump start" program for "worksites that want to do the right thing but need some assistance" and streamlined procedures. In addition, "we need to increase our program recognition and marketing strategies to encourage more sites to go for the STAR."[105]

Henshaw set an ambitious goal: to expand the number of VPP participants to 8,000, covering some 4 million workers. To encourage the rapid expansion of VPP, in 2003 OSHA introduced three new initiatives: (1) VPP Challenge, a pilot program designed to attract firms to VPP regardless of their current performance record; (2) VPP Corporate, a pilot program that streamlined the process for employers with sites already in the program that wish to bring other sites into VPP; and (3) VPP Construction, a pilot program for temporary construction sites that would not be able to meet existing requirements regarding the time a health and safety management system had to be in place. Collectively known as the 3-C demonstration programs, they were presented by Henshaw as "vehicles to dramatically expand and grow participation."[106]

As OSHA aggressively promoted its voluntary programs, two fundamental questions remained, both of which were addressed by a 2004 report by the

Government Accountability Office. First, did the performance record of the voluntary programs justify this renewed emphasis? While the GAO found some anecdotal evidence of improved occupational safety and health, there was simply insufficient data to arrive at an adequate evaluation. As the GAO reported:

> OSHA currently lacks the data needed to fully assess the effectiveness of its voluntary compliance programs. Developing outcome measures is difficult, particularly when factors other than program participation can affect key indicators such as injury and illness rates. However, agencies are required to develop such measures and it is especially important for OSHA, given its limited resources, to be able to evaluate the effectiveness of these programs. Currently, OSHA does not collect complete, comparable data needed to measure the value of its programs, including their relative impact, resource use, and effect on the agency's mission.[107]

Second, were the investments in voluntary programs coming at the expense of traditional enforcement? As the GAO noted: "The resources OSHA devotes to its voluntary compliance strategies consume a significant and growing portion of the agency's limited resources." In fiscal year 2003, OSHA had devoted 28 percent of its $450 million budget on voluntary programs, compared with 20 percent in 1996.

> During this same period, the proportion of resources OSHA dedicated to its enforcement activities fell by 6 percent, from about 63 percent to about 56 percent of the agency's total budget . . . . While it cannot be determined that resources were directly redistributed from enforcement to compliance assistance activities, funding for OSHA's other programs remained relatively stable.[108]

Given the resource constraints and the lack of evaluation, the GAO questioned whether the dramatic expansion of the voluntary programs could be justified by the empirical record. While OSHA acknowledged these concerns, it did not affect its advocacy of the VPP. The number of sites more than doubled, from 1,039 in 2003 to 2,174 in 2008. A new GAO analysis was released in 2009. As in 2004, the GAO found that OSHA had still "not developed goals or measures to assess the performance of the VPP, and the agency's efforts to evaluate the program's effectiveness." More concerning, the GAO's analysis concluded that the expansion of the program in a context of limited resources had easily predictable results:

> OSHA continues to expand the VPP, which adds to the responsibilities of staff who manage and maintain the integrity of the program and reduces the resources available to ensure that non-VPP sites comply with safety and health regulations and with OSHA's standards. In the absence of

policies that require its regional offices to document information regarding actions taken in response to fatalities and serious injuries at VPP sites, OSHA cannot ensure that only qualified sites participate in the program.[109]

Despite the promise that the VPP sites were capable of *de facto* self-regulation, the GAO found that some sites had experienced fatalities that stemmed from deficient systems. These facts led the GAO to question the integrity of the VPP and the adequacy of OSHA oversight.

The growth of VPP might have been less problematic if there were evidence that OSHA had succeeded in more effectively focusing its scarce enforcement resources. This had been the promise in 2003, when it implemented its Enhanced Enforcement Program (EPP). Under this program, OSHA would target high-risk employers (e.g., employers with previous citations for serious and high-gravity violations resulting in fatalities, willful or repeat violations). The program was amended in 2008 to require, in addition, a history of "similar in-kind" violations, further narrowing the universe of employers subject to the EPP. The program was audited at the end of the Bush presidency by the Department of Labor's Office of Inspector General, which examined a sample of 325 employers (282 of which qualified for EEP). It discovered that 53 percent of the EEP qualifying employers were not properly designated. Moreover, for 97 percent of the sample of cases that qualified for EEP, OSHA failed to comply with program requirements, either failing to designate the case correctly, inspect related worksites, conduct enhanced follow-up inspections, or implement enhanced settlement provisions (e.g., requiring additional reporting or implementing a comprehensive safety and health program). Of the 29 employers that OSHA correctly designated as EEP sites but failed to follow up with enhanced enforcement efforts, 20 subsequently had workplace fatalities, 14 of which were under circumstances similar to previous violations.[110] Clearly, the same lack of oversight that characterized the rapid expansion of VPP could be found in OSHA's efforts to target its enforcement efforts.

Obama and the Persistence of Partnerships

The 2008 election of Barack Obama promised to bring significant changes to OSHA. As a member of the Senate Health, Education, Labor and Pensions Committee, Senator Obama had been quite clear in his critique of OSHA and the need for reform. In a hearing on April 28, 2008, Obama had decried an agency that had used its authority "as if its mandate were to err on the side of corporations over the public interest—even when its decisions undermine the spirit of the law and put workers' lives at risk." Senator Obama called for increased budgetary resources and a better targeting of inspections to the most dangerous workplaces "to deter noncompliance among those employers who disregard worker protection in favor of production speed or profit." He argued that the Occupational Safety and Health Act must be amended to strengthen criminal penalties:

> OSHA must have the requisite authority to impose meaningful penalties for noncompliance, particularly in the case of serious, repeat, and egregious violations. The bottom line is that when an employer exposes workers to serious hazards, it should pay fines that are more than just an ordinary cost of doing business.[111]

On the campaign trail, Obama had emphasized these themes and promised to support OSHA's ergonomics rule and extend OSHA coverage to all public employees.[112]

In 2009, the Protecting America's Workers Act was introduced in the House of Representatives. The bill extended OSHA coverage to federal, state, and local employees. It provided additional protection for whistleblowers, mandated inspections for any incident resulting in the hospitalization of two or more workers, and significantly increased civil and criminal penalties. For example, it permitted criminal sanctions against any responsible corporate officer. Willful violations resulting in death could be punished with a maximum of ten years in prison.[113] The same bill had been introduced in every session of every Congress since 2004, with a range of impressive co-sponsors, which had included Obama, Senator Joe Biden (D-DL), and Hillary Clinton (D-NY). In the past, the bill had met with the opposition of the US Chamber of Commerce and languished in committee. The newest incarnation met the same fate, as business opposition was buttressed by the argument that the worst time to impose new regulatory costs on business was during a deep recession with record unemployment. The bill would be reintroduced in subsequent congresses, but with GOP control of the House after the 2010 midterm elections, there was little hope of passage.

Absent new statutory authority, the administration moved forward to alter priorities through administrative means. In the area of enforcement, it turned to the Enhanced Enforcement Program and, in response to the earlier critique by the Department of Labor's Office of Inspector General cited above, the Obama OSHA created a new Severe Violator Enforcement Program. The new program tightened the criteria for inspection with required follow-up inspections in every case.[114] Enforcement was further enhanced by additional resources from the American Recovery and Reinvestment Act of 2009, the Obama administration's stimulus program. Of the $80 million provided to the Department of Labor, $13.6 million was allocated to OSHA for enhanced inspection and enforcement.[115] While OSHA's budget would increase to an average of $562.2 million (2010–12), in subsequent years it would fall such that by 2016, it was $552.8 million (in inflation-adjusted terms, less than the average for the Bush presidency).[116]

As the administration sought to increase the priority of inspections and enforcement activities, it sought to reverse some of the policies of the Bush presidency that, according to successive GAO reports, had expanded the VPP beyond a level that could be supported administratively. Acting OSHA head Jordan Barab assured the VPPPA members in 2009 "We are not eliminating the Voluntary Protection Programs." However, "the days of signing companies into the VPP programs or Alliances just to fill arbitrary goals . . . as a replacement for standards, are over."[117] In 2010, Assistant Secretary of Labor Michaels went further, noting that agency resources were going to be shifted from compliance assistance and VPP to enforcement. He stated:

> given the choice of spending our limited resources on either supporting companies that are doing a great job protecting employees, or focusing on employers who willfully disregard workplace safety and allow workers to die in situations that could easily have been prevented our choice is clear.[118]

The decisions regarding resource allocations reveal some change in priorities. The share of the budget devoted to enforcement increased from 56.1 percent in 2009 to a high of 58.6 percent in 2011, before falling back to an average of 55.9 percent for the remainder of the Obama presidency. As one might expect, federal inspections increased from 39,004 in 2009 to a peak of 40,961, before declining to levels lower than during the Bush presidency. Whether these inspections were targeted more effectively remains an open question. With respect to federal compliance assistance and state consultation grants, the budgetary support fell. In 2009, 14.1 percent of the budget went to federal compliance assistance (a total of 24.5 percent if one includes state consultation grants). This share would fall in subsequent years, reaching a low in 2013 of 11.5 percent and 21.7 percent respectively, before gradually increasing.[119] While federal compliance assistance fell significantly, the Obama administration had hoped to eliminate OSHA funding altogether, making the VPP fully dependent on participation fees. In 2010, Assistant Secretary Michaels told the VPPPA that VPP "was very unlikely to continue under the current federal funding formula," and was exploring the option of relying solely on participation fees by the 2012 fiscal year.[120] The funding cuts were successfully avoided and by 2012, Jordan Barab as much as admitted defeat before the VPPPA ("You rejected that proposal, and we have taken it off the table. Nevertheless, the budget uncertainty remains").[121] In response to the uncertainty, new legislation was introduced in both chambers, the Voluntary Protection Program Act, to place the VPP on statutory foundations and ban the reliance on user fees. While the legislation failed to pass, it would be resubmitted in subsequent congresses. With 2,181 participants and a strong participant association actively lobbying on the program's behalf, the VPP appeared to be far stronger in 2016 than one would have imagined eight years earlier.[122]

Conclusion

President Nixon signed the Occupational Safety and Health Act on December 29, 1970, and OSHA officially opened for business in 1971. During the 1970s, the agency survived and even flourished, despite the chorus of critics linking regulation—and OSHA in particular—to the economic problems of high inflation and sluggish growth. Certainly, OSHA faced challenges during the Reagan presidency. Reagan and conservative critics of regulation had targeted OSHA as an agency that was renown for its zealotry and its adversarial posture toward business. The introduction of the Voluntary Protection Program—the cornerstone of the efforts to transform the agency into a cooperative regulator—seemed to have modest results, if measured in the number of firms that were enrolled as participants. By the presidency of George H. W. Bush, the assaults on OSHA appeared to be over. Enforcement actions were bearing new fruit and the agency was initiating important new standards. And with the election of Bill Clinton, the first Democratic president in more than a decade, there was every reason to believe that the agency would continue to thrive.

Yet, in the hostile environment that quickly emerged in Congress, two things became clear. First, any efforts to expand and update OSHA's mandate—to increase penalties, to enhance the role of labor, to extend coverage to public sector employees—would be impossible. Second, resources would be increasingly constrained, both in terms of the size of OSHA's budget and the restrictions placed on the funding it received. As with the EPA, the response was to be found in reinvention. The Reagan-era VPP became one of the vehicles of reinvention, as did a new set of strategic alliances and efforts to extend the reach of OSHA through the Cooperative Compliance Program. Corporations that had long fought against OSHA were now enlisted to invest in health and safety management systems that could not be mandated by regulation, and extend their efforts to address problems like repetitive stress injuries that, ultimately, could not survive the rulemaking process under the constraints imposed by Congress.

As the Clinton administration transitioned into the George H. W. Bush administration, further reductions in the vigor of enforcement were combined with the unprecedented expansion of the VPP and clear evidence that there were insufficient efforts on the part of OSHA to determine the extent to which voluntary programs contributed to its mission. While the Obama administration proved more skeptical of these programs than its predecessors, ultimately, its inability to secure new occupational safety and health statutes combined with sharp reductions in funding as the GOP once again assumed control of Congress, left few other options on the table. Even efforts to make the VPP self-funding, thereby relieving OSHA of the financial burdens of administering the program, proved impossible. As with environmental protection, regulatory voluntarism had become a seemingly permanent part of the regulatory state. As Obama's

OSHA chief, Assistant Secretary for Labor David Michaels, assured the VPPPA: "Administrations change, but our commitment to the program doesn't waver."[123]

Notes

1 Michael Levin, "Politics and Polarity: The Limits of OSHA Reform," American Enterprise Institute, December 6, 1979. Available at www.aei.org/publication/politics-and-polarity-the-limits-of-osha-reform/.

2 Jordan Barab, "Remarks to the Voluntary Protection Program Participants' Association Annual Meeting, August 24, 2015," Occupational Safety and Health Administration. Available at www.osha.gov/pls/oshaweb/owadisp.show_document?p_table=SPEECHES&p_id=3565.

3 Steven Kelman, "Occupational Safety and Health Administration," in *The Politics of Regulation*, ed. James Q. Wilson (New York: Basic Books, 1980), 239–40.

4 Ben A. Franklin, "Mine Safety: 78 Mute Witnesses for Reform," *New York Times*, December 1, 1968, E4.

5 Andrew Batista, *The Revival of Labor Liberalism* (Champaign, IL: University of Illinois Press, 2008), 46.

6 "Senate Approves Mine Safety Bill," *New York Times*, December 19, 1969, 31.

7 Richard Nixon, "Special Message to the Congress on Occupational Safety and Health," August 6, 1969. Available at www.presidency.ucsb.edu/ws/?pid=2181.

8 See Charles Noble, *Liberalism at Work: The Rise and Fall of OSHA* (Philadelphia, PA: Temple University Press, 1986), 90.

9 Quoted in "Occupational Safety and Health Legislation, 1970," *Social Service Review*, 45, 1 (1971): 94.

10 Walter Rugaber, "Job Safety Board Is Asked by Nixon: 5-Man Body Would Impose U.S. Standards if States Failed to Take Action," *New York Times*, August 7, 1969, 1.

11 "Congress Facing Job Safety Debate," *New York Times*, December 10, 1969, 26.

12 Noble, *Liberalism at Work*, 94.

13 Marc Allen Eisner, Jeffrey Worsham, and Evan J. Rinquist, *Contemporary Regulatory Policy*, 2nd ed. (Boulder, CO: Lynne Rienner, 2006), 194–95, Nicholas Askounes Ashford, *Crisis in the Workplace: Occupational Disease and Injury* (Cambridge, MA: MIT Press, 1976), 13–14.

14 David P. Currie, "OSHA," *American Bar Foundation Research Journal*, 1, 4 (1976): 1120–26.

15 Ibid., 1147–48.

16 John H. Stender, "Enforcing the Occupational Safety and Health Act of 1970: The Federal Government as a Catalyst," *Law and Contemporary Problems*, 38, 4 (1974): 648–49.

17 Noble, *Liberalism and Work*, 95.

18 Stender, "Enforcing the Occupational Safety and Health Act of 1970," 647.

19 This discussion draws on Governmental Accountability Office, *Workplace Safety and Health: Multiple Challenges Lengthen OSHA's Standard Setting*, GAO 12-330 (Washington DC: Government Accountability Office, 2012).

20 *Industrial Union Department, AFL-CIO v. American Petroleum Institute et al.*, 448 U.S. 607 (1980) and *American Textile Manufacturers Institute v. Donovan*, 452 U.S. 490 (1981).

21 GAO, *Workplace Safety and Health*, 8.

22 Thomas McGarity, Rena Steinzor, Sidney Shapiro, and Matthew Shudtz, "Workers at Risk: Regulatory Dysfunction at OSHA," Center for Progressive Reform White Paper no. 1003 (Washington DC: Center for Progressive Reform, 2010), 11.

23 See ibid., 10–11.

24 GAO, *Workplace Safety and Health*, 34.

25 W. Kip Viscusi, *Risk by Choice: Regulating Health and Safety in the Workplace* (Cambridge, MA: Harvard University Press, 1983), 11.

26 This section draws on Marc Allen Eisner, *Regulatory Politics in Transition*, 2nd ed. (Baltimore, MD: Johns Hopkins University Press, 2000), 162–65.

27 Judson MacLaury, "The Occupational Safety and Health Administration: A History of Its First Thirteen Years, 1971–1984," Occupational Safety and Health Administration. Available at www.dol.gov/dol/aboutdol/history/osha13guenther.htm.

28 Office of Management and Budget, Budget of the US Government, Appendix, 1975 Fiscal Year. On the impact of the "New Federalism," see Charles Culhane, "Administration Works to Shift Safety, Health Programs to States Despite Labor Criticism," *National Journal*, 4, 26 (1972): 1041–49.

29 David Burnham, "Work Safety Agency, Under Fire, Has Little Impact but Big Potential," *New York Times*, December 20, 1976, B6.

30 Occupational Safety and Health Administration, *Reflections on OSHA's History* (Washington DC: Occupational Safety and Health Administration, 2009), 16–18.

31 Ray Marshall, "The Labor Department in the Carter Administration: A Summary Report—January 14, 1981." Available at www.dol.gov/dol/aboutdol/history/carter-osha.htm.

32 436 U.S. 307 (1978).

33 Mark A. Rothstein, "OSHA Inspections after *Marshall v. Barlow's Inc.*" *Duke Law Journal*, 1979 (1979): 103.

34 465 F. Supp. 10 (1978).

35 448 U.S. 607.

36 Antonin Scalia, "A Note on the Benzene Case," *Regulation*, July/August 1980: 26–27.

37 Peter Milius, "OSHA: A 4-Letter Word," *Washington Post*, February 12, 1977.

38 Quoted in William F. Grover, *The President as Prisoner: A Structural Critique of the Carter and Reagan Years* (Albany, NY: State University of New York Press, 1989), 113.

39 "OSHA, E.P.A.: The Heyday Is Over," *New York Times*, January 4, 1981, 3. Available at www.nytimes.com/1981/01/04/business/osha-epa-the-heyday-is-over.html?pagewanted=all.

40 Budget data from Budget of the US Government, appendix, fiscal year 1982.

41 General Accounting Office, *Options for Improving Safety and Health in the Workplace*, HRD-90-66BR (Washington DC: US General Accounting Office, 1990), 21.

42 Philip Shabecoff, "Safety Agencies Find Their Common Ground Eroding," *New York Times*, November 28, 1982, 4. Available at www.nytimes.com/1982/11/28/weekinreview/safety-agencies-find-their-common-ground-eroding.html.

43 49 FR 25082, June 19, 1984.

44 William V. Warrant, "OSHA Safety and Health Consultation Services for Employers," *Job Safety & Health Quarterly*, 2, 2 (1991): 26–28.

45 47 FR 29025, July 2, 1982.

46 Gregory A. Huber, *The Craft of Bureaucratic Neutrality: Interests and Influence in Governmental Regulation of Occupational Safety* (Cambridge, UK: Cambridge University Press, 2007), 223–25.

47 For a discussion of VPP's history in its first two decades, see Judith Weinberg, "Happy Birthday, VPP!" *Job Safety & Health Quarterly*, 13, 4 (2002): 18–25.

48 50 FR 24804, October 29, 1985.

49 54 FR 3904, January 26, 1989.

50 Margaret R. Richardson and G. J. Catanzaro, "Introduction to the VPP," *Job Safety & Health Quarterly*, 1, 1 (1989): 16–18.

51 See Margaret R. Richardson, *Preparing for the Voluntary Protection Programs: Building Your Star Program* (New York: John Wiley & Sons, 1999), 8–11.

52 Data from Budget of the US Government appendices, various years.

53 "New OSHA Chief Is Praised by Industry, Criticized by Unions," *Wall Street Journal*, November 23, 1981.

54 GAO, *Options for Improving Safety and Health*, 28.

55 Patrick L. Knudsen, "OSHA: The Agency Nobody Loves: Old Business Nemesis Now Draws Labor's Fire," *CQ Weekly*, March 26, 1988, 783–85.

56 "Guarding the OSHA Chickens," *New York Times*, October 7, 1983. Available at www.nytimes.com/1983/10/07/opinion/guarding-the-osha-chickens.html.

57 Budget data from Budget of the US Government appendices, various years.

58 Jonathan Rauch, "The Regulatory President," *National Journal*, 23, 48 (1991): 2902–6.

59 William G. Laffer, "George Bush's Hidden Tax: The Explosion of Regulation," Heritage Foundation Backgrounder no. 905 on Regulation, July 10, 1992. Available at www.heritage.org/research/reports/1992/07/bg905nbsp-george-bushs-hidden-tax.

60 Budget data from Budget of the US Government appendices, various years.

61 Barbara Presley Noble, "At Work; Breathing New Life into OSHA," *New York Times*, January 23, 1994. Available at www.nytimes.com/1994/01/23/business/at-work-breathing-new-life-into-osha.html.

62 Cynthia Estlund, "Rebuilding the Law of the Workplace in an Era of Self-Regulation," *Columbia Law Review*, 105, 2 (2005): 344.

63 David Masci, "Labor: Overhaul of Job Safety Law Gains Committee Approval," *CQ Weekly*, March 12, 1994, 610. "Legislative Summary: OSHA Overhaul," *CQ Weekly*, November 5, 1994, 3185.

64 "Ballenger Bill Would Limit OSHA, Merge It with MSHA," *Congress Daily*, June 14, 1995.

65 Jonathan Weisman, "True Impact of GOP Congress Reaches Well Beyond Bills," *CQ Weekly*, September 7, 1996, 2515–20.

66 Allan Freedman, "Regulation: GOP's Secret Weapon against Regulations: Finesse," *CQ Weekly*, September 5, 1998, 2305–20.

67 All quotes are from "The New OSHA: Reinventing Worker Safety and Health, 1995." Available at www.osha.gov/archive/oshinfo/reinvent/reinvent.html.

68 "Vice President Highlights New OSHA at VPPA's Annual Conference," White House, Office of the Vice President, September 26, 1995. Available at http://govinfo.library.unt.edu/npr/library/speeches/2596.html.

69 Data from Budget of the US Government appendices, 1997 fiscal year.

70 Gregory A. Huber, *The Craft of Bureaucratic Neutrality: Interests and Influence in Governmental Regulation of Occupational Safety* (Cambridge, UK: Cambridge University Press, 2007), 226.

71 http://unionstats.gsu.edu/Private-Sector-workers.htm.

72 Judith Weinberg, "OSHA Cooperative Efforts: A Good Deal for Workers and Employers," *Job Safety & Health Quarterly*, 8, 4 (1997): 14.

73 Leigh Sherrill and Judith Weinberg, "OSHA's VPP Gets a Little Help from Its Friends," *Job Safety & Health Quarterly*, 9, 4 (1998): 29–33.

74 Figures on VPP sites from Occupational Safety and Health Administration Office of Partnerships and Recognition, "Growth of VPP, Federal and State." Available at www.osha.gov/dcsp/vpp/charts/slide9.html.

75 Sidney A. Shapiro and Randy S. Rabinowitz, "Punishment versus Cooperation in Regulatory Enforcement: A Case Study of OSHA," *Administrative Law Review*, 49, 4 (1997): 741–42. "Maine Top 200 Experimental Targeting Program," Harvard Kennedy School Ash Center for Democratic Governance and Innovation. Available at www.innovations.harvard.edu/maine-top-200-experimental-targeting-program.

76 Occupational Safety and Health Administration, "OSHA's Maine 200 Program Goes Nationwide," December 5, 1997. Available at http://govinfo.library.unt.edu/npr/library/misc/oshaccp.html.

77 Frank Kane, "OSHA Sees Partnerships as Key to Reducing Injuries and Illnesses," *Job Safety & Health Quarterly*, 10, 1 (1998): 20.

78 See Brian T. Bennett and Norman R. Deitch, *Preparing for OSHA's Voluntary Protection Programs: A Guide to Success* (Hoboken, NJ: Wiley, 2010), 25–26, and "OSHA Strategic Partnership for Worker Safety and Health," CSP 03-02-001 (1998). Available at www.osha.gov/pls/oshaweb/owadisp.show_document?p_table=directives&p_id=1889.

79 www.osha.gov/dcsp/partnerships/.

80 Cindy Skrzycki, "OSHA's Enforcement Plan Gets Stopped Short," *Washington Post*, April 17, 1998, F1.

81 *Chamber of Commerce v. Occupational Safety and Health Administration*, 174 F.3d 206 [D.C. Cir 1999].

82 Binglin Yang, *Regulatory Governance and Risk Management: Occupational Health and Safety in the Coal Mining Industry* (New York: Routledge, 2011), 80–81.

83 Cynthia Estlund, *Regoverning the Workplace: From Self-regulation to Co-regulation* (New Haven, CT: Yale University Press, 2010), 80–81.

84 This account draws on James C. Benton, "Ergonomics Debate: A Brief History," *CQ Weekly*, February 26, 2000, 404.

85 National Research Council, *Work Related Musculoskeletal Disorders: A Review of the Evidence* (Washington DC: National Academy Press, 1998), 21.

86 "New Release: Workplace Injuries and Illnesses in 1997," Department of Labor, Bureau of Labor Statistics, December 17, 1998. Available at www.bls.gov/news.release/history/osh_12171998.txt.

87 "Senate Key Vote: Ergonomics Rules (Vote 15)," *CQ Weekly*, December 22, 2001, 3059.

88 Michael Posner, "Ergonomics Proposal Pains Republicans," *National Journal*, January 22, 2000.

89 Ibid.

90 Charlie Mitchell, "Unions to Appeal to GOP Moderates to Sink Labor-HHS Bill," *Congress Daily*, June 7, 2000.

91 "Senate Key Vote: Ergonomics Rules (Vote 15)," *CQ Weekly*, December 22, 2001, 3059. See Steven Greenhouse, "Rules' Repeal Heightens Workplace Safety Battle," *New York Times*, March 12, 2001, A1.

92 George W. Bush, "Statement of Administration Policy: S.J. Res. 6 – Joint Resolution of Disapproval of Ergonomics Regulation," March 6, 2001. Available at www.presidency.ucsb.edu/ws/?pid=25633.

93 April Fulton, "Review Act Used to Repeal Workplace Regs," *National Journal*, March 10, 2001.

94 George W. Bush, "Statement on Signing Legislation to Repeal Federal Ergonomics Regulations," March 20, 2001. Available at www.presidency.ucsb.edu/ws/?pid=45790.

95 Mark Murray, "'Ergo Tour' Hits the Road," *National Journal*, July 14, 2001.

96 "Chao Outlines Ergonomic Principles," US Department of Labor, April 26, 2001. Available at www.osha.gov/pls/oshaweb/owadisp.show_document?p_table=NEWS_RELEASES&p_id=244.

97 April Fulton, "Administration Takes Voluntary Approach to Ergonomics," *Congress Daily*, April 5, 2002.

98 R. Jeffrey Smith, "Under Bush, OSHA Mired in Inaction," *Washington Post*, December 29, 2008, A1. Available at www.washingtonpost.com/wp-dyn/content/article/2008/12/28/AR2008122802124.html.

99 Alyssa Rosenberg, "Labor: Major Changes Are Due," *National Journal*, January 10, 2009, 26.

100 Budget of the US Government appendices, various years. Calculations by author.

101 Max Mihelich, "OSHA's Foulke Tale: Ed Foulke Reflects on His Tenure," *Workforce*, June 30, 2014. Available at www.workforce.com/articles/20592-oshas-foulke-tale.

102 Alex Wayne, "OSHA Changes Advance Only So Far," *CQ Weekly*, July 18, 2005, 1980.

103 Government Accountability Office, *Workplace Safety and Health: OSHA's Voluntary Compliance Strategies Show Promising Results, but Should Be Fully Evaluated before They Are Expanded*, GAO-04-378 (Washington DC: Government Accountability Office, 2004), 4–9.

104 See OSHA Active Alliances by Fiscal Year (through June 30, 2015). Available at www.osha.gov/dcsp/alliances/growthcharts.html.

105 John L. Henshaw, "Address to VPPPA 18th Annual Conference, Orlando, Florida, September 9, 2002," Occupational Safety and Health Administration. Available at www.osha.gov/pls/oshaweb/owadisp.show_document?p_table=SPEECHES&p_id=585.

106 John L. Henshaw, "Address to VPPPA 19th Annual Conference, Washington, DC, September 8, 2003," Occupational Safety and Health Administration. Available at www.osha.gov/pls/oshaweb/owadisp.show_document?p_table=SPEECHES&p_id=728.

107 GAO, *Workplace Safety and Health* (2004), 29.

108 Ibid., 21–22.

109 Government Accountability Office, *OSHA's Voluntary Protection Programs: Improved Oversight and Control Would Better Ensure Program Quality*, GAO-09-395 (Washington DC: Government Accountability Office, 2009), 18.

110 Department of Labor, Office of Inspector General, *Employers with Reported Fatalities Were Not Always Properly Identified and Inspected under OSHA's Enhanced Enforcement Program*, Report number 02-09-203-10-105 (Washington DC: Department of Labor, 2009).

111 "When a Worker Is Killed: Do OSHA Penalties Enhance Workplace Safety?" Hearing of the Senate Committee on Health, Labor, and Pensions, April 29, 2008, Senate Hearing 110-895 (Washington DC: Government Printing Office, 2008), 56.

112 Alexis Simendinger, "What's at Stake: Regulation," *National Journal*, October 2, 2008.

113 "Early Indicators of OSHA's Future Focus," *Industrial Safety & Hygiene News*, May 26, 2009. Available at www.ishn.com/articles/88620-early-indicators-of-osha-s-future-focus-5-28.

114 Occupational Safety and Health Administration, Severe Violator Enforcement Program. OSHA White Paper, January 2013. Available at www.osha.gov/dep/enforcement/svep_white_paper.pdf.

115 See Occupational Safety and Health Administration Office of Inspector General, *Recovery Act: OSHA Activities under the Recovery Act*, Report 18-13-004-10-105 (Washington DC: Department of Labor, 2013).

116 Budget of the US Government appendices, various years. Calculations by author.

117 "Labor Department Officials Seek to Sooth VPP Sites," *Industrial Safety & Hygiene News*, July 29, 2009. Available at www.ishn.com/articles/88998-labor-department-officials-seek-to-soothe-vpp-sites-7-29.

118 "OSHA Chief: The New Sheriff Is a Realist," *Industrial Safety & Hygiene News*, March 29, 2010. Available at www.ishn.com/articles/89855-osha-chief-the-new-sheriff-is-a-realist-3-29.

119 Budget of the US Government appendices, various years. Calculations by author.

120 "Remarks by David Michaels, Assistant Sectary of Labor for Occupational Safety and Health, Voluntary Protection Participants' Association Annual National Conference, Orlando, Florida, August 23, 2010," Occupational Safety and Health Administration. Available at www.osha.gov/pls/oshaweb/owadisp.show_document?p_table=SPEECHES&p_id=2287.

121 "Remarks by Jordan Barab, Deputy Assistant Secretary of Labor for Occupational Safety and Health, Voluntary Protection Participants' Association Annual National Conference, Anaheim, California, August 20, 2012," Occupational Safety and Health Administration. Available at www.osha.gov/pls/oshaweb/owadisp.show_document?p_table=SPEECHES&p_id=2860.
122 An updated list of participants by industry can be found at www.osha.gov/dcsp/vpp/sitebynaics.html.
123 David Michaels, "Remarks Prepared for Delivery by David Michaels, PhD, MPH, Assistant Secretary of Labor for Occupational Safety and Health," Voluntary Protection Programs Participants' Association Annual Meeting, National Harbor, MD, August 25, 2014. Occupational Safety and Health Administration. Available at www.osha.gov/pls/oshaweb/owadisp.show_document?p_table=SPEECHES&p_id=3256.

8

DEEPWATER DRIFT AND THE DISASTER IN THE GULF

On April 20, 2010, the BP Deepwater Horizon oil rig exploded off the coast of Louisiana, killing eleven workers. The *New York Times* conveyed a sense of the horror:

> Crew members were cut down by shrapnel, hurled across rooms and buried under smoking wreckage. Some were swallowed by fireballs that raced through the oil rig's shattered interior. Dazed and battered survivors, half-naked and dripping in highly combustible gas, crawled inch by inch in pitch darkness, willing themselves to the lifeboat deck . . . only to find the lifeboats "like smoke-filled ovens."[1]

As weeks and then months passed, the Deepwater Horizon quickly became the largest environmental catastrophe in the nation's history. Once again, regulatory failure would draw the attention of critics. But what makes this case interesting is that regulatory failure emanated from institutional failure. For two decades, Congress had failed to update the statutory framework for oil spills. Chapters 6 and 7 explored the administrative efforts to extend environmental protection and occupational safety and health in the face of polarization and gridlock. This chapter, in contrast, explores a single policy area as it evolved over the course of several decades. Beginning in 1970, Congress successfully passed a series of important laws extending and refining the policy for oil spills. But the last significant statute—the Oil Pollution Act of 1990—was passed in the wake of the 1989 Exxon Valdez disaster. From that point forward, Congress failed to pass new legislation and thus, the oil spill regime failed to evolve in tandem with the rapid and monumental technological changes in deep- and ultra-deepwater oil exploration. As a result, when the Deepwater Horizon disaster occurred, regulators and the industry were caught woefully unprepared to manage the risks of oil exploration and respond to an event that could have been anticipated. Although the policy area was not the target of deregulation, it was subject to the less obvious, more insidious, process of drift.

The Evolution of Oil Spill Policy

Policymakers can adopt various strategies to control risk. In some policy areas, like occupational safety and health, regulators reduce risk by prescribing technological standards that control exposure to hazardous chemicals in the workplace. In environmental policy, they can promulgate engineering standards to prevent leakage from chemical storage facilities. In contrast to risk reduction, policymakers can also engage in risk shifting. That is they can impose rules on liability in such a manner as to place the risks on corporations rather than on government, society, or individuals who would otherwise bear the costs. The underlying theory is simple: If liability is great enough, it can create incentives for corporations to invest in risk management, thereby preventing the frequency and magnitude of future liabilities.[2]

In the area of oil spill policy, risk reduction strategies have been an important part of the instrument mix. Various statutes have imposed design requirements (e.g., the requirement for double hulls in oil tankers under the Oil Pollution Act of 1990). But, arguably, assigning liability for damages and the costs of remediation have been far more important in shaping the behavior of owner/operators and their insurers. The history of oil spill policy is, in part, a history of liability. This is true in two senses. First, there has been an expansion of the conditions under which a responsible party would be liable for damages. Traditionally, owner/operators were liable only if they engaged in willful misconduct or were grossly negligent. By the post-1970 period, norms of strict liability prevailed, making parties liable regardless of whether their behavior met the above criteria. Second, whereas responsible parties were initially liable for relatively modest amounts, these amounts increased dramatically over time (indeed, becoming unlimited in many cases).

Although the use of liability as a policy instrument makes intuitive sense, its effectiveness can depend on the ability (1) to identify responsible parties, (2) measure and assess the damages, and (3) force responsible parties to pay for damages. Obviously, if there are weaknesses in any of these capacities, corporations may fail to have sufficient incentives to manage potential liabilities. Historically, common law liability has been too weak along multiple dimensions to have a deterrent effect. On the other hand, if a liability regime holds parties responsible for damages they did not cause or imposes too great a penalty, then actors may misallocate resources and invest too much in risk management or, alternatively, avoid any activities that could pose potential risks.[3]

The Comprehensive Environmental Response, Compensation, and Liability Act (CERCLA) of 1980 is commonly cited as an example of a liability regime that had unintended consequences for precisely this reason. It created strict, joint and several liability for hazardous waste sites. Strict liability means that parties can be held liable regardless of whether the damages arose from negligence or intent. Joint and several liability, in contrast, means that a defendant can be held liable for the entire damage, regardless of the degree of culpability.[4] Under CERCLA, liability was also retroactive, extending to activities that occurred before the passage of the Act. In the end, a firm that did not cause the environmental damage could be found liable for the damages when those who were responsible had limited assets or had long ago ceased to exist. Quite predictably, the resulting uncertainty and potentially unlimited liability has created disincentives to invest in sites that may have been contaminated in the past, leaving the nation's cities littered with unproductive brownfields. As Jason Scott Johnson notes:

> the lesson from the US experience with environmental liability under CERCLA is that while liability may indeed generate some strong incentives to avoid liability, on balance ex post environmental liability may be a very expensive and often counterproductive instrument for environmental protection.[5]

Modern oil spill policy can be traced to the response to the 1969 Santa Barbara oil spill, at that point, the largest offshore spill in US history.[6] The spill of some 230,000 barrels of oil emanated from a Union Oil platform, six miles off of coast of California. While the policy response was in some ways an extension of earlier policies that imposed civil liabilities for the discharge of oil, it was also shaped by the larger political context. This disaster, when combined with the already glaring evidence of environmental degradation (e.g., the burning Cuyahoga River, the Lake Eerie fish kills) contributed to a sustained period of legislative and administrative activism. As noted in Chapter 6, President Nixon created the Environmental Protection Agency and Congress passed a series of significant regulatory statutes that continue to provide the foundation for environmental regulation.

As the magnitude of the Santa Barbara oil spill became clear, President Nixon's Secretary of the Interior, Walter Hickel, quickly discovered that existing statutes were wholly inadequate to manage the disaster. Under the Clean Water Restoration Act of 1966, parties responsible for discharges on shorelines and navigable waters were required to remove it immediately. In the event that this did not occur, the Secretary of Interior could order removal, but the financial responsibility was limited (reasonable costs), fines were minimal ($2,500 per individual, $10,000 per vessel) and liability was capped (the lesser of $67 per gross ton of the vessel or $5 million). Moreover, the liability provisions were largely ineffective. The government would need to prove willful or gross negligence and there was no compensation to private parties impacted by the spill.[7] Under the provisions of the Act, the government could do little more than ask oil companies working off the coast of Santa Barbara to voluntarily suspend their operations and Union Oil to voluntarily assume the costs of the cleanup efforts.[8]

The Department of Interior acted unilaterally to impose new safety requirements on oil companies working under federal leases and impose higher standards of liability. These initiatives were quickly incorporated into the Water Quality Improvement Act of 1970. The Act accomplished several important things. Section 11 (b)(1) established the policy that "there should be no discharges of oil . . . into or upon the navigable waters of the United States, adjoining shorelines, or into or upon the waters of the contiguous zone." It directed the president to issue new regulations specifying the quantities of oil that would be harmful to the environment and mandating procedures for prevention and remediation. The president was also authorized to take charge of cleanup efforts, develop criteria for state and regional contingency planning, and develop a National Contingency Plan. Congress imposed new civil and criminal penalties, raised the statutory limits for federal government recovery of cleanup costs (now $100 per gross ton or $14 million per vessel). Larger vessels (over 300 gross tons) had to establish and maintain evidence of their ability to meet potential liability. Most important—and to the dismay of insurers, the oil industry, and the Nixon administration—the Act imposed strict liability "without regard to whether any such act or omission was or was not negligent." Indeed, if the government could establish willful negligence or misconduct, liability was unlimited.[9]

The oil spill related provisions of the Water Quality Improvement Act became §311 of the Federal Water Pollution Control Act Amendments (Clean Water Act) of 1972. At that time, Congress established a $35 million revolving fund in the US Treasury (the 311 Fund), under the control of the US Coast Guard, to finance cleanup and mitigation before liable parties could be forced to reimburse the federal government.[10] Six years later, when Congress passed the Clean Water Act Amendments of 1977, it used the opportunity to once again strengthen the regime for oil spills. It extended federal jurisdiction to 200 miles offshore and once again raised the liability caps ($150 per ton, with no cap). Most important, Congress extended liability to "any costs or expenses incurred by the Federal Government or any State government in the restoration or replacement of natural resources damaged or destroyed as a result of the discharge of oil."[11]

As the provisions of the Water Quality Improvement Act evolved via new statutes, Congress passed additional laws to regulate oil in specific venues. In 1973, Congress passed the Trans-Alaska Pipeline Authorization Act, imposing strict liability on pipeline operators and tankers transporting the oil. At that time, it created the Trans-Alaska Pipeline Liability Fund, an analog to the 311 Fund, to be maintained at $100 million through a tax on oil traveling through the pipeline.[12] In 1974, Congress passed the Deepwater Port Act, once again imposing strict liability and creating a Deepwater Port Liability Fund via fees collected by port licensees on oil.[13] Finally, in 1978, Congress passed the Outer Continental Shelf Lands Act that established strict liability for vessels and offshore facilities and imposed requirements that owner/operators maintain evidence of financial responsibility to cover their maximum liabilities. As with the previously mentioned legislation, the new Act created the Offshore Pollution Compensation Fund, to be capitalized at $200 million through a fee on oil from the Outer Continental Shelf.[14]

This brief history suggests three things. First, Congress acted with surprising speed and resolution in this policy area. Within less than a decade of the Santa Barbara spill, it had passed six significant statutes. As noted in Chapter 5, this was a period of low polarization and remarkable legislative productivity. Second, while there were command-and-control features in some of these statutes (e.g., design and construction specifications for deepwater ports), a far greater emphasis was placed on liability as a policy instrument. Strict liability, when combined with high caps on damages, could create incentives for the industry to invest more heavily in risk management that could prevent the frequency and severity of oil spills. At least this was the theory. Finally, given the temporal disjunction between the costs of cleanup and remediation, on the one hand, and the reimbursement by responsible parties, on the other, Congress created a variety of funds that could cover costs. In three of the four cases, these funds would be maintained through fees or taxes imposed on the industry itself, thereby creating additional incentives for risk management on an industry-wide basis.

It is important to note that these statutes were superimposed upon a patchwork of state laws. Several states had their own oil spill laws in place, and in the majority of cases, the laws set no caps on liability. There was ongoing support for creating a unified federal law that would preempt state laws, thereby imposing uniform caps on liability. While this would have been attractive to industry actors who faced great uncertainty over the unevenness of liability requirements, it would have proven weaker than many state laws. Senators from coastal states, in particular, were successful in blocking the creation of comprehensive federal statutes and, relatedly, preventing US participation in international conventions that would have had a similar effect.

Expanding Liability to Toxic Waste

For more than a decade following the passage of the Outer Continental Shelf Lands Act 1978, oil spill policy was at an impasse that was, at times reinforced by the Reagan administration's steadfast opposition to new regulatory statutes. There were periodic oil spills—the Burmah Agate in Galveston Bay, Texas (1979), a Mobil Oil spill on the Columbia River (1984), the Grand Eagle spill on the Delaware River (1985), the Ashland oil spill in Floreffe, Pennsylvania (1988)—but none was large enough to capture the public's attention. At the same time, Congress turned its attention to a related issue: the problem of toxic and hazardous waste sites. Toxic waste policy had two things in common with oil spill policy. First, it was born of crisis. Second, it relied heavily on the policy instruments that had been developed in response to the problem of oil spills. Let us address them in turn.

From the 1920s through the 1940s, Hooker Chemical Company had placed 21,000 tons of waste—a toxic mix of benzene, chlorinated compounds, dioxins, and mercury—in the abandoned Love Canal in Niagara Falls, New York. In 1953, Hooker sold it to the city of Niagara, fully disclosing the potential hazards. Municipal waste was added to the mix before it was covered. In the next few decades, the city developed the land, permitting a school, a playground, and residential construction above the canal. The contamination spread to the soil and groundwater, and with the heavy rains in 1978, it rose to the surface.[15] As the *New York Times* reported:

> A noxious brew of 82 chemicals bubbled up, scalding children and dogs, killing trees and eating through shoes. Pools of fuming liquids collected in yards. Poisons in the air reached dangerous levels in nearby homes. The chemical assault may have caused miscarriages, birth defects or other health problems—the basis for the health commissioner's recommendation that pregnant women and infants leave the area and that the public schools not open in the fall.[16]

Love Canal would become a salient symbol of a much larger problem. At the time, the EPA estimated that there were some 100,000 sites across the nation, 90 percent of which had been operated without safeguards. In the words of an EPA official quoted by the *New York Times*, these waste sites were "ticking time bombs . . . . We're mortgaging our future if we don't control them more carefully."[17]

Congress had addressed various aspects of toxic and hazardous chemicals in the past several years. Most recently, it had passed the Resource Conservation and Recovery Act in 1976 to regulate the generation, transportation, use, and disposal of toxic chemicals. The Act mandated rigorous record-keeping requirements and specified construction and performance standards for treatment and disposal facilities. But the problems encountered at Love Canal, and the other "ticking time bombs" across the country emanated from practices that predated this statute. As Congress turned to this issue, it did not begin with a blank slate. Rather, it drew on the model that had been developed over the previous decade to address the problem of oil spills. In the end, the Comprehensive Environmental Response, Compensation, and Liability Act of 1980 extended this model to a new, but related issue.

With CERCLA, Congress expanded the National Contingency Plan first established for oil spills. More importantly, it designed a system for the identification and prioritization of hazardous waste sites, assessing the liability for responsible parties, and financing remediation. In the latter two accomplishments, Congress drew on the oil spill regime. With respect to liability, CERCLA §101 (32) directly referenced the Clean Water Act's standard that had been incorporated from the Water Quality Improvement Act of 1970, thereby imposing strict liability.[18] As noted earlier, CERCLA went beyond this standard, however, to extend liability to any actor who had been connected with a site and potentially making any actor liable for complete damages regardless of the degree of culpability. While this model of liability could be traced back through the history of oil spill policy, ironically, CERCLA itself did not extend to petroleum. There were efforts in the House of Representatives to include petroleum, but the Senate version of the bill that ultimately became CERCLA contained an exclusion. Legislators in both chambers understood that this was a significant defect. But given the precarious timing—CERCLA was passed in a lame duck Congress, Ronald Reagan had recently been elected president, and the Republicans would soon take control of the White House and the Senate— there was insufficient time to eliminate the petroleum exclusion and develop a single unified regime for hazardous wastes.[19]

The problems of funding remediation were more complicated with CERCLA than with the kinds of damages created by oil spills. Oil spills, when they occur, are quickly discovered and it is not usually difficult to identify responsible parties and force them to assume the cleanup costs. Hazardous waste sites, in contrast, may have long and complicated histories, dating back decades or longer. Some responsible parties may no longer exist; they may have gone insolvent or were acquired by other firms. Given CERCLA's standard of strict, several, and joint liability, the identification of a hazardous waste site may generate a dense thicket of law suits as potentially responsible parties appeal to the legal system to shape the allocation of remediation costs. To fund remediation, Congress drew on the precedents set in oil spill policy, and created the Superfund trust fund. Between 1981 and 1995, $26.6 billion flowed into the trust fund. The primary sources of funding were excise taxes on crude oil and chemicals and an environmental tax on corporations (67.5 percent), budgetary appropriations (17.3 percent), interest (9 percent), and fines, penalties, and recoveries (6.1 percent). But by 1995, a polarized Congress refused to reauthorize the tax. Thereafter, the fund became far too dependent on appropriations.[20]

The Exxon Valdez and the Oil Pollution Act of 1990

By the 1980s, oil spill policy appeared to be locked into an intractable impasse. Commercial interests—oil companies, tanker companies, the insurance industry—would have welcomed a single federal law that placed caps on liability and reduced the complexities of negotiating myriad state and federal statutes. But any effort to override the patchwork of state laws raised the ire of members of Congress representing states with strict oil spill policies. Senate

Majority Leader George J. Mitchell (D-ME) was central to this dispute, warning that any federal statute that aspired to preempt stricter state laws like Maine's, which placed no limits on liability, would never reach the floor for a vote. As *Congressional Quarterly*'s George Hager observed: "For many of the 15 years that Congress has spent laboring in vain to produce a national oil-spill liability law, some frustrated backers have predicted it would take a catastrophic oil spill to break the legislative stalemate."[21] That catastrophic spill came in Prince William Sound, Alaska.

On March 23, 1989, the Exxon Valdez, a 987-foot, single-hulled tanker carrying 1.3 million barrels of North Slope crude oil, departed the Alyeska terminal in Valdez, to begin its journey from Alaska to Long Beach, California. The Valdez was captained by Joseph Hazelwood, a man with a record of drunk driving and alcohol treatment (a fact that was known by Exxon). After an afternoon celebrating with some of the other ships' officers, Hazelwood retired to his quarters and left the tanker under the direction of the third mate, who was not licensed by the Coast Guard to pilot a tanker in Prince William Sound. Just after midnight on March 24, 1989, the Exxon Valdez ran aground on Bligh Reef, tearing open eight of its eleven cargo bays. As the Alaska Oil Commission reported: "Hazelwood—perhaps drunk, certainly facing a position of great difficulty and confusion—would struggle vainly to power the ship off its perch on Bligh Reef." After attempts to free the ship failed, Hazelwood radioed the Valdez traffic center: "We've fetched up, ah, hard aground . . . and, ah, evidently leaking some oil and we're gonna be here for a while and, ah, if you want, ah so you're notified."[22]

Ultimately, the Valdez would dump some 250,000 barrels of crude oil into Alaska's Prince William Sound, making it the greatest oil spill thus far in the nation's history. In terms of sheer size, the official estimates of 250,000 barrels— a figure that remains contested—exceeded the size of the Santa Barbara oil spill. But because the spill occurred in an environmentally pristine area, the ecological effects were significant. As one report recounts:

> No one disputes the spill's death toll during the spring and summer of 1989 as thick oil spread over 10,000 square miles, contaminating a national forest, four national wildlife refuges, three national parks, five state parks, four "critical habitat areas," and a state game sanctuary along 1,500 miles of Alaska shoreline. Casualties included 2,800 sea otters, 300 harbor seals, 250 bald eagles, as many as 22 killer whales, and an estimated quarter-million seabirds. It's unclear how many billions of salmon and herring eggs and intertidal plants succumbed to oil smothering.[23]

None of this includes the severe economic, cultural and social disruptions to Alaska Native villages and commercial fishing communities. In addition to the obvious loss of commercial opportunities, research has documented effects that ranged from growing uncertainty to "increased drug and alcohol use and domestic violence; chronic feelings of helplessness, betrayal and anger; [and] elevated levels of depression, anxiety, and posttraumatic stress disorder."[24]

In part the story of the Exxon Valdez is one of human error. One can only imagine that a more competent crew could have averted the disaster. But human error is also a constant, and thus systems have to be developed to limit the extent to which it can give rise to catastrophic outcomes. The Exxon Valdez exhibited in the starkest of terms that the existing oil spill regime was deficient. At the time of the accident, there were six contingency plans in place, ranging from the National Contingency Plan to site-specific plans and an industry plan. But as the National Response Team's report to the president observed:

> Government and industry plans, individually and collectively, proved to be wholly insufficient to control an oil spill of the magnitude of the Exxon Valdez incident. . . . the various contingency plans did not refer to each other or establish a workable response command hierarchy. This resulted in confusion and delayed the cleanup.[25]

The 1987 contingency plan developed by Alyeska Pipeline Service (a consortium co-owned by Exxon, British Petroleum, Arco, Mobil, Amerada Hess, Phillips, and Unocal), unlike the others, included a scenario for a spill of the magnitude of the Exxon Valdez. However, as the *Wall Street Journal* reported, "The oil companies' lack of preparedness makes a mockery of a 250-page containment plan, approved by the state, for fighting spills in Prince William Sound" and "exposed a much deeper problem: the seeming inability of the oil industry to fight major oil spills."[26] Its ability to execute the plan was compromised by the lack of necessary supplies (barrier booms and dispersants) and the difficulties of summoning emergency response personnel during the Easter weekend. The containment barge, central to the contingency plan, was out of service at the time of the event. It had been used in a cleanup the previous January, unloaded for cleaning, and subsequently damaged in a winter storm. Efforts to reload it were hampered by the lack of qualified forklift operators. "Several feet of snow covered much of the response equipment, making it hard to find the yard."[27] None of this should have come as a surprise. Subsequent investigations revealed a history of inadequate equipment, training, and oil spill drills. Indeed, state records had described Alyeska's spill response capacity as having "regressed to a dangerous level."[28] State regulators responsible for overseeing the contingency plan could have forced changes, but the Alaska Oil Spill Commission concluded that a lack of staffing and policy instruments imposed serious constraints. Short of withdrawing approval of the contingency plan and shutting down the pipeline—the so-called "nuclear option," unpopular in a state that generated 85 percent of its revenues from royalties and taxes on the oil industry—it was difficult to leverage compliance.[29]

The poorly constructed contingency plans and the incapacity to implement them expeditiously allowed for an escalation of the crisis. Once the magnitude of the disaster became clear, a new question quickly emerged: Who would assume responsibility for the estimated $1 billion that would be required to fund cleanup, restoration, and economic damages. Congress had created four separate funds for this purpose, but three were location specific, and only the Trans-Alaska Pipeline Liability Fund was relevant. Under the Trans-Alaska Pipeline Authorization Act, owner/operators were responsible for the first $14 million. At that point, the fund would cover an additional $86 million. The revolving fund created under §311 (k) of the Clean Water Act would offer little help. It had a balance of $6.7 million, despite its authorized ceiling of $35 million.[30] Combined, the funds were unequal to the task. The cleanup was dependent on Exxon, that was spending $1 million per day on the clean up. Had the federal government sought to spend at these levels, the §311 revolving fund would have been exhausted in a week.[31] As the report on the Exxon Valdez prepared by Interior Secretary Samuel K. Skinner and EPA Administrator William K. Reilly concluded:

> Had Exxon not made vast sums of money available rather quickly, or had the discharger been unreachable, foreign, or less solvent, the patchwork of existing federal and state law applicable to a pollution incident of this magnitude would have been inadequate.[32]

The Exxon Valdez disaster attracted heavy coverage in the nation's newspapers and television broadcasts. The media was naturally drawn to the spill: It provided a dramatic symbol of the battle between Big Oil and the environment.[33] It was described, quite correctly, as "the 'Pearl Harbor' of the US environmental movement,"[34] serving as a rallying cry for environmental groups that had sought to preserve Alaska from development. In response to the Exxon Valdez, Congress moved quickly to sculpt new legislation to shore up the oil spill regime. The final product was the Oil Pollution Act (OPA) of 1990, passed by a wide margin in the House (375–5) and a voice vote in the Senate.

As noted earlier, the question of preemption had blocked progress on oil spill legislation for the previous decade, pitting the Senate, which was protective of states' rights, against the House. It prevented US participation in international conventions, including the Protocols to the International Convention on Civil Liability for Oil Pollution Damage and the Protocol to the International Fund for Compensation for Oil Pollution Damages, which would have capped liability at $260 million per vessel. The House of Representatives initially forwarded legislation that would have explicitly preempted state laws. The Senate, led by Majority Leader Mitchell, remained steadfast. Given the pressure for legislative action, the final version of the OPA imposed higher liability standards and endorsed but did not require participation in international conventions, without interfering with state laws.[35] Under the OPA, the standard of liability was the same as that adopted under CERCLA, which, as noted above, had largely evolved out of previous oil spill legislation. That is, the standard was strict, joint and several liability. Liability for cleanup costs was unlimited. However, liability for damages was capped at the greater of $1,200 per gross or $10 million, with a lower cap of $2 million for smaller vessels. The OPA imposed an expansive range of recoverable damages, including natural resources, real and personal property, the loss of profits or earning capacity, the loss of tax and other revenues, and the costs of additional public services. Owners of vessels in excess of 300 gross tons were required to maintain evidence of their ability to meet their maximum potential liability.[36] While comparable requirements were imposed in the past, the potential liability of responsible parties was far greater under the OPA.[37]

The Exxon Valdez had revealed the inadequacy of the exiting mechanisms for funding the cleanup of catastrophic oil spills. A patchwork of funds, some applicable others not, was combined with a dearth of resources. Ultimately, cleanup was dependent on the financial resources of Exxon. Three years before the disaster in Prince William Sound, Congress had drawn on the precedent of CERCLA to create a new Oil Spill Liability Trust Fund, albeit without simultaneously capitalizing it or providing a funding mechanism. Under the OPA, the four existing funds were consolidated into the Oil Spill Liability Trust Fund; $551 million in transfers from these funds were combined with a new five-cents per barrel excise tax on imported and domestic oil to raise the fund's balance to $1 billion. Within this fund, $50 million was made available annually as an Emergency Fund to allow for rapid response to spills and conduct initial assessments of damages. The remainder (the Principle Fund) was to pay claims to damaged parties in the event that responsible parties failed to make payment within 90 days. The Attorney General was authorized to recover these costs from the responsible parties and reimburse the fund (along with fines and civil penalties). The Principle Fund would also supplement the appropriations of agencies involved in implementing the OPA.[38]

The OPA also sought to prevent future spills through a variety of means. Some were technical: The Act required that new vessels be equipped with double hulls; the requirement was phased in for existing tankers, with all vessels over 5,000 gross tons in compliance by 2010 (or 2015, if they have double bottoms or sides). It also required participation in the USCG monitoring and tracking system and use of escort vehicles in Prince William Sound and Puget Sound. More important, the OPA mandated expanded contingency planning—a response to the chaotic state of affairs revealed by the Exxon Valdez spill. The National Contingency Plan had to be revised to include fish and wildlife and a realistic worst-case discharge response plan. It had to delegate more authority to the Federal On Scene Coordinators and a newly created National Strike Force Coordination Center that would work with strike teams in each of ten USCG districts. Similarly, owner/operators of vessels and facilities had to develop oil spill response plans, considering worst-case scenarios, and maintain (either directly or via contract) the personnel and equipment to implement the plans. Companies were required to file their plans with the USCG, the EPA, or the Department of Transportation by February 1993 and, unless approved by February 1995, they would be barred from transporting or storing oil.[39]

The Quiet Interregnum

The OPA imposed significant new restrictions on the petroleum industry. Unsurprisingly, there were initial claims from the industry that the economic consequences would be devastating. There were some short-term consequences, most of which were predictable. Several corporations, including Shell Oil, barred their tankers from operating in US waters, relying instead on charters. Other corporations pursued restructuring, creating subsidiaries to handle shipping in the hopes of sheltering the parent company from liability or divesting in inland fleets and contracting with third parties. Securing transportation in the price-sensitive spot market, ironically, gave an advantage to shipping firms that did not invest in double-hulled ships, which were up to 20 percent more expensive to operate due to their weight. And then there was the problem of OPA's requirements that shippers provide evidence of financial responsibility. While this requirement was not new, when coupled with a new liability regime, it created some initial difficulties. The Protection and Indemnity Clubs—mutual insurance associations of ship owners—proved hesitant to issue guarantees out of fear that they would expose members to unlimited liability. Ultimately, clubs provided coverage, but demanded a special surcharge for ships operating in the United States to cover the additional exposure.[40]

Despite the strategic responses to the new regime, the oil industry survived and flourished. The American Petroleum Institute moved quickly to develop a greater industry capacity to prevent, contain, and clean up spills. It created the Petroleum Industry Response Organization, which was ultimately chartered as the Marine Spill Response Corporation, funded by corporate dues paid by twenty oil companies and a pipeline company. Rather than requiring each company to maintain the equipment and personnel to implement their oil spill response plans, the new arrangement allowed companies to act collectively and pool their resources to manage spills as large as 216,000 barrels (i.e., roughly the size of the Exxon Valdez spill). Within five years, the Marine Spill Response Corporation would invest $900 million to establish five regional response centers with twenty-three equipment staging areas.[41]

It is striking to note that the two decades following the passage of the OPA were marked by a significant reduction in the number and size of spills. The US Coast Guard collects data on oil spills in US waters. Its Oil Spill Compendium is the best single source for analyzing trends since 1973. It is useful to preface the examination of the data with a few comments. The USCG provides data on the number of spills and the volume of spills. Unsurprisingly, the vast majority of spills are relatively small (e.g., under 10 gallons), whereas large spills (usually defined as in excess of 100,000 gallons or 238 barrels) are far rarer. While the cumulative effect of small spills should not be dismissed, they are geographically dispersed and thus far less significant than large spills from an environmental perspective.[42]

The total number of spills by spill size is presented in Figure 8.1. As the figure shows, there was a general decline in the total number of spills, and this decline was the greatest for spills over 1,000 gallons. As noted above, the vast majority of spills in any given year are relatively small. For the period in question (1973–2009), spills of 1–100 gallons constituted 88.5 percent of the total, whereas spills of over 1,000 gallons were a far more modest 3.4 percent. Large spills (over 100,000 gallons) were particularly infrequent, claiming .012 percent of the total. Yet, the large spills are the most significant with respect to overall volume. During the period 1973–2009, approximately 249.7 million gallons of oil were spilled in US waters. Of this amount, fully 85.6 percent came from spills greater than 100,000 gallons.

The total volume of oil spilled during the period 1973–2009 is presented in Figure 8.2. The most striking feature of this graph is the sharp decline in volume following the implementation of the OPA. Between 1973 and 1990, an average of 11.86 million gallons were spilled on an annual basis. From 1991 to 2009, in contrast, an annual average 1.9 million gallons were spilled. Much of this reduction can be attributed to the sharp decline of spills of over 1 million gallons. In the pre-OPA period, spills of greater than 1 million gallons occurred in

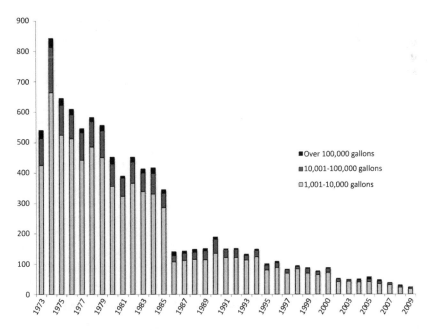

FIGURE 8.1   Number of Significant Spills by Spill Size

Source: US Coast Guard, *Polluting Incident Compendium* (2012).

fifteen of the eighteen years, cumulatively resulting in more than 82 million gallons discharged. In comparison, the period 1991–2009 witnessed spills of more than a million gallons in two years (2005 and 2006), cumulatively responsible for 10 million gallons. The spills in 2005 were largely a product of natural disasters: Hurricane Katrina, a category IV hurricane that damaged storage and pipeline facilities in Louisiana, and Hurricane Rita, which drove an integrated tug barge into a submerged platform in the Gulf of Mexico.[43]

While the data as presented in Figures 8.1 and 8.2 are suggestive, there is also a body of empirical research that has evaluated the impact of the OPA on oil spills. Anthony C. Hoffman and Todd Steiner have modeled oil spills as a function of vessel traffic, the amount of petroleum handled, and the price of petroleum for the period 1976–2004. After controlling for these causes, they conclude that OPA was the most significant factor explaining the sharp reduction of spills. When including relatively smaller spills, they conclude that the expected number of spills absent OPA would have been over 80 percent higher than in 1990. The new liability regime introduced under OPA had an immediate effect starting in 1991. The double-hull requirement, which was phased in beginning in 1996, only contributed to further reductions.[44] Yet, according to a subsequent analysis, this requirement was quite important. According to one study examining US oil spill data from 2001 to 2008, double-hull design reduced the size of spills in tanker accidents by 62 percent, with smaller reductions (20 percent) for tanker barges.[45]

As long as the economy is dependent on petroleum, some level of spillage is inevitable. The question is whether public policy creates the incentives for

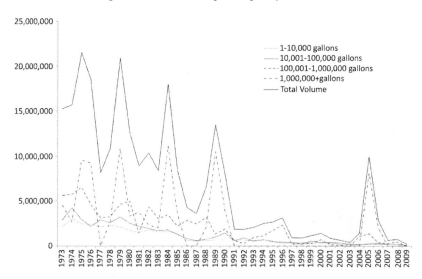

FIGURE 8.2 Total Volume of Spills by Spill Size

Source: US Coast Guard, *Polluting Incident Compendium* (2012).

corporations involved in the extraction and transportation of oil to develop the capacity to prevent spills, contain incidents before they grow in magnitude, and clean up any discharges. There is strong empirical evidence that the liability regime and regulatory changes had a major impact on the frequency and severity of spills. From the perspective of 2009, the regime put into place almost two decades earlier appeared to be a success. Whatever assurance the empirical record might have offered was shattered in 2010, when an explosion on BP's Deepwater Horizon mobile offshore drilling unit resulted, ultimately, in the largest spill in US history, accounting for 86 percent of all of the oil spilled from 1973 to 2010.

The Deepwater Horizon Disaster

On April 20, 2010, the Deepwater Horizon—a 33,000-ton, semisubmersible ultra-deepwater oil drilling rig—was positioned 49 miles off the Louisiana coast to drill a two-and-one-half mile deep exploratory well in the Macondo Prospect. Drilling was a technically complex matter. The Deepwater Horizon was located 5,000 feet above the ocean floor, and the well it drilled extended some 13,000 feet below the sea floor to a reservoir that contained an estimated 110 million barrels of oil. The well itself was connected to the seabed by a production casing, a steel pipe surrounded by additional casings to protect it from the rock formations. The drill pipe extended from the Deepwater Horizon through another pipe, known as a riser, and then passed through a 53-foot blowout preventer (or BOP). The oil and gas found in deep wells are under enormous pressure from the weight of the rock formations. The BOP was designed to contain the hydrocarbons in the event of a blowout. It consisted of a series of five devices that could seal the margins around the drill pipe and, in the case of the "blind sheer ram," actually cut through the drill pipe and seal the well.[46]

The organizational complexity and economic pressures exacerbated the technical complexity of deepwater oil exploration. The high costs of oil exploration in a deepwater environment requires the development of myriad partnerships and leasing arrangements. In the Macondo Prospect, BP had formed a partnership with Anadarko Petroleum and MOEX USA. The Deepwater Horizon oil rig, valued at $560 million, was owned by Transocean, which leased its services at a cost of up to $1 million per day. BP and its partners relied on the services of other companies to support its efforts (e.g., Halliburton was responsible for cementing the well; Oceaneering technicians controlled the remote operating vehicles necessary to work at the depths of the Gulf). BP had originally budgeted $96.2 million and 51 days to complete the well. But a host of challenges, including rig damage from Hurricane Ida and geological formations that required modifications of plans, had created significant delays. By April 20, the project was almost six weeks over schedule and $58 million over budget, but a successful conclusion appeared to be in sight.[47]

With the drilling completed, the only remaining task was to place a cement seal to secure the production casing for temporary abandonment until a production rig could be moved into place and conduct some pressure tests to verify the integrity of the well. Before the task could be completed, however, mud and then gas rushed past the BOP and ignited. Attempts to engage the BOP and close the blind sheer ram failed. The explosion in the well sent debris flying to the surface, engulfing the rig in flames and killing eleven workers. On April 22—ironically, the fortieth anniversary of Earth Day—the rig sank, beginning a five-month saga that would become the greatest environmental disaster in US history.

In its examination of the events leading up to the sinking of the Deepwater Horizon, the National Commission on the BP Deepwater Horizon Oil Spill and Offshore Drilling (hereafter, the Commission) identified and examined a number of discrete decisions that were made, many with the goal of cutting costs and saving time on a project that was already woefully over budget. While the Commission admitted the difficulty of determining the extent to which the various missteps were responsible, it concluded that "each of the mistakes made on the rig and onshore by industry and government increased the risk of a well blowout" and "the cumulative risk that results from these decisions and actions was both unreasonably large and avoidable."[48] The root causes of the disaster were easier to identify. They included the failure of management and the failure of government to effectively regulate offshore drilling. With respect to management, the Commission cited failures to identify and address risks and communicate them throughout the organization and to contractors, and ineffective training of key personnel. Moreover, it noted that many of the decisions that were made to save time and money created new risks that were not adequately addressed. The BP Commission report explained:

> Corporations understandably encourage cost-saving and efficiency. But given the dangers of deepwater drilling, companies involved must have in place strict policies requiring rigorous analysis and proof that less-costly alternatives are in fact equally safe. If BP had any such policies in place, it does not appear that its Macondo team adhered to them.[49]

On the regulatory side, the Commission observed that "regulations were inadequate" and "many critical aspects of drilling operations were left to industry to decide without agency review." This was not simply a product of poor regulatory decision-making by the Department of Interior's Mineral Management Service (MMS). Rather, the Commission placed the regulatory failure in a larger political context:

> The root cause can be better found by considering how . . . efforts to expand regulatory oversight, tighten safety requirements, and provide funding to equip regulators with the resources, personnel, and training needed

to be effective were either overtly resisted or not supported by industry, members of Congress, and several administrations. As a result, neither the regulations nor the regulators were asking the tough questions or requiring the demonstration of preparedness that could have avoided the Macondo disaster.

Even if the above had not been true, the MMS "would have still lacked personnel with the kinds of expertise to enforce those regulations effectively."[50] Under these conditions, regulators proved overly deferential to industry decisions.

The sinking of the Deepwater Horizon was a striking event. But it was eclipsed by the dramatic efforts to determine how to seal the hemorrhaging well. One might question why this proved so challenging, given that the Oil Pollution Act of 1990 had mandated that industry actors develop worst-case scenario contingency plans and maintain the equipment and personnel to implement them. Yet, it became clear in the immediate aftermath of the sinking that industry had failed in this task. When efforts to activate the BOP with remotely operated submersibles failed, it began a process of injecting chemical dispersants into the oil at its source. Attention turned to drilling relief wells to drain the oil from the underlying reservoir, thereby reducing the pressure. They could be employed subsequently to pump cement and mud into the well to seal it off. By May 2, work began on drilling a relief well; a second well would be initiated two weeks later. Unfortunately, this was viewed as a long-term solution that could require up to 100 days to complete. As a Commission staff paper notes: "Other than the lengthy process of drilling a relief well, BP had no available, tested technique to stop a deepwater blowout." It was thus forced to initiate "a massive effort to develop containment options, either by adapting shallow-water technology to the deepwater environment, or by designing entirely new devices." BP formed teams to consider different containment options, including activating the BOP, siphoning oil from the leaking riser, and "top kill" procedures involving pumping material into the well.[51]

On May 7, as drilling continued, a four-story containment dome was lowered over the riser, with the goal of channeling the oil into a pipe for collection at the surface. This effort was abandoned when the pipe became clogged. However, by May 16, a tube had been attached to the rise to collect some of the oil. The top kill strategy was deployed at the end of May, as BP tried to stem the flow of oil by pumping thick drilling mud into the well and, more inventively, injecting golf balls and pieces of tire rubber into the BOP (something creatively referred to as a "junk shot"). Various experiments in siphoning oil continued in June, with some positive effects. In July, a capping stack was lowered on to the BOP and, for the first time in 87 days, the flow of oil into the Gulf ceased. By early August, the decision was made to pump heavy drilling mud into the well, followed by cement. By September 19, some five months after the Macondo blowout, National Incident Commander Admiral Thad Allen announced that

BP had "successfully completed the relief well by intersecting and cementing the well nearly 18,000 feet below the surface . . . we can finally announce that the Macondo 252 well is effectively dead."[52]

In the end, the Deepwater Horizon disaster resulted in the release of 4.9 million barrels of oil into the Gulf of Mexico. The response effort was unprecedented. The On Scene Coordinator Report provides some indication of the magnitude of the effort

> Two drilling ships, numerous oil containment vessels, and a flotilla of support vessels were deployed to control the source of the well, while 835 skimmers and approximately 9,000 vessels were involved in the cleanup. On the single most demanding day of the response, over 6,000 vessels, 82 helicopters and 20 fixed wing aircraft and over 47,849 personnel/responders were assigned; 88,522 square miles of fisheries were closed . . . 3,795,985 feet of containment boom was deployed; 26 controlled in situ burns were conducted, burning 59,550 barrels of oil; 181 miles of shoreline were heavily to moderately oiled; 68,530 gallons (1,632 barrels) of dispersant were applied, and 27,097 barrels of oil were recovered.[53]

The total costs for the cleanup, borne by BP, were $32 billion. BP faced additional costs as a result of the Deepwater Horizon. In April 2016, a $20.8 billion settlement was granted, including BP, the federal government, and the states of Alabama, Florida, Louisiana, Mississippi, and Texas. The settlement included a $5.5 billion fine under the Clean Water Act, $8.1 billion for natural resources damages, $4.9 billion to the Gulf states, $1 billion to local governments, and another $700 million for as yet to be discovered problems. Befitting the magnitude of the disaster, this was the largest settlement with a single firm in US history and the largest civil penalty connected to the environment.[54] The news of the settlement brought an end to five years of litigation and sent its stock prices sharply upward. Investors had reason to celebrate. The settlement payments would be paid out over an eighteen-year period (roughly $1.1 billion annually). Moreover, the vast majority of its settlement could be deducted from its US tax returns, a *de facto* taxpayer subsidy.[55]

Making Sense of the Regulatory Failure

The Deepwater Horizon spill was the greatest environmental disaster in the nation's history. A spill of this magnitude may well have been viewed as a highly improbable event given the historical record of spills. Assuming that the regulatory budget is fixed, policymakers inevitably face tradeoffs. It is not necessarily a sign of regulatory failure if policymakers decide against imposing massive costs to prevent some low probability but potentially catastrophic events. Indeed, it may be a prudent decision if one wants to maximize the impact of scarce resources. But occasionally, low probability events happen. As Christopher Carrigan and Cary Coglianese note:

> the mere existence of an accident or disaster does not necessarily mean that the regulatory system has broken down . . . . Indeed, provided that such disasters occur infrequently, it may well be impossible to judge from their occasional occurrence whether the regulatory agency has struck the optimal balance in its risk management strategies. With any low-probability risk, we would not expect the hazardous event to occur anything but infrequently.[56]

If, in fact, policymakers made optimal decisions as a product of rational risk–cost–benefit tradeoffs and implemented policy effectively, there may still be the occasional disaster. Outcomes of policy will always be probabilistic.

Yet, there may be alternative explanations that cast the outcomes as the result of regulatory failure rather than bad luck. Following the Deepwater Horizon disaster, one of the hypotheses that garnered a great deal of attention involved lax regulatory oversight. The MMS was forced to execute incompatible duties—one regulatory, the other commercial—and it was this latter duty that served to magnify industry influence (or, in the extreme versions, created the preconditions for outright capture). Let us examine this explanation in somewhat greater detail before turning to an alternative hypothesis that is more persuasive; namely, that the failure stemmed from a political failure involving the recalibration of policy in light of dramatic changes in the industry.

Industry Influence and Conflicting Mandates

The primary regulator responsible for offshore drilling was the Department of Interior's Minerals Management Service, created in 1982.[57] The MMS emerged from a series of reforms designed, in part, to consolidate royalty collection. Under the preexisting arrangement, the US Geological Service had been responsible for revenue collection. The agency was not well suited for this task; systematic underreporting of production had resulted in a failure to collect royalties. Under the reorganization, MMS was assigned the task of revenue collection activities from oil and gas extracted under offshore and onshore leases. It could either collect the royalties in cash or in kind (under the royalties-in-kind program, the MMS would accept gas or oil and then sell it at a market price). In addition to collecting revenues, MMS was responsible for evaluating, leasing, and regulating offshore exploration and development. For critics, this combination of duties rendered the MMS overly accommodative to industry interests. Efforts to maintain rigorous regulatory oversight could suppress production, thereby compromising revenues. Maximizing revenues, in contrast, would involve sacrificing regulatory scrutiny. In essence, failed regulation emanated from poor institutional design decisions, the intermingling of duties that should have been segregated.

This was one of the core arguments made by the National Commission on the BP Deepwater oil spill. The Commission observed "internal tensions and confusion of goals that weakened the agency's effectiveness and made it more susceptible to outside pressures." It continues:

> At the core of this tension was a trade-off between, on the one hand, promoting "expeditions and orderly development" of offshore resources, as mandated by the Outer Continental Lands Act of 1978, while also ensuring, on the other hand, that offshore development proceeded in a manner that protected human health, safety, and the environment. Over the course of many years, political pressure to expand access and expedite permit approvals and other regulatory processes often combined to push MMS toward elevating the former goal over the latter.[58]

To this end, the Commission recommended assigning the duties formerly entrusted to the MMS to three new entities. It called for a statute to create a new independent agency within the Department of Interior to assume the regulatory functions. The leasing and scientific activities would be assigned to a second agency, with natural resource revenue management vested in a third agency. In essence, the organizational separation of functions could prevent the internal tensions and conflicts that led the MMS to prioritize resource development over competing goals.

As Christopher Carrigan has argued quite persuasively, a careful examination of the history of MMS leads one to question the force of this argument. The assumption that the two functions were closely integrated encounters some clear empirical problems. The two functions were geographically separated: Revenue collection (Revenue Management) was centralized outside of Denver, Colorado, whereas the regulatory functions implemented by MMS's Offshore Energy and Minerals Management (Offshore Energy) were located in close proximity to offshore resources, with a majority of staff located along the Gulf Coast (most notably, in New Orleans). Moreover, there were longstanding problems of coordination between Revenue Management and Offshore Energy. Their computer systems were not integrated; failures of Energy Management to provide Revenue Management with production data impeded the latter's ability to execute its functions, contributing to its ongoing difficulties in raising revenues.[59] As Carrigan explains, assumptions that revenue collection undermined regulation stands in stark contrast to the evidence:

> the vast majority of MMS's problems were connected to its function as an oil and gas revenue collector. Conversely, Offshore Energy received little critical attention from Congress throughout most of its existence . . . until

2010, the group was widely regarded as successfully performing its functions as demonstrated through the numerous awards and general approval it received politically.[60]

This is not to say that there were not problems. Indeed, there was a long history of unethical behavior and cozy relationships between some staff at MMS and the petroleum industry. The Department of Interior's Office of Inspector General, in revelations that predated the Deepwater Horizon, documented activities in the Denver office that ranged from the acceptance of gifts and gratuities to socializing with industry actors (a term that included incidents of drug and alcohol abuse and sexual relations). Some senior managers were "calculatedly ignorant of the rules governing post-employment restrictions" as they awarded contracts for disposing of payment-in-kind resources to former employees.[61] A subsequent Inspector General report found comparable problems with regulators overseeing activities in the Gulf of Mexico: "a culture of accepting gifts from oil and gas companies was prevalent." One employee had actually conducted inspections on a company's platforms while negotiating an employment contract with the same company. Clearly, there was a "sheer erosion of professional culture within some offices," to quote the Commission's report.[62] But incidences such as these, as troubling as they might be, do not make the case for an agency captured by industry.

A Technological Revolution and the Problem of Drift

In Chapter 5, we explored the problem of polarization. While Congress had proven quite successful in developing significant new regulatory statutes in the 1960s and 1970s, things would be quite different beginning in the 1990s. Legislative productivity declined markedly and significant regulatory statutes became a rarity, particularly if they expanded the reach of the regulatory state. Social regulatory agencies like the EPA and OSHA were not subject to explicit deregulation; rather, they were forced to function with increasingly dated mandates. They were subject to drift. A similar scenario appears to have occurred in oil pollution policy. From 1990 onward, Congress failed to recalibrate the oil spill regime despite the fact that the period witnessed nothing short of a technological revolution in oil exploration. The expedients embraced by the Oil Pollution Act of 1990, while clearly successful in preventing a recurrence of events like the Exxon Valdez, were ill suited for the industry as it subsequently evolved. Transporting oil in tankers or pipelines is fundamentally different from extracting oil from sources a mile or more below the surface.

Although offshore oil extraction in the Gulf of Mexico dates back to 1938, by 1980, most offshore oil production still came from relatively shallow water (e.g., 200 feet). Over the next several decades, the industry faced several challenges. First, the movement to deep water was far more expensive than production in shallow waters, and these costs could be difficult to justify in economic terms when oil prices were low, as they were for much of the 1980s and periodically thereafter. Second, and more important, deep and ultra-deep exploration was far more complex, and thus contingent on ongoing technological innovation. Advances in three-dimensional seismic imaging, combined with growing data processing power, enhanced the capacity for exploration and field development. Innovations in drilling and platform design were critical as well. The industry invested in vessels that could drill at greater depths (from 5,000 to 10,000 feet of water, and 20,000 to 30,000 feet below the surface). Working at new depths required the development of remote-operating vehicles that could be controlled from the surface. It also necessitated new platform designs, first tension-leg platforms that could be tethered to the seafloor with anchors and then, at greater depths, spar platforms that limited motion with deep-hulls and trusses that extend hundreds of feet below the surface.[63]

While the technological innovations were stunning, a staff working paper for the Commission noted that these "developments could not disguise the fact that the technical challenges" remained "unique and formidable" given the harsh conditions. "Water depths are extreme, down to 10,000 feet. Total well depths . . . can go beyond 30,000 feet. Well shut-in pressures can surpass 10,000 pounds per square inch. Bottom-hole temperatures can exceed 350 degree Fahrenheit." With respect to drilling, the long risers that connect drilling vessels to the blowout preventer "are exposed to strong ocean currents" and the severe pressures require a reliance on remote-operating vehicles when working thousands of feet below the surface.[64] As the report of the Commission noted "The remarkable advances that have propelled the move to deepwater drilling merit comparison with exploring outer space."[65]

Despite the challenges, the growth in deep and ultra-deep activity was impressive. The number of new wells drilled and producing for the period 1985–2015 is presented in Figure 8.3. In 1985, there were 82 deepwater wells drilled, with a total of 66 in active production. The number of new wells drilled would peak at 206 in 2001, whereas the number of active wells would reach a high of 501 in 2009. Ultra-deep activity lagged, as one might expect, given the greater technological complexity. The number of new wells drilled reached a peak of 71 in 2001, while the number of active wells would reach a high of 121 in 2015, the last year in the time series. During this same period, the amount of oil from deep and ultra-deep production in the Gulf of Mexico increased from 21 million barrels (1985) to 416.4 million barrels in 2014. To place things in broader perspective, in 1990, the year the Oil Pollution Act was passed, oil from deep and ultra-deep sources constituted 4.4 percent of the oil extracted from the Gulf of Mexico. By 2010, the year of the Deepwater Horizon disaster, it had reached 81.3 percent.[66] Clearly, the industry had changed in ways that few could have foreseen in the days of the Exxon Valdez.

The rapid expansion of deepwater drilling was undoubtedly accelerated by public policy. In 1995, Congress passed the Outer Continental Shelf Deep Water

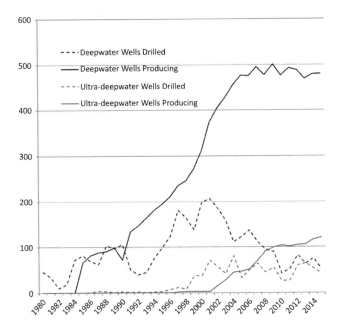

FIGURE 8.3   Deepwater and Ultra-deepwater Wells

Source: Bureau of Ocean Energy Management.

Royalty Relief Act to encourage exploration and development in deep water during a period of low oil and gas prices. Under the Act, firms that secured deepwater leases between 1996 and 2000 were given a waiver or reduction in royalty payments. The royalty suspension volumes increased with the depth of the wells (e.g., 17.5 million barrels for leases in waters between 200 and 400 meters, compared with 87.5 million barrels for leases in waters deeper than 800 meters). Although the Minerals Management Service imposed a price threshold above which royalty relief would not be granted, it did this inconsistently. Between 1996 and 2000, MMS failed to include price thresholds in 1,031 of the 3,401 leases it issued, an oversight that provided an additional subsidy of up to $10 billion.[67] Ultimately, an industry lawsuit challenging the Secretary of the Interior's authority to impose price-based thresholds was successful, further expanding the subsidy for deep water leases.[68] Certainly, there is evidence that industry responded to the incentives. In 1994, the year before the passage of royalty relief, 17 percent of leases were in deep water. By 1997, this figure had increased to 70 percent.[69]

In Search of Reform

The National Commission on the BP Deepwater Horizon Oil Spill and Offshore Drilling, co-chaired by Bob Graham (former Governor of Florida and

US Senator) and William K. Reilly (former EPA administrator), released its report and recommendations in January 2011. The Commission's recommendations envisioned a complete reconfiguration of oil spill policy, focusing on changes in regulation and industry governance that, in some important ways, employed some of the theoretical insights mentioned in Chapter 3's discussion of co-regulation. Let us review, albeit briefly, some of the key recommendations before discussing the legislative response.

The Commission premised its recommendations on the observation: "Neither the industry's nor the federal government's approaches to managing and overseeing the leasing and development of offshore resources have kept pace with rapid changes in the technology, practices, and risks associated with the different geological and ocean environments being explored and developed." While there had been efforts under successive administrations to promulgate new regulations regarding safety management and data reporting, they had been derailed by industry opposition or the Office of Management and Budget's concerns with compliance costs. The Commission argued that regulators must "reorient their regulatory approaches to integrate more sophisticated risk assessment and risk management practices" and "shift their focus from prescriptive regulations covering only the operator to a foundation of augmented prescriptive regulations."[70] In essence, the Commission recommended that existing regulations be subjected to expert review and benchmarked against international standards. The Department of Interior should work with other regulators and standard-setting organizations to "identify those drilling, production, and emergency-response standards that best protect offshore workers and the environment" and these standards should be updated "at least every five years as under the formal review process of the International Organization for Standardization."[71] Regulated parties, in turn, would be required to incorporate these standards into their exploration and production plans, implement Safety Environmental Management System Requirements, subject to third-party auditing and certification.[72] As explained in Chapter 3, the integration of regulations, standards, and internal management systems has a long pedigree in theoretical debates regarding alternatives to traditional command-and-control regulation.

The existing regulatory structure came under scrutiny. The Commission cited the "mingling of distinct statutory responsibilities"—most notably, safety and environmental regulation, on the one hand, and revenue generation and management on the other. The problems intrinsic in the competing missions were exacerbated by political and administrative problems. On the political side, there was "a tendency to defer to industry, which successfully sought congressional and political intervention to shorten time frames for plan and permit reviews, blocked royalty valuation rulemakings, and advocated to delay and weaken rules aimed at improving the safety management of operations." Administratively, the MMS was hampered by "an outdated organizational structure, a chronic shortage of resources, a lack of sufficient technical expertise, and the inherent difficulty of coordinating effectively with all the other government agencies."[73]

The Commission's recommendation was nothing short of a complete overhaul of the regulatory structure. It called for a new organic statute to create a new independent agency, the Offshore Safety Authority, in the Department of Interior to review and approve permits, inspect operations, and audit health, safety and environmental management systems. The new agency "should have the classifications and salary scales for engineering and technical staff similar to those of the Nuclear Regulatory Commission."[74] In addition, the Commission recommended the creation of a new Leasing and Environmental Science Office to manage leasing activities and the continuation of the Office of Natural Resources Revenues (created via a recent reorganization following the Deepwater Horizon spill). The budgets for these agencies (and others involved in overseeing the industry) "should come directly from fees paid by the offshore industry." Congress "could expressly oblige lessees to fund the regulation necessary to allow for private industry access to the energy resources on the [outer continental shelf]."[75]

As the Commission turned to the industry, it observed that it "has no discernible, broadly embraced culture of safety." While industry "devoted billions of dollars to the technologies required for deepwater drilling, it had devoted essentially nothing to creating alternative capabilities to deal with the foreseeable consequences of a disaster."[76] To remedy this situation, the Commission turned to the example of the nuclear power industry. In the wake of the Three Mile Island disaster, as noted in Chapter 3, it created the Institute of Nuclear Power Operators, a private organization devoted to developing and inculcating best practices and auditing the performance of its members.[77] The Commission recommended the creation of a comparable industry-run safety institute. Formally separate from the American Petroleum Institute, this organization would "drive continuous improvement in risk management practices, information sharing on accidents and near misses, and peer learning."[78] Members would be subjected to routine audits of their contingency plans, hazard assessments, training, and performance more generally, and this information would be shared with other members and serve as the basis for ongoing peer review. The Commission hinted at a move toward a system of co-regulation, making "participation in the industry organization mandatory for all well permit applicants."[79]

One of the more striking revelations of the Deepwater Horizon was the lack of sufficient contingency planning and preparation. In the Commission's words, it was "dismayingly clear that neither BP nor the federal government was prepared to deal with a spill of the magnitude and complexity of the Deepwater Horizon disaster."[80] Spill response plans "were not distributed to any federal agencies for review and comment outside of MMS" and once the spill occurred, "it was quickly evident that even the response capacity indicated in the industry's spill response plans did not exist."[81] To remedy this situation, the Commission proposed a far more vigorous system of interagency review, particularly when involving plans for spills of national significance. The Commission also turned to the need for additional research and development in spill response. Despite the technological revolution in oil exploration, response technology "has improved only incrementally since 1990." Oil companies have "committed minimal resources" and, despite the fact that the Oil Pollution Act on 1990 authorized funds for this purpose, "Congress has never appropriated even half the full amount authorized."[82] The Commission identified several specific areas for research and recommended that Congress authorize mandatory spending in this area ("Congress can comply with its pay-as-you-go rules by supporting increased research and development funding with a fee on offshore leases").[83] In keeping with the post-1994 thrust of environmental policy, the Commission also recommended incentivizing private sector research through tax credits and public–private partnerships.

Of course, investments in cleanup technology can be incentivized in other ways, most notably through increases in liability caps. The Oil Pollution Act of 1990 capped liability for damages at $75 million (there are no liability limits if the responsible party exhibited gross negligence, willful misconduct, violated regulations, or failed to report the incident). Similarly, the Oil Spill Liability Trust Fund could cover claims for damages of up to an additional $1 billion. Responsible parties are also required to maintain evidence of financial responsibility. For offshore facilities, the financial responsibility requirements range from $35 to $150 million. While these sums may have seemed sufficient in 1990, the Deepwater Horizon disaster imposed costs in the tens of billions of dollars. As the Commission noted, BP waived the liability caps and placed $20 billion in escrow. "But if a less well capitalized company had caused the spill, neither a multi-billion dollar compensation fund nor the funds necessary to restore injured parties would likely have been available."[84] The responsible party would have declared bankruptcy and the Oil Spill Liability Trust Fund would have been quickly depleted. Although the Commission did not suggest specific monetary limits, it recommended that Congress pass legislation to raise the liability cap for financial responsibility requirements, while authorizing larger per-incident limits on payouts. This latter step would likely require increases in the per-barrel tax from its current levels.

The Aftermath

The Commission's report and recommendations—some 380 pages, in total—were impressive in many regards. Yet, the immediate response was somewhat predictable. Industry representatives warned that new rules and regulations were unnecessary for firms with clean safety records. When combined with unspecified increases in liability caps, they warned that the proposed changes would force cuts in production and increases in fuel costs. President Obama welcomed recommendations that could be addressed through administrative means, but was skeptical that new regulatory statutes and additional spending could be extracted from Congress. Bob Graham, co-chair of the Commission, was more hopeful, suggesting that the magnitude of the Deepwater Horizon spill would "override an ideological preference for less government, less government intrusion, [and] less cost."[85] These hopes were quickly dashed. When the recommendations were presented before the House Natural Resources Committee, William K. Reilly described the environment as one of "venomous partisanship." Even among newly seated members of the new GOP majority—many of whom were attending their first committee meetings—"we were treated as if we were the enemy."[86]

In the immediate aftermath of the Deepwater Horizon, Interior Secretary Ken Salazar renamed the MMS the Bureau of Ocean Energy, Management, Regulation and Enforcement (BOEMRE), and then reorganized it into three new units (the Bureau of Safety and Environmental Enforcement, the Bureau of Ocean Energy Management, and the Office of Natural Resource Revenue) much as suggested by the Commission. New regulations were issued to impose more stringent requirements for well design, well casing and cementing, and blow out protectors. Much of this mattered little at the time, given that the Obama administration had imposed a moratorium on deepwater permits in May of 2010. With these regulations, the agency reached the limits of what could be accomplished without statutory authorization or the funding to hire additional personnel.[87]

In Congress, efforts to pass new liability legislation floundered. While the Obama administration and Democrats wanted to raise liability caps substantially, Republicans and oil-state legislators from both parties objected that it would only destroy smaller companies that could not afford the insurance. An alternative approach supported by the GOP and oil-state Democrats would have drawn on the model of the Price–Anderson Act of 1957, which limited liability for nuclear facilities and then relied on an industry-wide mutual insurance fund to cover additional claims. Such an arrangement, it was argued, would create incentives for industry investments in safety, while sheltering smaller firms. Nonetheless, these efforts failed to generate results.[88] Indeed, as Republicans assumed control of the House of Representatives, attention turned to expanded leasing in the Gulf of Mexico and permitting exploration and production in the Arctic National Wildlife Refuge (ANWR). While the efforts to open exploration in ANWR failed, by February 2011 the moratorium on deepwater drilling effectively ended when the Department of Interior granted a permit to Noble Energy. As a final point of irony, BP Exploration and Production, a wholly-owned subsidiary of BP America, held a 46.5 percent stake in the venture.[89]

"In 2010," Pam Radtke Russell notes,

> experts had predicted that the worst oil spill in American history would be a game changer that would spur fundamental changes in environmental policy—just like the 1969 Santa Barbara spill off California that helped lead to the creation of the EPA and the Exxon Valdez accident that resulted in the Oil Pollution Act of 1990.[90]

But the Deepwater Horizon met, in large part, with congressional inaction. The reasons are many. The American Petroleum Institution deployed its own registered lobbyists and hired eight lobbying and consulting firms, in an effort to shape the debates over reform. Of the 614 oil and gas industry lobbyists, some 53 percent had formerly worked on Capitol Hill and the executive branch.[91] Indeed, in the five-year period beginning in 2010, the oil and gas industry invested $726 million in lobbying, with BP responsible for $38.7 million.[92] As Russell explains, they undoubtedly found a ready audience in the new GOP majority, unified in part by its hostility toward regulation. But situational factors were important as well. With gas prices reaching record levels, there was pressure to maximize production. "And especially in a weak economy, residents of the Gulf Coast region dependent on the oil and gas industry for their livelihoods were eager to get back to drilling."[93]

Conclusion

Oil spills can be the most dramatic and salient environmental disasters. The images of despoiled beaches, extensive slicks, and oil drenched birds have commonly served as focusing events, drawing the attention of the media, the public, and policymakers. Two of the most significant oil spills in US history—the Santa Barbara spill and the Exxon Valdez—both followed this pattern. The Santa Barbara spill helped stimulate environmental concern on a national basis, giving rise to the modern environmental movement and one of the most productive periods of regulatory policymaking in the nation's history. Focusing only on legislation directly relevant to oil spills, Congress passed the Water Quality Improvement Act (1970), the Federal Water Pollution Control Act (1972), the Trans-Alaska Pipeline Authorization Act (1973), the Deepwater Port Act (1974), and the Outer Continental Shelf Lands Act (1978). While further action on oil spills was hampered by ongoing disputes over federal preemption of state laws that imposed unlimited liability, the Exxon Valdez spill shattered the impasse and revealed the limitations of the existing regime for oil spills. Seventeen months after the Exxon Valdez disaster, President George H. W. Bush signed into law the Oil Pollution Act, declaring that it "represents a continuation of my Administration's efforts to work with the Congress and other nations to protect the Earth's environment."[94]

  Three months after signing the Oil Pollution Act, President Bush signed the Clean Air Act Amendments of 1990, creating an innovating system of cap-and-trade to manage the problem of acid rain. A Republican president, working with a Democratic Congress, produced two landmark environmental statutes in a single year. Unfortunately, as detailed in Chapter 5, there would be little legislative productivity in subsequent years. As a product of polarization and gridlock, for the next several decades, the statutory foundations of environmental policy in general, and the oil spill regime in particular, would remain largely what they were in 1990. Bush's commitment "to work with Congress . . . to protect the Earth's environment" would not extend to subsequent presidential administrations and Congresses. As we saw in Chapters 6 and 7, there are various ways of managing the problem of drift, albeit none of them can substitute for significant new statutes that recalibrate the regulatory state in light of changes in the larger economic, technological, and physical environment.

When the Deepwater Horizon disaster occurred twenty years after the Exxon Valdez, the Oil Pollution Act proved painfully antiquated. It had been crafted before deepwater and ultra-deepwater oil exploration had come of age. The responsibility to engage in contingency planning and preparation had been devolved on to industry, and there was little evidence that industry had taken its responsibilities seriously. Regulatory supervision was anemic. Congress and successive administrations had blocked efforts on the part of regulators at the MMS to expand upon their authority and shore up regulation. In this case, regulatory drift was quickly translated into a regulatory disaster and the single largest oil spill in the nation's history. Like Santa Barbara and the Exxon Valdez before it, the Deepwater Horizon garnered heavy media coverage and became a salient issue. And yet, unlike these earlier disasters, it failed to translate into the passage of new statutes. The same political and institutional factors that created regulatory drift prevented Congress from formulating a response, even once the costs of drift became glaringly evident.

Notes

1 David Barstow, David Rohde, and Stephanie Saul, "Deepwater Horizon's Final Hours," *New York Times*, December 25, 2010, A1. Available at www.nytimes.com/2010/12/26/us/26spill.html?pagewanted=all.
2 See David A. Moss, *When All Else Fails: Government as the Ultimate Risk Manager* (Cambridge, MA: Harvard University Press, 2002).
3 Jason Scott Johnson, "Is the Polluter Pays Principle Really Fundamental? An Economic Explanation of the Relative Unimportance of Environmental Liability and Taxes in US Environmental Law," in *Marine Pollution Liability and Policy: China, Europe and the U.S.*, ed. Michael Faure, Han Lixin, and Shan Hongjun (Frederick, MD: Kluwer Law International, 2010), 116.
4 For a critique of joint and several liability, see D. R. Cooley, "Strict Joint and Several Liability and Justice," *Journal of Business Ethics*, 47, 3 (2003): 199–208.
5 Johnson, "Is the Polluter Pays Principle Really Fundamental?" 119.
6 This argument was previously presented as Marc Allen Eisner, "Crisis, Policy Learning, and the Emergence of a Regime for Oil Spill Risks," paper delivered at "Improving Risk Regulation: From Crisis Response to Learning and Innovation," OECD Conference Center, Paris, France, 13 October 2014. For a more detailed discussion,

see Marc Allen Eisner, "From Santa Barbara to the Exxon Valdez," in *Policy Shock: Regulatory Responses to Oil Spills, Nuclear Accidents, and Financial Crashes*, ed. Edward J. Balleisen, Lori S. Bennear, Kimberly D. Krawiec, and Jonathan B. Wiener (New York: Cambridge University Press, 2016).

7   Hui Wang, *Civil Liability for Marine Oil Pollution Damage: A Comparative and Economic Study of the International, US and Chinese Compensation Regimes* (Alphen aan den Rijn: Kluwer Law International, 2011), 191–92.

8   Walter J. Hickel, *Who Owns America?* (Englewood Cliffs, NJ: Prentice Hall, 1971), 92–93.

9   E. W. Kenworthy, "Curb on Oil Spills Is Signed by Nixon: New Law Raises Penalties and Expands Liability," *New York Times*, April 4, 1970, 28.

10   See Theodore L. Garrett, "Federal Liability for Spills of Oil and Hazardous Substances Under the Clean Water Act," *Natural Resources Lawyer*, 12, 4 (1979): 693–719.

11   As quoted in L. Diane Schenke, "Liability for Damages Arising from an Oil Spill," *Natural Resources & the Environment*, 4, 4 (1990): 14.

12   Alan G. Stone, "The Trans-Alaska Pipeline and Strict Liability for Oil Pollution Damage," *Urban Law Annual*, 9 (1975): 191–92.

13   Werner Pfennigstorf, "Environment, Damages, and Compensation," *American Bar Foundation Research Journal*, 4, 2 (1979): 413–14.

14   See Kenneth M. Murchison, Liability under the Oil Pollution Act: Current Law and Needed Revisions," *Louisiana Law Review*, 71 (2011): 922–25.

15   Harold C. Barnett, *Toxic Debts and the Superfund Dilemma* (Chapel Hill, NC: University of North Carolina Press, 1994), 57–58.

16   "Time Bomb in Love Canal," *New York Times*, August 5, 1978, 18.

17   Ibid.

18   Alexandra B. Klass, "From Reservoirs to Remediation: The Impact of CERCLA on Common Law Strict Liability Environmental Claims," *Wake Forest Law Review*, 39 (2004): 932–33.

19   See Christopher D. Knopf, "What's Included in the Exclusion: Understanding Superfund's Petroleum Exclusion," *Fordham Environmental Law Review*, 5, 1 (2011): 3–42.

20   Government Accountability Office, *Superfund: Funding and Reported Costs of Enforcement and Administration Activities*, GAO-08-841R (Washington DC: Government Accountability Office, 2008), 7.

21   George Hager, "Deadlock Likely to Continue," *CQ Weekly*, May 20, 1989, 1183.

22   Alaska Oil Spill Commission, *Spill: The Wreck of the Exxon Valdez. Alaska Oil Commission Final Report* (Juneau, AK: Alaska Oil Commission, 1990), 6, 13, Richard Mauer, "Unlicensed Mate Was in Charge of Ship That Hit Reef, Exxon Says," *New York Times*, March 27, 1989.

23   Brad Knickerbocker, "The Big Spill: An Ocean Struggles to Recover a Decade after the United States' Worst Environmental Disaster," *Christian Science Monitor*, March 22, 1999, 1.

24   Duane A. Gill, J. Steven Picou, and Liesel A. Ritchie, "The Exxon Valdez and BP Oil Spills: A Comparison on Initial Social and Psychological Impacts," *American Behavioral Scientist*, 20, 10 (2011): 5.

25   Samuel K. Skinner and William K. Reilly, *The Exxon Valdez Oil Spill: A Report to the President* (Washington DC: Environmental Protection Agency, 1989), ES-1.

26   Ken Wells and Charles McCoy, "How Unpreparedness Turned the Alaska Spill into Ecological Debacle," *Wall Street Journal*, April 3, 1989, A1.

27   Alaska Oil Spill Commission, *Spill*, 17.

28   Charles McCoy and Ken Wells, "Alaska, U.S. Knew of Flaws in Oil-Spill Response Plans," *Wall Street Journal*, April 7, 1989, A3.

29   Alaska Oil Spill Commission, *Spill*, 58–59.

30 Skinner and Reilly, *The Exxon Valdez Oil Spill*, 34–35.
31 George Hager, "Spill May Halt Drilling Bill, Help Liability Efforts," *CQ Weekly*, April 8, 1989, 742, and Hager, "Deadlock Likely to Continue," 1184.
32 Skinner and Reilly, *The Exxon Valdez Oil Spill*, 35.
33 See Thomas A. Birkland, "In the Wake of the Exxon Valdez: How Environmental Disasters Influence Policy," *Environment: Science and Policy for Sustainable Development*, 40, 7 (1998): 4–32.
34 Russell V. Randle, "The Oil Pollution Act of 1990: Its Provisions, Intent, and Effects," *Environmental Law Reporter*, 21 (1991): 10119.
35 Birkland, "In the Wake of the Exxon Valdez," 27–28.
36 See James E. Nichols, *Oil Pollution Act of 1990(OPA): Liability of Responsible Parties*, CRS Report for Congress R41266 (Washington DC: Congressional Research Service, 2010), and Benjamin H. Grumbles and Joan M. Manley, "The Oil Pollution Act of 1990: Legislation in the Wake of a Crisis," *Natural Resources & Environment*, 10, 2 (1995): 36.
37 Jeffrey D. Morgan, "The Oil Pollution Act of 1990," *Fordham Environmental Law Review*, 6, 1 (1994): 13.
38 See US Coast Guard, *Report on the Implementation of the Oil Pollution Act of 1990* (Washington DC: US Department of Homeland Security, 2010), 5–14.
39 Jonathan L. Ramseur, *Oil Spills in U.S. Coastal Waters: Background, Governance, and Issues for Congress*, CRS Report for Congress RL33705 (Washington DC: Congressional Research Service, 2010), 10–11, Randle, "The Oil Pollution Act of 1990," 10128–30.
40 See Morgan, "The Oil Pollution Act of 1990," and William Lovett, *United States Shipping Policies and the World Market* (Westport, CT: Praeger, 1996), 223–24.
41 Allanna Sullivan, "Oil Industry Maps Strategy to Combat Spills, Leaving Alaska out of the Picture," *Wall Street Journal*, September 7, 1990, A4. See Gerald O'Reilly, "Marine Spill Response Corporation (MSRC): How It Hopes to Fill the Oil Recovery Requirements of the Oil Pollution Act of 1990," paper submitted in partial fulfillment of the requirements for the degree of Master of Marine Affairs, University of Rhode Island, 1993.
42 Calculations in this and the next paragraph are by the author. Data from US Coast Guard, *Polluting Incidents in and around U.S. Waters. A Spill/Release Compendium: 1969–2011, Part I* (Washington DC: US Coast Guard, 2012), 16–17.
43 US Coast Guard, *Polluting Incidents in and around U.S. Waters. A Spill/Release Compendium: 1969–2011, Part II* (Washington DC: US Coast Guard, 2012), 192.
44 Anthony C. Hoffman and Todd Steiner, "OPA 90's Impact at Reducing Oil Spills," *Marine Policy*, 32 (2008): 711–18. Also see Inho Kim, "Ten Years after the Enactment of the Oil Pollution Act of 1990: A Success or a Failure," *Marine Policy*, 26 (2002): 197–207.
45 Tsz Leung Yip, Wayne K. Talley, and Di Jin, "The Effectiveness of Double Hulls in Reducing Vessel-Accident Oil Spillage," *Marine Pollution Bulletin*, 62 (2011): 2427–32.
46 This discussion draws on the National Commission on the BP Deepwater Horizon and Offshore Drilling, "Stopping the Spill: The Five-Month Effort to Kill the Macondo Well," Staff Working Paper no. 6, January 11, 2011.
47 National Commission on the BP Deepwater Horizon Oil Spill and Offshore Drilling, *Deep Water: The Gulf Oil Disaster and the Future of Offshore Drilling* (Washington DC: National Commission on the BP Deepwater Horizon Oil Spill and Offshore Drilling, 2011), 1–4.
48 Ibid., 115.
49 Ibid., 126.
50 Ibid., 126.
51 National Commission on the BP Deepwater Horizon and Offshore Drilling, "Stopping the Spill," 5.

52 Thad Allen, quoted in ibid., 35.
53 On Scene Coordinator Report, *Deepwater Horizon Oil Spill*. Submitted to the National Response Team, September 2011, v–vi. Available at www.uscg.mil/foia/docs/dwh/fosc_dwh_report.pdf.
54 "BP Deepwater Horizon Settlement Receives Final Approval," *Oil & Gas 360*, April 5, 2016. Available at www.oilandgas360.com/478337-2/.
55 Robert W. Wood, "In BP's Final $20 Billion Gulf Settlement, U.S. Taxpayers Subsidize $15.3 Billion," *Forbes*, April 6, 2016. Available at www.forbes.com/sites/robertwood/2016/04/06/in-bps-final-20-billion-gulf-settlement-u-s-taxpayers-subsidize-15-3-billion/#2be5c06f68fc.
56 Christopher Carrigan and Cary Coglianese, "Oversight in Hindsight: Assessing the U.S. Regulatory System in the Wake of Calamity," in *Regulatory Breakdown: The Crisis in Confidence in U.S. Regulation*, ed. Cary Coglianese (Philadelphia, PA: University of Pennsylvania Press, 2012), 11.
57 The discussion of MMS draws heavily on Christopher Carrigan, "Captured by Disaster? Reinterpreting Regulatory Behavior in the Shadow of the Gulf Oil Spill," in *Preventing Regulatory Capture: Special Interest Influence and How to Limit It*, ed. Daniel Carpenter and David A. Moss (Cambridge, UK: Cambridge University Press, 2014), 239–91.
58 National Commission on the BP Deepwater Horizon Oil Spill and Offshore Drilling, *Deep Water*, 255.
59 Carrigan, "Captured by Disaster?" 251–55.
60 Ibid., 269.
61 Earl E. Devaney, "OIG Investigations of MMS Employees," Memorandum, Office of Inspector General, US Department of Interior, 2008. Available at www.doioig.gov/sites/doioig.gov/files/SmithGregory-2008-09-10.pdf.
62 National Commission on the BP Deepwater Horizon Oil Spill and Offshore Drilling, *Deep Water*, 77–78.
63 National Commission on the BP Deepwater Horizon Oil Spill and Offshore Drilling, "The History of Offshore Oil and Gas in the United States," Staff Working Paper no. 22 (January 11, 2011), 31–32.
64 Ibid., 52.
65 National Commission on the BP Deepwater Horizon Oil Spill and Offshore Drilling, *Deep Water*, viii.
66 Bureau of Ocean Energy Management, "Deepwater Production Summary by Year." Available at www.data.boem.gov/homepg/data_center/production/production/summary.asp.
67 Mark Gaffigan, *Oil and Gas Royalties: Royalty Relief Will Likely Cost the Government Billions, but the Final Costs Have Yet to Be Determined*, GAO-07-369T (Washington DC: Government Accountability Office, 2007), 5–7.
68 Adam Vann, *Offshore Oil and Gas Development: Legal Framework*, CRS-RL33404 (Washington DC: Congressional Research Service, 2014), 19.
69 Lisa Breglia, *Living with Oil: Promises, Peaks, and Declines on Mexico's Gulf Coast* (Austin, TX: University of Texas, 2013), 252.
70 National Commission on the BP Deepwater Horizon Oil Spill and Offshore Drilling, *Deep Water: The Gulf Oil Disaster and the Future of Offshore Drilling. Recommendations* (Washington DC: National Commission on the BP Deepwater Horizon Oil Spill and Offshore Drilling, 2011), 3.
71 Ibid., 4.
72 Ibid., 5.
73 Ibid., 7.
74 Ibid., 11.
75 Ibid., 9.

76 Ibid., 12.
77 See Joseph V. Rees, *Hostages of Each Other: The Transformation of Nuclear Energy Safety since Three Mile Island* (Chicago, IL: University of Chicago Press, 1990).
78 National Commission, *Deep Water: The Gulf Oil Disaster and the Future of Offshore Drilling. Recommendations*, 15.
79 Ibid., 16.
80 Ibid., 24.
81 Ibid., 25, 26.
82 Ibid., 28.
83 Ibid., 29.
84 Ibid., 45.
85 John M. Broder, "Rougher Rules Urged for Offshore Drilling," *New York Times*, January 11, 2011, A12. Available at www.nytimes.com/2011/01/12/science/earth/12spill.html.
86 Pam Radtke Russell, "Oil Spill Legislation Shows Signs of Slip-Sliding Away," *CQ Weekly*, April 23, 2012, 798.
87 Amy Harder, "Safety Concerns Persist as Deepwater Drilling Resumes," *National Journal*, March 3, 2011, 15.
88 Amy Harder, "Congress Still Grappling with Oil Spill Liability," *National Journal*, April 2, 2011, 17.
89 "Noble Energy Announces Santiago Discovery and Increases Projected Galapagos Production." Available at http://investors.nobleenergyinc.com/releasedetail.cfm?ReleaseID=581819.
90 Russell, "Oil Spill Legislation Shows Signs of Slip-Sliding Away," 799.
91 Bara Vaida, "Oil's Three Mile Island?" *National Journal*, June 12, 2010, 18.
92 Data from www.opensecrets.org. Calculations by author.
93 Russell, "Oil Spill Legislation Shows Signs of Slip-Sliding Away," 799.
94 George Bush, "Statement on Signing the Oil Pollution Act of 1990," August 18, 1990. Available at www.presidency.ucsb.edu/ws/?pid=18772.

9

REGULATING THE WRONG THINGS AND THE FINANCIAL CRISIS

The 1970s was a decade of economic hardship for many. High inflation and sluggish growth were combined with mounting uncertainty about the relevance of well-established Keynesian theories, as noted in Chapter 4. Following the deep recession of the early 1980s, the nation entered a period commonly described as the great moderation. Policymakers eschewed active fiscal policy, placing greater faith in markets. For the next few decades, steady growth, low unemployment, and price stability led many to hope that the business cycle had been tamed. For many Americans, the period also brought a new affluence. The stock market rose to new levels and home ownership rates broke all records. President Clinton and President Bush both vigorously promoted the expansion of homeownership as a social policy goal. As Clinton explained when announcing his 1995 National Homeownership Strategy, an effort to leverage the resources of lenders, community groups, Fannie Mae, and Freddie Mac to meet ambitious housing goals:

> Home ownership encourages savings and investment. When a family buys a home, the ripple effect is enormous. It means new homeowner consumers. They need more durable goods, like washers and dryers, refrigerators and water heaters. And if more families could buy new homes or older homes, more hammers will be pounding, more saws will be buzzing. Homebuilders and home fixers will be put to work. When we boost the number of home-owners in our country, we strengthen our economy, create jobs, build up the middle class, and build better citizens.[1]

Seven years later, when President Bush unveiled his own effort to create an "ownership society," he told his audience that the American Dream is the ability to come from anywhere in our society and say, I own this home . . . we can put light where there's darkness, and hope where there's despondency in this country. And part of it is working together as a nation to encourage folks to own their own home.[2]

But in 2007, the speculative bubble in the real estate market burst and over the course of the next several months, defaults and foreclosures rapidly escalated, particularly among low- and moderate-income borrowers who had only recently started to enjoy the benefits of the ownership society. As one contemporaneous observer noted: "Foreclosure is replacing the American Dream of home ownership as a way of life. Foreclosure lawsuits were filed against 2,203,295 Americans in 2007, up 75 percent from 2006 and 148.83 percent from 2005."[3] By the summer of 2008, the real estate collapse had cascaded into a full-blown financial crisis, leaving well-established financial institutions and the US economy in ruins. The great moderation turned into the Great Recession and ultimately took on global proportions.

The financial collapse of 2007–8 is often presented as a story of excessive deregulation. Members of Congress and presidents of both parties and regulators from successive administrations had pursued deregulation relentlessly, from the late 1970s to the eve of the crash. Perhaps the pattern of action simply reflected the ascendance of neoliberalism and the growing faith in free markets? New financial instruments seemed to proliferate with a rapidity that outpaced the ability of the regulatory structure to adapt. But many believed—or claimed to believe—that those who ran the financial institutions were rational actors who possessed the incentives, the expertise, and the information to manage the risks they assumed. Perhaps in such a complex policy area, public officials were overly willing to defer to the judgment of industry actors? The industry employed an army of lobbyists to assure that its interests were recognized among policymakers. Or perhaps deregulation simply reflected the kinds of mutually beneficial exchanges that we have come to associate with capture? Certainly, the industry invested heavily in campaign finance, provided benefits like low-rate mortgages to congressional committee members and their staff, and held out the promise of lucrative post-government service employment. Undoubtedly, each of these factors was at play during the deregulatory era. Yet, what if deregulation—while part of the story—was not as important as many often assume? What if regulators were regulating, but regulating the wrong things?[4]

A Brief History of Financial Regulation

Chapter 2 argued that an expanded set of concepts drawn from comparative political economy and institutional analysis could prove quite useful in enriching our understanding of, and capacity to explain, significant changes in regulation. Subsequent chapters turned to an analysis of change in contemporary social regulation. A specific strategy of regulatory design—detailed statutes with minimal delegation to administrators—limited the flexibility to respond to emerging issues. When combined with growing polarization, it induced a process of drift. The deadlock in Congress prevented efforts to recalibrate policy and, as a result, regulators were often forced to rely on statutes that were dated and did not provide them with the authority or the flexibility to manage emerging problems. One response was to delegate greater responsibility to private sector parties in the hope of leveraging their resources and extending the reach of regulation. But as the past few chapters revealed, this strategy had distinct limitations.

Financial regulation provides an interesting case study for examining the dynamic described in Chapter 2 for several reasons. First, regulations play a far more fundamental role in finance than in most industries. The standard understanding of regulation presents policy as a response to market failure. For example, policy can be designed to reduce informational asymmetries (e.g., through required information disclosure) or reduce negative externalities (e.g., through mandated pollution control devices that force corporations to internalize the costs of pollution). While regulation still serves this function in finance, it serves a far more expansive function. Regulations literally constitute the market and the key institutional actors that comprise it. Formal financial intermediaries do not exist absent regulation. Rather, regulatory decisions regarding the conditions of chartering, for example, constitute these entities at their very conception.[5] To a great extent, regulatory decisions find their institutional articulation in financial intermediaries, and these decisions are reproduced in these organizations even after the focus of regulation has changed.

Second, finance has been unusually prone to crisis—a fact that was obscured by the quiescent decades following the passage of the New Deal banking laws. Since 1800, the United States has weathered thirteen banking crises, often with devastating results.[6] These crises have been of broader importance, in part, because of the political instability they produce, an instability that can carry ramifications for policies in multiple arenas. The Progressive Era, for example, emerged out of the electoral realignment of 1896, which was itself a response to a financial panic and resulting depression. The New Deal was a response to the Great Depression, which stemmed from the financial collapse of 1929. In each case, financial crises punctuated the equilibria that formed around public policies, creating opportunities to recast policy problems and introduce significant changes in policies, institutions, and the distribution of costs and benefits.

Third, because of the long history of financial regulation, one can learn quite a bit about the dynamics of layering through an examination of this policy area. Since the Civil War banking laws, new policies and institutions—often the product of crisis—have been layered upon the old. The great challenge has been to manage the tensions between existing and inherited policies and institutions. The national banking laws that emerged out of the Civil War stimulated free banking laws in the states and, in turn, a regulatory race to the bottom. The state banks, poorly capitalized with thin reserve requirements, bore the brunt of the financial collapse during the Great Depression. The New Deal regime sought to increase the stability of the banking system by creating distinct sub-industries, with regulations dictating interest rates, limiting services, and controlling the kinds of investments that institutions could engage in. The provision of deposit insurance, it was hoped, would both stem future panics and create incentives for state chartered banks to enter the Federal Reserve System. After a long period of stability, the system experienced another exogenous shock—the high and sustained inflation of the 1970s. Under the constraints imposed by the New Deal system, regulated depository institutions could not compete with so-called "nonbank banks" and state-chartered banks. Deregulation, in this context, can be understood as efforts to manage the friction between layered institutions.

Finally, the recent crisis can be understood, in part, as a product of drift. As policymakers fought a rear-guard action to manage the tensions described above, they failed to create a new regulatory architecture to manage new innovations in the financial economy. As will be argued later, this failure contributed to the depth and severity of the collapse of 2007–8. While it was convenient to ascribe the collapse to deregulatory zealotry, the most striking aspect of the collapse was that it stemmed from parts of the financial system that had never been subjected to regulation. Under existing laws, largely inherited from the New Deal, regulators were regulating depository institutions but not banking as an activity. Since the late 1980s, securitization and the shadow banking system had become far more prevalent. And yet, they evolved in the interstices between existing regulatory jurisdictions, much as one would expect.

This chapter begins with a historical review of three sequential but layered regimes: (1) the National Banking regime that began with the Civil War and evolved in the next several decades; (2) the New Deal regime that was forged in response to the Great Depression and extended through the immediate postwar decades; and (3) the deregulatory regime that emerged in response to inflation and disintermediation in the 1970s. It then turns to the financial collapse of 2007–8 and the regulatory response in light of this earlier history.

National Banking and Regulatory Competition

The crisis of war inevitably brings significant institutional and policy change. As Charles Tilly argued, state making is often a by-product of war making: "No one designed the principal components of national treasuries, courts, central administrations, and so on. They usually formed as more or less inadvertent by-products of efforts to carry out more immediate tasks, especially the creation and support of armed forces."[7] The exigencies of war were certainly the critical factor in the formation of the national banking system. As the Union faced the challenge of financing the war, it turned to the issuance of debt. Ultimately, the Civil War banking acts would meet the temporary demands of war finance, superimposing a new national banking system upon a chaotic collection of state banking laws. This, in turn, would create the foundations for a dual banking system and unleash decades of competition between federal and state regulators.[8]

Prior to the Civil War, the financial system was constituted and regulated by an uneven patchwork of state policies. Depending on the state, bank charters could be granted by a special act of the legislature or simply through meeting general requirements established under state laws. In some states (e.g., Tennessee and Indiana) public ownership was the norm. As for the money supply, it "consisted of various types of gold and silver coins along with paper notes issued in multiple denominations by each of the thousands of individual banks."[9] Any effort to introduce a national banking system would have to contend in one form or another with the system that had emerged in the decades following the demise of the Second Bank of the United States in 1836.

In 1862, Congress passed the Legal Tender Act, authorizing the issuance of $150 million of paper notes—fiat currency backed by Treasury securities—that had to be accepted as legal tender. Under the National Currency Act (1863) and the National Banking Act (1864), Congress authorized federally-issued national bank charters to create institutions that could issue the new currency. National banks were required to purchase government bonds, which could be used to meet their capital requirements, thereby creating a ready market for Union debt. A new Office of the Comptroller of the Currency (OCC) was established within the Treasury to regulate the national banks. The National Banking Act authorized new charters and a process for established state banks to convert to national banks. In the words of Senator John Sherman (R-OH), Chairman of the Senate Committee on Finance, the "national banks were intended to supersede the State banks"—they could "not exist together."[10] Many state banks proved hesitant initially to adopt national charters, rejecting federal oversight, more stringent capital requirements, and greater restrictions on the activities they could engage in (e.g., real estate loans, branching) than imposed under state law. In response, in 1865, Congress enacted a 10 percent tax on state bank notes. The number of state banks declined rapidly, from 1,089 (1864) to 247 (1868).[11] The seeming victory of the national banks would prove temporary, as state banks would soon enjoy a significant resurgence.

As state banks dwindled in number, the impact was most profound in agricultural regions and smaller communities that could not support a national bank. "In the rich States of the North, the vast preponderance in number, capital, and business is with the national banks," a contemporary analyst noted.

> In general, the rule holds that the older, richer, or more densely populated States, with varied industries, find it easier to use the national system than the more thinly settled communities, poor in capital and carrying on industries of slow return.[12]

Increasingly, the national banking system became politically salient, and was viewed (in combination with the gold standard and the Republican tariff) as means of privileging the concentrated wealth of the northeast over the relatively underdeveloped southern and western periphery.[13] During the last two decades of the nineteenth century, states responded to this situation in various ways, expanding "free banking" (i.e., allowing incorporation under general legal provisions), imposing minimal or in some cases no capital requirements, and few restrictions on bank activity. As a result of changes in state laws, the number of state banks grew rapidly (see Figure 9.1), increasing from 650 (1880) to 4,659 (1900). Indeed, by 1894, the number of state banks (3,810) actually surpassed the number of national banks (3,770), and controlled more assets ($4.87 billion versus $3.42 billion).[14]

The resurgence of state banks prompted a national response, unleashing a regulatory race to the bottom. How might one make national charters more appealing? One approach, an expansion of branching, was quickly abandoned as it invoked the ire of unit banks and their representatives. A second approach, the relaxation of capital requirements for national banks, was far more successful once embraced by Comptroller of the Currency Charles Dawes. Under the Gold Standard Act (1900), national bank charters would be issued to institutions serving small towns (population 3,000 or less) with capital of $25,000. As one might expect, state legislators responded in kind: Within the next decade, states with capital requirements above the newly established levels reduced them in hopes of preserving the advantages of a state charter.

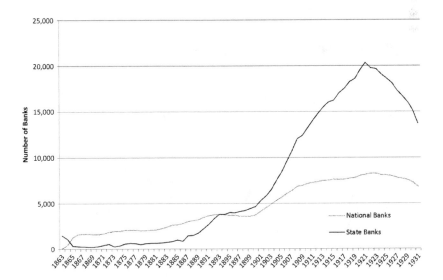

FIGURE 9.1 National and State Bank Charters

Source: Comptroller of the Currency Annual Report 1931, 3.

The 1907 panic and the subsequent revelations of the money trust in the Pujo hearings raised the salience of banking regulation and created a window of opportunity for institutional change. By 1913, the deliberations concluded with the creation of the Federal Reserve. The Federal Reserve Act created a decentralized structure in which power was vested in the regional reserve banks (something deemed important to avoid sectional antagonism and, in the wake of the Pujo hearings, ensure that the New York banking interests would not control the system). The new institution would serve a number of important functions, including serving as a lender of last resort (a function previously executed imperfectly by private clearing houses). The Fed was designed to serve national banks. They were required to become members of the Federal Reserve System, which obliged them to purchase the stock of, and place non-interest bearing reserves in, their regional reserve banks. However, state-chartered banks were invited to join the system, gaining access to the Fed's support as lender of last resort in exchange for Fed supervision.[15] As reserve requirements were subsequently reduced to draw more state banks into the Federal Reserve's orbit, states responded by refusing to authorize their state-chartered banks to participate and/or simultaneously lowering their own reserve requirements. The Fed responded, once again, by lowering member reserve requirements in 1921, only to stimulate another round of reductions in several of the states.[16]

The dual system of banking that emerged in the decades following the National Bank Act (1864) promoted a highly decentralized system. This decentralization was reinforced by state prohibitions on branch banking that proliferated in the first quarter of the twentieth century. Independent bankers, recognizing the threat posed by branching, successfully invoked populist arguments against the concentration of financial control in their quest for anti-branching legislation. The Federal Reserve Board understood that national banks, which had never been allowed to engage in branch banking, faced a disadvantage. When the first response—a restriction on branching by state-chartered members of the Federal Reserve system—created incentives to exit the system, Congress intervened. At the urging of Comptroller Joseph McIntosh, Congress passed the McFadden Act in 1927. Under the McFadden Act, banks with national charters were now allowed to establish branches, albeit only to the extent permitted by state laws. This was a limited victory at best, given that only eighteen states explicitly authorized some form of branch banking, and only two of these allowed intra-state branching (as contrasted to intra-city branching). The decentralization was further reinforced by the McFadden Act prohibition on interstate branching. In a further nod to the regulatory dynamic described above, the McFadden Act also reduced the capitalization requirements from $200,000 to $100,000 for national banks to incorporate in cities with populations of over 50,000, if state law permitted state-chartered banks to organize with capital of $100,000 or less.[17]

The New Deal Regime and Horizontal Fragmentation

The dual banking system that had emerged over the late nineteenth and early twentieth centuries was severely tested by the Great Depression. In the fall of 1932, thirty-eight states placed restrictions on withdrawals in hopes of stemming the panic. The day after his inauguration, Franklin Roosevelt declared a four-day national bank holiday. Under the authority of the Emergency Banking Act of 1933, the Treasury examined banks and reopened those deemed solvent. Other banks could be opened on a restricted basis under the supervision of the Comptroller of the Currency. The carnage is partially represented by the statistics on bank suspensions. Between 1929 and 1932, there were 5,454 bank suspensions; of this number, only 872 or 16 percent were national banks. Although the failed banks controlled $3.4 billion of deposits, only 24.3 percent of this sum was in the national banks. As the Comptroller reported in 1932, bank failures were the "most numerous among the smaller institutions . . . located in rural sections of the country." The "lax state laws" and reductions in the minimal capitalization required to charter national banks "facilitated the organization of thousands of small banks in small towns." These banks might have thrived under conditions of prosperity, "but with the turn of the times . . . we have come to realize the danger in permitting the organization of small under-capitalized institutions."[18]

The regime of the post-Civil War period unleashed vigorous competition between national and state banks and a regulatory race to the bottom that undoubtedly rendered the system more fragile to shocks. The regime that emerged during the New Deal focused more heavily on creating regulatory barriers between financial sub-industries, inducing a new horizontal fragmentation at the federal level. The Glass–Steagall Banking Act of 1933 forced the separation of commercial and investment banking and placed restrictions on interlocking directorates between commercial and investment banks, on the theory that the 1929 crash had been magnified by the comingling of the two activities. Glass–Steagall created a new Federal Deposit Insurance Corporation (FDIC) to guarantee deposits. All members of the Federal Reserve System were required to carry FDIC insurance. In hopes of drawing state-chartered banks into the orbit of federal supervision, they could access FDIC deposit insurance only if they joined the Federal Reserve System.

In theory, the provision of deposit insurance could open the door to problems of moral hazard. It is always a concern that parties will assume greater risks if the costs of failure are borne by other parties. Federal regulation of capitalization, reserves, and investments could reduce the vulnerability to these problems. Moreover, Glass–Steagall empowered the Fed, through Regulation Q, to fix interest rates for savings while prohibiting interest for demand deposits (i.e., checking). It was argued that banks would have fewer incentives to engage in destabilizing activities if they were not forced to compete for deposits by offering higher interest rates. Parallel institutions were created for savings and loans, which were regulated by the Federal Home Loan Bank Board, with deposit insurance provided by the Federal Savings and Loan Insurance Corporation (FSLIC).

Changes on the investment banking side of Glass–Steagall were equally profound and adopted a much different regulatory model than in commercial banking. Prior to 1933, securities regulation fell to the states. While the Securities Act of 1933 did not preempt state "blue sky" laws, issuers were now required to register securities with the Federal Trade Commission and disclose financial information. Rather than regulating securities based on their merit, the new statute assumed that it was sufficient to provide investors with the information necessary to make their own decisions. In 1934, Congress created a new agency, the Securities and Exchange Commission (SEC) to regulate the industry. The Securities and Exchange Act mandated that national exchanges register with the SEC, which also assumed the responsibility of registering all stocks sold on the exchanges. The SEC's regulatory model was one of government supervised self-regulation.[19] The SEC would oversee private associations which, in turn, functioned as surrogate regulators to govern the behavior of their members. Indeed, the SEC would use its authority to force the professionalization and reorganization of the New York Stock Exchange and to promote the self-regulation of the over-the-counter market through the National Association of Securities Dealers, which functioned very much like a regulatory agency.[20] Thus, by the end of the 1930s, regulations had constituted distinct financial sub-industries, each defined by the products and services it offered, each with its own set of regulators.

In 1933, the Federal Reserve System included 4,897 national banks (assets $20.8 billion) and 709 state banks (assets $12.2 billion); an additional 8,601 state banks (with assets of $7.5 billion) operated outside the system. By 1970, the system included 4,638 national banks (assets $314.3 billion) and 1,116 state banks (assets $117.2 billion), with 7,683 state banks (assets $98.4 billion) outside of the system. Following the Banking Act of 1935, however, FDIC insurance had become available for state banks that were not members of the Federal Reserve System. Thus, by 1970, 13,818 banks (with assets of $596 billion) were insured, whereas only 369 banks (with assets of $15.3 billion) were working outside of federal regulations. In short, the dual system of banking survived, but that vast majority of the country's banks were subject to federal regulations enforced by the OCC, the Federal Reserve, or the FDIC (with the FDIC as the only federal regulator for state banks that were not members of the Federal Reserve System).[21]

Deregulation: Managing Tensions between Regimes

To recap briefly, the post Civil War regime introduced national charters but, simultaneously, gave rise to a dual banking system where state and national banks competed, unleashing a dynamic that reduced levels of capitalization and reserves at both levels. The dual banking structure would survive the Great Depression, even if the financial collapse significantly changed the balance of national and state power. The New Deal regime layered a new set of institutions and policies on top of the old. On one side of the Glass–Steagall wall, investment banking was regulated through mandatory information disclosure and government-supervised self-regulation. On the other side of the wall, regulation constituted distinct financial sub-industries. Policy sought to instill stability through deposit insurance and tight regulatory restrictions over entry, products and services offered, and price competition.

The New Deal system provided stability in finance, a clear departure from the earlier history of financial turmoil. Indeed, following the creation of the FDIC, commercial bank suspensions plummeted, from an annual average of 566.2 during the period 1921–29, to an average of 49 a year for the decade following the creation of the FDIC (see Figure 9.2). By the immediate postwar decades, suspensions had become relatively rare (there were 43 in the decade of the 1950s, and 62 in the decade of the 1960s).[22] As Gary B. Gorton reminds us, this was highly unusual. From a long-term perspective, banking panics were routine events. The decades of stability following the introduction of the New Deal regime (the "Quiet Period" in US banking) "led to the view that banking panics were a thing of the past."[23] This belief would be shattered by subsequent events.

The New Deal regime extended regulations to nationally-chartered banks, defined as deposit-taking and loan-making entities. Firms that engaged in one

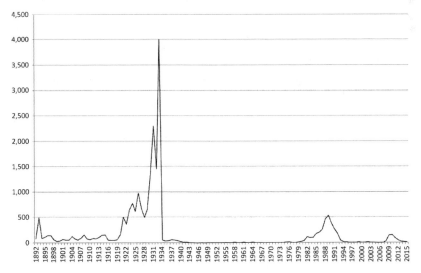

FIGURE 9.2   Bank Failures

Source: Federal Reserve, *Banking and Monetary Statistics* (7.1) and FDIC Failures and Assistance Transactions (BF02).

but not both of these activities and state-chartered banks that were not part of the Federal Reserve System were not subject to the same regulatory constraints. As noted earlier, interest was prohibited on demand deposits and, under Regulation Q, the Federal Reserve fixed the interest rates that banks could offer. In 1966, Regulation Q was extended to savings and loans (S&Ls). In hopes of channeling liquidity into real estate markets, S&Ls were allowed to offer a slightly higher interest.[24] Although the system appeared relatively stable, things changed dramatically once it was subjected to the high inflation of the 1970s. Depository institutions had an increasingly difficult time attracting funds. They faced new competition from money market mutual funds, which were deposit-taking, but not loan-making, and thus exempt from regulations. They could offer interest rates that exceeded those permitted under regulation. State-chartered institutions, moreover, could provide interest on demand deposits via negotiated order of withdrawal (or NOW) accounts. In short, the exogenous shock of stagflation exacerbated the friction between the two previous regimes.

Initially, regulators responded incrementally to the competitive threats, "trying to plug every new leak in the dike of regulation as it opened up, only to find a new leak elsewhere."[25] Soon, this proved insufficient to manage the friction between the earlier regimes. In 1980, Congress passed the Depository Institutions Deregulation and Monetary Control Act (DIDMCA), which had several important ramifications.[26] Most significantly, it mandated an orderly phase-out of interest rate controls. As DIDMCA noted: "all depositors, and particularly those with modest savings, are entitled to receive a market rate of return on their savings as soon as it is economically feasible for depository institutions to pay such rate."[27] Before DIDMCA, banks that were members of the Federal Reserve System had to place reserves at their district Federal Reserve Bank. Because the reserves were not interest bearing, this requirement also placed them at a competitive disadvantage and created growing incentives to exit the system. With DIDMCA, Congress mandated a phased reduction of these reserve requirements while requiring the uniform treatment of reserves of all depository institutions.

Interest rate deregulation could have the most profound consequences for the S&Ls. Even if they could now offer market-based interest rates, they carried the weight of portfolios burdened with long-term, fixed-rate mortgages. Congress responded by granting them greater discretion over their portfolios, allowing them to invest in commercial paper, corporate debt, and consumer loans and permitting the issuance of credit cards. NOW accounts—interest-bearing deposit accounts with checking privileges authorized by several states—were now available for all depository institutions.[28] Under Glass–Steagall, deposit insurance was combined with tight regulatory controls over the kinds of investments and services that could be offered as a means of controlling for potential moral hazard. Congress now seemed to discount the problem of moral hazard. With DIDMCA, it simultaneously provided greater latitude in investments while increasing the coverage of deposit insurance (from $40,000 to $100,000).

As the S&Ls proved particularly unfit to flourish in the complicated economic environment of the times, Congress passed the Garn–St. Germain Depository Institutions Act of 1982. Part of the Act focused on the near-term problems: It authorized the FDIC and FSLIC to make deposits in troubled institutions, and if necessary, assume their liabilities and engineer mergers with healthy institutions. But part of the act was designed to promote the long-term competitiveness of S&Ls. Savings and loans could now offer interest-bearing money market deposit accounts with checking services. They could further diversify their portfolios by holding a greater percentage of commercial and consumer loans and investing in state and local government revenue bonds. Furthermore, in response to the devastating impact that double-digit inflation had on institutions that made real estate loans, Congress authorized adjustable-rate mortgages.[29] Many states followed the lead of Congress, hoping to prevent their thrifts from pursuing federal charters. By 1984, one-third of the states gave their chartered S&Ls even more discretion over their investments than the federal government.[30] Unfortunately, the efforts came too late for many S&Ls. Some S&Ls that had participated in the real estate boom of the early 1980s responded to their shrinking portfolios by taking advantage of the greater latitude provided by regulators and assuming ever-riskier investments, essentially gambling for resurrection. As the Congressional Budget Office explained: "the problem of moral hazard took an especially virulent form. Having lost all of their equity, owners had nothing more to lose . . . the economic incentives essentially forced troubled institutions to undertake highly risky and even dangerous strategies."[31] This was a classic problem of moral hazard exacerbated by the fact that many S&Ls lacked the sophistication to negotiate the increasingly complex competitive environment.

The "Quiet Period" in US banking was apparently over. Congress responded to the S&L crisis by passing the Financial Institutions Reform, Recovery, and Enforcement Act of 1989. It eliminated FSLIC, which had gone bankrupt, reporting the largest losses ever incurred by a public or private corporation.[32] Its duties were transferred to the FDIC. It also eliminated the Federal Home Loan Bank Board—the S&L regulator—replacing it with a new Federal Housing Finance Board and the Office of Thrift Supervision. Congress created a new Resolution Trust Corporation to oversee the orderly disposal of the assets of the failed S&Ls. Between 1986 and 1995, 1,043 savings and loans, with total assets of over $500 billion, failed. As a result of failures and consolidations, the number of federally insured thrifts fell from 3,234 to 1,645. By 1995, when the Resolution Trust Corporation completed its work, the total cost of the S&L was $160 billion.[33]

In the wake of the S&L crisis, Congress returned to the task of deregulation, this time focusing on the Glass–Steagall Act. Calls for eliminating the regulatory separation of investment and commercial banking made sense to many advocates who noted that the Federal Reserve and the OCC had already permitted banks to offer mutual funds and participate in brokerage services. Recent mergers and acquisitions in the financial services industry had already permeated the Glass–Steagall firewalls.[34] Arguably, wholesale financial institutions could be better able to innovate and compete in a global financial market in which the largest competitors to the US did not function under comparable regulatory requirements.[35] In 1999, Congress passed the Gramm–Leach–Bliley Financial Services Modernization Act of 1999 (GLBA), authorizing the consolidation of commercial banks, investment banks, securities firms, and insurance companies into financial holding companies. GLBA did not eliminate existing regulatory authority nor did it create a new regulatory agency. Rather, functional regulation would continue much as it had before. The various activities that a firm engaged in would still remain within the jurisdiction of existing financial regulatory agencies.[36]

The Financial Crisis and the Limits of Regulation

If one marks the passage of GLBA as the end of the statutory deregulation of financial markets, less than a decade would pass before the nation experienced the greatest financial crisis and the deepest recession since the Great Depression. The losses were staggering. By 2010, inflation-adjusted household incomes had fallen to levels not seen since 1996. According to the Federal Reserve, the median net worth of American families fell by nearly 40 percent between 2007 and 2010.[37] The source of the collapse can be found in a speculative bubble in real estate that began to take hold in the late 1990s, although its escalation into a full-blown crisis was a product of profound changes in the financial system in the post-1980 period. In the broadest sense, there are two important questions. First, how can one explain the origins of the real estate bubble? Second, given that all speculative bubbles burst, why did policy fail to prevent this event from cascading into such an extraordinary crisis both in the US and globally? Let us address these questions in turn.

The Origins of the Housing Bubble

In the United States, the federal government has a long history of promoting home ownership. For most homeowners, the most immediate subsidies have been delivered through the tax code. Borrowers are allowed to deduct home mortgage interest and property taxes from their incomes, subsidies that reduced federal revenues by $73.9 billion and $33.9 billion respectively in 2015. Additionally, the tax code has promoted investment in real estate by providing special treatment for capital gains (another $56.5 billion in 2015).[38] Less visible, but nonetheless important, homeownership has been facilitated by intervention in capital markets. Two government-sponsored enterprises (or GSEs), the

Federal National Mortgage Association (Fannie Mae) and the Federal Home Loan Mortgage Corporation (Freddie Mac), have played a particularly important role. They raise capital by issuing debt, and then use the funds to purchase mortgages. The mortgages are then pooled and securitized (a subject we will return to below). By selling relatively illiquid assets (e.g., thirty-year mortgages) for cash, lenders can support a higher level of loan activity. Because the GSEs are quasi-public enterprises, investors believed that their debt is backed by the full faith and credit of the United States. This has allowed the GSEs to access funds at a lower rate than other institutions, and presumably this implicit subsidy is transferred to homeowners.

Increasing homeownership—particularly among low- and moderate-income households—was elevated as a social policy goal, beginning in the 1990s. For advocates of homeownership, the benefits for these households were obvious: Investments in appreciating assets could provide a means of building estates over time and would engender patterns of behavior (e.g., budgeting, punctuality in payments) that would engender greater stability. As Mechele Dickerson argues, the support for homeownership drew on a well-established narrative "that homeownership transforms renters into financially secure owners and then transforms them into stable, less transient and more actively involved citizens."[39] From an economic perspective, higher levels of homeownership could translate into higher demand for consumer durables like appliances and furnishings. Homeowners could also draw on the equity in their homes to finance higher levels of consumption, in essence borrowing from the future value of their real estate to finance current consumption. Given the departure from active fiscal policy beginning with the Reagan presidency and the growing fidelity to balanced budgets, this could provide a much-needed form of stimulus (something one scholar has described as "mortgage Keynesianism").[40]

Congress determined that the special treatment of GSEs (e.g., their exemption from certain regulations, lower capital requirements, and the implicit subsidy mentioned above) conveyed an affirmative obligation to meet national housing goals. In the aftermath of the S&L crisis, Congress contemplated tightening the capital requirements for the GSEs. But the GSEs lobbied effectively to block these requirements in exchange for their greater support for affordable housing goals. The Federal Housing Enterprises Financial Safety and Soundness Act of 1992 directed the Department of Housing and Urban Development (HUD) to create quantitative targets for the percentage of low- and moderate-income mortgages the GSEs had to purchase; between 1993 and 2007, the target grew from 30 to 55 percent. In 1995, at President Clinton's direction, HUD introduced a National Homeowner Strategy, with a number of objectives including cutting the costs of homeownership, facilitating access to mortgage financing, and eliminating barriers that had previously limited ownership among racial and ethnic minorities and low-income households. In a pattern of events similar to what was witnessed in social regulation (see Chapters 6 and 7), the

Clinton administration sought to leverage private sector resources to promote these goals. Its "Partners in the American Dream" enlisted affordable housing and civil rights advocacy groups, along with the GSEs, the American Bankers Association, the Mortgage Bankers Association of America, the National Association of Homebuilders, the National Association of Real Estate Brokers, the National Association of Realtors, and the National Bankers Association.[41] A similar framework was put into place during the subsequent Bush administration. All of this was facilitated by changes in the tax code. Under the Taxpayer Relief Act of 1997, home sellers were given a large capital gains tax exemption ($500,000 for married couples, $250,000 for individuals), thereby increasing the incentives for real estate investments.

The expansion of homeownership was promoted by significant changes in lending practices. Traditionally, banks and S&Ls made loans for mortgages and then held them in their portfolios, something that was referred to as the "originate-to-hold model." This model created incentives for conservative lending decisions: Banks that derived profitability from the stream of mortgage payments over thirty years, for example, would be hesitant to lend money unless they were satisfied with the quality of the real estate appraisals and the creditworthiness of borrowers. However, the "originate-to-distribute" model displaced the traditional model. That is, institutions and mortgage brokers issued loans and then sold them to investment banks or GSEs. The changes in incentives should be obvious. Lenders were less inclined to be concerned with appraisals or creditworthiness when they intended to sell the mortgages they issued only to search for new borrowers. Indeed, as the housing boom took hold, lenders increasingly failed to verify the income and credit of borrowers. To make matters worse, the weaker the underlying documentation—the greater the probability of default—the greater the incentive to sell the loan and transfer the risk to other parties.

Mortgages with novel features became far more common as lenders sought to access the new borrowers, upon whom the housing boom depended. These features included adjustable-rate mortgages (quite appealing in a period of low inflation) and mortgages that were designed to allow borrowers to make smaller initial payments (interest-only mortgages or pay-option mortgages whereby payments below the interest would be added to the principal, thereby increasing levels of indebtedness). Subprime mortgages—loans issued to people with poor credit histories—proliferated, increasing from 7–8 percent of the market in 2000–3, to some 18–20 percent in 2004–6. Alt-A loans, typically issued to those with incomplete documentation, increased as well, peaking at 13 percent of the market in 2006. Home equity loans, which allowed borrowers to draw on equity in their homes to fund current consumption, increased to 11–14 percent of the market between 2004 and 2007. Another novel innovation—the so-called "piggyback" loan—even allowed borrowers to get a first and second mortgage simultaneously, in essence drawing on equity that did not exist.[42]

As banks and GSEs purchased mortgage debt, they pooled the mortgages and sold shares to investors as mortgage-backed securities (MBSs)—the process of securitization. While GSEs did this directly, things were a bit more complicated with commercial banks, investment banks, mortgage banks, and S&Ls. They purchased the mortgages and then sold them to special purpose vehicles—in essence, subsidiaries with the sole function of holding and securitizing the pool or mortgages. The benefits were rather straightforward. By moving the assets off of their balance sheets, they could avoid higher capital requirements. In essence, this was an institutional adaptation to existing regulations that allowed securitizing institutions to function as more highly leveraged (and thus, more profitable) entities.[43]

Pooled mortgages were cut into "tranches" or slices to generate securities with different levels of risk and return. Credit rating agencies—Moody's Investor Service, Standard & Poor's, and Fitch—evaluated the risk associated with the different securities. Should borrowers fail to pay their mortgages, the losses would be borne by the holders of the lowest-rated MBSs (the junior tranches), and this risk was rewarded with the highest yields. Ratings provided one way to mitigate risk. However, there were others as well. When Fannie Mae and Freddie Mac issued MBSs (so-called agency MBSs), they charged a guarantee fee, which obliged the GSE to make the promised principal and interest payments if the underlying mortgages defaulted. When the sponsor of the MBS was not an agency, investors could mitigate risk by purchasing credit-default swaps, derivatives that provided *de facto* insurance by guaranteeing payments.

Securities with the highest ratings were viewed as being as safe an investment as US Treasury bonds and, as a result, they were deemed acceptable investments for pension funds, mutual funds, and insurance companies. Under the Secondary Mortgage Market Enhancement Act (1984), state regulated institutions, national banks, S&Ls, and credit unions were authorized to invest in private issue MBSs if the were rated AA or above by a nationally recognized credit rating agency.[44] For banks, investments in MBSs were preferable to holding traditional mortgages. Under prevailing regulations, capitalization requirements depend on the riskiness of the assets banks hold. A MBS with a AAA rating was deemed less risky than actual mortgages, creating a further incentive for banks to sell mortgages and hold MBSs in their portfolios, thereby freeing capital that would otherwise be used as reserves to generate higher levels of profitability.[45] In addition to serving as investments, the highest-rated securities were used routinely as collateral in financial transactions, for example, when companies took short-term loans from mutual funds as a means of managing routine cash flow issues. These transactions—a form of banking or "shadow banking"—occurred outside of regulated depository institutions and thus free from the same level of regulatory oversight.

In sum, two factors came together to promote rapid appreciation in real estate markets. Congress and successive presidential administrations elevated homeownership as a social policy goal, encouraging higher levels of lending and practices that promoted a deterioration of underwriting standards. Policies that were once designed to assure the stability of financial markets were now being leveraged to serve a social welfare function (a case of "conversion," to use the language introduced in Chapter 2). Innovations in financial markets promoted the conversion of illiquid assets (mortgages) into liquid assets (mortgage-backed securities), thereby providing lenders a steady stream of funds to support higher levels of lending. As one might expect, this combination drove record levels of homeownership. In the early 1990s, 64 percent of households owned their own homes. This rate would rise steadily after 1995, reaching a record peak of 69 percent by 2004.[46] Unsurprisingly, the period also brought sharp increases in debt. Household debt service payments as a percentage of disposable income peaked at 13.2 percent in 2007,[47] while net savings as a percentage of gross national income plummeted, approaching zero by 2008.[48] Americans owned more homes—a traditional sign of economic security—but they were, in fact, highly insecure by virtue of their indebtedness.

Public Policy to Prevent Contagion

As Chapter 8 explained in the context of oil spill policy, regulation can play an important role in preventing accidents from occurring in the first place. But it can also keep accidents from escalating into full-blown crises. As policymakers promoted an expansion of homeownership, easier access to credit invited speculation and real estate markets appreciated dramatically. The decision to press liquidity into the most fragile part of the market—low- and moderate-income households—and the amount of speculative purchases increased the risk that changing economic fortunes could result in a growing number of delinquencies, foreclosures, and the depreciation of real estate values. Given the growing importance of MBSs in the shadow banking system, there was a significant chance that this chain of events could lead to a broader financial crisis that, in turn, could have catastrophic ramifications for the economy.

What kinds of policies were being implemented to prevent this contagion from occurring? Surprisingly, events proved that there were few if any policies in place. Many of the key institutional actors were functioning either outside of existing regulations or with the lightest of regulatory supervision. The GSEs (Fannie Mae and Freddie Mac) were permitted to function with exemptions from existing securities regulations and to do so with modest capital requirements relative to banks. The credit rating agencies played an important role in serving as gatekeepers to financial markets insofar as the ratings they assigned determined the extent of the market for mortgage-backed securities. Yet, they were treated as self-regulating organizations with minimal supervision by the SEC. Indeed, even after Congress passed the Credit Agency Reform Act in 2006, following a wave of corporate scandals, it barred the SEC from regulating ratings or the procedures and methodologies used to arrive at the ratings.[49]

The American Insurance Group (AIG), the major issuer of credit-default swaps, was fully outside of the regulatory structure. And the process of securitization, the issuance of mortgage-backed securities, and so many of the institutions that were central to the shadow banking system, were functioning outside of regulations as well.

The shadow banking system is of particular interest here. Corporations, pension funds, and money market funds have large cash holdings. They need access to this cash to manage their regular obligations. At the same time, they want to earn interest and, to the extent possible, safeguard their cash in a world without deposit insurance. One way to place funds was in the commercial paper market. That is, investment banks could provide short-term unsecured loans to large corporations for a fee. In addition, there was the repo (or sale and repurchase) market, in which institutions provide cash to large commercial or investment banks at an interest rate, and accept collateral (often times, MBSs). These transactions constituted banking, even if much of it occurs outside of traditional depository institutions. In traditional banking, regulations serve to prevent liquidity crises. The FDIC provides deposit insurance to limit the risk that depositors will panic, withdraw their funds, and leave a bank insolvent. The Federal Reserve, moreover, serves a lender of last resort function. It stands ready to provide an infusion of funds to backstop banks in times of trouble. Taken alone, these protections could create problems of moral hazard. Banks could assume greater risk on the assumption that they would enjoy the benefits if successful, while taxpayers would pay the costs of failure. Thus, policies to mitigate liquidity risks were combined with regulations regarding capitalization, reserve requirements, and the kinds of investments and activities that banks could engage in. Unfortunately, as events would reveal, "the lack of these features in the shadow banking system led to substantial fragility."[50]

In the post-1980 period, the shadow banking system grew in prominence. The Financial Crisis Inquiry Commission, created by Congress to examine the causes of the collapse, reported: "The new parallel banking system—with commercial paper and repo providing cheaper financing, and money market funds providing better returns for consumers and institutional investors—had a crucial catch: its popularity came at the expense of the banks and thrifts."[51] In fact, the funds in the shadow banking system grew rapidly and, on the eve of the financial crisis, they actually exceeded the funds in the traditional banking system. The size of the shadow banking system remains something of a mystery, however. The Commission placed the value of the funds at approximately $7.3 trillion (2007–8), whereas the Bank for International Settlements reported that it exceeded $10 trillion. The differences in estimates reflects the fact that so much of what was going on in the shadow banking system occurred outside of the public eye and outside of established regulations. As Gary B. Gorton observes: "The size of the repo market is not known, because the government did not measure all of it, only part of it."[52]

The shadow banking system is a critical part of the story because it served as a transmission belt from the real estate market to the entire financial system and, ultimately, the economy as a whole. In late 2006 and early 2007, housing prices began to deteriorate and default rates began to rise in the $1.2 trillion subprime mortgage market. As the concerns over MBSs mounted—particularly those that were backed by subprime mortgages—they no longer served as a stable form of collateral in the repo market. What were once thought of as risk-free assets— bonds that had received the highest ratings by credit rating agencies—were now viewed as having a higher level of risk and thus lenders began demanding higher levels of collateral. If banks had to supplement the MBSs they were using as collateral, they were forced to sell off other assets to raise funds. As this response spread, the value of the assets—even those with no connection to real estate— began to plummet. Credit markets seized and what was essentially a bank run in the repo market spread into a full-fledged economic crisis.[53]

The US Treasury and the Federal Reserve were required to take extraordinary measures. Some financial firms were allowed to fail; other failing banks were acquired by healthier institutions via government-orchestrated mergers or placed into conservatorship. Some were rescued through heavy infusions of funds. At times, the actions fell well outside of existing regulatory jurisdictions, often justified by the Federal Reserve's reliance on section 13(3) of the Federal Reserve Act, which allowed it to lend to "any individual, partnership, or corporation" under "unusual or exigent circumstances." As one review of the events notes:

> Except for Lehman Brothers (and long-term debt holders of AIG and WaMu), there was a bailout of creditors of virtually all the heavily exposed financial intermediaries, including Bear Stearns, Fannie Mae, Freddie Mac, Merrill Lynch, Citigroup, Bank of America (through its purchase of Merrill Lynch), Wells Fargo (via Wachovia), and to a lesser extent, GMAC and GE Capital—as well as Goldman Sachs and Morgan Stanley—which were all in danger without government support.[54]

Congress responded to the crisis at the urging of Fed Chairman Ben Bernanke and Treasury Secretary Henry Paulson, and passed the Emergency Economic Stabilization Act of 2008. The Act authorized the Treasury to spend up to $700 billion to prevent the collapse of the financial system by purchasing distressed assets (e.g., MBSs that had lost their value) and providing funds to banks via a new Troubled Assets Relief Program. A few months later, the newly inaugurated Obama administration secured passage of a $787 billion stimulus bill, the American Recovery and Reinvestment Act of 2009. As the economy continued to deteriorate and unemployment ratcheted up to 10 percent, the federal government ran deficits of $1.4 trillion (2009) and $1.3 trillion (2010). As a percentage of GDP, these were the largest deficits since the end of World War II.

As the Republican Party—enlivened by the Tea Party movement—wrested control of the House of Representatives from the Democrats in the 2010 midterm elections, the period of expansive fiscal stimulus drew to a close. The next several years would witness extended budget battles, struggles over the debt ceiling, and a downgrading of the nation's credit rating. Things were only more complicated across the Atlantic, where the US financial crisis had cascaded into a global financial crisis, a sovereign debt crisis, and an extended recession.[55]

Making Sense of Failure

All of this raises an important question: How was it possible that regulations failed in such a tragic fashion? How could a collapse in a speculative bubble in real estate lead to the deepest recession since the Great Depression, wiping out a decade's worth of growth in household wealth, and a global financial crisis? Before developing an explanation that is in keeping with the larger argument of this book, let us consider in brief two of the more common explanations. Many critics on the right have gravitated toward the efforts to leverage credit markets to achieve social policy goals. Critics on the left, in contrast, have assigned responsibility to deregulation and the embrace of free markets. Both positions have some merits but prove unsatisfactory for reasons that will be developed below.

Many analysts on the right have assigned responsibility for the crash to failed efforts at social engineering. To be more precise, Congress and successive presidential administrations adopted increases in homeownership as a social policy goal, thereby circumventing markets. Traditionally, lenders made decisions based on the creditworthiness of borrowers, the quality of appraisal, and the size of a loan that could be supported at a given level of income. Certainly, the importance of these factors declined as lenders gravitated toward the originate-to-distribute model, and began selling loans for securitization rather than holding them in their portfolios. But the incentives to lower underwriting standards became far more powerful as financial regulators placed pressure on institutions to expand lending to low- and moderate-income households, using the Community Reinvestment Act to prevent racial discrimination in credit markets. Congress and HUD reinforced these efforts by directing Fannie Mae and Freddie Mac to push liquidity into the low and moderate portions of the market. While there may have been laudable goals associated with the efforts to promote homeownership—and here, unsurprisingly, there is much disagreement—the almost two-decade experiment in social policy had predictable results. Credit was extended to the most fragile part of the market, and on terms that were often predatory. As underwriting standards deteriorated, levels of speculation increased. With little money in the game, speculators and borrowers who had provided little in the way of down payments were among the first to exit once the market began to deteriorate.

The policies described above—when combined with other factors like the Federal Reserve's commitment to low interest rates—contributed to the rise in homeownership and the speculative bubble in real estate. Likewise, it would be difficult to make the case that low- and moderate-income households weren't particularly vulnerable to changing market conditions, thereby increasing the likelihood that a downturn in the market would have potentially devastating effects. But this does not provide an explanation of how the housing collapse cascaded into a full-blown financial crisis and a deep and prolonged recession. To provide a more complete explanation, one would need to incorporate the rise of the shadow banking system—the transmission belt between the securitization of mortgage debt and the larger economy. Moreover, one would need to incorporate the lack of regulation. As noted above, regulations are important precisely because they can limit the magnitude of damages.

This latter point would seem to favor the second explanation. For many critics on the left, the roots of the crisis are to be found in deregulation driven by an unbridled faith in free markets and the capacity of rational actors to manage risk without the intervention of the state and heavy industry investment in lobbying. As Chair of the House Financial Services Committee Rep. Barney Frank (D-MA) explained, the crisis was best understood as an indictment of "America's 30-year experiment with radical economic deregulation."[56] As noted in this chapter, beginning in the late 1970s, Congress and successive presidential administrations promoted deregulation that fundamentally altered the policies and institutions inherited from the New Deal, ending ultimately in the repeal of the Glass–Steagall Act's separation of commercial and investment banking. Had these policies been retained, the argument goes, the collapse could have been prevented or, at the very least, it could have been contained.

The argument has a certain appeal given that the dramatic growth in speculation and collapse closely followed the deregulation of financial markets. Yet, it flounders on a few counts. First, to acknowledge that deregulation occurred is not the same as making the case that an industry that was once highly regulated was now somehow free of regulation. In fact, banking remains the most regulated industry in the US economy. Between 1960 and 2010, the budget for finance and banking regulation (all figures expressed in 2005 dollars) increased more than tenfold, from $215 million to $2.873 billion. Of course, the "30-year experiment" cited above would lead us to focus on a shorter period. Between 1980 and 2007, the budget for finance and banking regulation increased from $802 million to $2.378 billion, in inflation-adjusted terms.[57] Regulators were regulating and doing so with historically unprecedented budgets. The key question was whether they were regulating the correct things—a point we will return to below.

Second, advocates of the argument that assigns primary importance to deregulation have a difficult time explaining precisely how the deregulatory actions directly contributed to the collapse. Exhibit one in the case against deregulation is GLBA's elimination of the Glass–Steagall firewall separating commercial and investment banking. Yet, even Joseph E. Stiglitz, Nobel laureate and sharp critic of financial deregulation, has a difficult time explicating the connection with precision. In his words:

> The most important consequence of the repeal of Glass–Steagall was indirect—it lay in the way repeal changed an entire culture. . . . When repeal of Glass–Steagall brought investment and commercial banks together, the investment-bank culture came out on top. There was a demand for the kind of high returns that could be obtained only through high leverage and big risk-taking.[58]

One might respond that the change in culture that Stiglitz attributes to GLBA existed prior to its passage, a factor that helps explain why the industry invested so heavily in lobbying to secure its passage. Moreover, many of the institutions that were central to the crisis—the GSEs, AIG, and large investment banks—were not engaged in activities that were directly restricted by Glass–Steagall. In short, the crisis did not emanate from the parts of the industry that had been deregulated by GBLA.

This does not mean that deregulation was irrelevant. The Garn–St. Germain Depository Institutions Act of 1982, for example, allowed banks to offer adjustable-rate mortgages. These mortgages may be more attractive to lower-income households—particularly if they take interest-only loans—and there is much evidence that they contributed to the rise of homeownership rates. But they transfer the risk of interest rate fluctuations from financial institutions to borrowers, many of whom ultimately proved incapable of making payments in an environment of rising interest rates. But the key question is whether deregulation permitted a collapse of the housing bubble to move rapidly through the rest of the economy. The evidence seems limited.

Regulation and the Problem of Drift

When making the case that deregulation provides an explanation for the collapse, advocates of this position frequently conflate deregulation and the absence of regulation. The two are not the same. Deregulation involves the repeal of existing laws or the loosening or elimination of restrictions on commercial behavior, not the absence of regulation. The deregulatory legislation and actions of the post-1970s period were designed, in part, to manage the friction between layered regimes. But taken as a whole, they did not constitute a new regulatory architecture for the rapidly evolving financial sector. As David Wessel correctly observes: "Congress had undone much of the New Deal legislation without finishing the job of reconstructing the financial regulatory apparatus, which was shared by a bewildering number of federal and state agencies of varying competence."[59] When looking at the shadow banking system—the process of securitization, the repo (or sale and repurchase) market, and many of the actors that participated in it—the striking fact is that most of it had never been subjected to regulation.

In part, the problem may have been cognitive. Policymakers view the activity of banking as something that occurs within the confines of regulated depository institutions. When it flows outside of these channels and thus outside of the jurisdiction of existing agencies, its significance as banking is only dimly understood. Moreover, the central actors in the shadow banking system—hedge funds, insurance companies, investment banks, money market mutual funds, pension funds, private equity funds—were not the kinds of organizations that one traditionally associated with banking. As Gary B. Gorton wrote in 2010:

> The shadow banking system is, in fact, banking. Banking is about the creation of information-insensitive debt. Securitized products serve the function of collateral for many purposes, but serve an especially important role in the repo market. Although the shadow banking system has been present for roughly 25 years, it was never understood to be "banking" because that was associated with chartered depository institutions. So while the development of this system was noted, the vulnerability to panic was not noted . . . . The shadow banking system was, as they say, "off the radar screen."[60]

In the end, a system that was not understood as banking would not be regulated as banking.

But even if the shadow banking system may have been "off the radar screen" for some, it is clearly the case that Congress had ample warning of the potential for disastrous outcomes. The General Accounting Office, for example, issued a report in 1994 at the request of Congress, where it expressed its concerns over the lack of regulation of derivatives (e.g., credit-default swaps). The Comptroller General warned that a failure of dealers or issuers could pose a risk to the financial system and force a government bailout.[61] In 2003, the International Monetary Fund warned that the GSEs had taken on too much risk with too little capital.[62] A year later, the Office of Management and Budget made the same argument and warned that "a misjudgment or unexpected economic event could quickly deplete this capital, potentially making it difficult for a GSE to meet its debt obligations . . . even a small mistake by a GSE could have consequences throughout the economy."[63] The warnings, spanning over a decade, suggest that the potential risks were recognized and brought to the attention of policymakers, but they nonetheless failed to precipitate a legislative or regulatory response.

Indeed, they often had the opposite impact. Consider the case of derivatives like the credit-default swaps that were issued to insure the MBSs that were central to the shadow banking system. As noted above, as early as 1994, the GAO had warned of the lack of regulation and questioned whether issuers had sufficient capital to back their guarantees. In 1997, the Commodity Futures Trading Commission solicited comments on tightening the regulation of derivatives to set the foundations for rulemaking. Federal Reserve Chairman Alan Greenspan, Treasury Secretary Robert Rubin, SEC Chair Arthur Levitt, and Deputy Secretary of the Treasury Lawrence Summers rebuffed these efforts and testified in opposition before Congress.[64] As Greenspan testified: "participants in financial futures markets are predominantly professionals that simply do not require the customer protections that may be needed by the general public. Regulation that serves no useful purpose hinders the efficiency of markets to enlarge standards of living."[65] Despite the recent collapse of Long Term Capital Management, a highly leveraged hedge fund with some $1 trillion in derivatives, Congress responded by blocking the regulatory efforts through the passage of an appropriations rider. A few years later, the reports identifying the fragility of the highly leveraged GSEs—issued in the wake of revelations about accounting problems stemming from the misreporting of $450 billion of profits over a three-year period—resulted in hearings, but on each occasion, Congress refused to enact significant reforms.[66]

The story of financial regulation has a strong dose of path dependency and drift—the failure, under conditions of polarization, to recalibrate policy and institutions to reflect the challenges posed by changes in the larger environment. In Chapter 2, we noted that one of the critiques of path dependency theory is that it often focuses on stability in policy and institutions without paying sufficient attention to the intense political battles that occur to reinforce the path. In the case of finance, it is clear that regulated interests invested heavily in their efforts to prevent the introduction of new regulations. It is difficult to arrive at any other conclusion when looking at the record of campaign contributions. Total contributions by the finance, insurance, and real estate industries expanded dramatically during the period in question. In presidential electoral cycles, between 1991–92 and 1999–2000, industry spending increased from $126.2 million to $320.2 million, increasing again to $518 million by 2007–8. In congressional electoral cycles, the figures grew as well, from $110.9 million (1993–94) to $292.6 million (2005–6). As one might expect, the contributions reflected support for both parties, with a slight preference for the GOP (55 percent). The GSEs may have started slowly, but they rapidly became major participants in campaign finance. In 1991–92, they gave a combined $229,075. By 2001–2, when Freddie and Fannie were under investigation for accounting irregularities, their joint investment in elections hit a peak of $6.7 million.[67]

Election spending pales in comparison to the investment in lobbying. In the decade leading up to the financial collapse (1998–2007), Fannie Mae and Freddie Mac, the two GSEs that were deeply involved in securitization and effectively avoided the imposition of additional regulatory restraints as their portfolios grew in size, spent $74.4 million and $88.4 million, respectively, on lobbying. The American Insurance Group, the firm responsible for issuing credit-default swaps on MBSs, invested $66.2 million in lobbying activities. All told, the industry (finance, insurance, and real estate) spent $3 billion on lobbying during this period. Although the GSEs and AIG largely exited the lobbying game in the aftermath of the collapse, industry totals continued to increase, largely one expects, as a means of shaping the legislative and regulatory response. In the period 2008–15, the industry spent an additional $3.85 billion, roughly 160 percent per year of the pre-crisis annual average.[68]

In Chapter 3, we briefly discussed regulatory capture as the situation where agencies nurture the very interests they are charged with regulating. Often capture is viewed as the product of an explicit *quid pro quo*. In the standard account, corporate interests provide vote-maximizing politicians with the resources they need to secure reelection in exchange for policies that allow them to maximize their own profits. Of course, it may also involve preventing the introduction of policies that could hinder profitability, thereby contributing to drift. Certainly, the heavy industry investment in campaigns would reinforce this model, as would the ubiquitous revolving door in finance. Regulators and legislators alike could look to lucrative post-government employment in the industry they were charged with overseeing. Of course, there is a reverse revolving door as well, particularly in finance, with industry actors moving into regulatory positions and then returning to the private sector.[69]

But lobbying is an important part of regulatory politics as well. In recent years, terms like "cognitive capture" and "cultural capture" have been used to describe the process by which elected officials, staffers, and administrators internalize the interests of an industry, framing the problems encountered by industry actors and the validity of competing responses (and nonresponses) in ways that reinforce these very interests.[70] Lobbyists made the case that rational actors in the financial industry had the expertise, knowledge, and the incentives to manage the risks they assumed. Those in charge of overseeing the industry and adjusting the regulatory architecture came to believe them—or in the face of extraordinary complexity, deferred to their judgment—thereby reinforcing the material and electoral interests identified earlier and contributing to the pattern of drift.

Whatever the precise mechanism, two things are clear. First, Congress failed to pass new statutes to extend the reach of regulations to the most dynamic and rapidly expanding parts of the industry. The ongoing regulation of traditional depository institutions was simply insufficient given the dramatic expansion of securitization and the shadow banking system. Here we have a classic case of path-dependent development. Second, however, path dependency doesn't just happen. To simply suggest that the developments of prior decades were "off the radar screen" is to ignore the dramatic levels of industry spending in campaigns and lobbying designed to keep things off the radar screen, reinforcing path dependency. Drift was not the inevitable product of polarization, although polarization was an important part of the story. Instead, it was the product of political action extending over decades.

The Congressional Response

In the wake of the collapse, Congress passed the Dodd–Frank Wall Street Reform and Consumer Protection Act of 2010, the most significant piece of financial regulatory legislation since the New Deal, and thus something of an anomaly in an age of polarization and gridlock. Dodd–Frank is a complex statute—some 848 pages in length—but a few of its key features are worth reviewing.[71] Prior to Dodd–Frank, the regulatory system consisted of a set of agencies that regulated specific kinds of institutions (e.g., commercial banks, investment banks, savings and loans). Differences in regulatory requirements created opportunities for regulatory arbitrage; financial actors would assume institutional forms that would subject them to less stringent regulations, even if they still engaged in the same forms of behavior. While the old regulatory agencies would survive, a new Financial Stability Oversight Council, chaired by the Treasury Secretary, was created to monitor risk on an economy-wide basis and coordinate the efforts of its members. It was charged with identifying firms that were potential sources of financial risk regardless of their corporate form. Nonbank financial companies, if considered a source of risk, can be subjected to regulation by the Federal Reserve. Institutions that are deemed systemically important can be forced to meet higher capital and liquidity requirements and subjected to annual "stress tests" to determine whether they could survive under trying conditions. One of the great concerns that emerged in the years leading up to the financial crisis was that consumers were being tempted to assume levels of indebtedness that were unsustainable, and often on terms that left them vulnerable. To address these issues, Dodd–Frank created a new independent agency, the Consumer Financial Protection Bureau, housed in the Federal Reserve.

One of the persistent concerns in financial regulation is that large, systemically important firms that are "too-big-to-fail" engage in riskier behavior on the assumption that regulators (or taxpayers) will cover any downside risk. Under Dodd–Frank, the moral hazard problems were addressed in a few ways. First, as noted above, systemically important firms can be required to meet higher capital and liquidity requirements. Second, they can be forced to develop "living wills," that is, plans for their orderly resolution (the underlying assumption, of course, is that they will be liquidated). Resolution processes had long been established for regulated depository institutions to manage failure. But as the financial crisis revealed, similar powers were absent for nonbank financial companies, forcing the government to orchestrate emergency *ad hoc* bailouts (e.g., AIG, Bear Stearns) or permit a firm to fall into bankruptcy (e.g., Lehman Brothers), a decision that only exacerbated the crisis. Under Dodd–Frank, the government's liquidation authority was extended to financial firms that fell outside of the traditional regulatory silos.

With respect to shadow banking, several reforms were introduced by Dodd–Frank. Institutions involved in securitization will be required to disclose information on the structure of the securities they issue. Major actors in the repo market can be forced to meet liquidity requirements. With respect to derivatives (like credit-default swaps), Dodd–Frank mandated regulations intended to standardize them, bring the trading on to established exchanges under regulatory supervision, and increase reporting requirements. Dodd–Frank authorized the creation of a new Office of Credit Ratings in the SEC and mandated new rules on reporting, disclosure, and examination requirements and required a GAO study of alternatives to the "issue pays" compensation model.[72] As for the GSEs, Dodd–Frank did little more than note that "the hybrid public–private status of Fannie Mae and Freddie Mac is untenable and must be resolved" and stated that financial reforms "would be incomplete without enactment of meaningful structural reforms." That task was put off for another day.[73]

The formal provisions of Dodd–Frank may be an improvement over what existed prior to the financial crisis, but its long-term performance remains uncertain as of this writing. Much will depend on the specific regulations promulgated by the agencies involved. Dodd–Frank mandated 390 rulemakings, 271 of which had to be completed by a statutory deadline. By the fifth anniversary of the Act, agencies had met 70.8 percent of the deadlines, and had promulgated a total of 247 final rules.[74] Given that the rules are intrinsically complex and notice-and-comment rulemaking is a protracted process, delay should not be a surprise. The slow pace of rulemaking is unsurprising for another reason. In some cases, the demands of rulemaking have exceeded agency capacities and budgetary resources. In the years preceding the financial crisis, for example, the SEC promulgated 9.5 rules per year; under Dodd–Frank, it was required to complete 59 rulemakings in the next calendar year. Similarly, the CFTC, which had produced an average of 5.5 rules per year, was required to complete work on 37 rules.[75] Given the number and complexity of the rules, no one can predict with certainty how they will perform and interact once implemented. Unquestionably, the rulemaking mandated under Dodd–Frank is only the beginning. Each significant rule will generate court challenges and many of these challenges may, when combined with experience, result in rule modifications.

The future is also muddied by the ongoing impact of polarization. In the past, significant regulatory statutes were passed with overwhelming bipartisan majorities, even when they were not the result of a crisis of the magnitude of the financial collapse. Dodd–Frank, in contrast, was passed along strict party lines, attracting no Republican votes in the House and three votes in the Senate. Following the GOP victories in the 2010 midterm elections, the next several years would witness ongoing attempts to deny agencies increased appropriations to implement the act and legislative efforts to block the implementation of the financial reforms. Bills were passed in 2012 to narrow the regulation of derivatives and to prohibit the SEC and the CFTC from proposing new rules without conducting a cost–benefit analysis that would support the rule. Neither effort survived the Senate.[76] The next year, the House passed four bills to weaken various parts of Dodd–Frank, two of which focused on derivative regulation. Once again, the Senate did not take the bills up for consideration.[77] In 2014, opponents succeeded by attaching a rider on a $1.1 trillion spending bill for Fiscal Year 2015 that repealed a prohibition on banks from making certain derivative trades in their units that were backed by federal deposit insurance. Calls for an outright repeal of Dodd–Frank are unlikely, however, given the continued anger at Wall Street, the investments that financial institutions have already made in compliance, and the reality that the most effective and least visible avenues will remain in agency rulemaking and the courts.[78]

Conclusion

The financial crisis of 2007–8 was arguably the greatest regulatory failure in the nation's history. While many analysts blame the crisis on excessive deregulation, it has been the core argument of this chapter that deregulation was but one part of the story. Finance has been subject to regulation for most of the nation's history. This chapter departed from the contemporary focus of other chapters in this volume to situate the financial crisis in this history, beginning with the Civil War banking laws. What becomes clear is that the history of financial regulation is one of path-dependent layering. The tensions between layered regimes have generated new regulatory problems over time. Deregulation was a response to the problems of inflation and the growing competitive challenge from financial firms that fell outside of the regulatory structure inherited from the New Deal. Money market mutual funds could compete for deposits, free from the interest rate regulations imposed on regulated depository institutions subject to Regulation Q. So-called nonbank banks could offer products and services denied their regulated counterparts. With a series of deregulatory statutes, Congress removed many of the restrictions that impeded competition, at times with painful results (e.g., the S&L crisis). But Congress failed to build a new regulatory architecture for the emerging practice of securitization, the issuance of credit-default swaps, and the repo market. As noted earlier in the chapter, regulators were regulating (indeed, by most measures the resources devoted to financial regulation had never been greater than in the years preceding the collapse). But they were regulating the wrong things. Shadow banking remained largely outside of the existing regulatory structure. Regulated depository institutions, to the extent that they participated in the repo market or held securitized debt in their portfolios, were left highly vulnerable.

The financial crisis is a story of regulatory drift resulting in disaster. Of course, drift doesn't just happen. In the case of finance, many key actors assumed that financial institutions behaved like rational actors. They had the knowledge and the incentives to manage the risks they assumed. For those who may have been less enamored of the industry's capacity for self-regulation, heavy investments in lobbying and campaign contributions also proved instrumental in preventing the extension of regulatory authority to the shadow banking system and its key components. Successive warnings about the fragility of the system seemed to gain little if any traction in Washington in the decade leading up to the crisis. While Congress ultimately responded to the disaster with the passage of the most significant financial regulatory statute since the New Deal, it did not use the opportunity to build a new regulatory architecture. Rather, it created new mechanisms to coordinate the actions of existing regulatory agencies and authorized hundreds of rulemakings. Given the history leading up to the crisis, one can question whether these rulemakings will be subject to the same forces that blocked reforms in the past. Much has yet to be determined.

Notes

1 William J. Clinton, "Remarks on the National Homeownership Strategy, June 5, 1995." Available at www.presidency.ucsb.edu/ws/?pid=51448.
2 "President Hosts Conference on Minority Homeownership, George Washington University, Washington, DC, October 15, 2002." Available at georgewbush-white house.archives.gov/news/releases/2002/10/20021015-7.html. See Jo Becker, Sheryl Gay Stolberg, and Stephen Labaton, "White House Philosophy Stoked Mortgage Bonfire," *New York Times*, December 20, 2008, A1. Available at www.nytimes. com/2008/12/21/business/21admin.html.
3 Shari Olefson, *Foreclosure Nation: Mortgaging the American Dream* (Amherst, NY: Prometheus Books, 2009), 12.
4 This argument was first presented in Marc Allen Eisner, "Policy Regimes in Political Time: Path Dependency, Regime Change and the Case of US Financial Regulation," paper delivered at the International Conference on Public Policy, Grenoble, France, June 26, 2013.
5 See Marc Allen Eisner, "Markets in the Shadow of the State: An Appraisal of Deregulation and Implications for Future Research," in *Government and Markets: Toward a New Theory of Regulation*, ed. Edward J. Balleisen and David A. Moss (Cambridge, UK: Cambridge University Press, 2010), 512–37. On the constitutive role of regulatory policy, see Lauren B. Edelman and Mark C. Suchman, "The Legal Environments of Organizations," *Annual Review of Sociology*, 23 (1997): 479–515, and Neil Fligstein, *The Architecture of Markets: An Economic Sociology of Twenty-First Century Capitalist Societies* (Princeton, NJ: Princeton University Press, 2001).
6 Carmen M. Reinhart and Kenneth S. Rogoff, *This Time Is Different: Eight Centuries of Financial Folly* (Princeton, NJ: Princeton University Press, 2009), 153.
7 Charles Tilly, *Coercion, Capital, and European States: AD 990–1992* (Cambridge, UK: Blackwell, 1992), 26.
8 Richard Franklin Bensel, *Yankee Leviathan: The Origins of Central State Authority in America, 1859–1877* (Cambridge, UK: Cambridge University Press, 1990), 238–302.
9 Office of the Comptroller of the Currency, *Office of the Comptroller of the Currency: A Short History* (Washington DC: Comptroller of the Currency, 2011), 1.
10 Quoted in Howard H. Hackley, "Our Baffling Banking System," *Virginia Law Review*, 52, 4 (1966): 571.

11 Office of the Comptroller of the Currency, *Office of the Comptroller of the Currency*, 6–7, 9; Office of the Comptroller of the Currency, *Comptroller of the Currency Annual Report 1931* (Washington DC: Government Printing Office, 1931), 3.

12 Charles F. Dunbar, "The National Banking System," *The Quarterly Journal of Economics*, 12, 1 (1897): 5, 7.

13 See Richard Franklin Bensel, *The Political Economy of American Industrialization, 1877–1900* (Cambridge, UK: Cambridge University Press, 2000), 133–43.

14 Eugene Nelson White, "The Political Economy of Banking Regulation, 1864–1933," *The Journal of Economic History*, 42, 1(1982): 34–35, Office of the Comptroller of the Currency, *Comptroller of the Currency Annual Report 1931*, 3, US Census Bureau, *Historical Statistics of the United States*, series X, 657, 635.

15 Marc Allen Eisner, *The American Political Economy: Institutional Evolution of Market and State*, 2nd ed. (New York: Routledge, 2014), 55–57. Although the case can be made that the Federal Reserve Act (1913) was sufficiently important to constitute a new regime, here it is treated as a means of shoring up the national banking system—an example of regime maintenance.

16 White, "The Political Economy of Banking Regulation," 35–36.

17 See ibid., 37–39; Verle B. Johnson, "The McFadden Act: A Look Back," *FRB SF Weekly Newsletter*, Federal Reserve Bank of San Francisco, August 19, 1983, and H. H. Preston, "The McFadden Banking Act," *The American Economic Review*, 17, 2 (1927): 202.

18 Office of the Comptroller of the Currency, *Comptroller of the Currency Annual Report 1933* (Washington DC: Government Printing Office, 1933), 3–4.

19 See Marc Allen Eisner, *Regulatory Politics in Transition* (Baltimore, MD: Johns Hopkins University Press, 1993), 106–11.

20 Thomas K. McCraw, "With the Consent of the Governed: SEC's Formative Years," *Journal of Policy Analysis and Management*, 1, 3 (1982): 359.

21 Census Bureau, *Historical Statistics of the United States*, series X, 610–15, 620–23.

22 Figures on banks suspensions from Milton Friedman and Anna Jacobson Schwartz, *A Monetary History of the United States, 1867–1960* (Princeton, NJ: Princeton University Press, 1963), 438–39, and Census Bureau, *Historical Statistics of the United States*, series X, 741.

23 Gary B. Gorton, *Slapped by the Invisible Hand: The Panic of 2007* (New York: Oxford University Press, 2010), 14.

24 For a brief history of Regulation Q, see R. Alton Gilbert, "Requiem for Regulation Q: What It Did and Why It Passed Away," Federal Reserve Bank of St. Louis, February 1986.

25 George G. Kaufman, Larry R. Mote, and Harvey Rosenblum, "Consequences of Deregulation for Commercial Banking," *The Journal of Finance*, 39, 3 (1984): 790.

26 For an overview of financial deregulation, see Jeffry Worsham, *Other People's Money: Policy Change, Congress, and Bank Regulation* (Boulder, CO: Westview Press, 1997), 107–28.

27 Depository Institutions Deregulation and Monetary Control Act (1980), title II, §202 (a).

28 See Paul R. Allen and William J. Wilhelm, "The Impact of the 1980 Depository Institutions Deregulation and Monetary Control Act on Market Value and Risk: Evidence from the Capital Markets," *Journal of Money, Credit and Banking*, 20, 3 (1988): 364–80.

29 For an overview of Garn–St. Germain, see David Allardice, Herbert L. Baer, Elijah Brewer III, Thomas F. Cargill, John Dobra, Gillian Garcia, Anne Marie Gonczy, George G. Kaufman, Robert D. Laurent, and Larry R. Mote, "The Garn–St. Germain Depository Institutions Act of 1982," *Federal Reserve Bank of Chicago Economic Perspectives*, 7, 2 (March 1983): 3–31.

30 Yomarie Silva, "The Credit Crisis of 2008," *Review of Banking & Financial Law*, 28 (2009): 34.

31 Congressional Budget Office, *The Economic Effects of the Savings & Loan Crisis* (Washington DC: The Congressional Budget Office, 1992), 10.

32 Richard J. Cebula and Chao-Shun Hung, "Barth's Analysis of the Savings and Loan Debacle: An Empirical Test." *Southern Economic Journal*, 59, 2 (1992): 307, 305, and Mark Carl Rom, *Public Spirit in the Thrift Tragedy* (Pittsburgh, PA: University of Pittsburgh Press, 1996), 3.

33 Timothy Curry and Lynn Shibut, "The Cost of the Savings and Loan Crisis: Truth and Consequences," *FDIC Banking Review*, 13, 2 (2000): 26, 31, 33.

34 Michelle Clark Neely, "Commercial & Investment Banking: Should This Divorce Be Saved?" *The Regional Economist* (Federal Reserve Bank of St. Louis), April 1995.

35 Robert D. Hershey, Jr., "Plan Is Offered to Reorganize Finance Sector," *New York Times*, May 22, 1997, D1. Available at www.nytimes.com/1997/05/22/business/plan-is-offered-to-reorganize-finance-sector.html.

36 James R. Barth, R. Dan Brumbaugh, and James A. Wilcox, "The Repeal of Glass–Steagall and the Advent of Broad Banking," *Journal of Economics Perspectives*, 14, 2 (2000): 196.

37 Jesse Bricker, Arthur B. Kennickell, Kevin B. Moore, and John Sabelhaus, "Changes in U.S. Family Finances from 2007 to 2010: Evidence from the Survey of Consumer Finances," *Federal Reserve Bulletin*, 98, 2 (June 2012).

38 Office of Management and Budget, *Analytical Perspectives, Budget of the United States Government, Fiscal Year 2015*, March 4, 2014, 206. See Dennis J. Ventry, Jr., "The Accidental Deduction: A History and Critique of the Tax Subsidy for Mortgage Interest," *Law and Contemporary Problems*, 73 (2010): 232–84.

39 Mechele Dickerson, *Homeownership and America's Financial Underclass: Flawed Premises, Broken Promises, New Prescriptions* (New York: Cambridge University Press, 2014), 37.

40 See Monica Prasad, *The Land of Too Much: American Abundance and the Paradox of Poverty* (Cambridge, MA: Harvard University Press, 2012).

41 Marc Allen Eisner, "Before the Third Act: Crony Capitalism and the Origins of the Financial Crisis," *Georgetown Journal of Law & Public Policy*, 11 (2013): 399, 395–96.

42 Michael Simkovic, "Competition and Crisis in Mortgage Securitization," *Indiana Law Journal*, 88 (2013): 225–27.

43 Matthew Richardson, Joshua Ronen, and Marti Subrahmanyam, "Securitization Reform," in *Regulating Wall Street: The Dodd–Frank Act and the New Architecture of Global Finance*, ed. Viral V. Acharya, Thomas F. Cooley, Matthew Richardson, and Ingo Walter (Hoboken, NJ: John Wiley & Sons, 2011), 473.

44 Edward L. Pittman, "Economic and Regulatory Developments Affecting Mortgage Related Securities," *Notre Dame Law Review*, 64 (1989): 512–21.

45 Financial Crisis Inquiry Commission, "Securitization and the Mortgage Crisis," Preliminary Staff Report, April 7, 2010, 18. Available at http://fcic-static.law.stanford.edu/cdn_media/fcic-reports/2010-0407-Preliminary_Staff_Report_-_Securitization_and_the_Mortgage_Crisis.pdf.

46 US Bureau of the Census, "Homeownership Rate for the United States." Available at https://research.stlouisfed.org/fred2/series/USHOWN.

47 Federal Reserve Bank of St. Louis, "Household Debt Service Payments as a Percent of Disposable Personal Income." Available at https://research.stlouisfed.org/fred2/series/TDSP.

48 US Bureau of Economic Analysis, "Net Savings as a Percentage of Gross National Income." Available at https://research.stlouisfed.org/fred2/series/W207RC1Q156SBEA.

49 John C. Coffee, "Rating Reform: The Good, the Bad, and the Ugly," *Harvard Business Law Review*, 1 (2011): 246–49.

50 Financial Crisis Inquiry Commission, "Shadow Banking and the Financial Crisis," Preliminary Staff Report, May 4, 2010, 16. Available at http://fcic-static.law.stanford.edu/cdn_media/fcic-reports/2010-0505-Shadow-Banking.pdf.

51 Financial Crisis Inquiry Commission, *The Financial Crisis Inquiry Report: Final Report of the National Commission on the Causes of the Financial and Economic Crisis in the United States* (New York: Public Affairs, 2011), 31.

52 Gary B. Gorton, *Misunderstanding Financial Crises: Why We Don't See Them Coming* (New York: Oxford University Press, 2012), 132.

53 This discussion draws on Gorton, *Misunderstanding Financial Crises*, 182–99.

54 Matthew Richardson, Roy C. Smith, and Ingo Walter, "Large Banks and the Volcker Rule," in *Regulating Wall Street: The Dodd–Frank Act and the New Architecture of Global Finance*, ed. Viral V. Acharya, Thomas F. Cooley, Matthew Richardson, and Ingo Walter (Hoboken, NJ: John Wiley & Sons, 2011), 184.

55 The paragraph draws on James J. Gosling and Marc Allen Eisner, *Economics, Politics, and American Public Policy* (Armonk, NY: M. E. Sharpe, 2013), 200–11.

56 Barney Frank, "Why America Needs a Little Less Laissez-Faire," *Financial Times*, January 13, 2008, 11. Available at www.ft.com/cms/s/0/d001b2c6-c20a-11dc-8fba-0000779fd2ac.html#axzz4GBqbnQF5.

57 Susan Dudley and Melinda Warren, *Fiscal Stalemate Reflected in Regulators' Budget: An Analysis of the U.S. Budget for Fiscal Years 2011 and 2012* (St. Louis, MO: Murray Weidenbaum Center of the Economy, Government, and Policy, Washington University; Washington DC: George Washington University Regulatory Studies Center, 2011), Appendix A2.

58 Joseph E. Stiglitz, "Capitalist Fools," *Vanity Fair*, December 9, 2008. Available at www.vanityfair.com/news/2009/01/stiglitz200901-2.

59 David Wessel, *In Fed We Trust: Ben Bernanke's War on the Great Panic* (New York: Crown Business, 2009), 150.

60 Gorton, *Slapped by the Invisible Hand*, 58.

61 See General Accounting Office, *Financial Derivatives: Actions Needed to Protect the Financial System*, GAO/T-GDD-94-15 (Washington DC: General Accounting Office, 1994).

62 International Monetary Fund, *Global Financial Stability Report: Market Developments and Issues* (Washington DC: International Monetary Fund, 2003).

63 Office of Management and Budget, *Analytical Perspectives, Budget of the United States Government, Fiscal Year 2005* (Washington DC: Government Printing Office, 2004), 82.

64 Peter S. Goodman, "Taking a Hard New Look at the Greenspan Legacy," *New York Times*, October 8, 2008, A1. Available at www.nytimes.com/2008/10/09/business/economy/09greenspan.html.

65 Alan Greenspan, "The Regulation of OTC Derivatives," Testimony of Chairman Alan Greenspan before the Committee on Banking and Financial Services, US House of Representatives, July 24, 1998. Available at www.federalreserve.gov/board docs/testimony/1998/19980724.htm.

66 See Gretchen Morgenson and Joshua Rosner, *Reckless Endangerment: How Outsized Ambition, Greed, and Corruption Led to Economic Armageddon* (New York: Times Books, 2011), 238–62.

67 These figures include direct donations, donations by employees, and political action committees. All figures are from Federal Election Commission statistics at opensecrets.com, calculations by author.

68 All figures are from Federal Election Commission statistics at opensecrets.com, calculations by author.

69 See Gretchen Morgenson, "A Revolving Door Helps Big Banks' Quiet Campaign to Muscle out Fannie and Freddie," *New York Times*, December 7, 2015, A1. On the industry more generally, see David Lucca, Amit Seru, and Francesco Trebbi, "The Revolving Door and Worker Flows in Banking Regulation," Federal Reserve Bank of New York Staff Report no. 678, June 2014.

70 See James Kwak, "Cultural Capture and the Financial Crisis," in *Preventing Regulatory Capture: Special Interest Influence and How to Limit It*, ed. Daniel Carpenter and David Moss (Cambridge, UK: Cambridge University Press, 2013), 71–98.

71 This discussion draws on Michael S. Barr, "The Financial Crisis and the Path of Reform," *Yale Journal on Regulation*, 29 (2012): 91–119.

72 For a discussion of Dodd–Frank's provisions on credit rating agencies, see Edward I. Altman, T. Sabri Öncü, Matthew Richardson, Anjolein Schmeits, and Lawrence J. White, "Regulation of Rating Agencies," in *Regulating Wall Street: The Dodd–Frank Act and the New Architecture of Global Finance*, ed. Viral V. Acharya, Thomas F. Cooley, Matthew Richardson, and Ingo Walter (Hoboken, NJ: John Wiley & Sons, 2011), 443–67. A requirement that the SEC create a Credit Rating Agency Board to assign credit rating agencies to rate issuances was passed by the Senate but was not included in the final version of Dodd–Frank. See Government Accountability Office, *Credit Rating Agencies: Alternative Compensation Models for Nationally Recognized Statistical Rating Organizations*, GAO-12-240 (Washington DC: Government Accountability Office, 2012).

73 See Viral V. Archarya, T. Sabri Öncü, Matthew Richardson, Stijn Van Nieuwerburgh, and Lawrence J. White, "The Government Sponsored Enterprises," in *Regulating Wall Street: The Dodd–Frank Act and the New Architecture of Global Finance*, ed. Viral V. Acharya, Thomas F. Cooley, Matthew Richardson, and Ingo Walter (Hoboken, NJ: John Wiley & Sons, 2011), 429–42.

74 DavisPolk, "Dodd–Frank Progress Report," July 16, 2015. Available at http://prod. davispolk.com/sites/default/files/Q4_2015_Dodd-Frank_Progress_Report.pdf.

75 R. Glenn Hubbard, John L. Thornton, and Hal S. Scott, "The Pace of Rulemaking Under the Dodd–Frank Act," December 15, 2010. Available at http://capmktsreg. org/news/pace-of-rulemaking-under-the-dodd-frank-act/.

76 James B. Stewart, "As a Watchdog Starves, Wall Street Is Tossed a Bone," *New York Times*, July 15, 2011, A1, Suzy Khimm, "What Really Causes 'Regulatory Uncertainty'? Budget Cuts," *Washington Post*, November 16, 2011, and Ben Weyl, "2012 Legislative Summary: Banking Overhaul Rollback," *CQ Weekly*, January 14, 2013, 76.

77 Ben Weyl, "2013 Legislative Summary: Dodd–Frank Changes," *CQ Weekly*, January 6, 2014, 34.

78 Ben Weyl, "Dodd–Frank: Wall Street Reform, Round 3," *CQ Weekly*, January 5, 2015, 24, and George Cahlink, "Dodd–Frank: Turning 5 and Hanging Tough," *CQ Weekly*, July 20, 2015, 32.

10

BEYOND DEREGULATION

For the first three-quarters of the twentieth century, the dominant story with respect to regulation was one of dramatic expansion. Congress passed a long series of statutes creating new agencies and extending regulation to a host of industries. In key industries (e.g., banking, air and surface transportation, communications), important economic decisions formerly made by private sector actors were now shaped, and in some cases dictated, by regulations that sought to govern prices, flow to market, permissible products and services, and the conditions of entry and exit. Up until the immediate postwar decades, it may have made some sense for analysts to speak of the "regulated" and "unregulated" sectors of the economy. But by the 1970s, with the introduction of environmental protection and occupational safety and health regulations and the creation of new agencies with economy-wide jurisdictions, simple distinctions between the regulated and unregulated industries were no longer relevant. The United States might have reveled in its celebration of free markets, but market activity was embedded in a dense network of public policies. Indeed, to the extent that regulations shaped the expectations that transactions could occur without fraud, discrimination, or unnecessary risks, regulations created "the very possibility of marketplaces."[1]

The 1970s brought unprecedented regulatory expansion and, ironically, regulatory contraction. As the problems of high inflation and sluggish growth eluded traditional macroeconomic policy instruments, attention turned to deregulation. Some of the policies that were inherited from the Progressive Era and the New Deal were revoked by Congress or administrators; others were revised to provide a greater role for market forces. The deregulatory statutes and administrative decisions, when combined with new regulatory review processes that forced agencies to subject significant regulations to cost–benefit analysis, seemed to mark a genuine sea change. Many concluded that the era of regulatory expansion had drawn to a close; the deregulated society had arrived. When combined with changes in macroeconomic policy, taxation, social welfare, and trade, deregulation would be presented as a central component of a new neoliberal policy mix premised on the centrality of free markets.

While deregulation and regulatory review were important, they by no means marked the end of regulation. As suggested by the brief statistical portrait of regulation in Chapter 2, there is much evidence that the regulatory state has continued to expand. Whether one looks to inflation-adjusted regulatory budgets or the continuous growth of the Code of Federal Regulations, there is little evidence that the late 1970s and the 1980s marked a transition from a regulated economy to some idyllic world of free markets. However, something else quite profound was occurring. As levels of polarization increased in Congress and gridlock ensued, legislative productivity plummeted, and with it, the passage of significant new regulatory statutes. Yes, regulators were regulating, but they were often regulating the wrong things, drawing on statutes that had been passed decades earlier. In many cases, these statutes failed to provide the legal authority or the flexibility to shift the focus of regulation to emerging issues and problems. The end result was a problem of drift.

The potential costs of regulatory drift were veiled in the 1990s. A Congress under unified Republican control may have been unwilling to pass new regulatory statutes or support budgetary growth, but the Clinton administration offered a novel solution in regulatory reinvention. President Clinton proclaimed: "It is time to move from a process where lawyers and bureaucrats write volumes of regulations to one where people work in partnership" and called on agencies "to promote better communication, consensus building, and a less adversarial environment."[2] Reinvention was premised on the belief that agencies and private sector actors could work cooperatively to extend regulatory capacity. It was in the enlightened self-interest of corporations to promote environmental responsibility, healthy workplaces, and safe consumer products as means of reducing waste, preventing future liabilities, and supporting long-term profitability. It was in the interest of agencies to devolve some responsibilities onto the regulated via partnerships and voluntary programs as a means of going beyond antiquated statutes, mitigating regulatory adversarialism, and leveraging private sector resources. While these initiatives would be a legacy of the Clinton presidency, many would be retained by subsequent presidents.

The consequences of drift at EPA and OSHA may have been subtle. Agencies introduced partnerships and voluntary programs in the hope of managing the constraints imposed by dated statutes and increasingly stressed budgets. In many cases, one could question whether these adjuncts to the regulatory state made verifiable contributions to agency performance or simply depleted resources that might have been better used for inspections and enforcement. In other cases, drift had more tragic consequences, as revealed by the two most stunning regulatory failures of the new millennium: the greatest financial collapse since the Great Depression and the largest environmental disaster in the nation's history. In each case, the failure of Congress to recalibrate regulation through the passage of new statutes created extraordinary gaps and provided few means of managing the levels of risk that emanated from new industry practices like securitization and deepwater oil exploration. Institutional failure created the preconditions for regulatory failure, leaving a nation and much of the world in financial ruin and despoiling the ecosystem of the Gulf of Mexico.

In Search of Lessons

Much of this book has been devoted to making sense of contemporary regulation. What happens when Congress fails as an institution and becomes increasingly incapable of passing significant new regulatory statutes? How do agencies respond when they were empowered with detailed statutes and complex procedures that placed hard limits on their flexibility to adapt to a changing environment? To what extent can the larger institutional story help us understand some of the most tragic regulatory failures in US history? Several important lessons can be gleaned from these crises and the book more broadly. Let us consider them in brief before concluding with a few reflections on the future of regulation.

1. Gradual Forms of Change Are Critically Important to an Understanding of Contemporary Regulatory Dynamics

Scholars of regulation often focus on large-scale change, major alterations in the regulatory state that occur in response to crises and are at the core of new regulatory regimes. Large crises or dramatic changes in issue salience can trigger rapid regulatory change. In the extreme, change may cut across multiple institutions and policy areas. The emergence of the modern industrial economy in the late-nineteenth century and the financial panic and depression of the 1890s led to an electoral realignment and a series of Progressive Era reforms, many of which were regulatory. The 1929 financial collapse generated a realignment of the party system once again, and the introduction of new regulations in commercial and investment banking, agriculture, industrial relations, civil aeronautics, trucking, communications, and public utility holding companies. The changes are even more profound if one turns to the creation of the welfare state and the introduction of macroeconomic management during this same period. Four decades later, highly publicized environmental disasters generated new concerns over environmental risks that cascaded rapidly across multiple issue areas. Congress and President Nixon responded with an unprecedented wave of new social regulatory statutes addressing air and water pollution, toxic wastes, occupational safety and health, and consumer product safety.

While these are dramatic events, equally important are the more gradual forms of change that occur on an ongoing basis, often veiled by the superficial stability of policies and institutions. In Chapter 2, we investigated several forms of change drawn from the research in historical institutionalism, including displacement, layering, conversion, drift, and devolution. To recap, displacement occurs when one set of rules renders old rules obsolete or inoperative (e.g., the Occupational Safety and Health Act's general duty clause, as discussed in Chapter 7). Layering occurs when new policies or processes are superimposed on the old because supporters lack the power or the will to implement more thoroughgoing change. Layering can occur both within a single policy area (e.g., finance, as shown in Chapter 9) or across multiple agencies (e.g., regulatory review, as discussed in Chapter 4). Conversion occurs when existing institutions appear stable but begin to serve other purposes (e.g., capture, as noted in Chapter 3, results when agencies begin to promote the profitability of the interests they are charged with regulating). Drift occurs when institutions lack the flexibility to adapt to a changing environment and Congress is incapable of passing significant new statutes. Devolution, finally, involves the assignment of governmental duties to private sector actors (e.g., the voluntary programs and partnerships discussed in Chapters 6 and 7).

Change can take a variety of forms, and an expanded analytical vocabulary is much needed in regulation, where prevailing accounts of change have been framed as a movement between two poles: regulatory expansion and deregulation. In some ways, this mirrors the state–market dichotomy that was long used as an organizing schema in political economy. As the latter chapters of this volume demonstrate, this continuum provides few insights into contemporary regulation. Rather than deregulation, the cases of the Environmental Protection Agency and the Occupational Safety and Health Administration exhibited a combination of drift (the lack of new statutory authority), layering (the imposition of regulatory review), and devolution. The Deepwater Horizon disaster stemmed from a combination of drift and devolution without sufficient regulatory oversight. Finance was the most complicated case, involving the layering of successive regimes, conversion (the use of credit regulation to promote social policy goals), devolution (the reliance on credit rating agencies, the assumption that financial institutions were capable of managing the risks they incurred), and drift (the failure to extend regulation to the shadow banking system).

Arguably, in an era of polarization and gridlock, there are strong institutional barriers to the passage of the kinds of significant statutes that were so central to the history of regulation. In this context, a broader analytical framework is far more important than ever before. The superficial stability of regulatory institutions under conditions of drift can veil important changes in administration that can undermine the efficacy of policy. Regulators may continue to regulate, without regulating the right things (the very scenario that was exhibited in the Deepwater Horizon and financial crisis).

2. Regulatory Drift Does Not Simply Happen

Much of this volume has dealt with regulatory drift. In the area of social regulation, the problems of regulatory drift occurred as a result of two factors, as argued in previous chapters. First, Congress—often reinforced by the courts and to a lesser extent presidents—made a specific set of institutional design decisions that limited the discretionary authority of administrators. Second, polarization and gridlock in Congress dramatically compromised the capacity of Congress to pass significant new statutes that could recalibrate existing policies and institutions. As shown in Chapter 3, the design decisions were intentional responses to growing concerns about the representational capacity of the administrative state and the vulnerability of policy in an uncertain environment. Institutions and policies had to be designed to ensure that regulation would not be derailed by business interests and potentially hostile presidential appointees while simultaneously providing adequate representation for citizens and affected interests. To this end, Congress wrote highly detailed statutes that limited bureaucratic discretion and designed complex policy processes that provided avenues for interest group participation. All of this made great sense given the normative concerns that framed the debates in Congress and the larger public interest community. If the skeletal statutes that were passed by earlier generations of reformers created the structural preconditions for agency capture or indolence, far more detailed mandates might provide a potent remedy. Yet, Congress was launching bold and ambitious regulatory experiments; in many cases, there was uncertainty as to how, precisely, the goals and timetables could be met given current technologies. Unquestionably, there would be a need for amendments as agencies gained experience with their new regulatory duties, policy instruments, and implementation timetables.

From the perspective of the late 1960s and early 1970s when the most significant regulatory statutes in the nation's history passed with large, bipartisan majorities, few would have anticipated what the future would hold. As detailed in Chapter 5, by the 1990s, Congress became increasingly polarized, with the effect that the bipartisan coalitions that were so instrumental in passing the core regulatory statutes would prove elusive. While polarization was a product of a number of factors, the gridlock that came to dominate the policy process emanated from a variety of strategies adopted by majorities and minorities of both parties. The commitment of the Republican majority in the House to prevent a vote on any legislation that fails to attract a majority of the majority (the Hastert rule) effectively forecloses legislation that might well pass with bipartisan support. In the Senate, the Democrat's practice of filling the amendment tree precludes participation by the GOP minority, creating incentives to use parliamentary procedures like the filibuster to stall the policy process, thereby requiring supermajorities to pass even minor statutes. Additional strategies, like passing appropriations riders (e.g., to prevent work on new ergonomic standards or initiate the regulation of derivatives) are explicitly designed to lock in the status quo and prevent agencies from responding to the changing environment they face. Drift, in short, is not a simple function of polarization. It has been the product of political struggles and explicit strategies to prevent the recalibration of the regulatory state.

What has driven these strategies? In part, they may have been driven by ideology. Certainly, the 1998 decision to prevent the Commodity Futures Trading Commission regulation of derivatives began with the intense lobbying of Treasury Secretary Robert Rubin, Deputy Treasury Secretary Larry Summers, and Fed Chair Alan Greenspan, three influential policymakers who argued vigorously that financial institutions were rational and possessed information and incentives to manage the risk they assumed that were far superior to whatever regulators could amass.[3] Congress may have been predisposed to accept these claims. The regulatory issues at stake were enormously complicated, creating incentives to defer to those who could make a claim to specialized expertise. Moreover, incessant lobbying can give rise to problems of cognitive or cultural capture. That is, regulators and members of Congress alike may internalize the values and heuristics promoted by industry representatives, ultimately coming to understand the merits of policy proposals in ways that reinforce the material interests of the industry rather than the larger public.[4] Of course, it is difficult to separate ideology from material interest. The revolving door remains ubiquitous. Both Rubin and Summers would benefit greatly from their post-government service employment in the financial industry—Rubin as Chairman of Citibank, Summers as a managing director at a hedge fund. Similarly, as noted in Chapter 9, the same Congress that stripped the CFTC of its authority to regulate derivatives via an appropriations rider and refused to tighten regulation of the government-sponsored enterprises and the credit rating agencies was subject to massive and ever-increasing industry investments in campaign finance. Whatever the proximate cause, this and so many other efforts to prevent an extension of regulation did not simply happen as the function of some impersonal processes.

3. The Consequences of Drift Can Be Misdiagnosed as Problems Arising from Deregulation

The high inflation and low growth of the 1970s spurred a period of deregulatory change, as noted in Chapter 4, one that focused most heavily on economic regulations. With the exception of finance, most of the deregulatory policy changes were initiated during the Ford and Carter presidencies, and to a lesser extent the Reagan presidency. Yet, there is a pervasive sense that deregulation remains the dominant theme and it often enters into policy debates as the default explanation for policy failure. The environmental and financial disasters that were the subject of Chapter 8 and Chapter 9, most notably, have been portrayed by many as a product of deregulation, although the role that deregulation played is rarely developed with precision. Often, the events are simply presented as emblematic of larger deregulatory trends. For example, one analysis of the Deepwater Horizon incident notes:

> The BP disaster marks the failure of deregulation itself. For two decades, the American people have repeatedly been told that private actors could be trusted to protect public interests. Coupled with a naïve faith in technology, the assumption that market forces could replace government oversight drove calls for deregulation, voluntary compliance, and cooperative regulation—the hallmarks of recent United States regulatory policy.[5]

Another analyst, when explaining the 2010 oil spill, noted that a "vortex of corporate power, hubris, and governmental deregulation . . . set the stage for the Deepwater Horizon." They were part of "the deregulatory tide in Washington . . . that began with the Reagan administration's backlash against environmental enforcement."[6]

To be fair, the analyses cited above also consider a host of factors including a lack of congressional attention to safety problems, successful efforts to forestall more rigorous regulations by the Minerals Management Service, and anemic regulatory oversight, all reinforced by the flow of money into politics. These are important parts of the story. There is much evidence that regulation was lax and the MMS was functioning without adequate resources and faced strong opposition from Congress and presidential administrations when it attempted to draw attention to the inadequacy of existing regulations. But here is where clarity in our terminology is important. These are actions taken to prevent the adaptation and recalibration of regulation in the face of changing circumstances. They create a situation of drift, which is not simply part of some amorphous deregulatory tide that began during the Reagan presidency (but mysteriously dissipated briefly to permit the passage of the Oil Pollution Act of 1990).

Similarly, the financial crisis is often attributed to deregulation. Unlike the case of the oil spill policy, Congress did in fact pass a series of deregulatory laws, including the Gramm–Leach–Bliley Financial Services Modernization Act of 1999, which eliminated the Glass–Steagall Act's separation of investment banking, commercial banking, and insurance. As the Financial Crisis Inquiry Commission reported: "the new regime encouraged growth and consolidation within and across banking, securities, and insurance." The new financial holding companies "could compete directly with the 'big five' investment banks . . . in securitization, stock and bond underwriting, loan syndication, and trading in over-the-counter derivatives."[7] The argument seems to hinge on the belief that when financial firms were allowed to merge at will, they took on far higher levels of risk on the assumption that they were simply "too big to fail." Even if this is the case, nations with unified banking—those that never separated commercial and investment banking in the wake of the Great

Depression—did not seem any more vulnerable to financial crises than the United States. Deregulation, in this case, may have played some role in exacerbating the crisis as it unfolded. But a far more persuasive argument would focus on the fact that the shadow banking system had never been subjected to regulation in the first place. Once again, Congress failed to pass statutes to create a new regulatory architecture for banking as it had evolved in the preceding decades. Indeed, "fail" is the wrong verb, given that key actors intentionally blocked the extension of regulation. Deregulation is not the same as a lack of regulation, nor is it synonymous with drift.

Is there anything more than semantics at stake? Deregulation is commonly used in the broadest possible fashion (e.g., the "deregulatory tide" cited above). Presumably, if deregulation did not occur, crises would not have resulted. But as a thought experiment, imagine that the financial deregulatory statutes of the 1980s and 1990s had not passed. The rigid lines of demarcation between financial industries remained largely as they were in earlier years. The securitization process, the issuance of credit-default swaps, and the repo market would have grown unimpeded and would have remained outside of regulation. The politically driven decisions to promote high levels of home ownership via credit markets and tax expenditures, the overleveraging of the government-sponsored enterprises which always received the lightest of regulation, and the promotion of low interest rates by the Federal Reserve would have created a housing bubble. Perhaps there would have been less contagion once the housing bubble burst—and this is an important issue—but to attribute the crisis as a whole to deregulation seems a bit simplistic. And it may well result in a framing of the crisis that leads to solutions that are no solutions at all.

4. The History of Contemporary Regulation Has Been Shaped by Inter-branch Conflict

Regulatory politics have been heavily shaped by ongoing struggles between the Congress and the president. During the formative decades of the modern administrative state, Congress provided broad grants of authority to administrative agencies and, by implication, the president. Bolstered by a faith in neutral expertise, Congress was willing to grant agencies enormous flexibility in their pursuit of "the public interest," a term that appears repeatedly in core regulatory statutes. By the 1960s and 1970s, the faith in administrative neutrality and the willingness to delegate had diminished significantly. Henceforth, Congress would write far more detailed regulatory statutes, granting minimal discretionary authority to regulators. In so doing, Congress simultaneously sought to limit both the president's control over executive branch agencies and the president's ability to depart from congressional policy preferences. As shown in Chapter 4, the imposition of regulatory review processes centralized in the Office of Management and Budget's Office of Information and Regulatory Affairs constituted one important and enduring response to this assertion of legislative power. Congress could direct agencies to regulate in a particular manner, but the new cost–benefit-analysis-based regulatory review processes provided presidents with a means of thwarting congressional will.

Congress objected to the assertion of presidential power, seeking to constrain the extent to which presidents could circumvent congressional will. When President Reagan's OMB began vigorously enforcing Executive Order 12291, Congress responded by withholding authorization and funding for OIRA. Congress ultimately reauthorized OIRA in 1986, but extracted a high price: From this point forward, the OIRA administrator would be subject to Senate confirmation. Threats of statutory restrictions on OIRA that same year forced it to agree to introduce higher levels of transparency (e.g., to place some restrictions on communications with outside parties and enhanced disclosure of written materials).[8] While the battles between Congress and the president over the role of OIRA would continue, the threat of a legislative response diminished as Congress became increasingly mired in gridlock.

As argued in Chapter 5, the same institutional failure that prevented Congress from passing new regulatory statutes simultaneously created the preconditions for presidential unilateralism. A Congress that is hobbled by high levels of partisan polarization and gridlock cannot effectively defend its institutional prerogatives. Presidents can introduce voluntary programs that rest on tenuous legal foundations. They can extract agreements from private parties that exceed the power delegated by Congress. They can engage in rulemaking that goes beyond what was authorized under existing statutes. The courts may provide something of an obstacle, but Congress no longer serves the function it has historically in shaping affirmatively the regulatory state. Certainly, unilateral actions may be attractive to presidents who face the conditions presented earlier in this volume, but they may not be as effective as regulations that find a firm statutory foundation.

5. Administrative Responses to Drift Are of Questionable Effectiveness

As the social regulatory agencies entered the contemporary period, it was evident that they were in an increasingly difficult environment. Congress would not pass new statutes that expanded authority to accommodate emerging regulatory issues or the cumulative experience with existing policies. Budgets would be constrained, both in their inflation-adjusted growth and in the restrictions placed on their use. OSHA, in particular, was hampered by an overly complex rulemaking process, a product of the original design, judicial oversight, and congressional restrictions on its use of funds. Agencies were subjected to regulatory review processes that imposed an additional level of oversight. Due to highly detailed legislative mandates, agencies found themselves without the flexibility and resources to adjust their regulatory foci. Under these conditions, they experimented with various forms of regulatory voluntarism. Agencies devolved authority on to regulated parties in the hope of leveraging resources and extending their authority, often in an extra-legal fashion.

At the EPA, Clinton's Partners for the Environment incorporated a host of public–private partnerships that could leverage private sector resources to address issues ranging from the toxicity of high production volume chemicals to climate change. At OSHA, authority was increasingly devolved on to regulated parties through the Reagan-era Voluntary Protection Program and a variety of voluntary alliances. These initiatives, while arguably a strategic response to the seemingly unique conditions of the new GOP-controlled Congress in the 1990s, would continue in one form or another in subsequent presidential administrations. During the Bush presidency, they may have been attractive because they provided the illusion of active regulation in a period of declining enforcement. During the Obama presidency, they may have been retained because they had gained political constituents and, under unified Republican control of Congress, there were few other options. Regardless of the explanations, one can now view them as more or less permanent parts of the regulatory state.

Perhaps the growing network of voluntary programs and partnerships should be celebrated. Contemporary regulatory theories laud the importance of various models of regulation that synthesize public and private sector activities, leverage private sector expertise and resources, and deploy a broader array of policy instruments ranging from traditional command-and-control standards to forms of management-based regulation combined with third-party auditing. Obviously, enlisting the support of the regulated and working cooperatively to achieve shared goals is superior to ongoing conflict, although there may be little reason to believe that firms that participate are less inclined to lobby against regulation or file suit in court. But contemporary regulatory theory also emphasizes the importance of integration and administrative oversight. Given the detailed nature of the statutes and rules, integration was impossible. Rather than creating a system of co-regulation, regulatory voluntarism was layered on top of existing policies and institutions, often in a haphazard fashion.[9]

The importance of administrative oversight is evident when we consider the differences between public and private sector actors. Regulators, one assumes, execute mandates that are a product of political deliberation in representative institutions. They seek to use public authority to promote optimal levels of environmental protection, workplace safety, and consumer product safety. Corporate managers, in contrast, have a fiduciary responsibility to maximize shareholder wealth, and thus focus on issues of profitability. When regulators delegate responsibilities to corporate participants in voluntary programs, we have the potential for classical principal–agent problems. As noted in Chapter 3, the potential for shirking or outright opportunistic behavior increases under conditions of information asymmetry. In this case, corporations have the best-quality information on their own practices and performance. If regulators do not have the legal authorization or the resources to engage in inspections or compel the disclosure of verified data, they cannot effectively monitor behavior and make meaningful distinctions between firms based on their performance. Some corporations may participate in partnerships only because it reinforces profitability (e.g., by delivering reputational advantages with critical stakeholders). Some may seek these advantages without making the requisite investments, veiling their behavior by self-reporting inaccurate or biased information (e.g., reporting on those dimensions of a firm's activities that have improved while failing to disclose accidents). If shirking behavior becomes widespread, participants who are genuinely committed to furthering regulatory goals may conclude that ongoing participation does not deliver any reputational advantages (indeed, it may have the opposite effect). Under these conditions, they would be rational to exit the program. The program might continue to exist. It might be allowed to survive because it creates the impression of success in achieving gains in the environment or workplace safety or because it retains the support of participants or members of Congress. But it has done little to further the goals of regulation.[10]

Administrative oversight has been uneven at best, given the resource constraints. As Chapters 6 and 7 revealed, there have been persistent concerns over the agencies' success in evaluating the performance of key voluntary programs. In the case of the EPA, the determination of what constituted a voluntary program was so opaque that the Inspector General had a difficult time determining how many programs actually existed.[11] External analyses of key programs like the National Environmental Performance Track could generate little evidence that participants had levels of performance that were superior to nonparticipants.[12] At OSHA, the rapid expansion of the Voluntary Protection Program during the Bush administration occurred without the simultaneous investment in oversight, which was perfunctory at best. Firms were often allowed to participate even though they had serious violations—some resulting in fatalities—that should have led to their exclusion.[13]

Given the lack of statutory authorization and the ongoing budgetary constraints faced by the agencies, one can rightfully question whether the partnerships and voluntary programs make a genuine contribution to the expansion of regulatory authority and, even when they do, whether they can be justified given the opportunity costs. Moreover, one must recognize the limits that necessarily arise from the lack of statutory foundations. The existing statutes simply do not provide even the most entrepreneurial agencies with the flexibility or the authority to use voluntary programs and partnerships to achieve significant goals. Voluntary programs necessarily make limited demands on participants because they can offer meager inducements.[14]

6. Administrative Responses to Drift Raise Serious Concerns about Accountability

Concerns over performance closely track additional problems of transparency and accountability. As Chapter 3 explained, the design of new regulatory institutions in the 1960s and 1970s was premised on a commitment to participation, transparency, and accountability—values that many believed had been compromised in the past. Statutes mandating quasi-judicial proceedings complete with testimony and cross-examination, and in some cases providing intervener funding, bolstered the Administrative Procedure Act's requirements of advance notice of rulemaking and the solicitation of public comments. All of this had important implications for administrative efficiency. The procedural complexity and multiple forms of review elongated the policy process and imposed high costs and lengthy delays (as noted in Chapter 7, the OSHA rulemaking process can extend for close to a decade).[15] But Congress, one assumes, understood the tradeoffs and some of the delays were foreseeable consequences of institutional design decisions.

Democratic government is grounded in norms of procedural regularity and transparency. Once authority is delegated, there are mechanisms in place to secure access to information (e.g., Freedom of Information Act requests, open meeting requirements), force accountability (e.g., congressional oversight), and punish poor performance (e.g., budget cuts, removal of officials). None of these mechanisms are perfect. But public–private partnerships and voluntary programs are largely free from these processes.[16] In this respect, they are similar to other arrangements that have proliferated with the rise of "government by proxy" or "third-party government," that is, the growing tendency to rely on firms, contractors, and nonprofits to deliver public services.[17] On the one hand, this immunity from traditional mechanisms of oversight can permit a higher level of flexibility and entrepreneurial activity. Presidents can act unilaterally to achieve goals that Congress is reticent to endorse. Regulatory agencies can pursue goals that are beyond those authorized by antiquated statutes and give their private sector partners far greater latitude to experiment. But critics note that the avoidance of accountability can carry significant costs. Citizens and interest groups lack the legal means to force private parties to disclose verifiable performance data. The lack of data, in turn, can compromise the role of interest groups in promoting more vigorous congressional oversight. Agencies can create the impression that partnerships are delivering results, often by aggregating self-reported data on their websites, when in fact there is insufficient oversight to evaluate actual performance.[18]

A Future Uncertain

The history of regulation in the United States has witnessed periods of rapid and substantial change followed by periods of stable, path-dependent development. Stable equilibria form around policies, locking in a dominant policy image, a shared understanding of policy goals and instruments, and a set of institutions and actors. But these equilibria can be punctuated. Crises can stimulate mass and elite mobilization and open the door to a redefinition of policy.[19] Often these events occur on a policy-specific basis in response to a salient case of regulatory failure. Other times, they can spread across multiple policy areas almost simultaneously. In each case, these episodes of change have required the passage of significant new statutes by Congress. This raises an important question: What are the ramifications for the future of regulation if the polarization and gridlock that have beset Congress become enduring features of the institution?

The most obvious outcome of a continuation of the status quo is institutional ossification and ongoing regulatory drift. That is, polarization and gridlock will continue to impede the passage of significant new regulatory statutes. In cases where Congress wrote detailed laws that limited bureaucratic flexibility and agencies are blocked from extending their authority through a lack of budgetary growth or riders that constrain new rulemaking, regulations will become increasingly irrelevant and the regulatory system will become more sclerotic. Regulation will continue, but policy will fail to address the most pressing problems. Perhaps some of the gaps in policy will be filled as they have in the past few decades, albeit imperfectly, through a greater reliance on regulatory voluntarism. As the proliferation of public–private partnerships suggest, corporations and trade associations are willing to cooperate, as long as the demands are modest and participation is compatible with profitability or the demands of key stakeholders. As in the past, budgetary constraints will raise the opportunity costs of active administrative oversight of voluntary programs and partnerships. One might expect that these opportunity costs will only grow over time, creating disincentives to assure that they are, in fact, generating verifiable results that extend regulation.

Perhaps public regulation will become less relevant as alternative forms of private governance grow in importance. As noted in Chapter 1, many analysts have argued that market liberalization and deregulation have occurred at the same time that there has been a proliferation of private governance arrangements that are outside public regulation but serve a regulatory function. Steven K. Vogel states it concisely: "we have wound up with a world of freer markets and more rules."[20] Firms routinely employ environmental management systems, conduct testing, and submit results to third-party auditors in response to pressures imposed by finance, insurers, customers, and other actors in the supply chain. A dense network of so-called second-order agreements exists in the shadow of the law. Corporations self-regulate to meet requirements that are embedded in corporate acquisition, credit, commercial real estate, product sale and service agreements.[21] Corporations also participate in forms of self-regulation through their trade associations, which may prescribe codes of conduct and internal management systems for their members. They may receive certification under any number of international standards that have become necessary to gain access to key markets or supply chains. Congress may fail to pass climate change legislation and the EPA may struggle to establish meaningful regulations under dated statutes, but the International Organization for Standardization has already developed over 570 environmental standards, including standards for greenhouse gas accounting (ISO 14064 and 14065) and energy management systems (ISO 5001).[22] In sum, even in the absence of a regulatory system that is routinely recalibrated to address changes in the larger environment, a dynamic system of private governance exists and serves some of the same functions as public regulation.

Although analysts have identified an emerging system of regulatory capitalism, there is nonetheless recognition that the role of the state varies cross-nationally.[23] Some states use public policy to reinforce the mechanisms described above, integrating them with regulatory policies to create systems of co-regulation. Others, like the United States, have been far more disengaged.[24] This disengagement, initially premised on a separation of the market and the state and the priority attached to efficiency, has now become a product of necessity for reasons described in this volume. Disengagement renders regulators incapable of forcing the transparency and accountability of private–private agreements that occur in the shadow of the law, often with minimal disclosure. It also frustrates the attempts to evaluate the impact of regulatory policies that may generate a network of second-order agreements.[25] Moreover, given that private governance often arises out of the self-interest of commercial parties, one can question whether it can prove robust across the business cycle. In prosperous times, consumers may reward firms that engage in socially responsible practices, creating incentives for self-regulation. Conversely, when economic difficulties arise, consumers may become more price sensitive, thereby creating disincentives for social responsibility. Without the reinforcement of public policy, there is no reason to believe that private governance will exhibit the features that have been the hallmarks of public regulation.[26]

While private governance may fill some of the gaps created by regulatory drift, the failure of industry actors to manage their own levels of risk in the two case studies that concluded this volume should give us room for pause. As the disjunction between policy and the underlying environment continues to generate new problems, some will prove increasingly catastrophic. If these problems are sufficient to generate a sustained legislative response—to punctuate the equilibrium that has formed around Congress—the current period may be viewed in historical context as the protracted decay of a regulatory regime that preceded a new era of regulatory change. If not, we should anticipate that the kinds of regulatory failures that marked the first decade of the twenty-first century will become more common.

Notes

1 Daniel Carpenter, "Confidence Games: How Does Regulation Constitute Markets?" in *Government and Markets: Toward a New Theory of Regulation*, ed. Edward J. Balleisen and David A. Moss (Cambridge, UK: Cambridge University Press, 2010), 164.
2 William J. Clinton, "Memorandum on Regulatory Reform," March 4, 1995. Available at www.presidency.ucsb.edu/ws/?pid=51062.

3 See Peter S. Goodman, "Taking a Hard New Look at a Greenspan Legacy," *New York Times*, October 9, 2008, A1. Available at www.nytimes.com/2008/10/09/business/economy/09greenspan.html?_r=0.

4 See James Kwak, "Cultural Capture and the Financial Crisis," in *Preventing Regulatory Capture: Special Interest Influence and How to Limit It*, ed. Daniel Carpenter and David A. Moss (Cambridge, UK: Cambridge University Press, 2014), 71–98.

5 Rebecca M. Bratspies, "Regulating by Regulators, Not Industry," *The Environmental Forum*, 27, 5 (2010): 48.

6 Anthony E. Ladd, "Pandora's Well: Hubris, Deregulation, Fossil Fuels, and the BP Oil Disaster in the Gulf," *American Behavioral Scientist*, 56, 1 (2012): 110.

7 Financial Crisis Inquiry Commission, *The Financial Crisis Inquiry Report: Final Report of the National Commission on the Causes of the Financial and Economic Crisis in the United States* (New York: Public Affairs, 2011), 56.

8 Curtis W. Copeland, *Federal Rulemaking: The Role of the Office of Information and Regulatory Affairs*, CRS Report for Congress, RL32397 (Washington DC: Congressional Research Service, 2009), 7–8.

9 See Edward J. Balleisen and Marc Eisner, "The Promises and Pitfalls of Coregulation: How Governments Can Draw on Private Governance for Public Purposes," in *New Perspectives on Regulation*, ed. David Moss and John Cisternino (Cambridge, MA: The Tobin Project, 2009), 127–49.

10 Matthew Potoski and Aseem Prakash, "Voluntary Programs, Compliance and the Regulation Dilemma," in *Handbook on the Politics of Regulation*, ed. David Levi-Faur (Cheltenham, UK: Edward Elgar, 2011), 91–92.

11 See Environmental Protection Agency Office of Inspector General, *Voluntary Programs Could Benefit from Internal Policy Controls and a Systematic Management Approach* (Washington DC: Environmental Protection Agency, 2007).

12 Cary Coglianese and Jennifer Nash, "Performance Track's Postmortem: Lessons from the Rise and Fall of EPA's 'Flagship' Voluntary Program," *Harvard Environmental Law Review*, 38 (2014): 1–86.

13 See Department of Labor, Office of Inspector General, *Employers with Reported Fatalities Were Not Always Properly Identified and Inspected under OSHA's Enhanced Enforcement Program*, Report number 02-09-203-10-105 (Washington DC: Department of Labor, 2009).

14 See Coglianese and Nash, "Performance Track's Postmortem," for a development of this argument.

15 See Government Accountability Office, *Workplace Safety and Health: Multiple Challenges Lengthen OSHA's Standard Setting*, GAO 12-330 (Washington DC: Government Accountability Office, 2012).

16 Chris Skelcher, "Public–Private Partnerships and Hybridity," in *The Oxford Handbook of Public–Private Management*, ed. Ewan Ferlie, Laurence E. Lynn, and Christopher Pollitt (New York: Oxford University Press, 2005), 361–62.

17 H. Brinton Milward and Keith G. Provan, "Governing the Hollow State," *Journal of Public Administration Research and Theory: J-PART*, 10 (2000): 359–80.

18 See Ronald C. Moe, "The Emerging Federal Quasi Government: Issues of Management and Accountability," *Public Administration Review*, 61, 3 (2001): 290–312.

19 See Frank R. Baumgartner and Bryan D. Jones, *Agendas and Stability in American Politics*, 2nd ed. (Chicago, IL: University of Chicago Press, 2009).

20 Steven K. Vogel, *Freer Markets, More Rules: Regulatory Reform in Advanced Industrial Countries* (Ithaca, NY: Cornell University Press, 1996), 3.

21 Michael P. Vanderbergh, "The Private Life of Public Law," *Columbia Law Review*, 105, 7 (2005): 2029–96.

22 Sandra Tranchard, "How ISO Standards Can Help Act against Climate Change," *ISO News*, November 30, 2015. Available at www.iso.org/iso/home/news_index/news_archive/news.htm?Refid=Ref2028.

23 See John Braithwaite, *Regulatory Capitalism: How It Works, Ideas for Making It Work Better* (Cheltenham, UK: Edward Elgar, 2008).

24 Vogel, *Freer Markets, More Rules*, 260–65.

25 Vanderbergh, "The Private Life of Public Law."

26 See Marc Allen Eisner, "Private Environmental Governance in Hard Times: Markets for Virtue and the Dynamics of Regulatory Change," *Theoretical Inquiries in Law*, 12 (2011): 489–515.

INDEX